Menallen [Pennsylvania] Minutes, Marriages and Miscellany

Quaker Records, 1780-1890

Margaret B. Walmer

HERITAGE BOOKS
2007

HERITAGE BOOKS
AN IMPRINT OF HERITAGE BOOKS, INC.

Books, CDs, and more—Worldwide

For our listing of thousands of titles see our website
at
www.HeritageBooks.com

Published 2007 by
HERITAGE BOOKS, INC.
Publishing Division
65 East Main Street
Westminster, Maryland 21157-5026

Copyright © 1992 Margaret B. Walmer

Other books by the author:

*100 Years at Warrington: York County, Pennsylvania
Quaker Marriages, Removals, Births and Deaths*

All rights reserved. No part of this book may be reproduced or transmitted in any form or by any means, electronic or mechanical, including photocopying, recording or by any information storage and retrieval system without written permission from the author, except for the inclusion of brief quotations in a review.

International Standard Book Number: 978-1-55613-656-6

CONTENTS

Maps	4
Abbreviations	8
History	9
Minutes	37
Burials	165
Marriages	189
Sources	261
Index	263

MENALLEN MINUTES, MARRIAGES AND MISCELLANY

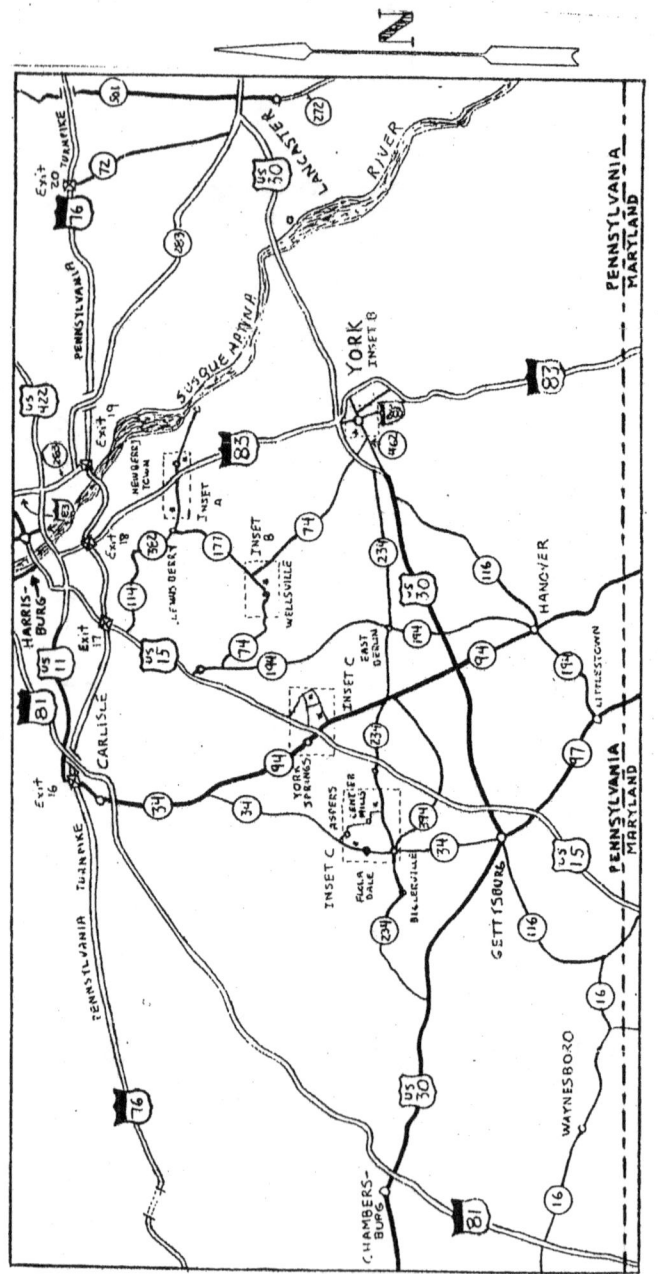

Map of South Central Pennsylvania

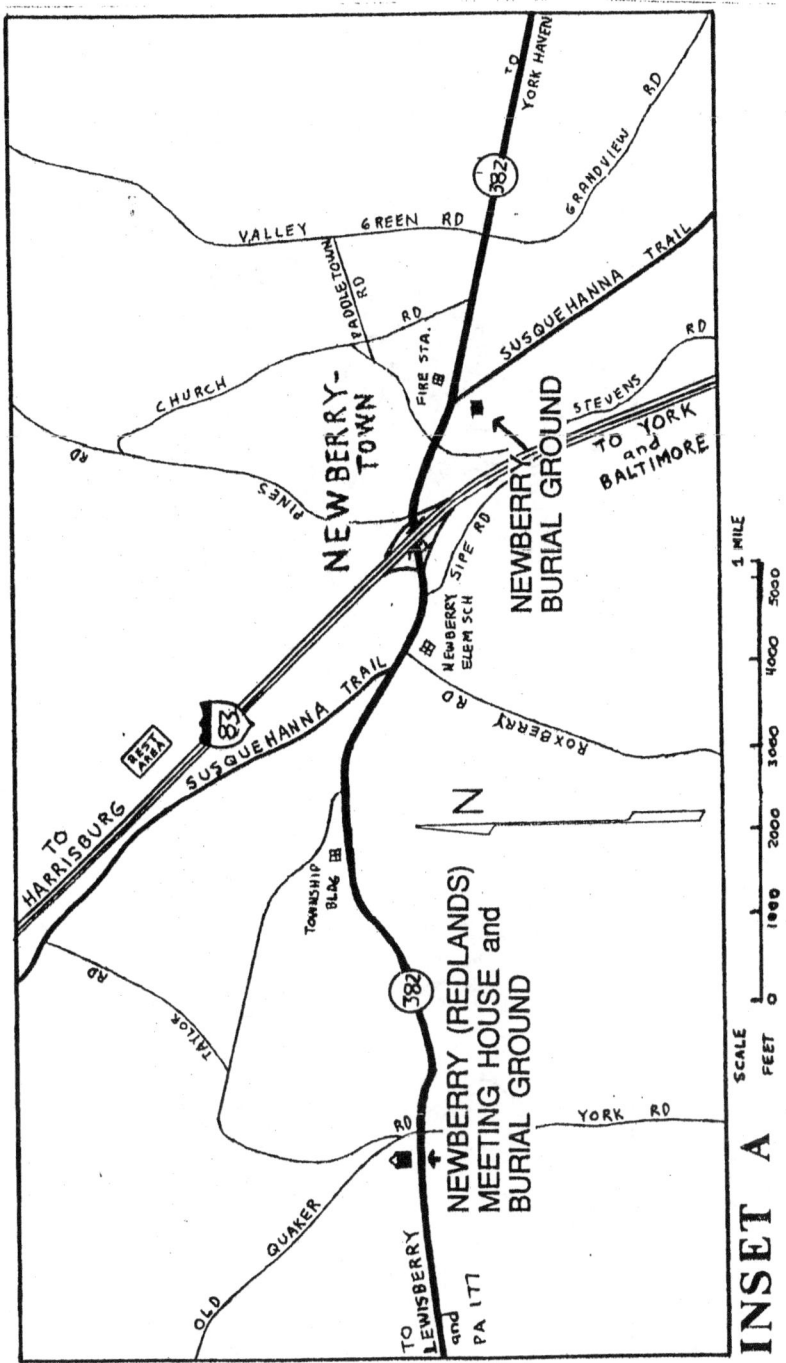

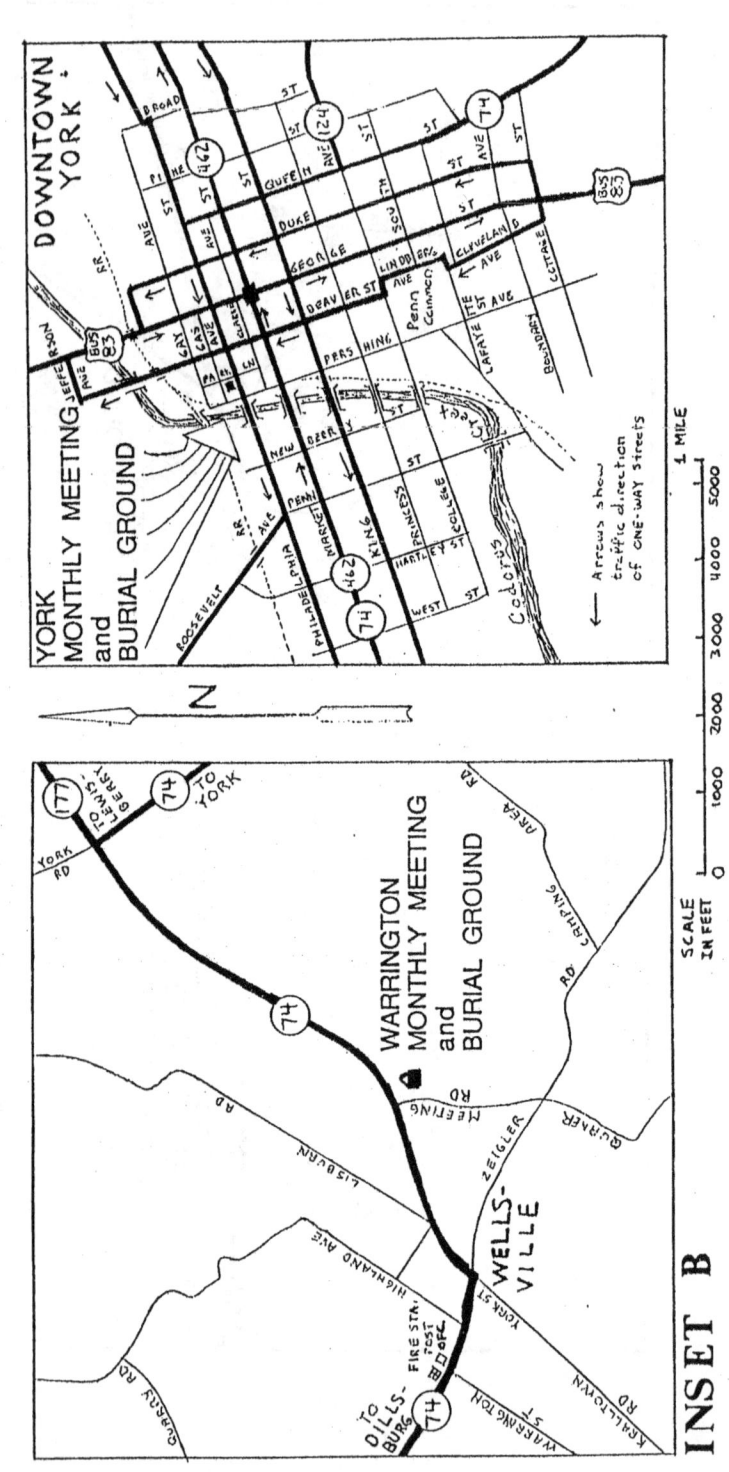

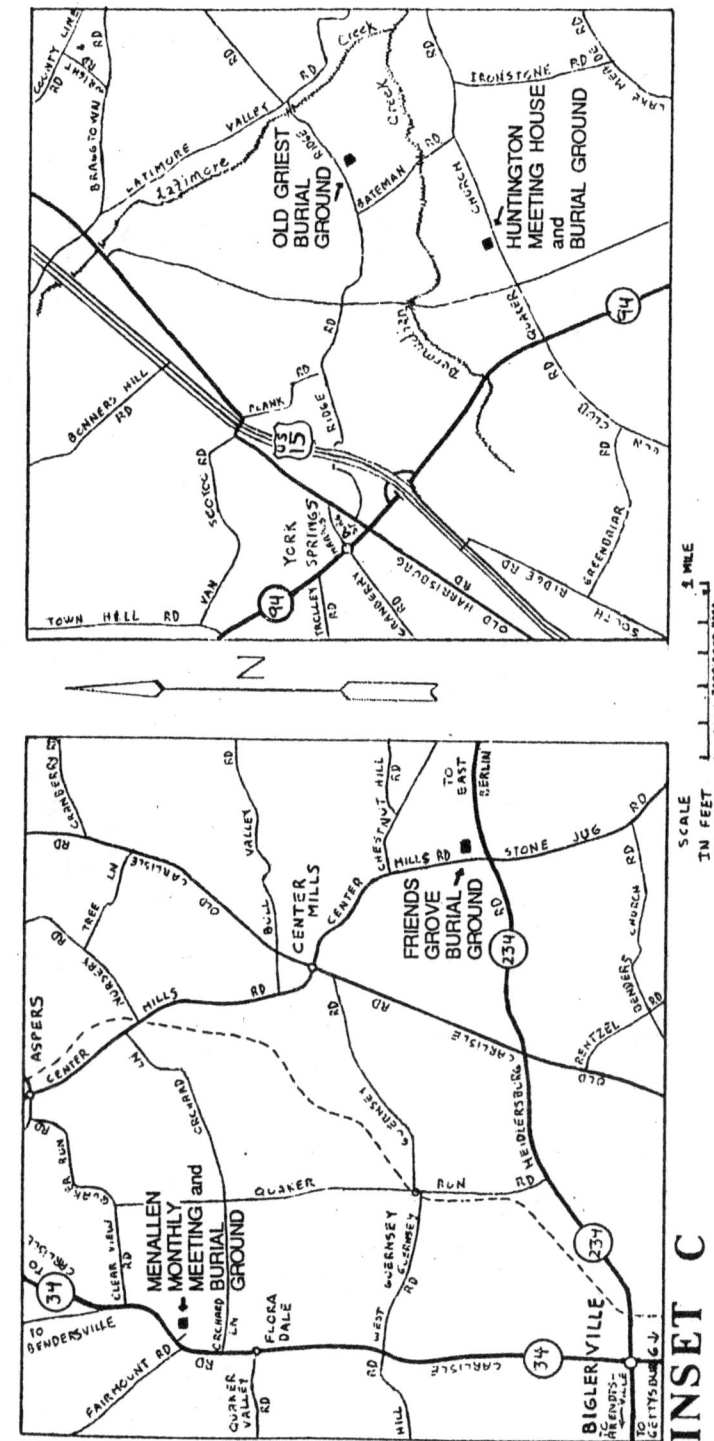

ABBREVIATIONS

appt	appointed
appt comm	appointed to a committee
cert	certificate
comm	committee
compl of	complained of
mou	married out of unity
dis	disowned
gct	granted certificate to
rct	requested certificate to
read ack	read acknowledgment
read test	read testimony
rec	received
rep to	representative to
req	requested
roc	received on certificate
rocf	received on certificate from
[w]	from the Women's Minutes

HISTORY

The people of Menallen Township were still living very much on the frontier at the time Menallen Monthly Meeting was formed, in 1780. They were located almost forty miles from their county seat at York. Adams County would not come into existence for another twenty years. Travel was by stage, wagon or horseback and the country was mountainous. Cornwallis had not yet surrendered to Washington, and the westward movement had begun.

In 1737 enough Quakers had moved across the Susquehanna River to form a new Monthly Meeting at Warrington in York County. By 1780 the congregation had grown so large that the decision was made to set off two of the Preparative Meetings to form the new Menallen Monthly Meeting, to be held alternately between Menallen and Huntington.

The Minute Book for Menallen Meeting begins with an excerpt from the Minutes of the Quarterly Meeting, as follows:

> The Monthly Meeting of Warrington being greatly Increased in Number and the Business thereof very Extensive and many Friends believing it Necessary to Consider of Some way to Shorten the Same: in the third Month 1779 appointed a large Number of Friends to take the Same under their weighty and Deliberate Consideration and propose such means as to them might appear best: Who after divers

Deliberations thereon proposed to the Monthly Meeting the Division thereof: which after some months Time was proposed to the Quarterly Meeting for their Deliberation, and the Minutes and proceedings of that Meeting thereon is as Follows. Viz:

. . . At a Quarterly Meeting held at Fairfax the 19th of the 6th month 1780. . . . The Committee appointed on the Proposal from Warrington Monthly Meeting respecting the Division thereof made the following Report Viz: We of the Committee appointed by the Quarterly Meeting, on the Request of Warrington Monthly Meeting agree to Report that we have Visited three of their Preparative Meetings: were at York first-day Meeting and attended the Service of Said Monthly Meeting, had a Solid Conference with Friends there— also had an opportunity to view the minutes of that Monthly Meeting, Which Expressed their Deliberate and Weighty Care on that Subject . . . have sollidly Considered the Same, and do give it as our judgment that it would be profitable to Divide that Monthly Meeting, and that we think it will be most agreeable that Monalin and Huntington Preparative Meetings do Constitute the New Monthly Meeting; all which is Nevertheless Submitted to the Quarterly Meeting.
5th mo 15th 1780 John Hough
Mahlon Janney
Abel Walker
Joseph Wright

. . . Which being Considered in this Meeting is Concurred With, with a desire and Trust that the Establishment of that Meeting will tend to the advancement of the Cause of Truth and it is desired that Friends of Warrington Monthly Meeting, and Monalin and Huntington Preparative Meetings fix on suitable Time and Place for holding the New Monthly Meeting, and Report to Next Quarter; and it is now concluded that the Members of the Select Meeting belonging to both Monthly Meetings, Continue United in on as

HISTORY

heretofore. . . .

At a Quarterly Meeting held at Warrington the 18th of 9th mo 1780

By a Coppy of a Minute of Warrington Monthly Meeting dated the 9th Instant, it appears that that Meeting appointed a Committee to unite with Friends of Monalin and Huntington Meetings in fixing on Time and Place for holding the New Monthly Meeting, who Reported that they all attended to the Service Except one and conferred with Friends there; and find there still Remains a Difference and fear with Some of the Members of Huntington Preparative Meeting respecting their ability to hold Such a Meeting; Yet agreed to propose for that meeting to be held Circular between Monalin and Huntington, on Seconday after the Second first-day in every month, the first to be held at Monalin in Next Month, and to be Called Monalin Monthly Meeting; Which being considered in this Meeting is concurred with and in order for the help and Encouragement of Friends of that Meeting Especially those who from a Sence of the Weight and importance of Such a Trust are under discouragements (with whome a Near Simpathy is felt by a number now present) the following Named Friends are appointed to sit with them at their first Monthly Meeting Viz: James Steer, Michael Shion, William Pickering, Mahlon Janney, John Hough, Joseph Janney, Alen Farquhar and Joseph Wright, who are desired to Report their Care to Next Quarterly Meeting; and it is now desired that Friends of Warrington Monthly Meeting may Endeavour to keep in a feeling Simpathy with Friends of that meeting and from Time to Time attend it for their help and Incouragement. . . .

MENALLEN MINUTES, MARRIAGES, & MISCELLANY

WARRINGTON IS LAID DOWN

Eighty two years later the congregation of Warrington Meeting had dwindled to the point that it was decided to "lay the meeting down." Again, the Quarterly Meeting assisted in transferring the remaining members of Warrington and Newberry Meetings to Menallen, unless they indicated their desire to go elsewhere, or discontinue their membership altogether. In doing so they produced a list of families with ages of parents and children, which is reproduced here in its entirety, including the message accompanying it:

> To Monallin Monthly Meeting to be held this 20th of 2nd mo 1862. The committee of the Yearly Meeting that attended this meeting in the eleventh month last having felt it to be in the line of their duty to assemble with you again at this time, think it proper to state, that after attending the Quarterly Meeting at Pipe Creek, they prepared an address to the Friends who had formerly constituted Warrington Monthly Meeting; Which together with the minutes of Monallen Monthly Meeting and the Quarterly Meeting they had printed, and a copy thereof is herewith presented to the Monthly Meeting. The committee have since visited all the members of Newberry and Warrington Meetings who are now in those neighborhoods at their homes, placed a copy of the address in the hands of every one who was of sufficient age to be benefited thereby, and in most cases, the address was read to the assembled family, we have reason to believe that the address, and the minutes of the meeting referred to, were well received, as giving renewed evidence of the tender care and concern of Friends on their behalf. Where deviations from our order have occurred the committee have extended such care and labour as the respective case, under circumstances seemed to demand. Every case of deviation that became known to us, has received the

attention of the committee and we are gratified to believe they were all satisfactorily adjusted; those who wish to retain their rights, being, as a general thing, in a frame of mind favorable for future usefulness. The names of those members who have deviated from our order, and who wish not to remain members of our religious Society are herewith reported, being seven in number.

Some cases are still under care of the Committee.

We find that a number of the members both at Newberry and Warrington have removed from the neighborhood to settle. Of these individually we have obtained the Postoffice Address and the committee will endeavour to communicate with them, and make known to the monthly meeting the result on a future occasion. We herewith present to the monthly meeting fifty-two (52) names of the members of Newberry Meeting and fifty seven (57) names of the members of Warrington Meeting.

The committee would respectfully suggest to the Monthly meeting the propriety of appointing some Friends to be overseers, at both Newberry and Warrington if, as we believe is the case, judicious Friends suitable for the station may be found there.

Also as Trustees of the Property of both meetings are very few in number and quite aged, that new Trustees, of younger men, be appointed to take charge of the Properties and that those or some other Friends be appointed to have charge of the Books, records, deeds, and other papers that belonged to Warrington Monthly Meeting. The committee having been authorized by the Yearly meeting to visit this meeting in furtherance of the object entrusted to us, and having recently mingled with the Friends of those meetings in social and religious communion at their homes, as well as at their meetings they are willing so far as they are desired by the monthly meeting to communicate to the committees that may be appointed on those subjects any such information as we are in possession of to aid in accomplishing satisfactorily the important objects in view.

We may further inform the monthly meeting, that the Friends of Newberry propose to hold their First day meetings regularly and a mid week and Preparative meeting, once a month, but not the other mid week meetings. A Preparative meeting has been accordingly held, and representatives appointed to attend this meeting.

The committee are unitedly of the opinion under all the circumstances of the case, that the Friends don't feel prepared to undertake more at this time, and as this will be the means of establishing an official connexion between those friends and the monthly meeting it would be best for the Monthly Meeting to recognize I sent in this arrangement on the part of Friends of Newberry with a hope too that Warrington Friends, who now propose to hold a First day meeting regularly, may adopt a similar arrangement.

Signed, Thomas P. Stabler, Benj'n P. Moore, Benj'n Hallowell, Chalkley Gillingham, George Reese, Mary G. Moor, Elizabeth S. Cixon.

MEMBERS TRANSFERRED

The Names, with the ages of the members of Newberry Meeting brought to Monallen Monthly Meeting as members thereof by the committee of the Yearly Meeting, 2nd mo 20th 1862:

Names	Ages
Israel Garretson	64
Ruth Garretson his wife	58
Children of Israel and Ruth:	

HISTORY

Jacob Garretson	36
Mary Garretson	29
Martha Garretson	26
Maria Garretson	23
James Wickersham	78
Mary Wickersham his wife	68
Ross Wickersham, their son	35
Benjamin Garretson	62
Rhoda Garretson, his wife	66
Children of Benjamin:	
Ezra Garretson	28
Jesse Garretson, now in the west	23
Josiah Garretson	22
Ann Garretson, now in Chester Co	38
Asenith Garretson	30
Anna Wickersham	65
Children of Anna:	
Mary Ann Wickersham	30
Edith Wickersham	26
Lydia Mills	44
Joel V. Garretson	28
Hannah Ann Garretson, his wife	29
Children of Joel & Hannah:	
Frank G. Garretson	4
Eli Penn Garretson	2
infant not named	7 weeks
Elizabeth V. Garretson (died 2nd mo 13 1862, aged 68)	
Children of Elizabeth:	
Louisa Garretson	41
Mary Garretson	37
Israel Garretson, Jr	32
Rachel Garretson, his wife	34
Joel Hoopes	37
Thomas Jones	36
Martha Jones, his wife	36
Children of Thomas and Martha:	
Hiram Benjamin Jones	11
Barzilla Jones	6
Edwin Thomas Jones	2

MENALLEN MINUTES, MARRIAGES, & MISCELLANY

Rebecca Cleaver, wife of John Cleaver   27
  Their daughter:
  Malinda G. Cleaver   3
Hannah Kirk, widow of Jacob   60
John B. Wright   42
Mary W. Wright, his wife   39
  Living children of John and Mary
  They have buried four:
  Robert W. Wright   17
  Chapman A. Wright   9
  Ida L. Wright   7
  Howard L. Wright   6
  Richard M. Wright   8 months
Hannah Thomas   67
  Daughters of Rhoda Garretson:
  Phebe Jane Eppley, widow
  Hannah Hoopes
  Elizabeth N. Hoopes
Maria W. Cook, daughter of Anna
  Wickersham   40
  Members of Newberry Meeting who wish not to continue members of our Religious Society:
Ruth Anna Gunkle   29
  daughter of Israel and Ruth
  Garretson married out of our order
  and wishes not to continue a member

Esteemed Friend: Monallen 2nd mo 21st 1862
  I neglected to mention to thee yesterday that I would have to request thee to insert the ages of the following named friends in the list we handed to the Monthly Meeting as we could not obtain them till we came here. Please to do so—also put a "W" in Maria Cooks name add that she has an infant son 3 weeks old not named.

                Thy Sincere Friend,
                Benjamin Hallowell
                Martha H. Smith

HISTORY

Phebe Jane Eppley	30
Hannah A. Hoopes	25
Elizabeth N. Hoopes	23
Edith Wickersham	25
Maria W. Cook	40
Infant son not named	3 weeks

The names with the ages of the members of Warrington Meeting brought to Monallen Monthly Meeting as members thereof by the committee of the Yearly Meeting 2nd mo 20th 1862:

Eli Cookson	57
Phebe Cookson, his wife	61
Sons of Eli and Phebe:	
Franklin Eli Cookson	31
Milton V. Cookson	26
Sarah Vale	69
Martha Cook, widow of Walker	53
Children of Martha:	
John W. Cook	23
Elizabeth Cook	19
Sarah Cook	17
Martha J. Cook	15
Walker Cook	13
Joseph Cook	11
Daniel Garretson	60
Anna Cook Garretson, his wife	56
Children of Daniel and Anna:	
Israel Garretson	26
Eliza Ann Garretson	21
Abel Garretson	19
Arnold Garretson	17
Melissa Garretson	12
Asahel W. Cook	
Hannah C. Cook, his wife	29
Children of Asahel and Hannah:	
Theressa Caroline Cook	28 [sic]
Anna Elizabeth Cook	6

MENALLEN MINUTES, MARRIAGES, & MISCELLANY

George W. Cook	4
Twins not named	7 weeks
Daughters of Thos. Griest:	
Martha Griest	50
Anna Griest	48
John Cook	80
Hannah Cook, his wife	77
Children of John and Hannah:	
John Cook, Jr	49
Leah Cook	42
Mary Griest	61
Daughter of Mary:	
Belinda Griest	40
Esther Morthland	60
Sarah E. Vale, daughter of Esther	38
William Cadwalader	80
Waln Hoopes	46
Sarah Ann Hoopes, his wife	44
Children of Waln and Sarah Ann:	
Phebe Ann Hoopes	22
Mary Elizabeth Hoopes	20
Maria W. Hoopes	19
Reuben Hoopes	17
Amanda Rhoda Hoopes	16
Joseph Ellis Hoopes	14
Lucinda Hoopes	12
Thomas L. Hoopes	10
Angelina Hoopes	7
Amy B. Hoopes	5
Franklin Waln Hoopes	3
Elmira Hoopes	1
Joshua Vale	33
Mary G. Vale, his wife	30
Oliver G. Vale, their son	2
Asahel Walker	76
Lydia G. Walker, his wife	66
Lydia Walker, widow of John Walker	82

HISTORY

Members of Warrington meeting who have married out of our order and wish not to continue members of our Religious Society:

Sons of Martha Cook:
    Isaac Cook   30
    Hezekiah Cook   25
Children of Asahel Walker:
    Garretson Walker   27
    Lewis P. Walker   29
    Phebe Angeline Smith   24
John G. Garretson, son of
    Daniel Garretson   29

In 1888 a committee was appointed to find the location of absent members. They submitted the following report:

To Menallen Monthly Meeting to be held the 18th of 7th mo 1888

Dear friends.
We the comm appointed some months ago to look up the where-abouts of our absent members make the following report, to wit:

Reuben Hoopes—deceased
Joseph Ellis Hoopes, Thomas L. Hoopes, Franklin Waln Hoopes: children of Waln and Sarah Ann Hoopes
Joshua Vale—In Iowa
Oliver Vale (his son)—In Iowa

Transferred from Warrington to Menallen:
Franklin Eli Cookson, Milton Cookson, sons of Eli and Phebe Cookson, Rossville, York Co, Pa.

Transferred from Warrington to Menallen: Walker Cook, Joseph Cook, John W. Cook, children of Walker and Martha Cook
Israel Garretson, Abel Garretson, Arnold Garretson, children of Daniel and Anne Garretson

MENALLEN MINUTES, MARRIAGES, & MISCELLANY

John Cook, son of John and Hannah

Jacob Garretson, son of Israel and Ruth, Lewisbury, York Co, Pa
Joel Hoopes, Kansas
Jesse Garretson, Josiah Garretson, sons of Benjamin, in Illinois
Robert N. Wright, Lewisbury, York Co
Chapman A. Wright, Elmira, NY
Franklin Wright, Elmira, NY
Richard M. Wright, Curwensville, Pa
Hadley Griest, Fort Bridge, Wyoming
Robert Wickersham, Va
William McCreary, Hunterstown, Adams Co, Pa
Samuel McCreary, Hunterstown, Adams Co, Pa
Aaron Bishop, Littlestown, Pa
Z. Hibbard Moore, Oketo, Kansas

We have not been able to get the P.O. address of all of them up to this time, which we submit to the meeting.
Hiram Griest, Samuel H. Harris

HISTORY

THE MINUTES

Because their religious beliefs forbade taking their disputes to a court of law, swearing oaths, or using the services of "an hireling priest," the Quakers have always felt it important to keep meticulous records of their actions. Although regular weekly meetings for worship were held at various locations, known as Preparative Meetings, they came together for a Monthly Meeting for Business in which clerks, elders, overseers, trustees and ministers were appointed, marriages approved, disputes settled, and backsliding members were "treated with, in love," and given the opportunity to publically testify to error and promise to reform, or be disowned. Members were disowned for swearing oaths, attending muster, quarreling, and, most often, for marrying out of order.

The first minute at Menallen is an example of the way minutes were written, and it includes a rather intriguing story:

> And on the 9th of the 10th Month 1780 the first Monthly Meeting was held at Monalin, the Minutes and proceedings thereof are as follows viz:
>
> At Monalen Monthly Meeting held the 9th of the 10th Month 1780 the Representatives being called all appeared. . . .
>
> This meeting taking into Consideration the appointment of a clerk makes Choice of Jonathan Wright for that service, and it is likewise agreed that a Friend Should be Chose annually for that Service. . . .
>
> Huntington meeting informs this that Henry Wierman Senior hath been guilty of Unchristian Conduct to People Passing through his land, to dig a grave and Bury the Corps of a Deceased Person in a Time of deep Snow, which rendered it difficult to pass along the Common way: and that in the 8th month last he took a Woman into his House to whom he Said

MENALLEN MINUTES, MARRIAGES, & MISCELLANY

he was married in the 3rd month and he produced two Papers Signed by him and the Woman Expressive of their taking each other for Husband and Wife but neither of the Papers were Witnessed: and he saith that Some Time after they for Some reasons Went to a Minister and got their marriage confirmed: Which Conduct of his appeared So Scandalous to the Profession we make; this Meeting appoints Abel John, William Griffith, James McGrail, Jonathan Wright, Daniel Griest and Elias Pearson, to inspect Closely into those several matters, treat with him therefor, and if they find it so let him know the Necessity there is for Friends to bear their Testimony against him and his conduct and report to next Meeting.

The Minutes section of this book consists of an every-name abstract of the Minutes of Menallen Monthly Meeting from 1780 to 1890, for the Men's Minutes, and from 1835 to 1890 for the Women's Minutes. In early Quaker Meetings, the men sat on one side of the building and the women on the other, with a movable partition separating them. Each side held its own meeting for business, kept its own minutes, and frequently referred matters to each other for consideration. It is apparent from reading the men's minutes that the women held meeting from the beginning, but their minutes prior to 1835 seem to have been lost.

Although Menallen continues today as an active Monthly Meeting, I chose the cutoff date of 1890 because at that time the decision was made to discontinue holding a separate Women's Meeting and for the men and women to conduct business and worship together.

The names are arranged in alphabetical order and are not included in the index at the end of the book. Whenever possible, women who married are listed both by maiden name and married name.
For example:
    Mary Smith, [date], dis, mou. Formerly Jones

HISTORY

Mary Jones, [date], dis, mou. Now Smith means that Mary Jones was disowned on a certain date for marrying a man named Smith, out of unity with Friends.

Because there were some members who seemed to be appointed month after month to committees, it seemed useless to list every instance and they are shown as having been appointed x many times between two dates. A [w] following a listing indicates that the information was found in the women's minutes. Most entries should be self-explanatory (see abbreviations), but in a few cases, the text of the minute is entered in full for a clearer understanding of what happened.

THE BURIALS

As with the minutes, the burials are also listed in alphabetical order. I found eight Quaker graveyards in York and Adams counties. In the very early days, Quakers' graves were marked with a plain stone or rock, with no inscription on it at all. Around 1811, there is an indication in the Warrington Minutes that some members requested that the Quarterly Meeting rule on whether they could at least have initials and a date on the stone. At a later time Warrington raised the question of non-Quaker members of the community placing stones on graves that were too fancy and out of keeping with Friends' beliefs. At that time, after much discussion, it was decided to pass flyers around the community asking people to keep the stones rather plain.

FRIENDS GROVE
The original Menallen Meeting was held in a log structure east of Biglerville. In 1838, this building was moved to the present location of Menallen, and in 1884, replaced by the brick structure in use today. The original land was sold, all but the burial ground which has come to be known as Friends Grove. Some of the stones are just rocks with no inscriptions, while some have initials and a date. Others have been replaced with modern, professionally made tombstones. In recent years, the Blackburn family placed a monument here in memory of their ancestors, many of whom are buried here.

MENALLEN MINUTES, MARRIAGES, & MISCELLANY

MENALLEN
The burial ground at Menallen adjoins the meeting house and is still in use, as is the meeting house. The inscriptions on the gravestones are almost all easy to read and the grounds are kept mowed and trimmed.

HUNTINGTON
Huntington meeting house must look the same today as it did when it was built, perhaps as early as 1766 when the land was acquired. The building is stone and the interior is bare wood and plaster, with facing benches, a movable partition, and backless, handmade benches. A meeting for worship is held here annually and sometimes monthly. The burial ground beside the building is neatly trimmed and, like Friends Grove, has many unmarked rocks as well as a number of more modern stones.

NEWBERRY
The first Quaker Meeting House in York County was at Newberry and the burial ground connected with it is thought to be the oldest graveyard west of the Susquehanna River. The first building was of logs and was replaced in 1792 with a stone building across the road from the burial ground. This building was sold in 1811 and a new stone building was built two miles to the west. The graveyard at Newberrytown was not sold and suffered many years of neglect after Warrington Meeting was laid down.

The names listed as being buried in Newberry come from a photocopy of a handwritten document in the possession of Menallen Meeting. It begins as follows:

"Inscriptions on tombstones in Friends' graveyard, Newberrytown, Newberry Township, York County, Pa, copied 7 mo. 26, 1897, by Albert Cook Myers, of Kennett Square, Pa. This old graveyard, situated at the end of the little village of Newberrytown, is an almost impenetrable wilderness of locust trees, sumac, and blackberry briars. There are very many

HISTORY

unmarked graves, and many having low stones but no inscriptions. Old Newberry Meeting House, built in 1792, stands just across the road. It has been remodeled on the inside and is now occupied by two families."

In 1988, the Trustees of Menallen hired Kaminek Nursery, Inc. of Etters, PA to restore the old burial ground. It was impossible to identify most of the markers. Many were rocks, many were broken, some had sunk into the ground. Today the burial ground at Newberry is a place of serenity and beauty, thanks to the efforts of Ray Kaminek, who made a meticulous chart of the location of every marker he was able to find. After completely removing all weed and stumps and smoothing out the irregular ground, he reseeded the grass and replaced the surviving markers as nearly where they might have been as possible. He not only restored it but also keeps it beautiful.

REDLANDS

The little meeting house at Redlands, a nickname for the "new" Newberry meeting, looks very much like the one at Huntington. When Warrington Meeting was laid down, Newberry (Redlands) was a preparative meeting. The building was placed under the care of Menallen Trustees, but for the next 70 years it seems to have been pretty much neglected. A neighbor, Malinda Miller and her husband, although not Quakers, became concerned about the sad condition of the property. The roof leaked, windows were broken, and it was subject to occasional vandalism. They offered to be caretakers for a small fee and spent the rest of their lives struggling to keep the building and grounds in a decent state. Rather than abandon it, the Menallen members hold a meeting for worship at least once a year at Redlands and see to it that it is kept clean and repaired, while retaining its original simplicity. There is a monument to Malinda Miller in front of the building, honoring her efforts.

The graveyard is similar to the one at Huntington, with many unmarked or unidentified graves and quite a few old but legible stones.

MENALLEN MINUTES, MARRIAGES, & MISCELLANY

WARRINGTON

Warrington graveyard presents a much different appearance from the others. It is a little larger and is surrounded by a stone wall. Almost half of the stones are "un-Quakerly" in that they are of fancy shapes, or have poems or pictures inscribed on them. It is evident that, although the land was held in the name of the trustees of the meeting, it was shared with the community and families of other religious beliefs.

The inscriptions in this book are from a list in the possession of Menallen Meeting. It is not known whether it consists of all the stones or only the members of the meeting.

YORK

York Monthly Meeting was formed from Warrington in 1786. It is located in downtown York very near the buildings used by the first government of the United States at the time of the Revolution. Although it is very small and crowded by a modern city, it is still in use and is kept in good repair. It is on a small plot and the meeting house is surrounded on three sides by the gravestones.

Again, the names in this book are from a list in possession of Menallen Meeting, of unknown date and origin.

OLD GRIEST

The source of names for Old Griest Graveyard is a chart drawn in Oct, 1941, showing measurements, locations and names but no other information. It is believed that it was originally located on the John Griest homestead farm in Latimore Township. The farm has been subdivided and apparently the graveyard has been moved. Today there exists only a very small fenced plot with four or five modern stones enclosed within.

HISTORY

THE MARRIAGES

When a couple decided to be married within the Meeting, they had first to submit their intentions in writing to a Monthly Meeting. A committee would be appointed to visit them and see to it that they were sincere, that they were free to marry and, if they were minors, that they had the permission of their parents. The committee would make a report to the next monthly meeting, and, if it was favorable, the couple was free to marry and a committee was then appointed to attend the wedding and make sure that it was properly conducted and report back to the Monthly meeting following. A certificate was read at the wedding and all the guests signed it as witnesses. The certificate was copied into the permanent record, and returned to the newlyweds.

Because no preacher conducted the service, the bride and groom spoke their vows to each other before witnesses. A typical certificate is shown here. As a rule, the husband signed his name on the lower right side just above the witnesses, with his bride signing her new name just below his. Often, but not always, the first witness' signatures in the right column were the parents of the new couple, followed by brothers and sisters and then all the others attending.

> Whereas <u>Nicholas Wierman</u> son of <u>William Wierman</u> of Huntington Township York County State of Pennsylvania and <u>Hannah</u> his wife and <u>Jane Underwood</u> Daughter of <u>John Underwood</u> late of Warrington Township County and State afforesaid (deceased) and <u>Mary</u> his wife having Declared their intentions of Marriage with Each Other before several Monthly Meetings of the People called Quakers at Warrington in the County of York aforesaid and having consent of Parents and Parties concerned Their said Proposals were allowed of by the said Meetings. Now these are to Certify whom it may concern that for the full accomplishment of their said Intentions this twenty fourth day of the twelfth month in the year of our Lord one thousand seven hundred and Ninety five they the

said <u>Nicholas Wierman and Jane Underwood</u> appeared in a Public Meeting of the said People at their meeting house at Warrington in the County afforesaid, and he the said <u>Nicholas Wierman</u> taking the said <u>Jane Underwood</u> by the Hand did in a Solemn manner openly declare that he took her to be his Wife Promising through Divine Assistance to be unto her a Loving and Faithful Husband untill Death should separate them (or words to the same effect) and then and there in the same Assembly the said <u>Jane Underwood</u> did in the like manner declare that she took him to be her Husband Promising through Divine Assistance to be unto him a Loving and Faithful Wife untill Death should Separate them (or words to that purpose) And MOREOVER they the said <u>Nicholas Wierman and Jane Underwood</u> she according to the Custom of Marriage Assuming the Name of Her Husband as a further Confirmation thereof, did then and There to these Presents set their Hands.

                                        Nicholas Wierman
                                        <u>Jane Wierman</u>

And we whose Names are Hereunder also Subscribed being Present at the Solemnization of said Marriage and Subscription have as Witnesses thereto Subscribed our Names.

Daniel Griest	Susanna Morthland	William Wierman
Thos Thornburgh	Michael Morthland	Nicholas Wierman
Phebe Thornburgh	Mary McMillan	Sarah Wierman
Thomas Griest	Content Garretson	Isaac Everitt
Ann Griest	Susanna Griest	Charles Underwood
Robert Vale Jr	John Marsh Jr	Samuel Underwood
Robert Morthland	Benjamin Walker	Alexander Underwood
Phebe Morthland	Ruth Walker	Benjamin Underwood
Mary Beals	John Kettlewell	Stephen Hendricks
Jane Hussey	Thos Pearson	Sarah Hendricks
David Griest	Joshua Ash	William Nevitt
Jesse Comly	Charles Kettlewell	Susanna Wierman
Samuel Morthland	James Marsh	Ann Marsh
John Wierman	Susanna Everitt	Hannah Everitt
Samuel Comly	Robert Morthland	Jonathan Marsh
Isaac Wierman	John Packer	John Everitt
Nicholas Wierman	John Garretson	

HISTORY

COMMITTEE ON SUFFERING

Another record maintained by Menallen was that of the Committee on Suffering. The following is a reproduction of the entire contents of the surviving Minute Book kept by the committee. The names mentioned are also included in the Index at the end of this book.

Minutes of the Comitee relative to suffering Cases appointed 1842

page 1
5th month 29th 1842

We the comitee appointed in relation to sufferings of a military nature having met and taken the subject of our appointment under our serious consideration.

Cyrus Griest was appointed clerk of the comitee. Nine members present, to wit, Josiah Garretson, Jesse Cook, Isaac Tudor, John Griest, Joel Wright, Isaac T. Garretson, Elijah Wright, Cyrus Griest, William H. Wright. Absent William Ellis.

The members are requested to Collect and forward to our next meeting Such cases of suffering for noncompliance with demands of a Military nature as may come under their notice since the Monthly meeting of the 8th mo last.

Then adjourned to meet at Huntington on the 14th of the 8th month next.

8th month 14th 1842

Pursuant to adjournment the comitee again met 8 members present, Elijah Wright and Joel Wright absent.

The following cases of Suffering were reported (to wit) Taken from Elijah Wright one saddle valued at $7.00 for $2.00 muster fine by Christian Stout Constable—

From Oliver Garretson on Sleigh valued at $2.00 for $2.00 muster fine By—

The clerk is directed to forward the substance of the foregoing in a report to the Monthly meeting.

Then adjourned to meet again at Manallen on first day the 11th of 9th month next at 2 o'clock PM.

9th month 11th 1842 pursuant to adjournment the comitee again met. 9 members present [?] absent Isaac [?] Garretson absent.

The clerk informed that he attended to his appointment.

The members are requested to forward such cases of suffering as shall come under their notice to our next meeting.

Then adjourned to meet at Huntington the second first day in the 11th mo next at 2 o'clock PM if so permitted.

12th month 11th 1842 pursuant to adjournment the comitee again met.

Six members present. William Ellis, William H. Wright, Elijah Wright, and Joel Wright absent.

Josiah Garretson is appointed to inform the absent members that a reason would be secured for their absence.

Then adjourned to meet again at Manallen at 2 o'clock on the PM of the day preceeding the monthly meeting in the first month.

1st mo 16th 1843 pursuant to adjournment the comitee again met.

8 members present. Absent Isaac H. Garretson and Joel Wright. The former of whom gave a reason for his absence.

The minutes of the last meeting were read.

Josiah Garretson informs that he attended to his appointment and most of the absent members of last meeting gave satisfactory reasons for their non-attendance.

Several written and printed documents were read

to the edification of many and calculated to strengthen and encourage our members in the support of our righteous Testimony against war. We being favoured with the company of many friends not members of the comitee.

The subject of addressing the Legislative body of this Commonwealth having claimed our serious consideration Cyrus Griest, Josiah Garretson, William Ellis, John Griest and Isaac Tudor are appointed to prepare and produce to our next meeting an essay containing our views and feelings on the Subject of war in form prepared to Lay before the members of the Legislature.

Then adjourned to meet 11 o'clock of the day preceeding our next Monthly Meeting.

2nd mo 22nd 1843 according to adjournment the comitee again met. Six members present. Absent William Ellis, Jesse Cook, Joel Wright and Elijah Wright.

The comitee appointed to prepare an essay Containing our views and feelings on the subject of war report they have attended to their appointment in much harmony and condescension [?] and produced an essay in form prepared to lay before the Legislature which was united with and Cyrus Griest is appointed to forward the same to the Monthly Meeting for its approbation or otherwise and report to next meeting.

The clerk is directed to furnish the Monthly Meeting with the Substance of the above minute signed on behalf of the Comitee. Then adjourned to meet at Manallen on the 2nd first day in the 8th mo next at 2 o'clock PM.

The Comitee through misunderstanding having failed to meet according to adjournment have again met the 10th of the 9th mo.

The clerk informs that he attended to his appointment laid the address before the Monthly Meeting which united therewith and returned the same to the comitee for their further care which not yet having been forwarded William Ellis, Josiah Garretson, and Elijah Wright are appointed to take charge of the same and present it to our neighbouring Monthly Meeting in this State as way opens and report to our next meeting.

An address under the title of War and Christianity was received and read and was referred to the Care of Josiah Garretson and Cyrus Griest to be corrected, preserved and produced to our next meeting.

Then adjourned to meet again at Huntington the first firstday in the 1st mo 1844

1st mo 7th 1844 pursuant to adjournment the comitee again met.

9 members present to wit Wm Ellis, Josiah Garretson, Isaac Tudor, William H. Wright, Elijah Wright.

The following named friends have been added to the comitee, to wit: Nathan Griest, Jacob B. Hewett, Mahlon Garretson and Able T. Wright who are also present. Absent Jess Cook, Joel Wright, Cyrus Griest and Isaac P. Garretson.

Josiah Garretson on behalf of the Comitee appointed at our last meeting to lay the address before our neighbouring Monthly Meeting report that they have attended to their appointment.

The address under the title of War and Christianity referred to the care of Cyrus Griest and Josiah Garretson for correction was now produced read and approved and directed to be preserved.

There being no Book to preserve the minutes of the comitee Able T. Wright is appointed to procure a suitable one for that purpose and produce it next meeting.

William Ellis and Nathan Griest are appointed to take charge of the memorial of Friends prepared by this Comitee present it to the Legislature now in session and report to our next meeting.

HISTORY

Then adjourned to meet again at Menallen on the 2nd first day in the fourth month next.

4th mo 14th 1844 pursuant to adjournment the Comitee again met.

9 members present. Absent Jesse Cook, William H. Wright, Mahlon Garretson and Isaac F. Garretson.

The friend appointed to procure a blank book for the use of the comitee produced one, price 15 cts.

The comitee appointed to lay the memorial of friends before the Legislature report they attended to their appointment and it appeared to meet with a favourable reception.

An essay on war and peace was produced and read to our edification and Conformation.

Then adjourned to meet again at Huntington the 2nd first day in the 8th mo next.

8th mo 11th 1844 pursuant to adjournment the Comitee again met 9 members present absent Joel Wright, Elijah Wright and Jacob B. Hewett.

The following case of Suffering was reported (to wit) forcible detained from Mahlon Garretson $3.00 for $3.00 muster fine by John Berkholder and Thomas Plocher (constables).

The subject of Civil government having claimed our consideration the comitee agreed to request that the portion of discipline relative to that subject be read in our Monthly Meeting.

The clerk is directed to furnish the Monthly Meeting with a coppy of the above minute.

Then adjourned to meet at Menallen the 2nd first day in the 4th mo 1845.

4th mo 13th 1845 pursuant to adjournment the comitee again met. 6 members present. Absent Nathan Griest, Mahlon Garretson, Wm Ellis, Jacob B. Hewett, Elijah Wright, Jesse Cook and Isaac T. Garretson.

The clerk informs he complied with his appointment then adjourned to meet at Huntington on the

MENALLEN MINUTES, MARRIAGES, & MISCELLANY

1st first day in the 8th mo next.

At a meeting of the Comitee on Military concerns held the 28th of the 3rd mo 1846 8 members present. Absent Wm Ellis, Isaac Tudor, Elijah Wright and Josiah Garretson.

The following cases of suffering has been reported at this time to wit Taken from Jacob B. Hewett three flower barrels for $1.00 muster fine—

Taken from Isaac J. Wright 1 bushel of wheat for one dollar muster fine.

Taken from Mahlon Garretson one sack full of corn for $1.00 muster fine.

Taken from Elijah Wright a quantity of corn for $1.00 muster fine.

Retained on Settlement from John B. Wright $1.00 for muster fine.

The foregoing were all taken and Retained by Joseph Cline collector of taxes.

The comitee adjourned to meet at Huntington on the 1st first day in the 8th mo next.

At a meeting of the comitee on Military Concerns held at Huntington the 20th of the 8th mo 1846.

The clerk is directed to forward to the Monthly meeting the cases of suffering contained in the minutes of our last meeting.

At a meeting of the comitee appointed in relation to suffering on account of our testimony against military Exercises held at Menallen the 1st of the 8th mo 1847, 7 members present.

The clerk informed he attended to his appointment.

The following cases of suffering were reported at this time which the clerk is directed to forward to the Monthly Meeting to wit

Taken from Elijah Wright 5 bushels of corn ears for $1.00 muster fine.

Taken from Isaac J. Wright 4 bushels of corn ears for $1.00 muster fine.

HISTORY

Taken from Samuel Hanns 1/2 bushel timothy seed for $1.00 muster fine.

Taken from John B. Wright a quantity of leather for $1.00 muster fine.

The above distraints were made by Daniel Plank collector of taxes.

Taken from Nathan Griest one whip worth $1.00 for muster fine.

An address from Kennet Monthly meeting to its members, was presented to this comitee which was read and the clerk was directed to forward the same to our next monthly meeting as containing some of our Views and feeling on the subject in relation to which we have been appointed.

Then adjourned to meet at Huntington on the first 1st day in the 8th month of next year.

At a meeting of the committee appointed in relation to suffering on account of our testimony against Military exercises held at Huntington the 6th of the 8 month 1848, 6 members present. The clerk not being present T. Wright was appointed clerk for the day.

The following case of suffering was reported at the time which the clerk is directed to forward to the Monthly Meeting to wit. Taken from Isaac J. Wright 4 bushels corn ears for one dollar muster fine. Taken from Samuel H. Hamms 6 bushels corn ears for 1 dollar muster fine for the year 1847.

The above distraints were made by Daniel Plank collector of Taxes.

An Essay on War Inconsistent with Christianity was produced and read and was satisfactory and the clerk is directed to forward it to the Monthly Meeting. Then adjourned to meet at Menallen on the first 1st day of the 8th month 1849.

ABSTRACTS OF THE MINUTES OF MENALLEN MONTHLY MEETING

1780-1890

ADAMS, Elijah, 07-14-1788, req membership
    Elijah, 12-15-1788, appt comm 8 times thru 4-20-1797
    Rachel, 2-14-1791, compl of: mou; unchastity. Formerly Potts
        Rachel, 6-13-1791, dis: mou; unchastity; child too soon after marriage
    Ruth, 8-23-1798, compl of: mou. Formerly Williams
    Ruth, 11-21-1798, dis: mou; formerly Williams

ALBERT, Addeson Edwin, 3-19-1845, req membership thru father, David
    Addison, 2-24-1859, rct Prairie Grove MM, Iowa, with father, David
    David, 7-17-1844, requests membership
    David, 2-20-1845, rep to QM 5 times thru 8-19-1847
        David, 2-20-1845, req a meeting be held near him in Cumberland Co, Pa.
    David, 3-19-1845, req membership for his 4 children
        David, 3-19-1845, comm report re opening a new meeting in the brick meeting house situate in Allen Township, Cumberland Co., Pa., a half mile west of Center Square . . . it would be right to grant the meeting as requested . . . 3rd first day in the 4th mo and to be held every 4 weeks

MENALLEN MINUTES, MARRIAGES, & MISCELLANY

ALBERT, David, 4-20-1848, appt comm 4 times thru 3-21-1849
    David, 8-24-1848, rep to MM
    David, 2-24-1859, rct Prairie Grove MM, Iowa with 2 minor children [w]
    Emmanuel Erb, 3-19-1845, req membership thru father David [w]
    Maria, 2-24-1859, rct Prairie Grove MM, Iowa with father David
    Maria Margaret, 3-19-1845, req membership thru father David [w]
    Serina Amelia, 3-19-1845, req membership thru father David
ALLEN, Priscilla, 11-20-1844, req membership
    Priscilla, 10-25-1845, req marriage with Benjamin W. Vanscyoc
    Rebecca, 10-13-1783, dis: mou; formerly Shipherd
ALLESON, James, 5-13-1793, req membership. He is of Bedford, Pa
ALLISON, James, 1-13-1794, req marriage with Sarah Bowen
ALTEMUS, Hanah, 8-20-1818, compl of: mou per report from Darby MM
    Hanah, 5-19-1819, rct Warrington MM
ANTHONY, Melissa, 7-20-1887, dis: mou, joined Methodists; formerly
    Garretson [w]
    William, 4-17-1889, appt comm to raise money to repair Warrington
        Meeting House
    William, 4-17-1889, on comm requesting repairs to Warrington Meeting
        House
BAILEY, William, 11-23-1825, rocf London Grove MM as Minister
BAILS, Elizabeth, 2-23-1797, read testimony. Retained
BAIR, Ruth Emma, 7-17-1889, req membership [w]
BALE, Sarah, 2-22-1888, rep to QM [w]
BARBER, Eliza, 2-24-1825, rocf Grace Church St, London MM, endorsed by
    Alexandria
    Eliza, 2-24-1825, rocf Grace Church St, London MM, endorsed by
        Alexandria
    Jonathan, 2-24-1825, rocf Grace Church St, London MM, endorsed
        by Alexandria
    Mary, 2-24-1825, rocf Grace Church St, London MM, endorsed by
        Alexandria
BARKSTER, Sarah, 8-21-1800, compl of: mou. Formerly McGrail
    Sarah, 10-23-1800, dis: mou. Formerly McGrail
BATEMAN, Anne, 8-24-1815, rct Miami MM, Ohio
    Elizabeth, 7-22-1801, rocf Exeter MM with husband William and 3
        children
    Elizabeth, 7-22-1801, rocf Exeter MM with father William and
        family
    Elizabeth, 7-20-1814, rct Miami MM, Ohio with husband William
    Hannah, 6-21-1804, rocf Dunnings Creek MM
    Jacob, 5-20-1801, rocf Uwchlan MM
    Jacob, 11-19-1806, rep to QM
    Jacob, 12-19-1811, compl of: fornication
    Jacob, 3-18-1812, dis: fornication
    Jacob, 4-24-1817, case revived
    Joel, 2-22-1810, rct Dunnings Creek MM with father John and
        family
    John, 7-22-1801, rocf Exeter MM

MINUTES

BATEMAN, John, 3-23-1803, rct Dunnings Creek MM for marriage with
    Hannah Thomas
    John, 2-21-1805, appt comm 16 times thru 10-9-1809
    John, 2-21-1805, rep to QM 6 times thru 2-22-1810
    John, 2-22-1810, rct Dunnings Creek MM with wife and 3 children
    John, 8-22-1811, exempt fines: "Taken from John Bateman by George
        Gilbert for exempt fine of 4 dollars, one pair of saddel bags and
        one blind bridle valued at $4.75. Also taken from ditto by George
        Smyser for exempt fine of 5 dollars, 1 back band, 1 belly band, 1
        blind bridle, and 3 riding bridles at $5.13"
    Lydia, 2-22-1810, rct Dunnings Creek MM with father John and family
    Mary, 7-22-1801, rocf Exeter MM with father William and family
    Mary, 2-20-1806, req marriage with Jonathan Wright
    Maryann, 2-22-1810, rct Dunnings Creek MM with father John and
        family
    Rachel, 7-22-1801, rocf Exeter MM with father William and family
    Rebecka, 4-23-1807, req marriage with John Garretson
    William, 7-22-1801, rocf Exeter MM with wife Elizabeth and 3 children
    William, 4-19-1804, appt comm
    William, 2-21-1805, appt comm
    William, 7-20-1814, rct Miami MM, Ohio with wife Elizabeth
BEALES, Daniel, 7-22-1812, certificate to New Hope (Tenn) MM refused
    Daniel, 4-22-1813, dis: refused to give certificate to Newhope MM
    Mary, 7-22-1812, certificate to New Hope (Tenn) MM refused
    Mary, 4-22-1813, dis: refused to give certificate to Newhope MM
BEALS, Ann, 12-24-1801, rct New Hope MM, Tenn with father Solomon and
    family
    Caleb, 3-13-1786, compl of: fighting and dancing. Son of William
    Caleb, 5-15-1786, dis: fighting and dancing
    Daniel, 12-10-1781, mou to 1st cousin, Mary Squibb
    Daniel, 1-14-1782, dis: mou, hireling teacher and as 1st cousins
    Elizabeth, 11-23-1796, compl of: unchastity; child in unmarried state.
        Formerly Elizabeth Loan
    Hannah, 12-24-1801, rct New Hope MM, Tenn with father Solomon and
        family
    Jacob, 4-14-1783, req marriage with Elizabeth Blackburn
    Jacob, 9-14-1795, roc for self and family
    Jacob, 12-24-1801, rct New Hope MM, Tenn with father Solomon and
        family
    Jane, 12-24-1801, rct New Hope MM, Tenn with father Solomon and
        family
    John, 12-24-1801, rct New Hope MM, Tenn with father Solomon and
        family
    Lydia, 5-20-1807, compl of: mou to first cousin. Now Underwood
    Martha, 12-24-1801, rct New Hope MM, Tenn with father Solomon and
        family
    Mary, 1-14-1782, dis: mou. Formerly Squibb
    Mary, 5-10-1784, compl of: unchastity. Daughter of William
        Beals
    Mary, 7-12-1784, dis: unchastity. Daughter of William Beals

MENALLEN MINUTES, MARRIAGES, & MISCELLANY

BEALS, Mary, 9-21-1796, req marriage with David Griest
    Moses, 4-13-1789, compl of: non-attendance; threats; attending musters
    Moses, 7-13-1789, dis: joined another Society
    Moses, 2-15-1790, dis: non-attendance; attending musters; threats
    Rebecca, 12-24-1801, rct New Hope MM, Tenn with husband Solomon and 7 children
    Samuel, 12-24-1801, rct New Hope MM, Tenn with father Solomon and family
    Solomon, 4-11-1791, appt comm
    Solomon, 5-9-1791, appt comm
    Solomon, 12-24-1801, rct New Hope MM, Tenn with wife Rebecca and 7 children
    Stephen, 6-19-1800, compl of: swearing profanely
    Stephen, 10-23-1800, dis: swearing profanely
    William, 10-11-1784, compl of: non-payment of debt
    William, 7-11-1785, comm reports matter settled, he having paid debt
    William, Jr, 8-12-1782, compl of: no attendance, etc.
    William, Jr, 9-9-1782, dis: non-attendance and dancing
    William, Jr, 2-11-1782, compl of: dancing
BEAR, Ruth Emma, 10-23-1889, req membership
BELL, Harvey, 4-17-1889, on comm requesting repairs to Warrington Meeting House
BERNARD, Elihu, 2-24-1842, rocf New Garden MM, Chester Co, Pa as Minister [w]
    Elihu, 2-24-1853, rocf Penns Grove as Minister [w]
BISHOP, Aaron L., 8-18-1864, req membership
BLACK, Alice L., 9-23-1886, rocf Pipe Creek MM with mother Emilie W.
    Annie M., 9-23-1886, rocf Pipe Creek MM with mother Emilie W.
    Emilie W., 1-17-1872, ack mou to William H. Black. Formerly Wright [w]
    Emilie W., 5-20-1874, gct Wapsononoc MM, Beder Co, Iowa
    Emilie W., 9-23-1886, rocf Pipe Creek MM with four children [w]
    Emilie W., 2-24-1887, appt comm 5 times thru 8-20-1890
    Emilie W., 5-18-1887, appt clerk [w]
    Emilie W., 5-18-1887, rep to QM 5 times thru 5-21-1890 [w]
    Emilie W., 5-23-1888, appt clerk [w]
    Emily, 2-21-1872, ack mou. Retained. Formerly Wright
    Emily W., 4-22-1874, rct Wopsinonoc MM, Cedar Co, Iowa [w]
    Emily W., 8-20-1890, appt Elder
    Mabel E., 9-23-1886 rocf Pipe Creek MM with mother Emilie W. [w]
    Susan E., 9-23-1886 rocf Pipe Creek MM with mother Emilie W. [w]
BLACKBOURN, Ann, 10-22-1802, rct Redstone MM with father Moses and mother
    Anthony, Jr, 2-18-1802, compl of: mou
    Anthony, Jr, 6-24-1802, dis: mou and attending muster
    Deborah, 10-22-1802, rct Redstone MM with father Moses and mother
    James, 4-22-1802, rct Redstone MM
    James, 6-24-1802, compl of: mou since moving to Redstone MM
    James, 2-24-1803, dis: mou to first cousin

MINUTES

BLACKBOURN, John, 2-14-1791, compl of: mou
    John, 1-9-1792, dis: mou. Is son of Thomas of Bedford Co, Pa
    John, 10-19-1797, dis: carnal knowledge; mou
    Moses, 8-13-1792, rep to QM
    Moses, 11-12-1792, compl of: "case of difficulty"
    Moses, 10-22-1802, rct Redstone MM with wife and 3 children
    Moses, 12-23-1802, dis: mou
    Moses, Jr, 1-20-1802, compl of: mou; moved to virge of Redstone MM
    Samuel, 8-15-1785, compl of: dancing
    Samuel, 12-12-1785, dis: dancing
    Thomas, 11-12-1792, compl of: "case of difficulty"
    Thomas, 5-19-1802, appt comm
    Thomas, 10-22-1802, rct Redstone MM with father Moses and mother
BLACKBURN, Alice, 7-12-1784, req marriage with Samuel Garretson of Warrington
    Alice, 10-22-1818, req marriage with Samuel Way
    Anthony, 4-9-1781, rct Pipe Creek MM with wife and 4 children
    Anthony, 6-10-1782, rocf Pipe Creek MM with wife Mary and 5 children
    Anthony, 10-13-1783, gct Hopewell MM with father Joseph and family
    Anthony, 10-13-1783, gct Hopewell MM
    Anthony, 12-15-1788, req indulged meeting for Bedford, Pa
    Anthony, 3-20-1799, appt comm
    Anthony, 3-20-1799, compl of: drinking to excess. Son of Thomas
    Anthony, 8-22-1799, read testimony. Retained
    Deborah, 8-13-1781, daughter mou
    Deborah, 10-13-1783, gct Hopewell MM with husband Joseph and 9 children
    Deborah, 10-13-1783, gct Hopewell MM with father Joseph and family
    Elizabeth, 4-9-1781, rct Pipe Creek MM with father Anthony and family
    Elizabeth, 6-10-1782, rocf Pipe Creek MM with father Anthony and family
    Elizabeth, 4-14-1783, req marriage with Jacob Beals
    Elizabeth, 6-9-1794, compl of: mou. Now Wirecarver
    Elizabeth, 8-11-1794, dis: mou. Now Wirecarver
    Elizabeth, 4-24-1800, compl of: mou. Now Rouzer
    Elizabeth, 8-21-1800, dis: mou. Now Rouzer
    Eve, 4-9-1781, rct Pipe Creek MM with father Anthony and family
    Eve, 6-10-1782, rocf Pipe Creek MM with father Anthony and family
    Finly, 10-13-1783, gct Hopewell MM with father Joseph and family
    Finly, 6-9-1794, compl of: mou
    Finly, 9-15-1794, dis: mou
    Isabell, 8-22-1799, req marriage with Thomas Ginnings
    Isaiah, 8-22-1850, rocf Dunnings Creek MM
    James, 10-13-1783, gct Hopewell MM with father Joseph and family
    Jesse, 12-24-1818, rct Dunnings Creek MM with mother Mary
    John, 10-13-1783, gct Hopewell MM with father Joseph and family
    John, 8-11-1788, req marriage with Mary Morton
    John, 2-23-1797, compl of: mou
    John, 2-18-1819, req reinstatement at Smithfield MM, Ohio
    Joseph, 8-13-1781, daughter mou

MENALLEN MINUTES, MARRIAGES, & MISCELLANY

BLACKBURN, Joseph, 2-11-1782, daughter Mary mou to Brannan
    Joseph, 10-13-1783, gct Hopewell MM with wife Deborah and 9 children
    Joseph, 10-13-1783, gct Hopewell MM with father Joseph and family
    Josiah, 3-23-1853, rct Dunnings Creek MM, Bedford Co, Pa
    Mary, 8-13-1781, mou, "Mary, the daughter of Joseph and Deborah Blackburn, who resides on the West Side of the Alegainy Mountains has accomplished her marriage out of the unity of Friends"
    Mary, 2-11-1782, ack mou, now Brannan daughter of Joseph Blackburn, in West Moreland County, Pa, retained
    Mary, 6-10-1782, rocf Pipe Creek MM with husband Anthony and 5 children
    Mary, 6-10-1782, rocf Pipe Creek MM with father Anthony and family
    Mary, 7-13-1795, req marriage with John McGrail
    Mary, 12-24-1818, rct Dunnings Creek MM with son Jesse
    Moses, 3-10-1788, absent from MM
    Moses, 9-15-1794, appt comm
    Rachel, 4-15-1782, to marry Thomas Griffith
    Rachel, 10-13-1783, gct Hopewell MM with father Joseph and family
    Rebecca, 4-9-1781, rct Pipe Creek MM with father Anthony and family
    Rebecca, 5-14-1781, mou: now Hendricks
    Rebecca, 6-10-1782, rocf Pipe Creek MM with father Anthony and family
    Rebecca, 6-22-1797, compl of: mou to first cousin. Now Griffith
    Rebekah, 3-23-1797, req marriage with Thomas McGrail
    Thomas, 4-9-1781, rct Pipe Creek MM with father Anthony and family
    Thomas, 6-10-1782, rocf Pipe Creek MM with father Anthony and family
    Thomas, 10-13-1783, gct Hopewell MM with father Joseph and family
    Thomas, 3-18-1784, rep to QM 5 times thru 5-17-1797
    Thomas, 9-4-1787, appt comm
    Thomas, 9-9-1793, req marriage with Sarah Griffith
    Thomas, 6-9-1794, appt comm
    Thomas, 2-23-1797, compl of: fighting. Son of Thomas
    Thomas, 8-24-1797, compl of: striking a man. Son of Thomas
    Thomas, 3-21-1798, released as recorder of Certificates
    Thomas, 4-10-1799, appt comm
    Thomas, 10-22-1801, req marriage with Elizabeth Bowen
    William, 3-23-1797, req marriage with Amy Kenworthy
    Zachariah, 10-13-1783, gct Hopewell MM with father Joseph and family
BOING, Jonathan, 1-14-1782, appt comm
BONEN, Hannah, 6-20-1833, formerly Wierman, now separated from Hicksites
BONNER, Margaret, 12-21-1815, compl of: mou. Formerly Everitt
    Margaret, 3-20-1816, dis: mou. Formerly Everitt
BONSALL, Ann H., 8-19-1850, appt comm [w]
BOON, Esther C., 12-20-1821, rocf Warrington MM
    Isaac, 11-17-1819, rocf Exeter MM
    Isaac, 4-19-1821, rct Warrington MM for marriage with Esther Starr
    Isaac, 1-18-1826, appt comm
BOON, Isaac, 11-22-1826, appt comm
BORTON, William, 11-17-1847, rocf Chester MM, NJ, as Minister

MINUTES

BOWEN, Abraham, 8-7-1784, compl of: non-attendance
    Elizabeth, 10-22-1801, req marriage with Thomas Blackburn
    Jane, 6-9-1794, compl of: mou. Formerly Mickel. Retained
    Jane, 2-21-1799, compl of: mou. Now Gorden
    John, 7-11-1785, compl of: mou to first cousin
    John, 8-15-1785, dis: mou to first cousin
    Jonathan, 11-11-1782, rep to QM 10 times thru 10-24-1803
    Jonathan, 7-14-1783, appt comm 43 times thru 11-17-1802
    Jonathan, 3-14-1785, appt Overseer in place of Finly McGrew
    Jonathan, 12-15-1788, rct Bedford with wife and family
    Jonathan, 2-23-1797, released as Overseer at Dunnings Creek
    Lidia, 8-10-1789, compl of: mou. Now Mather
    Lydia, 10-12-1789, dis: mou. Now Mather
    Lydia, 7-14-1794, read ack. Retained. rct Exeter MM
    Lydia, Sr, 8-13-1787, req marriage with Thomas Oldham
    Rebecca, 2-10-1794, compl of: allowing daughter to mou
    Rebekah, 8-11-1794, read ack: attended marriage out of unity. Retained
    Sarah, 5-13-1793, compl of: mou. Now Millinger, of Bedford
    Sarah, 1-13-1794, req marriage with James Allison
    Thomas, 10-14-1793, appt comm 9 times thru 11-17-1802
    Thomas, 2-10-1794, compl of: allowing daughter to mou
    Thomas, 8-11-1794, read ack: attended marriage out of unity. Retained
    Thomas, 8-18-1796, rep to QM
    Thomas, 3-23-1797, req marriage with Susanna Smith
    Thomas, 2-20-1800, appt Overseer at Dunnings Creek PM
    Thomas, Jr, 2-10-1783, req marriage with Rebecca Mickle
    Thomas, Jr, 4-14-1794, req membership
BOWER, Abraham, 9-13-1784, disowned: non-attendance
    Michel, 8-11-1783, compl of: mou; non-attendance. Now Pizel
    Michel, 10-13-1783, dis: mou and non-attendance. Now Pizel
BOWIN, Jonathan, 11-10-1783, rep to QM
    Jonathan, 11-15-1784, appt comm
BRACKEN, Caleb, 2-14-1791, req membership
    Caleb, 2-11-1793, rct York MM
BRANNAN, Mary, 2-11-1782, mou: read testimony; retained. Formerly
    Blackburn, daughter of Joseph Blackburn, living in
    Westmoreland County, Pa
BRANNON, Mary, 10-13-1783, gct Hopewell MM; wife of George Brannon
BROOKS, Edward, 7-21-1847, req marriage with Sarah Ann Griest
    Edward, 8-19-1847, rocf Deer Creek MM
    Sarah Ann, 9-20-1848, gct Deer Creek MM
BROUGH, Alice F., 4-20-1870, req membership be discontinued. Mou.
    Formerly Shugh [w]
BROWN, Angelina, 2-22-1855, compl of: mou. Formerly Griest [w]
    Angelina, 3-21-1855, ack error. Retained [w]
    Louisa, 6-18-1857, compl of: mou. Formerly Hewitt [w]
    Maria, 8-19-1868, compl of: mou. Formerly Hoopes [w]
    Maria, 2-17-1869, compl of: mou
    Maria, 3-17-1869, dis: mou. Formerly Hoopes [w]
    Susana, 3-22-1848, req membership thru father Thomas

MENALLEN MINUTES, MARRIAGES, & MISCELLANY

BROWN, Susannah, 7-23-1823, compl of: fornication. Read testimony.
    Retained
    Thomas, 1-19-1848, req membership
    Thomas, 3-22-1848, req membership for daughter Susanna
BRUGH, Alice S., 4-20-1870, relinquishes membership. Formerly Shugh
BUSHONG, Carlane, 8-22-1822, rocf York MM with father Henry and family
    Caroline, 9-23-1829, rct Sadsbury MM, with father Henry and family
    Henry, 8-22-1822, rocf York MM with wife Sarah and 5 children
    Henry, 10-24-1822, appt comm 23 times, thru 8-23-1827
    Henry, 2-20-1823, rep to QM 7 times thru 1-18-1826
    Henry, 8-19-1824, appt assistant clerk
    Henry, 9-23-1829, rct Sadsbury MM, with wife Sarah and 4 children
    Jacob, 8-22-1822, rocf York MM with father Henry and family
    Jacob, 9-23-1829, rct Sadsbury MM, with father Henry and family
    Jesse, 8-22-1822, rocf York MM with father Henry and family
    Jesse Gibbert, 9-23-1829, rct Sadsbury MM, with father Henry and family
    John, 8-22-1822, rocf York MM with father Henry and family
    John, 9-23-1829, rct Sadsbury MM with father Henry and family
    Lydia, 8-22-1822, rocf York MM with father Henry and family
    Sarah, 5-18-1814, rct York MM
    Sarah, 8-22-1822, rocf York MM with husband Henry and 5 children
    Sarah, 9-23-1829, rct Sadsbury MM with husband Henry and 4 children
BUTTERWORTH, Paulina, 5-23-1883, rocf Indiana YM as Minister [w]
    Pauline, 5-23-1883, rocf Miami MM, Ohio as companion to Ann Packer
CADWALLADER, Clara Jane, 1-22-1862, gct Center MM, Center Co, Pa with father William [w]
    David, 4-17-1889, on comm requesting repairs to Warrington Meeting House
    Maria Jane, 12-19-1861, rct Centre MM with father William S.
    Oscar S., 1-22-1862, gct Center MM, Center Co, Pa with father William S. [w]
    William, 6-19-1851, req membership
    William, 1-22-1862, gct Center MM, Center Co, Pa with 2 children [w]
    William, 6-23-1864, rep to MM
    William S., 9-17-1851, req marriage with Rebecca Griest
    William S., 10-18-1860, compl of: mou
    William S., 10-24-1861, ack transgression. Retained
    William S., 12-19-1861, rct Centre MM with two children
CARSON, Hannah, 4-19-1849, ack error. Retained [w]
    Jean, 11-12-1781, compl of: dancing
    Jean, 1-14-1782, continued under care of friends
    Jean, 3-11-1782, compl of: dancing; retained
    Jean, 6-9-1783, compl of: unchastity
    Jean, 8-11-1783, dis: unchastity
CINKLER, John, 4-13-1795, rocf Bradford MM
CLEAVER, Andrew, 11-22-1837, roc as Minister
    Edith W., 1-19-1870, ack mou. Retained [w]
    Edith W., 1-19-1870, rct Centre MM, Centre Co, Pa [w]

MINUTES

CLEAVER, Elizabeth, 8-23-1810, rocf Warrington MM with husband Isaac and 1 child
    Isaac, 8-23-1810, rocf Warrington MM with wife Elizabeth and 1 child
    John, 9-13-1784, req marriage with Susanna Everitt. He of Warrington
    Louisa, 1-17-1855, rct West Branch MM with Amanda, Martha & Mary Garretson [w]
    Louisa W., 8-24-1854, gct West Branch MM with daughter Lydia G. Garretson
    Malinda G., 8-21-1862, resigned membership thru mother Rebecca J. Cleaver [w]
    Mary, 9-9-1782, of Warrington MM, to marry Jonathan Potts
    Rachel, 8-23-1810, rocf Warrington MM with father Isaac and family
    Rebecca J., 8-21-1862, resigned membership with daughter Malinda G. Cleaver [w]
    Susanna, 11-15-1784, rct Warrington MM
    William, 11-23-1853, req marriage with Louisa W. Garretson
    William, 12-22-1853, rocf West Branch MM
    William, 1-17-1855, rct West Branch MM with Amanda, Martha & Mary Garretson [w]
CLEVER, Edith W., 1-19-1870, ack mou. Retained
    Edith W., 2-23-1870, gct Center MM, Center Co, Pa
CLINE, Joseph, 8-20-1846, collector of taxes, collected muster fines
COLLEY, Thomas, 10-10-1785, visiting from Great Brittain
COLLINS, Isaac, 8-10-1789, of Trenton, proposed new edition of Bible to Monthly Meetings
COMBLEY, Samuel, 11-22-1826, has subscribed to establishment of a seminary
COMELY, Jacob, 1-18-1797, appt comm
    Jacob, 11-20-1799, rep to QM
    Samuel, 2-21-1822, rep to QM 4 times thru 1-20-1830
    Samuel, 3-20-1822, appt comm 26 times thru 1832
    Samuel, 8-19-1824, appt clerk
    Samuel, 8-19-1824, appt clerk
    Samuel, 3-23-1831, appt clerk for the day
    Samuel, 12-22-1831, appt clerk for the day
    Samuel, 2-23-1832, appt comm to list names re separation at Baltimore Yearly Meeting
COMER, Mary, 5-12-1788, compl of: neglecting attendance
    Mary, 7-14-1788, dis: non-attendance and contention against practice
    Richard, 5-12-1788, compl of: neglecting attendance, also "attending Musters, charged with being guilty of fornication, used no endeavour to clear himself of the charge and when he was spoke to in these accounts discharged friends on pain of death from coming to treat with him any further on that occasion"
COMLEY, Jacob, 5-23-1798, appt comm 45 times thru 6-23-1814
    Jacob, 8-21-1800, rep to QM 11 times thru 8-20-1812
    Jacob, 4-22-1802, appt to prepare memorial for Isaac Everitt, dec'd
    Jacob, 2-24-1803, released as Overseer at Huntington
    Jesse, 6-21-1810, compl of: mou
    Jesse, 8-23-1810, read testimony. Retained

MENALLEN MINUTES, MARRIAGES, & MISCELLANY

COMLEY, Samuel, 3-23-1808, req marriage with Susannah Wierman
    Samuel, 2-20-1817, appt Guardian for Benjamin Tomlinson
    Samuel, 4-24-1817, appt comm re Benjamin Tomlinson
    Samuel, 6-19-1817, appt to standing comm re care of Benjamin Tomlinson
    Samuel, 8-21-1817, rep to QM
    Samuel, 6-24-1819, appt comm
    Samuel, 12-21-1820, appt comm
    Susanna, 2-20-1806, req marriage with Isaac Wierman
COMLY, Ezra, 6-21-1832, rct Gunpowder MM
    Isaac W., 2-23-1837, rct Westland MM with father Samuel and family
    Jacob, 5-14-1792, rocf Horsham MM with wife Sarah and 3 children
    Jacob, 8-13-1792, rep to QM 13 times thru 8-20-1807
    Jacob, 1-14-1793, appt comm 60 times thru 9-18-1816
    Jacob, 5-11-1795, appt Overseer at Huntington
    Jacob, 7-19-1797, appt Elder at Huntington
    Jacob, 9-18-1816, offers to pay Mary Robinson expenses to date
    Jesse, 5-14-1792, rocf Horsham MM with parents Jacob and Sarah
    Jesse, 5-24-1832, has been absent from meeting for some time
    Lydia, 2-23-1837, rct Westland MM with father Samuel and family
    Phebe, 3-22-1837, rct Westland MM [w]
    Samuel, 5-14-1792, rocf Horsham MM with parents Jacob and Sarah
    Samuel, 12-21-1815, appt comm 18 times thru 3-22-1837
    Samuel, 5-19-1819, appt Overseer
    Samuel, 8-19-1819, rep to QM 5 times thru 5-24-1832
    Samuel, 8-18-1825, appt Overseer
    Samuel, 11-23-1825, appt clerk
    Samuel, 9-18-1833, rep to MM 3 times thru 9-21-1836
    Samuel, 3-22-1837, rct Westland MM with wife Susanna and 2 children [w]
    Sarah, 5-14-1792, rocf Horsham MM with husband Jacob and 3 children
    Sarah, 4-13-1795, appt comm
    Sarah, 3-21-1832, req marriage with Lewis Harry
    Susanna, 5-14-1792, rocf Horsham MM with parents Jacob and Sarah
    Susanna, 10-22-1835, appt Elder
    Susanna, 2-23-1837, rct Westland MM with husband Samuel and 2 children
    Susannah, 5-24-1832, appt Elder
    Susannah, 2-18-1836, appt comm [w]
    Susannah, 8-18-1836, rep to QM [w]
    Susannah, 2-23-1837, rep to QM [w]
COOK, A. G., 5-18-1887, assessed $2.00 for fuel for Ann & Martha Griest
    Adella J., 6-22-1876, req membership. Born 9-11-1879 [w]
    Albert J., 2-19-1873, released from membership
    Amos G., 5-27-1884, rep to MM
    Amos W., 12-23-1874, appt comm
    Amos W., 12-23-1885, assessed $1.00 for Yearly Meeting
    Ann Elizabeth, 8-20-1863, rct Fallcreek MM, Ind with father Asahel W. and family [w]

MINUTES

COOK, Anna, 8-21-1862, formerly Warrington MM member, now removed
    Anna, 8-21-1862, dtr of Martha Cook. Removed from neighborhood [w]
    Anna Eliza, 2-22-1871, compl of: mou. Now Rinehart [w]
    Anne Elizabeth, 8-20-1863, rct Fall Creek MM, Ind with father Asahel and family
    Annie M., 6-22-1876, minor child of one member. Born 9th mo 7th 1873
    Annie M., 6-22-1876, req membership. Born 9-7-1873 [w]
    Ardella, 8-20-1890, appt Elder
    Ardella J., 8-20-1890, appt comm [w]
    Asahel W., 8-20-1863, rct Fall Creek MM, Ind with wife Hannah and 4 children
    Cyrus G., 9-19-1866, compl of: mou; non-attendance
    Cyrus G., 2-21-1867, ack mou. Retained
    Cyrus G., 12-23-1874, requests release from membership
    David, 11-20-1844, req membership
    David, 7-18-1849, appt comm
    David E., 10-24-1844, req membership
    David E., 3-18-1846, rep to MM 5 times thru 10-21-1852
    David E., 5-17-1848, req marriage with Mary McGrail
    David J., 1-20-1858, compl of: mou
    David J., 2-18-1858, read ack. Retained
    Edith Ann, 4-18-1861, req marriage with Franklin W. Cook
    Edith Ann, 10-23-1862, rep to MM [w]
    Edith Ann, 12-17-1862, appt comm [w]
    Edith Ann, 10-22-1863, rep to MM [w]
    Elizabeth, 1-11-1796, compl of: mou. Formerly Wright
    Elizabeth, 4-21-1796, dis: mou
    Ellis, 12-23-1885, assessed $1.00 for Yearly Meeting
    Ellis, 5-18-1887, compl of: mou
    Ellis, 7-20-1887, ack mou. Retained
    Ellis W., 7-20-1887, ack mou. Retained [w]
    Elmira, 2-19-1879, rep to QM [w]
    Elmira J., 4-21-1869, ack mou. Retained
    Elmira J., 1-23-1878, appt comm 7 times thru 4-23-1890 [w]
    Elmira J., 10-20-1880, rep to MM 11 times thru 5-19-1886 [w]
    Elmira J., 4-23-1884, appt assistant clerk [w]
    Elmira J., 4-22-1885, appt assistant clerk [w]
    Elmira J., 4-21-1886, appt assistant clerk [w]
    Elmira J., 12-18-1889, hired to care for meeting house
    Elmira J., 2-20-1878, rep to QM 13 times thru 8-20-1890 [w]
    Elmira Jane, 6-18-1840, rocf Warrington MM with father Jesse and family
    Elmira Jane, 3-23-1881, appt comm [w]
    Fannie, 4-17-1889, on comm requesting repairs to Warrington Meeting House
    Fannie M., 7-17-1889, req membership [w]
    Fanny M, 10-23-1889, req membership
    Franklin W., 2-21-1861, req membership
    Franklin W., 4-18-1861, req marriage with Edith Ann Cook
    Franklin W., 1-23-1863, rep to MM

MENALLEN MINUTES, MARRIAGES, & MISCELLANY

COOK, Franklin W., 3-23-1864, appt comm
    George, 1-21-1891, invalid Friend in need of assistance
    George, 1-21-1891, appt comm [w]
    George H., 5-19-1869, rep to QM
    George H., 5-22-1872, rep to MM
    George H., 5-21-1873, rep to QM
    George H., 5-20-1874, appt comm
    George M., 6-18-1840, rocf Warrington MM with father Jesse and family
    George M., 10-24-1861, compl of: mou
    George M., 11-20-1861, ack transgression. Retained
    George W., 10-22-1863, rct Fall Creek MM, Ind with father Asahel W. and family [w]
    George W., 12-21-1870, rep to MM
    George W., 12-17-1873, rep to MM
    Gideon, 1-18-1843, appt Overseer
    Hannah, 8-21-1862, was Warrington MM member, now removed. Daughter of Martha
    Hannah, 8-20-1863, rct Fallcreek MM, Ind with husband Asahel W. and 4 children [w]
    Harry J., 6-22-1876, minor child of one member. Born 12th mo 16th 1868
    Harvey J., 6-22-1876, req membership. Born 12-16-1868 [w]
    Henry, 8-19-1824, rocf Warrington MM with wife Mary and 2 children
    Henry, 12-23-1824, appt comm
    Henry, 4-19-1827, rct Warrington MM with wife Mary
    Henry, 5-18-1831, rct York MM
    Henry, 8-18-1869, ack mou. Retained
    Henry W., 8-19-1824, rocf Warrington MM with father Henry and family
    Israel, 12-18-1834, req membership
    Israel, 6-18-1835, rep to MM 28 times thru 9-17-1845
    Israel, 11-18-1835, rep to QM 6 times thru 8-21-1845
    Israel, 6-23-1836, appt comm 17 times thru 11-19-1845
    Isreal, 11-21-1838, rep to QM
    Isreal, 12-22-1842, appt comm
    Jacob, 11-13-1786, req marriage with Susanna Speakman. He of Warrington
    Jane, 8-19-1824, rocf Warrington MM with father Henry and family
    Jane, 5-23-1827, gct Warrington MM
    Jennie May, 6-22-1876, minor child of one member. Born 9th mo 8th 1871
    Jennie May, 6-22-1876, req membership. Born 9-8-1871 [w]
    Jess, 6-18-1840, rocf Warrington MM with wife Ruth M. and 4 children [w]
    Jesse, 6-21-1821, rocf Warrington MM. Son of Henry
    Jesse, 12-19-1822, rct Warrington MM
    Jesse, 7-21-1831, rct Warrington MM
    Jesse, 8-23-1832, req membership with wife Rebecca and son William
    Jesse, 8-20-1835, rep to QM, 89 times thru 8-20-1879

MINUTES

COOK, Jesse, 6-23-1836, appt comm 135 times thru 8-20-1879
    Jesse, 8-24-1837, appt comm in charge of graveyards
    Jesse, 5-22-1839, rep to MM 263 times thru 9-18-1879
    Jesse, 6-18-1840, rocf Warrington MM with wife Ruth M. and 4 children
    Jesse, 7-22-1840, appt Elder 26 times thru 4-23-1879
    Jesse, 5-18-1842, appt comm on military demands
    Jesse, 1-18-1843, appt Overseer 7 times thru 7-19-1876
    Jesse, 1-18-1843, rct Fairfax QM as Minister
    Jesse, 1-22-1845, req membership for foster child Sarah Wierman [w]
    Jesse, 1-20-1847, on comm against settling new meeting at Mechanicsville
    Jesse, 4-18-1850, appt clerk
    Jesse, 8-21-1851, appt to care for burying grounds
    Jesse, 4-19-1866, rct Philadelphia YM as Minister
    Jesse, 6-20-1867, appt Trustee at Newberry
    Jesse, 8-18-1880, died 10th of 2nd mo 1880 in his 89th year
    Jesse Harry, 6-18-1840, rocf Warrington MM with father Jesse and family
    Jesse W., 8-22-1822, rocf Warrington MM
    Jesse W., 9-18-1822, has returned to Warrington virge
    Jesse W., 2-19-1824, rocf Warrington MM
    Jesse W., 6-23-1825, rct Warrington MM
    Jesse Wilbert, 6-22-1876, minor child of one member. Born 8th mo 7th 1872
    Jesse Wilbert, 6-22-1876, req membership. Born 8-7-1872 [w]
    Jesse, Jr, 10-19-1842, appt comm 4 times thru 3-22-1848
    Jesse, Jr, 11-23-1842, rep to QM
    Jesse, Jr, 8-24-1843, rep to MM 6 times thru 7-17-1850
    Jesse, Jr, 1-16-1849, appt Overseer
    Jesse, Jr, 4-24-1851, appt clerk
    Jesse, Sr, 9-17-1851, appt comm
    Jesse, Sr, 11-19-1851, rep to QM
    Jesse, Sr, 10-19-1842, appt comm
    John, 4-17-1889, on comm requesting repairs to Warrington Meeting House
    Josiah, 4-19-1827, rocf Warrington MM
    Josiah, 7-23-1834, rct Warrington MM
    Josiah, 2-22-1838, rocf Warrington MM
    Josiah, 4-19-1838, rct Warrington MM to marry Mary Griest
    Josiah, 5-23-1838, appt comm 17 times thru 4-17-1878
    Josiah, 1-23-1839, rep to MM 43 times thru 10-23-1878
    Josiah, 11-19-1856, rep to QM 11 times thru 8-20-1879
    Josiah, 3-22-1871, appt Elder
    Josiah, 7-19-1876, appt Overseer
    Josiah, 4-23-1879, appt Elder
    Josiah, 12-23-1885, assessed $1.00 for Yearly Meeting
    Leah, 8-21-1851, rep to QM [w]
    Leah, 10-18-1854, appt comm [w]

MENALLEN MINUTES, MARRIAGES, & MISCELLANY

COOK, Margaret, 11-19-1851, rep to QM [w]
    Margaret, 2-17-1869, rep to QM [w]
    Margaret, 10-20-1869, rep to MM [w]
    Margaret, 7-20-1870, rep to MM [w]
    Martha, 4-19-1850, appt comm [w]
    Martha, 8-21-1862, formerly of Warrington, now removed with 3 children [w]
    Martha, 5-18-1887, compl of: mou to Ellis W. Cook. Formerly Harris [w]
    Martha, 6-23-1887, ack mou. Retained. Formerly Harris
    Martha, 4-18-1888, req release from membership
    Martha, 4-18-1888, dis: joined another society. Widow of Walker Cook [w]
    Martha Jane, 1-18-1865, rep to MM [w]
    Martha Jane, 5-17-1865, rep to QM [w]
    Martha Jane, 11-18-1868, rep to MM [w]
    Martha Jane, 11-18-1868, rep to QM [w]
    Martha Jane, 1-19-1870, appt comm [w]
    Martha Jane, 1-17-1872, req marriage with Gideon Smith
    Mary, 8-19-1824, rocf Warrington MM with husband Henry and 2 children
    Mary, 4-19-1827, rct Warrington MM with husband Henry
    Mary, 5-23-1827, gct Warrington MM
    Mary, 2-21-1839, rocf Warrington MM
    Mary, 6-18-1840, rocf Warrington MM with father Jesse and family
    Mary, 2-20-1845, appt Elder
    Mary, 11-19-1845, rep to QM 10 times thru 8-23-1866 [w]
    Mary, 7-23-1851, appt Elder
    Mary, 7-19-1854, appt Elder
    Mary, 3-19-1856, appt Overseer [w]
    Mary, 8-21-1862, formerly Warrington MM member, now removed
    Mary, 8-21-1862, daughter of Martha Cook. Removed from neighborhood [w]
    Mary, 1-21-1863, rep to MM 4 times thru 8-23-1867 [w]
    Mary, 1-21-1863, appt comm 36 times thru 5-22-1867 [w]
    Mary, 12-22-1869, compl of:mou. Now Hardy [w]
    Mary Ellen, 8-20-1863, rct Fallcreek MM, Ind with father Asahel W. and family [w]
    Miller G., 6-22-1876, req membership. Born 5-18-1870 [w]
    Milton W., 6-22-1876, req membership. Born 4-24-1874 [w]
    Morton W., 6-22-1876, minor child of one member. Born 7th mo 24th 1874
    Rebecca, 8-23-1832, req membership with husband Jesse and son William
    Rebecca, 7-22-1840, appt Elder 7 times thru 11-21-1855 [w]
    Rebecca, 3-20-1843, appt Overseer [w]
    Rebecca, 1-22-1845, req membership for foster child Sarah Wierman [w]
    Rebecca, 3-18-1846, appt Overseer [w]
    Rebecca, 5-20-1849, appt Overseer [w]
    Rebecca, 6-23-1836, appt comm 40 times thru 6-19-1856 [w]
    Rebecca, 8-20-1835, rep to QM 30 times thru 11-21-1856 [w]

MINUTES

COOK, Rebecca, 8-19-1858, women's meeting produced memorial to her, deceased [w]
    Ruth, 2-23-1839, rep to QM [w]
    Ruth, 5-18-1841, appt comm 4 times thru 5-23-1860 [w]
    Ruth, 5-23-1860, rep to QM [w]
    Ruth G., 2-22-1838, rocf Warrington MM
    Ruth G., 7-19-1843, appt comm [w]
    Ruth M., 6-18-1840, rocf Warrington MM with husband Jesse and 4 children
    Sallie E., 1-22-1873, ack mou. Retained. Now Petry [w]
    Samuel, 8-20-1829, appt comm 3 times thru 3-21-1832
    Samuel, 1-23-1833, rep to MM 3 times thru 7-22-1874
    Samuel, 5-22-1872, rep to QM
    Samuel C., 10-17-1877, rep to MM
    Samuel E., 6-24-1824, rocf Warrington MM
    Samuel E., 8-19-1824, req marriage with Margaret Joice
    Samuel E., 3-17-1858, appt comm 6 times thru 12-20-1876
    Samuel E., 8-19-1868, rep to QM
    Samuel E., 7-21-1841, rep to MM 26 times thru 1-18-1882
    Sarah, 4-21-1837, req membership [w]
    Sarah, 6-24-1841, compl of: mou. Now Griest [w]
    Sarah, 5-23-1888, released from membership. Now Harbold
    Sarah A., 4-17-1878, ack mou. Retained. Now Myers
    Sarah G., 5-17-1837, req membership
    Susanna, 1-15-1787, rct Warrington MM
    Susannah, 1-19-1820, compl of: fornication
    Susannah, 3-22-1820, dis: fornication
    Teressa C., 8-20-1863, rct Fallcreek MM, Ind with father Asahel W. and family [w]
    Thomas, 12-22-1842, appt comm
    Thomas, 3-29-1844, rep to MM
    Thomas, 4-18-1844, appt comm
    Thomas, 12-23-1868, rep to MM
    Thomas E., 2-24-1842, requests membership
    Thomas E., 7-22-1857, appt Overseer 5 times thru 12-17-1873
    Thomas E., 11-22-1843, rep to QM 17 times thru 11-17-1875
    Thomas E., 1-18-1843, appt comm 37 times thru 9-20-1877
    Thomas E., 12-22-1842, rep to MM 68 times thru 5-22-1878
    Thomas Elwood, 6-22-1876, minor child of one member. Born 1st mo 16th 1869
    Thomas Elwood, 6-22-1876, req membership. Born 1-16-1869 [w]
    Thos. E., 8-19-1852, rep to MM
    Thos. E., 10-20-1853, rep to MM
    W. W., 4-24-1862, read ack. Retained
    William, 8-23-1832, req membership with parents Jesse and Rebecca
    William, 11-18-1840, rep to QM
    William, 10-24-1844, rep to MM
    William E., 9-20-1854, appt comm
    William H., 11-21-1860, relinquishes membership

MENALLEN MINUTES, MARRIAGES, & MISCELLANY

COOK, William K., 4-17-1889, appt comm to raise money to repair Warrington Meeting House
    William R., 4-17-1889, on comm requesting repairs to Warrington Meeting House
    William R., 8-21-1889, req membership
    William R., 10-23-1889, req membership [w]
    William W., 2-23-1837, req membership
    William W., 6-22-1837, rct Warrington MM to marry Ruth Griest
    William W., 5-19-1841, rep to QM
    William W., 2-24-1853, rep to QM
    Willie G., 6-22-1876, minor child of one member. Born 5th mo 18th 1870
COOKSON, Daniel, 8-13-1781, rocf Pipe Creek MM with father Samuel
    Daniel, 5-12-1783, rct Warrington MM with father Samuel
    Daniel, 3-23-1825, appt comm 3 times thru 6-23-1825
    Eli, 3-19-1828, req marriage with Phebe Vail
    Eli, 7-23-1862, appt comm 3 times thru 8-20-1863
    Eli, 8-21-1862, rep to QM
    Eli, 4-24-1862, rep to MM 11 times thru 8-24-1865
    Elizabeth, 11-11-1782, req marriage with Ambrose Updegraff
    Franklin, 6-19-1862, appt Overseer at Warrington
    Franklin, 4-17-1889, on comm requesting repairs to Warrington Meeting House
    Franklin W., 5-21-1863, appt comm
    Mary, 8-13-1781, rocf Pipe Creek MM with husband, Samuel
    Phebe, 7-23-1828, rct Warrington MM
    Phebe, 7-23-1862, appt comm [w]
    Samuel, 8-13-1781, rocf Pipe Creek MM, for himself, his wife Mary, Daniel, his youngest child, and his wife's children, namely Samuel, Deborah, and Isaac Haines
    Samuel, 4-15-1782, appt comm
    Samuel, 5-12-1783, rct Warrington MM for self and son Daniel
COOL, Josiah W., 8-22-1877, ack mou. Retained
COX, Amy, 2-15-1790, dis: mou; now Morton
    Amy, 4-12-1790, read acknowledgment
    Amy, 11-17-1813, req membership for 6 minor children
    Amy, 11-17-1813, req membership thru parents Joshua and Amy
    Amy, 3-21-1821, rct New Garden MM, Ind with husband Joshua and family
    Amy, Jr, 4-19-1821, gct New Garden MM, Ind
    Anna, 11-17-1813, req membership thru parents Joshua and Amy
    Anna, 3-21-1821, rct New Garden MM, Ind with father Joshua and family
    Benjamin, 11-17-1813, req membership thru parents Joshua and Amy
    Benjamin, 3-21-1821, rct New Garden MM, Ind with father Joshua and family
    Eamy, 5-11-1789, req marriage with Jesse Morton
    Elizabeth, 9-20-1797, rct Goose Creek MM with 3 daughters
    Elizabeth, 3-21-1821, rct New Garden MM, Ind with father Joshua, Jr and family

MINUTES

COX, Elizabeth, Jr, 1-13-1783, req marriage with Abenezer Speakman
Eme, 7-13-1789, compl of: mou
Eme, 8-10-1789, compl of: mou. Now Morton
Emey, 8-19-1813, retained with husband Joshua. Had been disowned years ago
Emma, 6-11-1787, compl of: married 1st cousin. Formerly Wierman
Emma, 8-13-1787, dis: marrying 1st cousin Joshua Cox
Emy, 9-20-1797, rct Goose Creek MM with mother Elizabeth and family
Ephraim G., 5-18-1842, req marriage with Mary Kettlewell
Isaac, 9-20-1797, rct Goose Creek MM, Bedford Co, Va
Jean, 6-10-1782, cert to Warrington MM with children
Jean, 6-11-1787, compl of: mou. Now Moody
Jean, 9-10-1787, dis: mou. Now Moody
Jesse, 2-10-1783, compl of: horseracing, betting, etc
Jesse, 7-14-1783, dis: drinking; betting; horse racing, etc
Jesse, 3-12-1787, compl of: dancing
Jesse, 2-15-1790, compl of: mou to Rebekah Squibb
Jesse, 1-10-1791, dis: mou
Joseph, 6-11-1787, compl of: marrying 1st cousin, Emma Wierman
Joshua, 8-13-1787, dis: marrying 1st cousin Emma
Joshua, 4-12-1790, read acknowledgment
Joshua, 8-19-1813, retained with wife Emey. Had been disowned some years ago
Joshua, 11-17-1813, req membership for 6 minor children
Joshua, 12-24-1818, appt comm
Joshua, 3-21-1821, rct New Garden MM, Ind with wife Amy and 3 children
Joshua, Jr, 11-17-1813, requests membership
Joshua, Jr, 7-22-1818, req marriage with Maria McGee
Joshua, Jr, 3-21-1821, rct New Garden MM, Ind with wife Mariah and child
Mariah, 3-21-1821, rct New Garden MM, Ind with husband Joshua, Jr and child
Mary, 8-19-1813, req membership. Daughter of Joshua
Mary, 4-19-1821, gct New Garden MM, Ind
Mary, 12-21-1843, rct Pipe Creek MM [w]
Mary, 1-17-1844, gct Pipe Creek MM
Mary L., 2-22-1838, rocf Green St. MM, Phila
Mary L., 1-22-1840, compl of: creating disturbance in Phila MM [w]
Mary L., 11-18-1840, rct Spruce St. MM, Philadelphia, Pa [w]
Phebe, 9-20-1797, rct Goose Creek MM with mother Elizabeth and family
Rebekah, 2-15-1790, compl of: mou to Jesse Cox. Formerly Squibb
Rebekah, 1-10-1791, dis: mou
Ruth, 8-11-1783, mou to John Wireman
Ruth, 10-13-1783, disowned: mou to John Wireman
Samuel, 11-17-1813, req membership thru parents Joshua and Amy
Samuel, 2-24-1820, rct Center MM, Ohio
Sarah, 9-20-1797, rct Goose Creek MM with mother Elizabeth and family

MENALLEN MINUTES, MARRIAGES, & MISCELLANY

COX, Sarah, 8-22-1816, compl of: mou. Formerly Wierman
    Sarah W., 8-22-1816, read testimony. Retained
    Solomon, 11-17-1813, req membership thru parents Joshua & Amy
    Solomon, 3-21-1821, rct New Garden MM, Ind with father Joshua and family
    Susanna, 1-14-1793, compl of: mou. Now Stretch
    Susanna, 3-17-1793, dis: mou. Now Stretch
    Susanna, 11-17-1813, req membership thru parents Joshua & Amy
    Susannah, 4-19-1821, gct New Garden MM, Ind
    Thomas, 11-17-1813, requests membership
    Thomas, 5-18-1814, rct Warrington MM
    Thomas, 8-21-1817, rocf Warrington MM
    Thomas, 8-20-1818, rep to QM
    Thomas, 7-21-1819, appt comm
    Thomas, 4-19-1821, rct New Garden MM, Ind
    William, 3-12-1787, compl of: dancing and disturbing school, son of Widow Cox
    William, 6-11-1787, dis: disturbing school and dancing, son of Nathaniel Cox, deceased
    William, 4-10-1799, compl of: carnal knowledge with woman he is now married to
    William, 7-17-1799, dis: carnal knowledge with woman he is now married to
    William, 1-20-1813, rct Warrington MM
    William, Jr, 10-24-1811, req membership
CYCLAIR, John, 7-20-1796, roc
DAVIS, Sarah, 4-23-1801, compl of: unchastity. Formerly Hendrix
    Sarah, 6-18-1801, dis: unchastity. Formerly Hendrix
DAY, Mary, 6-9-1794, req membership
    Phebe, 7-22-1829, compl of: mou. Formerly Wierman
    Phebe, 8-20-1829, dis: mou. Formerly Wierman
    Rachel W., 7-20-1870, ack mou. Retained
    Rachel W., 8-22-1888, absent member
    Sylvanus, 8-18-1796, rct New Garden MM
DELAP, Catrine, 3-12-1787, req membership
    John, 8-12-1782, compl of: non-attendance etc
    John, 10-14-1782, dis: non-attendance and dancing
    Mary, 7-12-1784, dis: mou to 1st cousin; unchastity. Now Williamson
    Samuel, 12-13-1790, compl of: mou
    William, 5-12-1788, compl of: disturbance, "for publickly opposing friends in a meeting of worship who were reproving a man not of our society who was disturbing the meeting by his publick declaration"
    William, 2-11-1793, compl of: making attempts on chastity of a woman
    William, 5-13-1793, read acknowledgement. Retained
    William, 9-20-1797, compl of: Monallin Preparative meeting informs that the Overseers of the Poor of Tyrone Township on behalf of the township complains of William Delap that he refuses to settle agreeable to his trust
    William, 5-20-1801, compl of: non-attendance; quarrelling, profanity

MINUTES

DELAP, William, 8-20-1801, dis: quarrelling and profane swearing
DENNIN, Abigail, 10-13-1783, gct Hopewell MM with father Andrew and family
    Andrew, 10-13-1783, gct Hopewell MM with wife Rachel and 8 children
    Anthony, 10-13-1783, gct Hopewell MM with father Andrew and family
    Elinor, 10-13-1783, gct Hopewell MM with father Andrew and family
    John, 10-13-1783, gct Hopewell MM with father Andrew and family
    Joseph, 10-13-1783, gct Hopewell MM with father Andrew and family
    Rachel, 10-13-1783, gct Hopewell MM with husband Andrew and 8 children
    Rachel, 10-13-1783, gct Hopewell MM with father Andrew and family
    Susanna, 10-13-1783, gct Hopewell MM with father Andrew and family
    William, 10-13-1783, gct Hopewell MM with father Andrew and family
DERBY, Sarah, 6-21-1888, ack mou. Retained. Formerly Ellis
DETTES, Angeline, 2-22-1888, dis: mou & joined another society. Formerly Hoopes
DINGEE, Charles, 11-12-1787, clerk of Hopewell MM
ELGAR, Elizabeth, 5-15-1786, rocf Warrington MM with father Joseph and family
    John, 5-15-1786, rocf Warrington MM with father Joseph and family
    John, 5-14-1794, rct Pipe Creek MM with father Joseph and family
    Joseph, 5-15-1786, rocf Warrington MM with wife Margaret and 6 children
    Joseph, 5-15-1786, rocf Warrington MM with father Joseph and family
    Joseph, 1-12-1787, rct York MM as Minister
    Joseph, 2-9-1789, rct Goose Creek MM, Va as Minister
    Joseph, 5-11-1789, appt comm, to visit Bedford Co Meeting
    Joseph, 6-15-1789, ret cert from Goose Creek as Minister
    Joseph, 11-9-1789, rct Fairfax QM as Minister
    Joseph, 8-15-1791, rct Pipe Creek MM for son Joseph, an apprentice
    Joseph, 8-13-1792, rocf Fairfax MM
    Joseph, 9-11-1786, rep to QM 15 times thru 11-11-1793
    Joseph, 7-10-1786, appt comm 29 times thru 4-14-1794
    Joseph, 5-14-1794, rct Pipe Creek MM with wife Margaret and 3 children
    Margaret, 5-15-1786, rocf Warrington MM with husband Joseph and 6 children
    Margaret, 11-13-1786, to serve as Elder at Monallin
    Margaret, 2-15-1790, released as Elder and appt Minister
    Margaret, 3-12-1792, expressed a concern
    Margaret, 7-9-1792, rct York MM and Pipe Creek MM as Minister
    Margaret, 7-15-1793, rct Blackwater YM in Va as Minister
    Margaret, 5-14-1794, rct Pipe Creek MM with husband Joseph and 3 children
    Margret, 3-14-1791, rct Indian Springs MM as Minister
    Mary, 5-15-1786, rocf Warrington MM with father Joseph and family
    Mary, 4-14-1794, req marriage with Amos Farquar
    Nathan, 5-15-1786, rocf Warrington MM with father Joseph and family
    Nathan, 5-14-1794, rct Pipe Creek MM with father Joseph and family
    Samuel, 5-15-1786, rocf Warrington MM with father Joseph and family

MENALLEN MINUTES, MARRIAGES, & MISCELLANY

ELGAR, Samuel, 5-15-1786, rocf Warrington MM with father Joseph and family
    Samuel, 5-14-1794, rct Pipe Creek MM with father Joseph and family
ELIOT, Alice, 4-11-1785, rct Warrington with husband Isaac and family
    Benjamin, 4-11-1785, rct Warrington MM with father Isaac and family
    Elizabeth, 4-11-1785, rct Warrington MM with father Isaac and family
    Isaac, 4-11-1785, rct Warrington MM with wife Alice and 3 children
    Joseph, 4-11-1785, rct Warrington MM with father Isaac and family
ELLET, Benjamin, 1-12-1784, rocf Warrington MM with father Isaac and family
    Elice, 1-12-1784, rocf Warrington with husband Isaac and family
    Isaac, 1-12-1784, rocf Warrington MM with wife Elice and 2 children
    Joseph, 1-12-1784, rocf Warrington MM with father Isaac and family
ELLIOTT, Eli, 3-23-1825, appt comm
    Eli, 3-23-1825, appt comm
    Eli, 6-23-1825, appt comm
ELLIS, Elizabeth, 1-21-1835, req membership for 3 children
    Elizabeth, 4-23-1835, req membership
    Elizabeth, 4-23-1835, rocf Pipe Creek MM [w]
    Elizabeth, 2-20-1845, appt Elder
    Elizabeth, 9-21-1836, appt comm 9 times thru 3-19-1845 [w]
    Elizabeth, 5-17-1848, appt Elder
    Elizabeth, 11-18-1835, rep to QM 14 times thru 8-19-1852 [w]
    Louisa, 1-21-1835, req membership thru parents William and Elizabeth
    Louiza, 12-21-1848, req marriage with Hiram Griest
    Mary, 3-20-1861, rocf Wilmington MM, Del
    Mary, 5-22-1861, rep to QM 19 times thru 8-22-1871 [w]
    Mary, 4-24-1862, appt Overseer [w]
    Mary, 4-20-1865, appt Overseer [w]
    Mary, 12-23-1868, appt Overseer [w]
    Mary, 1-19-1870, appt comm 20 times thru 1-19-1870 [w]
    Mary, 4-20-1870, appt Elder
    Mary, 12-17-1862, rep to MM 21 times thru 10-19-1870 [w]
    Mary, 5-22-1872, gct London Grove MM, Chester Co, Pa
    Mary Ann, 1-21-1835, req membership by parents William and Elizabeth
    Mary Ann, 1-22-1845, appt comm [w]
    Mary Ann, 5-21-1845, rep to QM 7 times thru 8-19-1874 [w]
    Mary Ann, 11-21-1849, appt assistant clerk [w]
    Mary Ann, 9-17-1862, rep to MM 3 times thru 12-17-1873 [w]
    Mary Ann, 6-20-1867, appt assistant clerk [w]
    Mary Ann, 8-19-1868, appt assistant clerk [w]
    Sarah, 6-21-1888, ack mou. Retained. Now Derby
    Sarah J., 11-18-1857, appt comm [w]
    Sarah Jane, 1-21-1835, req membership by parents William and Elizabeth
    Sarah Jane, 1-19-1853, appt comm [w]
    Sarah Jane, 4-23-1857, appt comm [w]
    William, 2-18-1830, req membership

MINUTES

ELLIS, William, 2-23-1832, appt comm to list names re separation at Baltimore Yearly Meeting
    William, 1-21-1835, req membership for 3 children
    William, 2-19-1835, rct Western Pa with Joel Garretson
    William, 6-22-1837, rct parts of Ohio as Minister
    William, 11-22-1837, named as Minister
    William, 12-20-1838, rct Fairfax MM as Minister [w]
    William, 8-20-1840, rct Philadelphia YM as Minister
    William, 7-21-1841, rct Fairfax MM as Minister
    William, 5-18-1842, appt comm on military demands
    William, 7-20-1842, rct Sandy Spring MM as Minister
    William, 1-17-1843, rct Fairfax MM as Minister [w]
    William, 4-20-1843, rct York MM as Minister
    William, 2-22-1844, rct Frederick Co, Md as Minister [w]
    William, 8-22-1844, rct Forrest and York as Minister
    William, 8-22-1844, rct York Co as Minister [w]
    William, 7-23-1845, gct Fairfax QM as Minister
    William, 1-21-1846, gct Fairfax QM as Minister
    William, 1-22-1846, rct Fairfax QM as Minister [w]
    William, 7-22-1846, rct Chester, Cumberland, York Cos, Pa as Minister
    William, 1-19-1848, rct Frederick Co, Md as Minister
    William, 5-23-1849, rct Baltimore QM as Minister
    William, 2-21-1850, gct Philadelphia YM as Minister
    William, 9-19-1860, rct Wilmington MM, Del to marry Mary Fisher
    William, 1-22-1862, rct Gettysburg Area as Minister
    William, 1-22-1862, rct Gettysburg to appoint a meeting [w]
    William, 9-24-1863, rct Philadelphia and Delaware as Minister
    William, 9-24-1863, rct Philadelphia etc as Minister [w]
    William, 7-17-1867, rct Nottingham QM as Minister
    William, 12-23-1830, appt comm 62 times thru 4-22-1868
    William, 5-18-1831, rep to QM 51 times thru 11-18-1868
    William, 3-20-1833, rep to MM 65 times thru 2-17-1869
    William, 4-19-1869, rct Philadelphia YM as Minister [w]
    William, 8-17-1870, a Minister, died 14th of 2nd mo 1870
EPLEY, Rebecca, 8-22-1877, requests membership
EPPLEY, Jane, 2-20-1868, rep to QM [w]
    Jane, 7-22-1869, appt comm 4 times thru 3-23-1881 [w]
    Jane, 11-17-1875, rep to QM [w]
    Jane, 2-23-1876, req membership for daughter Rebecca [w]
    Jane, 5-22-1866, rep to MM 15 times thru 8-22-1883 [w]
    Jane, 8-22-1883, appt Overseer [w]
    Phebe J., 8-22-1888, absent member. Now in New Carlisle, Ohio
    Phebe Jane, 2-20-1878, rep to MM 5 times thru 10-18-1882 [w]
    Phebe Jane, 2-20-1878, appt Overseer [w]
    Phebe Jane, 10-18-1882, appt comm [w]
    Phebe Jane, 11-22-1882, rep to QM [w]
    Phebe Jane, 2-21-1883, rep to QM [w]
    Rebecca, 2-23-1876, req membership thru mother Jane [w]
    Rebecca, 8-22-1888, absent member. Now in New Carlisle, Ohio [w]
    Rebecca M., 12-22-1880, rep to MM [w]

MENALLEN MINUTES, MARRIAGES, & MISCELLANY

EPPLEY, Jane, 1-19-1870, rep to MM 8 times thru 3-18-1874 [w]
    Jane, 3-22-1871, appt comm 6 times thru 10-21-1871 [w]
    Phebe Jane, 8-22-1871, rep to QM [w]
ERB, Beulah, 10-23-1889, rct Pipe Creek MM [w]
    Beulah H., 9-17-1872, ack mou. Retained. Formerly Shugh [w]
    Beulah H., 11-20-1889, gct Pipe Creek MM. Formerly Shugh
EVANS, Jane, 8-21-1862, formerly Warrington MM member, now removed
EVERETT, Elizabeth, 6-22-1826, req marriage with Joel Garretson
    Isaac, 5-12-1783, appt comm
    Isaac, 3-9-1789, appt comm
    John, 5-17-1826, rep to QM
EVERIT, Isaac, 4-13-1789, rct Eastward on this Continent as Minister
EVERITT, Elizabeth, 2-18-1802, dis: unchastity. Daughter of Joseph
    Elizabeth, 9-15-1783, req marriage with Isaac Pearson
    Elizabeth, 11-19-1800, Womens meeting reports, that she has "left the parts in a privet unbecoming manner without the knowledge of parent or friends"
    Elizabeth, 12-18-1823, req marriage with Eli Griest
    George W., 5-17-1837, rct Westland MM, Pa
    Hamilton, 3-23-1831, req marriage with Rebeckah R. Garretson
    Hamilton, 11-23-1853, compl of: allowing daughter to mou; non-attendance
    Hamilton, 2-23-1854, dis: daughter mou; non-attendance
    Hannah, 9-21-1796, req marriage with Charles Underwood
    Isaac, 10-15-1781, rct several meetings as Minister
    Isaac, 5-13-1782, rep to QM
    Isaac, 4-10-1786, rct Baltimore QM and London Grove QM as Minister
    Isaac, 5-12-1788, rct Fairfax Quarter as Minister, also Maryland meetings
    Isaac, 7-14-1788, returned cert endorsed by Westland MM and Fairfax QM
    Isaac, 4-12-1790, rocf Nine Partners MM, NY, as Minister returning
    Isaac, 8-9-1790, rocf meetings in New England as Minister
    Isaac, 1-13-1794, rocf Pipe Creek MM with Uncle William Kenworthy
    Isaac, 4-13-1795, rct Philadelphia QM as Minister
    Isaac, 11-23-1796, rct Fairfax QM as Minister
    Isaac, 3-23-1797, rct friends up the Susquehanna as Minister
    Isaac, 11-21-1798, compl of: mou
    Isaac, 12-20-1798, read testimony. Retained
    Isaac, 8-22-1799, rct Baltimore QM as Minister
    Isaac, 10-9-1780, appt comm 46 times thru 12-19-1799
    Isaac, 1-22-1800, rct MMs in NY, NJ and PA as Minister
    Isaac, 5-14-1781, rep to QM 15 times thru 11-19-1800
    Isaac, 11-19-1800, report from Dunnings Creek PM, that "Isaac Everitt of Joseph has left the neighborhood in a reproachful manner and took his sister with him unknown to his parent"
    Isaac, 1-21-1801, rct Southern States as Minister
    Isaac, 2-18-1802, dis: left area in reproachful manner. Son of Joseph
    Isaac, 8-18-1808, compl of: fighting
    Isaac, 1-18-1809, dis: fighting

MINUTES

EVERITT, John, 1-13-1794, rocf Pipe Creek MM with Uncle William Kenworthy
    John, 8-18-1808, compl of: fighting. Read acknowledgment. Retained
    John, 8-23-1821, appt comm
    John, 6-24-1824, compl of: attending a marriage by hireling minister
    John, 6-24-1824, read testimony. Retained
    John, 6-24-1824, compl of: attending a marriage by hireling minister
    John, 6-24-1824, read testimony. Retained
    John, 10-20-1825, appt comm
    John, 4-19-1827, appt to settle with Benjamin Tumbleson's trustees
    John, 8-20-1829, rep to QM
    John, 5-17-1837, rct Westland MM, Pa with wife Susanna
    John, Jr, 8-23-1827, compl of: married first cousin
    Joseph, 6-9-1794, rocf Pipe Creek MM for self and wife Sarah
    Joseph, 7-14-1794, cert returned to Pipe Creek, not accepted here, [The committee] on inspection are of the mind that in a short time his wife will be chargeable to friends she not being capable of receiving advice or taking care of herself
    Julia, 12-20-1832, compl of: mou. Now Welsh
    Malinda, 11-20-1833, req marriage with Barzillai Garretson
    Margaret, 12-21-1815, compl of: mou. Now Bonner
    Margaret, 3-20-1816, dis: mou. Now Bonner
    Martha, 4-11-1791, req marriage with Thomas Pearson
    Rebecca, 8-22-1839, rep to QM [w]
    Rebecca, 8-18-1853, compl of: attending mou of her minor daughter [w]
    Rebecca, 1-18-1854, ack error. Retained [w]
    Rebecca R., 5-17-1854, req membership be discontinued [w]
    Sarah, 6-9-1794, rocf Pipe Creek MM with husband Joseph
    Sarah, 7-14-1794, cert returned to Pipe Creek, not accepted here, [see Joseph Everitt]
    Susanna, 9-13-1784, req marriage with John Cleaver of Warrington
    Susanna, 3-10-1794, rocf Warrington MM
    Susanna, 5-17-1837, rct Westland MM, Pa with husband John
    Susannah, 6-18-1835, appt comm [w]
    Susannah, 6-27-1837, gct Westland MM with husband John [w]
FARQUAR, Amos, 4-14-1794, req marriage with Mary Elgar
    Benjamin, 4-14-1794, req marriage with Rachel Wright
FARQUER, Mary, 7-14-1794, roc
FARQUHAR, Rachel, 9-20-1815, compl of: mou. Formerly Wright
    Rachel, 1-17-1816, dis: mou. Formerly Wright
    Sarah, 3-12-1792, of Pipe Creek MM, expressed a concern
    Sarah, 2-23-1804, rct this area as Minister
FAULK, Sarah, 9-14-1795, compl of: was baptized in Episcopal Church
    Sarah, 12-14-1795, dis: partook of Baptism in Episcopal Church
FISHER, Alice, 6-9-1794, rocf Warrington MM. Child of Isaac Fisher
    Alice, 8-21-1800, rct Westland MM with father Abel John and family
    Ann, 4-15-1863, rocf Short Creek MM, Ohio as Minister
    Elizabeth, 2-15-1796, req membership thru father Samuel
    Elizabeth, 7-19-1797, rct Westland MM with father Samuel and family
    Frances, 7-19-1797, rct Westland MM with father Samuel and family

MENALLEN MINUTES, MARRIAGES, & MISCELLANY

FISHER, Isaac, 6-9-1794, children rocf Warrington MM
    Isaac, 6-9-1794, rocf Warrington MM. Child of Isaac Fisher
    Isaac, 9-15-1794, rocf Warrington MM
    Isaac, 5-17-1797, appt comm
    Isaac, 2-21-1799, rep to QM
    Isaac, 5-22-1799, appt comm
    Isaac, 8-22-1799, req marriage with Elizabeth Hancock
    Joel, 10-23-1851, rocf York MM with wife Mary [w]
    Joel, 1-21-1852, rep to MM 6 times thru 5-23-1855
    Joel, 5-23-1855, rep to QM
    John, 6-9-1794, rocf Warrington MM. Child of Isaac Fisher
    Mary, 6-9-1794, rocf Warrington MM. Child of Isaac Fisher
    Mary, 2-15-1796, req membership thru father Samuel
    Mary, 7-19-1797, rct Westland MM with father Samuel and family
    Mary, 10-23-1851, rocf York MM with husband Joel [w]
    Mary, 11-17-1852, rep to QM 4 times thru 5-19-1858 [w]
    Mary, 5-19-1852, appt comm 10 times thru 5-19-1858 [w]
    Mary, 2-24-1859, gct Wilmington MM, Del
    Rachel, 7-19-1797, rct Westland MM with father Samuel and family
    Ruth, 6-9-1794, rocf Warrington MM. Child of Isaac Fisher
    Ruth, 4-13-1795, rct Kennet MM
    Ruth, 8-10-1795, rocf Kennett MM
    Ruth, 7-19-1797, rct Westland MM with husband Samuel and 4 children
    Ruth, 8-21-1800, rct Westland MM with father Abel John and family
    Samuel, 6-15-1795, rocf New Garden MM
    Samuel, 2-15-1796, req membership thru father Samuel
    Samuel, 8-18-1796, compl of: wagering
    Samuel, 7-19-1797, rct Westland MM with wife Ruth and 4 children
FLETCHER, Mary, 1-9-1786, compl of: mou to 1st cousin. Formerly Loan, now residing in Bedford Co, Pa
    Mary, 2-13-1786, dis: mou to 1st cousin. Formerly Loan
FOULK, John, 12-20-1827, attended as Minister
FRENCH, Thomas, 2-19-1818, rocf Salem MM, Ohio, as minister
FULLER, Elizabeth, 7-22-1846, rocf Baltimore MM, W. Dist. Daughter of Elizabeth M.
    Elizabeth, 10-18-1849, rct Roaring Creek MM, thru mother Elizabeth M. [w]
    Elizabeth M., 3-20-1844, rocf Baltimore MM, Western District [w]
    Elizabeth M., 8-22-1844, appt Minister
    Elizabeth M., 8-22-1844, frequently appears as Minister [w]
    Elizabeth M., 9-18-1844, appt comm 4 times thru 4-24-1845 [w]
    Elizabeth M., 5-21-1845, rep to QM [w]
    Elizabeth M., 10-18-1849, rct Roaring Creek MM, Columbia Co, Pa for daughter [w]
GARRETSON, A. W., 4-17-1889, on comm requesting repairs to Warrington Meeting House
    Abel, 4-17-1889, appt comm to raise money to repair Warrington Meeting House
    Alice, 9-13-1784, rct Warrington MM

MINUTES

GARRETSON, Amanda M., 1-17-1855, rct West Branch MM thru William Cleaver [w]
    Amanda M., 2-22-1855, gct West Branch MM
    Amos, 9-23-1801, rct Pipe Creek MM
    Amos, 6-23-1803, rocf Pipe Creek MM with wife Mary
    Amos, 3-21-1811, rct Pipe Creek MM with wife Mary and 3 children
    Ann H., 7-20-1870, gct Clear Creek MM, Putnam Co, Ill
    Anna, 4-23-1863, req to be excused from serving as Overseer [w]
    Anna, 6-19-1863, rep to MM [w]
    Anne, 8-19-1850, appt comm [w]
    Anne, 4-17-1889, on comm requesting repairs to Warrington Meeting House
    Annie, 4-24-1862, appt Overseer [w]
    Annie, 5-19-1886, rep to QM [w]
    Annie M., 2-18-1885, rep to MM [w]
    Annie M., 2-24-1887, appt comm
    Aquilla G., 11-17-1858, gct Penns Grove MM, Chester Co, Pa
    Arnold, 11-22-1871, appt Trustee in place of Franklin Cookson
    Arnold, 11-22-1882, req release as Trustee of Warrington property
    Arnold, 4-17-1889, appt comm to raise money to repair Warrington Meeting House
    Arnold, 4-17-1889, on comm requesting repairs to Warrington Meeting House
    Aron, 6-9-1794, rocf Warrington MM with father John and family
    Aron, 2-21-1799, rocf Warrington MM with wife Mary and 8 children
    Aron, 2-21-1799, rocf Warrington MM with father Aron and family
    Barzilla, 2-23-1837, rocf Warrington MM with wife Malinda and 2 children [w]
    Barzilla, 6-22-1837, appt comm
    Barzilla, 3-21-1838, rep to MM
    Barzilla, 8-23-1838, appt assistant clerk
    Barzilla, 11-21-1838, rep to MM
    Barzilla, 2-24-1842, rct Warrington MM with wife Malinda and 2 children
    Barzillai, 11-20-1833, req marriage with Malinda Everitt
    Barzillai, 12-19-1833, rocf Warrington MM
    Benjamin, 2-21-1799, rocf Warrington MM with father Aron and family
    Benjamin, 6-19-1862, appt Overseer at Newberry
    Charles, 11-18-1857, rct Prairie Grove MM, Iowa with father Mahlon and family
    Content, 12-18-1800, req marriage with Jesse Russel
    Daniel, 6-19-1862, appt Overseer at Warrington
    Daniel, 6-23-1864, appt Overseer
    Daniel, 7-20-1864, appt comm
    Daniel, 8-18-1864, declines to serve as Overseer
    Eli, 1-21-1885, rep to MM
    Eli, 2-18-1885, rep to QM
    Eli, 3-18-1885, rep to MM
    Eli P., 4-18-1888, req membership be discontinued [w]
    Eliza, 3-21-1811, rct Pipe Creek MM with father Amos and family

MENALLEN MINUTES, MARRIAGES, & MISCELLANY

GARRETSON, Eliza, 6-23-1842, appt comm 9 times thru 8-18-1853 [w]
    Eliza, 12-22-1842, rocf Warrington MM with husband Mahlon and son Isaac [w]
    Eliza, 11-20-1844, rep to QM 4 times thru 8-18-1853 [w]
    Eliza, 5-17-1848, appt Elder
    Eliza, 11-18-1857, rct Prairie Grove MM, Iowa with husband Mahlon and 6 children
    Elizabeth, 6-9-1794, rocf Warrington MM with father John and family
    Elizabeth, 2-21-1799, rocf Warrington MM with father Aron and family
    Elizabeth, 12-22-1808, rocf Sadsbury MM
    Elizabeth, 4-19-1838, appt comm 4 times thru 4-24-1845 [w]
    Elizabeth, 8-22-1844, rep to QM [w]
    Elizabeth, 5-22-1857, gct Penns Grove MM, Chester Co, Pa
    Elizabeth C., 2-20-1845, appt comm [w]
    Elizabeth E., 11-21-1838, appt clerk [w]
    Elizabeth E., 9-18-1839, appt Overseer [w]
    Elizabeth E., 7-22-1840, declined appointment as Elder
    Elizabeth E., 7-22-1840, appt Elder [w]
    Elizabeth E., 7-22-1840, req release as Elder [w]
    Elizabeth E., 8-24-1843, appt clerk [w]
    Elizabeth E., 5-21-1835, rep to QM 21 times thru 8-19-1852 [w]
    Elizabeth E., 3-18-1835, appt comm 37 times thru 12-22-1853 [w]
    Hannah, 11-18-1835, rep to QM 7 times thru 11-22-1854 [w]
    Hannah, 3-18-1846, appt Overseer [w]
    Hannah, 6-18-1835, appt comm 17 times thru 7-18-1855 [w]
    Hannah, 8-18-1869, rep to MM [w]
    Hannah A., 7-23-1862, appt comm [w]
    Hannah A., 6-19-1863, rep to MM [w]
    Hannah A., 11-19-1864, rep to MM [w]
    Hannah A., 5-22-1867, rep to MM [w]
    Hannah A., 5-22-1867, appt comm [w]
    Hannah Ann, 10-23-1862, rep to MM 9 times thru 11-22-1876 [w]
    Hannah Ann, 2-20-1867, appt comm 5 times thru 12-23-1874 [w]
    Hannah Ann, 2-17-1869, rep to QM 6 times thru 8-18-1875 [w]
    Hannah M., 11-21-1860, gct Penns Grove MM, Chester Co, Pa
    Hannah S., 12-17-1862, rep to MM [w]
    Isaac, 5-9-1785, rep to QM
    Isaac, 10-10-1785, rct Darby MM
    Isaac, 6-12-1786, rocf Darby MM
    Isaac, 8-14-1786, appt comm
    Isaac, 7-9-1787, rct Fairfax MM
    Isaac, 8-13-1787, roc
    Isaac, 12-22-1842, rocf Warrington MM with parents Mahlon and Eliza [w]
    Isaac B., 2-18-1836, rep to QM
    Isaac Elwood, 11-18-1857, rct Prairie Grove MM, Iowa with father Mahlon and family
    Isaac N., 11-22-1837, rep to QM
    Isaac P., 12-18-1834, read testimony. Retained
    Isaac P., 7-18-1838, rep to MM 11 times thru 2-20-1845

MINUTES

GARRETSON, Isaac P., 2-21-1839, rep to QM 5 times thru 8-21-1845
    Isaac P., 11-17-1841, appt comm
    Isaac P., 12-23-1841, appt Overseer
    Isaac P., 5-18-1842, appt comm on military demands
    Isaac P., 12-22-1842, req release as Overseer
    Isaac P., 2-22-1844, appt comm
    Isaiah, 4-19-1827, appt comm
    Isaiah, 6-24-1852, rep to MM
    Israel, 6-20-1867, appt Trustee at Newberry
    Israel, 3-17-1875, appt assistant clerk 8 times thru 3-19-1884
    Israel, 2-22-1882, appt Overseer
    Israel, 2-21-1883, appt to comm to plan and build new meeting house
    Israel, 4-19-1882, appt Elder 4 times thru 4-22-1885 [w]
    Israel, 6-19-1862, rep to MM 20 times thru 11-18-1885
    Israel, 11-18-1885, appt custodian of old records
    Israel, 12-23-1885, assessed $3.50 for Yearly Meeting
    Israel, 8-18-1886, rep to Yearly Meeting
    Israel, 3-23-1887, only surviving trustee at Newberry
    Israel, 3-23-1887, surviving trustee at Warrington
    Israel, 5-18-1887, assessed $3.00 for fuel for Ann and Martha Griest
    Israel, 6-23-1887, clerk for the day
    Israel, 2-21-1872, rep to QM 21 times thru 8-17-1887
    Israel, 9-22-1887, clerk for the day
    Israel, 10-19-1887, clerk for the day
    Israel, 7-23-1873, appt comm 25 times thru 11-23-1887
    Israel, 12-21-1887, appt recorder of Certificates of Removal [w]
    Israel, Jr, 4-24-1862, rep to MM
    Israel, Jr, 4-24-1862, appt Trustee at Newberry
    Israel, Jr, 4-24-1862, appt to care for Newberry graveyard
    Israel, Sr, 9-17-1862, rep to MM
    Jacob, 6-22-1848, rep to QM
    Jacob, 4-24-1862, appt to care for Newberry graveyard
    Jacob B., 12-23-1885, assessed $1.00 for Yearly Meeting
    Jacob Blair, 3-23-1887, appt Trustee for Warrington & Newberry
    James W., 11-18-1857, rct Prairie Grove MM, Iowa with father Mahlon and family
    Jesse B., 1-21-1864, ack mou. Retained
    Jesse B., 3-23-1864, rct Clear Creek MM, Ill
    Jno, 8-13-1787, rep to QM
    Joel, 9-23-1807, req marriage with Martha Pearson
    Joel, 6-23-1814, appt recorder of Births and Deaths in place of Isaac Pearson, decd
    Joel, 6-19-1817, appt assistant clerk 4 times thru 6-19-1834
    Joel, 5-19-1819, appt clerk for the day
    Joel, 8-19-1819, approved as Minister
    Joel, 8-19-1819, plans to attend YM at Mt. Pleasant, Ohio
    Joel, 4-20-1820, rct Centre MM as Minister with Ruth McMilin
    Joel, 1-22-1823, rct Baltimore Quarter as Minister
    Joel, 12-18-1823, rct Washington and Indian Springs as Minister
    Joel, 6-22-1826, req marriage with Elizabeth Everitt

MENALLEN MINUTES, MARRIAGES, & MISCELLANY

GARRETSON, Joel, 3-21-1827, rct Warrington Quarter as Minister
    Joel, 3-23-1831, rct Warrington as Minister
    Joel, 2-23-1832, appt clerk for the day
    Joel, 2-23-1832, appt comm to list names re separation at Baltimore Yearly Meeting
    Joel, 5-24-1832, appt recorder of Marriages, to replace George Wilson
    Joel, 2-21-1833, appt clerk for the day
    Joel, 4-24-1834, appt clerk for the day
    Joel, 1-21-1835, rct Western Pa as Minister
    Joel, 7-20-1836, rct Centre QM as Minister
    Joel, 2-22-1838, rct Baltimore and Western Quarter as Minister
    Joel, 2-22-1838, gct Baltimore YM as Minister [w]
    Joel, 6-21-1838, rct Ohio YM as Minister [w]
    Joel, 3-17-1841, gct York, Adams and Cumberland Cos, Pa as Minister
    Joel, 3-17-1841, rct York, Cumberland and Adams Cos, Pa as Minister [w]
    Joel, 4-21-1842, rct appoint meetings in Pa and Md
    Joel, 2-23-1843, rct Pa, Md, and Va as Minister [w]
    Joel, 5-22-1844, rct Adams, York, Cumberland Cos as Minister
    Joel, 5-24-1844, rct Pa and Md as Minister [w]
    Joel, 7-17-1844, appt to record Marriage Certificates
    Joel, 4-24-1845, rct adjacent counties as Minister
    Joel, 5-21-1845, rct Fishing Creek Half Year Meeting as Minister [w]
    Joel, 9-23-1846, rct Western Pa and Ohio as Minister
    Joel, 9-22-1847, gct surrounding counties as Minister
    Joel, 8-24-1815, rep to QM 23 times thru 11-20-1850
    Joel, 10-24-1811, appt comm 88 times thru 7-23-1851
    Joel, 6-19-1834, rep to MM 18 times thru 10-20-1853
    Joel, 11-23-1853, compl of: deception in obtaining money
    Joel, 12-22-1853, comm reports no wrong. Complaint to be erased
    Joel, 5-17-1854, case appealed to QM for assistance
    Joel, 5-23-1855, dis: obtaining money under false pretenses
    Joel, 8-23-1855, notifies of intention to appeal to QM
    Joel B., 4-20-1864, appt comm
    Joel T., 10-23-1862, rep to MM 5 times thru 8-20-1863
    Joel V., 7-23-1862, rep to MM 16 times thru 4-21-1875
    Joel V., 2-22-1866, rep to QM
    Joel V., 1-23-1867, appt comm 9 times thru 2-24-1887
    Joel V., 2-20-1868, rep to QM
    Joel V., 5-19-1875, rep to QM
    Joel V., 3-23-1887, appt Trustee for Warrington and Newberry
    Joel V., 5-18-1887, assessed $2.00 for fuel for Ann and Martha Griest
    Joel V., 8-20-1890, appt Elder
    Joel V., 8-20-1890, appt comm [w]
    Joel, Jr, 11-19-1851, compl of: mou
    Joel, Jr, 3-17-1858, compl of: drinking, non-attendance; poor conduct
    Joel, Jr, 8-19-1858, comm reports he is in Salem, Iowa
    Joel, Jr, 2-24-1859, dis: drinking; nonattendance
    Joel, Jr, 11-21-1862, rep to MM
    Joel, Jr., 3-23-1853, comm reports not guilty; retained

MINUTES

GARRETSON, John, 10-9-1780, appt comm 55 times thru 4-20-1815
John, 3-11-1782, rep to QM
John, 7-15-1782, released as Overseer at Huntington
John, 9-9-1793, released as recorder of Marriage Certificates
John, 6-9-1794, rocf Warrington MM with wife Tamer and 5 children
John, 2-22-1798, compl of: non-attendance; muster; suing at law
John, 10-10-1798, dis: non-attendance; muster; suing a member at law
John, 2-21-1799, rocf Warrington MM with father Aron and family
John, 4-23-1807, req marriage with Rebecka Bateman
John, 10-9-1809, req marriage with Rebecca Thomas. Son of Samuel
John, 3-11-1782, rep to QM 14 times thru 5-17-1815
John, 7-19-1815, released as recorder of Marriage Certificates
John, 7-19-1815, rct Miami MM, Ohio with wife Rebekah and 4 children
John, 2-23-1837, rocf Warrington MM with father Barzilla and family
John, 2-24-1842, rct Warrington MM with father Barzilla and family
John, 2-24-1842, rct Warrington MM thru mother Malinda [w]
John, Jr, 5-18-1796, rep to QM 5 times thru 11-19-1806
John, Jr, 2-22-1798, appt comm 4 times thru 1-18-1809
John, Jr, 8-21-1800, appt to record Marriage Certificates
John, Jr, 9-23-1807, appt assistant clerk
John, Jr, 10-20-1808, appt assistant clerk
Jonah, 6-21-1821, appt comm
Jonah, 1-23-1822, appt comm
Jonah, 6-19-1823, appt comm
Jonathan, 12-11-1780, appt comm
Joseph, 2-21-1799, rocf Warrington MM with father Aron and family
Joseph Griest, 7-17-1816, appt comm
Josiah, 3-21-1798, rct Pipe Creek MM as apprentice to Thomas Russel
Josiah, 12-18-1800, rocf Pipe Creek MM
Josiah, 7-20-1808, rct Sadsbury MM to marry Elizabeth Rakestraw
Josiah, 2-20-1817, appt to represent B. Tomlinson's case in court
Josiah, 6-19-1817, appt to standing comm for care of Benj. Tomlinson
Josiah, 5-19-1819, appt Overseer
Josiah, 7-21-1819, appt Overseer
Josiah, 9-18-1822, appt Overseer
Josiah, 12-22-1825, appt caretaker for Thomas Mickle
Josiah, 6-22-1837, appt to report to Pipe Creek re Abel N. Russell
Josiah, 1-23-1839, appt Elder [w]
Josiah, 3-17-1841, appt Minister
Josiah, 7-17-1844, appt to revise, record and care for MM records
Josiah, 11-20-1816, rep to QM 34 times thru 2-21-1850
Josiah, 7-17-1816, appt comm 118 times thru 4-24-1851
Josiah, 2-21-1833, rep to MM 53 times thru 4-15-1863
Josiah C., 12-17-1862, rep to MM
Josiah G., 8-21-1862, rep to MM
Josiah S., 4-24-1862, rep to MM
Josiah T., 6-19-1862, rep to MM
Josiah T., 8-21-1862, rep to QM
Josiah T., 11-21-1862, rep to MM
Josiah T., 2-22-1866, rep to QM

MENALLEN MINUTES, MARRIAGES, & MISCELLANY

GARRETSON, Lavinia, 12-18-1834, gct Short Creek MM, Jefferson Co, Ohio
    Louisa, 12-17-1862, rep to MM [w]
    Louisa, 11-18-1863, rep to MM [w]
    Louisa, 2-18-1864, rep to MM [w]
    Louisa, 4-21-1864, appt comm [w]
    Louisa W., 2-19-1835, req membership
    Louisa W., 3-18-1835, accepted in membership [w]
    Louisa W., 11-23-1853, req marriage with William Cleaver
    Lydia, 7-19-1815, rct Miami MM, Ohio with father John and family
    Lydia, 5-17-1848, gct Warrington MM
    Lydia G., 8-24-1854, gct West Branch MM with mother Louisa W. Cleaver
    Lydia L., 7-19-1854, rct West Brook MM thru mother Louisa W. Cleaver [w]
    Mahlon, 12-22-1842, rocf Warrington MM with wife Eliza and son Isaac [w]
    Mahlon, 7-17-1844, appt to revise, record and care for MM records
    Mahlon, 8-22-1844, forced to pay muster fine of $3.00 by sheriff
    Mahlon, 12-19-1844, clerk for the day
    Mahlon, 12-18-1845, appt Overseer
    Mahlon, 8-20-1846, forced to pay $1.00 muster fine
    Mahlon, 1-16-1849, appt Overseer
    Mahlon, 11-20-1844, rep to MM 11 times thru 2-21-1850
    Mahlon, 4-18-1850, req release as Overseer
    Mahlon, 12-22-1842, appt comm 23 times thru 8-21-1851
    Mahlon, 2-22-1844, rep to QM 13 times thru 8-19-1853
    Mahlon, 11-18-1857, rct Prairie Grove MM, Iowa with wife Eliza and 6 children
    Mahlon Edwin, 11-18-1857, rct Prairie Grove MM, Iowa with father Mahlon and family
    Malinda, 2-23-1837, rocf Warrington MM with husband Barzilla and 2 children [w]
    Malinda, 1-22-1840, appt comm [w]
    Malinda, 2-24-1842, rct Warrington MM with husband Barzilla and 2 children
    Maria, 10-22-1873, released from membership
    Maria, 10-22-1873, req membership discontinued [w]
    Maria M., 2-23-1837, req marriage with Edwin G. Vancise
    Martha, 1-18-1888, req release from membership. Now Otmyer
    Martha, 1-18-1888, dis: joined another society [w]
    Martha P., 1-17-1855, rct West Branch MM thru William Cleaver [w]
    Mary, 2-21-1799, rocf Warrington MM with husband Aron and 8 children
    Mary, 2-21-1799, rocf Warrington MM with father Aron and family
    Mary, 6-23-1803, rocf Pipe Creek MM with husband Amos
    Mary, 3-21-1811, rct Pipe Creek MM with husband Amos and 3 children
    Mary, 8-18-1825, req marriage with Isaac Tudor
    Mary, 4-24-1862, resigns membership. Daughter of Israel Garretson
    Mary, 4-24-1862, req membership be discontinued [w]

MINUTES

GARRETSON, Mary, 11-19-1862, rep to MM 8 times thru 1-18-1871 [w]
    Mary Ann, 3-21-1811, rct Pipe Creek MM with father Amos and family
    Mary Elizabeth, 1-17-1855, rct West Branch MM thru William Cleaver [w]
    Mary Elizabeth, 11-18-1857, rct Prairie Grove MM, Iowa with father Mahlon and family
    Melinda, 2-23-1837, rocf Warrington MM with husband Barzilla and 2 children
    Melissa, 7-20-1887, dis: mou; joined Methodists; now Anthony [w]
    Nathan, 6-9-1794, rocf Warrington MM with father John and family
    Oliver, 4-22-1841, rep to MM 3 times thru 10-25-1847
    Oliver, 2-22-1844, rep to QM 4 times thru 2-18-1847
    Orpha Jane, 8-21-1862, formerly of Warrington, now removed from this area [w]
    Rachel, 4-20-1815, req marriage with Josiah Penrose
    Rachel, 5-20-1874, appt comm 10 times thru 4-18-1888 [w]
    Rachel, 4-19-1882, appt Elder
    Rachel, 4-22-1885, appt Elder
    Rachel, 10-23-1862, rep to MM 9 times thru 6-18-1885 [w]
    Rachel, 2-20-1845, rep to QM 15 times thru 8-22-1888 [w]
    Rachel F., 5-18-1859, compl of: mou. Now Mercer [w]
    Rebecca Clarisa, 11-18-1857, rct Prairie Grove MM, Iowa with father Mahlon and family [w]
    Rebecca Jane, 2-23-1837, rocf Warrington MM with father Barzilla and family [w]
    Rebecca Jane, 2-24-1842, rct Warrington MM with father Barzilla and family
    Rebecca Jane, 2-24-1842, rct Warrington MM thru mother Malinda [w]
    Rebeckah R., 3-23-1831, req marriage with Hamilton Everitt
    Rebekah, 7-19-1815, rct Miami MM, Ohio with husband John and 4 children
    Rheuben T., 7-19-1815, rct Miami MM, Ohio with father John and family
    Rhoda, 7-19-1815, rct Miami MM, Ohio with father John and family
    Rhoda, 2-19-1862, appt comm [w]
    Rhoda, 9-17-1862, rep to MM 4 times thru 7-22-1868 [w]
    Rhoda, 11-19-1862, appt comm [w]
    Rhoda H., 11-22-1865, rep to MM [w]
    Ruth, 9-17-1862, rep to MM [w]
    Ruth, 3-19-1863, rep to MM [w]
    Ruthanna, 7-19-1815, rct Miami MM, Ohio with father John and family
    Samuel, 7-12-1784, req marriage with Alice Blackburn. He of Warrington
    Samuel, 8-21-1862, formerly of Warrington, now removed from this area [w]
    Sarah, 6-9-1794, rocf Warrington MM with father John and family
    Sarah, 2-21-1799, rocf Warrington MM with father Aron and family
    Susannah, 4-12-1790, req marriage with John Pidgeon
    Talbott, 3-21-1811, rct Pipe Creek MM with father Amos and family

MENALLEN MINUTES, MARRIAGES, & MISCELLANY

GARRETSON, Tamer, 6-9-1794, rocf Warrington MM with husband John and 5 children
    William, 6-9-1794, rocf Warrington MM with father John and family
    William, 2-21-1799, rocf Warrington MM with father Aron and family
GARRISON, John, 1-14-1788, appt comm 5 times thru 9-15-1788
GERBER, Sarah Jane, 11-21-1862, ack mou. Retained
GIBBONS, Daniel, 3-22-1815, req marriage with Hannah Wierman
    Daniel, 4-20-1815, rocf Sadsbury MM for marriage
    Hannah, 6-22-1815, rct Sadsbury MM
GILLINGHAM, Chalkley, 2-19-1862, rocf Alexandria MM, Va as Minister
GINLER, Sarah Jane, 8-21-1862, daughter of Waln Hoops, now removed from neighborhood [w]
GINNINGS, Thomas, 8-22-1799, req marriage with Isabell Blackburn
GITT, Hannah, 10-20-1842, compl of: mou. Formerly Wierman [w]
    Hannah, 12-22-1842, ack error. Retained [w]
GIVLER, Lucinda, 2-22-1888, compl of: mou. Formerly Hoopes [w]
    Lucinda, 5-23-1888, req membership
    Lucinda, 5-23-1888, ack mou. Retained [w]
    Sarah Jane, 11-19-1862, ack mou. Retained [w]
GORDEN, Jane, 2-21-1799, compl of: mou. Formerly Bowen
    Jane, 7-17-1799, dis: mou
GOVE, Mary E., 8-22-1888, absent member. Now in Herman, Neb [w]
    Mary Elizabeth, 8-21-1878, ack mou to J. Howard Gove. Formerly Griest [w]
    Mary Lizzie, 8-21-1878, ack mou. Retained. Formerly Griest
    Miriam, 12-21-1845, rocf Fairfax MM as Minister [w]
GOVES, Miriam, 12-18-1845, rocf Fairfax MM, Va as Minister
GRAIDY, Ann, 9-13-1784, compl of: mou. Formerly Potts
    Ann, 11-15-1784, dis: mou
GREIST, Thomas, 4-24-1817, appt comm
GRIESS, Daniel, 10-9-1780, appt comm
GRIEST, A. W., 5-27-1884, rep to QM
    A. W., 5-18-1887, assessed $3.00 for fuel for Ann and Martha Griest
    A. W., 8-17-1887, rep to QM
    Adella J., 12-21-1887, ack mou to Richard M. Wright. Retained [w]
    Alcetta, 8-19-1847, req membership thru her mother Sarah T. Griest
    Alcetta B., 1-18-1860, dis: mou. Now Rutzer
    Alexandra, 3-21-1827, rct Warrington MM with father Solomon and family
    Allen, 10-25-1845, dis: mou
    Alvina, 4-18-1833, req marriage with William Underwood
    Amos, 12-22-1808, rct York MM
    Amos, 2-22-1810, rocf York MM with wife Phebe
    Amos, 2-18-1819, appt comm 5 times thru 10-23-1889
    Amos, 4-19-1827, compl of: joined Methodists
    Amos, 7-19-1854, rocf York MM with wife Margaret and 2 children [w]
    Amos, 8-24-1854, rep to MM 15 times thru 9-21-1859
    Amos, 2-21-1856, rep to QM
    Amos, 7-22-1857, appt Overseer

MINUTES

GRIEST, Amos, 5-22-1861, rct Penns Grove MM, Chester Co, Pa with wife Margaret [w]
    Amos W., 12-22-1869, appt comm 13 times thru 8-20-1890
    Amos W., 11-23-1870, rep to QM 9 times thru 11-20-1889
    Amos W., 11-22-1871, rep to MM 4 times thru 5-27-1884
    Amos W., 12-23-1874, req marriage with Eliza R. Wright
    Amos W., 4-23-1879, clerk for the day
    Amos W., 5-21-1879, appt clerk
    Amos W., 8-18-1880, appt clerk
    Amos W., 2-21-1883, appt to comm to plan and build new meeting house
    Amos W., 5-20-1885, appt recorder
    Amos W., 11-18-1885, appt clerk
    Amos W., 12-23-1885, assessed $3.00 for Yearly Meeting
    Amos W., 11-17-1886, appt comm to aid Ann and Martha Griest
    Amos W., 2-24-1887, appt clerk
    Amos W., 4-23-1890, appt clerk
    Amos W., 8-20-1890, appt Elder
    Amy, 6-19-1823, rct Miami MM, Ohio with father Joseph and family
    Andrew J., 5-21-1879, rep to MM
    Angelina, 7-19-1837, rec as member. Minor child of Gideon and Martha
    Angelina, 3-19-1845, membership requested by father Gideon
    Angelina, 7-18-1849, req membership [w]
    Angelina, 2-22-1855, compl of: mou. Now Brown [w]
    Angelina P., 11-17-1852, rct Centre MM, Pa [w]
    Angeline, 8-18-1836, req membership with mother Martha and father [w]
    Angeline, 8-23-1849, req membership
    Angeline P., 12-23-1852, gct Centre MM, Centre Co, Pa
    Ann, 2-18-1808, compl of: fornication. Daughter of Willing
    Ann, 7-19-1820, appt comm
    Ann, 7-23-1823, gct Miami MM, Ohio
    Ann, 9-18-1884, req pecuniary assistance for self and sister Martha
    Ann, 9-18-1884, requests aid from MM [w]
    Ann, 11-17-1886, req aid from MM [w]
    Ann M., 4-18-1839, rocf Warrington MM with father Cyrus and family
    Ann M., 6-21-1866, rep to MM [w]
    Annie M., 10-22-1873, rep to MM [w]
    Annie M., 3-19-1884, rep to MM [w]
    Balinda, 3-21-1827, rct Warrington MM with father Solomon and family
    C.S., 9-23-1880, clerk for the day
    C.S., 9-23-1880, appt comm 4 times thru 9-24-1885
    C.S., 11-22-1882, appt Trustee for Warrington property
    C.S., 2-20-1884, rep to QM 3 times thru 2-20-1884
    C.S., 4-21-1886, clerk for the day
    Caroline, 2-20-1884, req membership thru father Charles W. Griest
    Caroline A., 2-20-1884, req membership thru father Charles W. Griest [w]

MENALLEN MINUTES, MARRIAGES, & MISCELLANY

GRIEST, Caroline A., 6-18-1884, comm reports she was born 11th mo 12th 1865 [w]
    Charles, 5-17-1865, gct Centre MM
    Charles, 6-21-1883, rep to MM
    Charles H., 5-20-1874, rep to MM
    Charles J., 6-18-1884, comm reports he was born 10th mo 5th 1868 [w]
    Charles Jacob, 2-20-1884, req membership thru father Charles W. Griest
    Charles W., 4-22-1868, req membership
    Charles W., 8-19-1868, rep to QM 12 times thru 8-20-1884
    Charles W., 2-17-1869, rep to MM 128 times thru 4-22-1885
    Charles W., 3-23-1870, appt comm 13 times thru 9-24-1885
    Charles W., 7-19-1876, appt Overseer
    Charles W., 2-20-1884, req membership for 2 children: Caroline and Charles J [w]
    Content, 7-18-1804, compl of: mou to first cousin once removed
    Content, 11-21-1804, dis: mou to first cousin once removed
    Content, 2-20-1840, appt comm 34 times thru 9-17-1872 [w]
    Content, 3-17-1852, appt clerk [w]
    Content, 6-20-1852, appt Overseer [w]
    Content, 4-21-1853, appt clerk [w]
    Content, 5-17-1854, appt clerk [w]
    Content, 3-19-1856, appt Overseer [w]
    Content, 8-18-1859, appt Overseer [w]
    Content, 4-19-1860, appt Elder [w]
    Content, 4-24-1862, appt Overseer [w]
    Content, 4-20-1865, appt Overseer [w]
    Content, 12-23-1868, appt Overseer [w]
    Content, 4-19-1871, appt Overseer [w]
    Content, 6-18-1874, appt Overseer [w]
    Content, 8-21-1862, rep to MM 19 times thru 8-19-1874 [w]
    Content, 11-21-1835, rep to QM 35 times thru 8-19-1874 [w]
    Content, 9-21-1876, clerk for the day [w]
    Content, Jr, 4-20-1837, req membership
    Content, Jr., 1-17-1838, appt comm [w]
    Cornelius, 8-19-1813, compl of: accompanied sister when she mou
    Cornelius, 11-17-1813, read testimony. Retained
    Cornelius, 6-23-1814, compl of: mou
    Cornelius, 1-18-1815, dis: mou
    Cyrus, 4-18-1839, rocf Warrington MM with wife Mary Ann and 6 children
    Cyrus, 4-18-1839, rocf Warrington MM with father Cyrus and family
    Cyrus, 7-17-1839, appt assistant clerk
    Cyrus, 1-20-1841, appt clerk for the day 9 times thru 6-17-1863
    Cyrus, 6-20-1839, rep to MM 69 times thru 6-20-1878
    Cyrus, 5-18-1842, appt comm on military demands
    Cyrus, 4-20-1848, appt clerk
    Cyrus, 4-19-1849, appt clerk
    Cyrus, 1-21-1852, appt Overseer

MINUTES

GRIEST, Cyrus, 4-22-1852, appt clerk
    Cyrus, 4-21-1853, appt clerk
    Cyrus, 4-19-1855, appt Overseer
    Cyrus, 11-21-1855, appt Elder
    Cyrus, 12-24-1857, appt Elder
    Cyrus, 4-21-1859, gct Philadelphia YM as Elder with wife Mary Ann
    Cyrus, 4-19-1860, appt Elder
    Cyrus, 1-23-1861, rct Penns Grove MM to marry Letitia B. Broomell
    Cyrus, 12-21-1863, appt Elder
    Cyrus, 6-23-1864, appt Overseer
    Cyrus, 2-20-1867, appt Elder [w]
    Cyrus, 8-20-1840, rep to QM 46 times thru 5-20-1868
    Cyrus, 8-17-1870, an Elder, died 3rd of 11th mo 1869
    Cyrus, 3-18-1840, appt comm 98 times thru 8-21-1878
    Cyrus G., 8-21-1878, rep to MM
    Cyrus S., 3-21-1866, appt comm 48 times thru 1-21-1891
    Cyrus S., 2-21-1872, appt recorder of Marriage Certificates
    Cyrus S., 2-19-1873, appt clerk
    Cyrus S., 4-23-1873, appt Trustee at Menallen
    Cyrus S., 2-18-1874, appt clerk
    Cyrus S., 12-23-1874, compl of: difficulty with contract with Elisha Penrose
    Cyrus S., 2-17-1875, charge against him carried to QM
    Cyrus S., 8-19-1875, dis: refusing to submit to arbitration
    Cyrus S., 9-21-1876, clerk for the day 16 times thru 10-23-1890
    Cyrus S., 4-18-1877, appt clerk
    Cyrus S., 5-18-1881, appt clerk
    Cyrus S., 1-17-1883, appt clerk
    Cyrus S., 2-21-1883, appt to comm to plan and build new meeting house
    Cyrus S., 8-22-1883, appt representative to YM
    Cyrus S., 3-19-1884, appt clerk
    Cyrus S., 12-17-1884, appt Overseer
    Cyrus S., 12-23-1885, assessed $3.50 for Yearly Meeting
    Cyrus S., 2-17-1886, appt to Firstday School comm
    Cyrus S., 9-22-1858, rep to MM 41 times thru 4-21-1886
    Cyrus S., 5-19-1886, superintendent of First Day School [w]
    Cyrus S., 3-23-1887, surviving trustee at Warrington
    Cyrus S., 3-23-1887, surviving trustee at Menallen
    Cyrus S., 3-23-1887, appt Trustee for Menallen and Huntington
    Cyrus S., 5-18-1887, assessed $3.00 for fuel for Ann and Martha Griest
    Cyrus S., 5-23-1888, appt Elder [w]
    Cyrus S., 7-22-1890, appt Overseer
    Cyrus S., 10-23-1890, appt comm to aid Ann and Martha Griest
    Cyrus S., 5-22-1872, rep to QM 34 times thru 11-19-1890
    Cyrus S., 1-21-1891, appt comm
    Daniel, 3-12-1781, appt comm 51 times thru 3-22-1876
    Daniel, 11-13-1780, appt Elder
    Daniel, 3-12-1781, appt Elder
    Daniel, 9-12-1785, appt Overseer at Huntington in place of H. Wierman

MENALLEN MINUTES, MARRIAGES, & MISCELLANY

GRIEST, Daniel, 12-19-1799, compl of: carnal knowledge with wife Elizabeth pre-marriage
Daniel, 2-20-1800, dis: carnal knowledge before marriage
Daniel, 7-23-1817, req marriage with Soosan Swain
Daniel, 10-22-1818, compl of: false advertising re an apprentice
Daniel, 11-18-1818, read testimony. Retained
Daniel, 3-23-1825, compl of: mou
Daniel, 5-18-1825, dis: mou
Daniel, 3-23-1864, gct Whitewater MM, Ind
Daniel, 4-21-1869, rocf White Water MM, Ind
Daniel, 9-23-1874, req membership for children Emily and Mary Lizzie [w]
Daniel, 8-19-1858, rep to MM 28 times thru 2-23-1876
Daniel, 12-18-1889, rct Genoa MM, Nebraska with wife Rose D. and 2 children
Daniel, 2-19-1890, rct Lincoln Executive Mtg, Neb instead of Genoa
Daniel, 2-19-1890, gct Lincoln Executive MM, Neb instead of Genoa MM [w]
David, 9-21-1796, req marriage with Mary Beals
David, 11-23-1803, compl of: paying an exempt fine
David, 4-19-1804, dis: paid an exempt fine
David, 9-23-1818, dis: mou
David, 6-21-1860, rep to MM
David, Jr, 4-23-1818, compl of: mou
Della E., 2-20-1884, req membership thru father Charles W. Griest
Edith, 5-19-1841, req marriage with Nathan Smith
Edith, 10-18-1855, rocf Warrington MM [w]
Edith, 2-21-1856, rep to QM 18 times thru 2-20-1868 [w]
Edith, 5-21-1856, appt comm 17 times thru 5-22-1867 [w]
Edith, 7-23-1856, rct Fairfax MM as Minister
Edith, 4-21-1859, gct Philadelphia YM as Minister
Edith, 4-21-1859, rct Phila YM as Minister [w]
Edith, 7-17-1861, rct Ohio YM as Minister
Edith, 1-21-1863, rep to MM 5 times thru 4-22-1868 [w]
Edith, 6-17-1863, rct Centre MM as Minister
Edith, 10-20-1864, rct Nottingham QM as Minister
Edith, 8-24-1865, gct Fishing Creek Half Years Meeting as Minister
Edith, 8-19-1868, a Minister, died 4th mo 17th 1868, aged 68
Eli, 1-19-1820, appt comm 6 times thru 2-18-1830
Eli, 11-21-1821, rep to QM
Eli, 12-18-1823, req marriage with Elizabeth Everitt
Eli, 1-21-1824, decides not to marry Elizabeth Everitt
Eli, 2-19-1824, committee reports his reasons for not marrying, "We had an opportunity with Eli and by a free communication with him he informs us his reasons for declining to proceed in marriage is altogether from Impressions of uneasiness in his own mind and not from any slight or dislike to the young woman nor discouragement or persuasion of any other person yet he acknowledges he is sensible of having committed an error by

MINUTES

  laying his proposals of marriage before the monthly meeting after having such impressions of uneasiness."
GRIEST, Eli, 12-23-1824, read testimony. Retained
  Eli, 3-18-1829, appt for care of burying grounds
  Eli, 8-20-1829, rep to QM
  Eli L., 12-18-1889, req membership
  Eli L., 8-20-1890, rep to QM
  Eli L., 1-21-1891, appt comm
  Eli L., 1-21-1891, appt comm [w]
  Elisha, 4-19-1838, rct Warrington MM with father Uriah and family
  Elisha, 3-18-1840, rocf Warrington MM with father Uriah and family
  Elisha, 5-30-1846, compl of: mou
  Elisha, 7-22-1846, read testimony. Retained
  Elisha, 9-21-1853, rct Smithfield MM
  Elisha William, 4-19-1838, rct Warrington MM with father Uriah and family [w]
  Eliza, 9-21-1836, rct Center MM, Centre Co, Pa [w]
  Eliza, 4-18-1839, req membership thru parents Gideon and Martha
  Eliza, 4-20-1843, rct Warrington MM with father John and family
  Eliza, 3-21-1855, compl of: mou. Now Thomas [w]
  Eliza E., 1-17-1883, appt comm [w]
  Eliza Hewitt, 11-17-1852, rep to QM [w]
  Eliza J., 2-20-1889, req membership [w]
  Eliza R., 4-17-1878, appt comm 11 times thru 10-23-1889 [w]
  Eliza R., 8-17-1881, rep to MM [w]
  Eliza R., 8-17-1881, clerk for the day [w]
  Eliza R., 1-23-1884, rep to MM [w]
  Eliza R., 11-19-1884, rep to QM 4 times thru 5-22-1889 [w]
  Eliza R., 5-22-1889, appt clerk [w]
  Eliza R., 5-21-1890, appt clerk [w]
  Elizabeth, 12-19-1799, compl of: carnal knowledge with husband Daniel pre marriage
  Elizabeth, 2-20-1800, dis: carnal knowledge before marriage
  Elizabeth, 5-23-1810, compl of: fornication
  Elizabeth, 10-18-1866, discontinues membership. Joined another society [w]
  Elizabeth M., 5-23-1866, ack mou. Retained. Now Koser
  Ella M. G., 8-17-1887, ack mou to Josiah W. Prickett. Retained [w]
  Ellis, 8-22-1888, absent member. Now in Kansas [w]
  Elmer Mahlon, 4-19-1838, rct Warrington MM with father Uriah and family [w]
  Elmer Malon, 3-21-1840, rocf Warrington MM with father Uriah and family [w]
  Elmer Malon, 4-22-1841, rct Warrington MM with father Uriah and family [w]
  Elmira, 7-19-1837, rec as member. Minor child of Gideon and Martha
  Elmira, 3-19-1845, membership requested by father Gideon
  Emily, 4-20-1843, rct Warrington MM with father John and family
  Emily, 9-23-1874, req membership thru parents Daniel and Rose D. Griest [w]

MENALLEN MINUTES, MARRIAGES, & MISCELLANY

GRIEST, Esther, 10-23-1817, rct Warrington MM. Daughter of Isaac Griest
    Esther H., 11-19-1884, rep to QM [w]
    Esther H., 8-19-1885, rep to MM [w]
    Florence, 9-22-1887, req marriage with Charles Michener
    Florence, 12-18-1889, rct Genoa MM, Neb with father Daniel and mother [w]
    Florence, 3-19-1890, hired as school teacher in 1887; $35.00 per month [w]
    Florence T., 12-18-1889, rct Genoa MM, Neb with father Daniel and family
    George, 4-18-1839, rocf Warrington MM with father Cyrus and family [w]
    George, 2-22-1849, clerk for the day
    George Espey, 3-19-1856, rct Center MM with father Nathan and family
    George Espy, 11-17-1852, rct Centre MM with father Nathan and family
    George M., 4-18-1839, rocf Warrington MM with father Cyrus and family
    George M., 2-22-1849, rep to MM
    George M., 4-18-1850, appt assistant clerk
    Gideon, 6-19-1817, req marriage with Jesse M. Swain
    Gideon, 1-23-1833, compl of: fornication with woman he has since married
    Gideon, 9-21-1836, produced acknowledgment
    Gideon, 4-20-1837, comm reports he should be received as member
    Gideon, 4-18-1839, req membership for daughter Eliza with wife Martha [w]
    Gideon, 7-17-1844, appt to record Births and Deaths
    Gideon, 1-20-1847, on comm against settling new mtg at Mechanicsville
    Gideon, 8-24-1820, rep to QM 15 times thru 11-22-1848
    Gideon, 6-20-1850, appt Overseer
    Gideon, 1-19-1820, appt comm 40 times thru 6-19-1851
    Gideon, 4-19-1838, rep to MM 40 times thru 9-20-1854
    H., 6-18-1885, rep to MM
    Hannah, 8-20-1840, rep to QM [w]
    Hannah, 2-24-1842, appt comm [w]
    Hannah, 4-20-1843, rct Warrington MM with husband John and 6 children [w]
    Harriet, 3-21-1827, rct Warrington MM with father Solomon and family
    Hiram, 4-18-1839, rocf Warrington MM with father Cyrus and family
    Hiram, 12-21-1848, req marriage with Louiza Ellis
    Hiram, 3-22-1854, appt assistant clerk
    Hiram, 4-19-1855, appt assistant clerk
    Hiram, 4-25-1857, appt assistant clerk
    Hiram, 8-20-1857, clerk for the day 8 times thru 3-20-1889
    Hiram, 4-22-1858, appt assistant clerk
    Hiram, 4-21-1859, appt assistant clerk
    Hiram, 4-19-1860, appt assistant clerk

MINUTES

GRIEST, Hiram, 7-22-1863, appt assistant clerk
    Hiram, 8-18-1864, appt assistant clerk
    Hiram, 8-24-1865, appt assistant clerk
    Hiram, 8-23-1866, appt assistant clerk
    Hiram, 12-23-1874, compl of: difficulty with contract with Elisha Penrose
    Hiram, 2-17-1875, charge against him carried to QM
    Hiram, 4-22-1885, appt Elder [w]
    Hiram, 12-23-1885, assessed $2.50 for Yearly Meeting
    Hiram, 2-17-1886, appt to Firstday School comm
    Hiram, 4-21-1859, rep to MM 26 times thru 5-19-1886
    Hiram, 5-18-1887, assessed $3.00 for fuel for Ann and Martha Griest
    Hiram, 3-20-1889, appt clerk
    Hiram, 4-17-1889, appt comm to raise money to repair Warrington Meeting House
    Hiram, 10-22-1890, recommended to be a Minister [w]
    Hiram, 10-23-1890, appt comm to aid Ann and Martha Griest
    Hiram, 10-23-1890, appt Minister
    Hiram, 11-18-1857, rep to QM 29 times thru 11-19-1890
    Hiram, 1-21-1891, appt comm to care for George Cook
    Hiram, 12-18-1851, appt comm 47 times thru 1-21-1891 [w]
    Hiram S., 10-18-1871, appt comm
    Hiram S., 1-21-1874, appt comm
    Hiram S., 8-20-1879, appt comm
    Hiram S., 9-18-1879, rep to MM
    Isaac, 10-19-1797, rct Warrington MM for marriage with Mary Cook
    Isaac, 3-23-1808, compl of: paid muster fine; mou
    Isaac, 6-23-1808, dis: paying muster fine; mou
    Isaac, 6-19-1823, rct Miami MM, Ohio with father Joseph and family
    Jacob, 8-15-1791, compl of: mou
    Jacob, 12-12-1791, dis: mou
    Jacob, 4-21-1825, compl of: married cousin
    Jacob, 6-23-1825, dis: mou
    Jacob, 8-18-1825, dis: married first cousin
    Jacob, 11-20-1833, req membership
    Jacob, 9-17-1834, appt comm 55 times thru 5-21-1856
    Jacob, 6-18-1835, appt assistant clerk
    Jacob, 7-19-1837, appt assistant clerk
    Jacob, 1-23-1839, clerk for the day
    Jacob, 1-20-1847, on comm against settling new meeting at Mechanicsville
    Jacob, 5-20-1835, rep to QM 17 times thru 2-19-1857
    Jacob, 11-19-1834, rep to MM 41 times thru 3-18-1857
    Jane C., 4-18-1839, rocf Warrington MM with father Cyrus and family
    Jane C., 4-21-1853, appt assistant clerk [w]
    Jane C., 6-23-1853, appt comm [w]
    Jane C., 9-20-1854, req marriage with Abel T. Wright
    Jesse, 5-18-1859, rep to QM
    Jesse W., 4-18-1839, rocf Warrington MM with father Cyrus and family
    Jesse W., 3-17-1863, rct Redford MM, Burlington Co, NJ to marry

MENALLEN MINUTES, MARRIAGES, & MISCELLANY

GRIEST, Jesse W., 9-18-1867, appt assistant clerk
    Jesse W., 9-24-1868, appt assistant clerk
    Jesse W., 2-17-1869, rct New Garden MM, Pa to marry Sibilla E. More
    Jesse W., 4-21-1869, clerk for the day 5 times thru 5-18-1881
    Jesse W., 11-17-1869, appt assistant clerk
    Jesse W., 11-23-1870, appt assistant clerk
    Jesse W., 12-20-1871, appt assistant clerk
    Jesse W., 12-23-1874, compl of: difficulty with contract with Elisha Penrose
    Jesse W., 2-17-1875, charge against him carried to QM
    Jesse W., 8-19-1875, dis: refusing to submit to arbitration
    Jesse W., 2-21-1883, appt to comm to plan and build new meeting house
    Jesse W., 2-18-1864, rep to MM 16 times thru 9-18-1884
    Jesse W., 7-20-1864, appt comm 26 times thru 11-19-1884
    Jesse W., 11-21-1862, rep to QM 22 times thru 2-18-1885
    Jno, 11-12-1787, appt comm
    Joel, 2-23-1854, rep to QM
    John, 12-11-1780, appt comm
    John, 3-12-1787, rct Warrington MM to marry Miriam Cleaver, Jr [John is son of Daniel Griest]
    John, 2-15-1790, rep to QM 8 times thru 11-23-1842
    John, 2-20-1806, compl of: quarrelling and striking his wife
    John, 9-17-1806, dis: quarrelling with wife
    John, 6-19-1823, rct Miami MM, Ohio with father Joseph and family
    John, 2-21-1833, rct Pipe Creek MM to marry Hannah Edmundson
    John, 3-23-1836, appt Trustee for Menallen & Huntington properties
    John, 6-23-1836, appt assistant clerk
    John, 6-22-1837, appt to report to Pipe Creek re Abel N. Russell
    John, 7-19-1837, appt clerk
    John, 8-24-1837, appt comm in charge of graveyards
    John, 8-23-1838, appt clerk
    John, 10-18-1838, appt Overseer
    John, 7-17-1839, appt clerk
    John, 8-19-1841, appt clerk
    John, 5-18-1842, appt comm on military demands
    John, 5-20-1835, rep to MM 19 times thru 12-22-1842
    John, 12-15-1794, appt comm 24 times thru 1-18-1843
    John, 4-20-1843, rct Warrington MM with wife Hannah and 6 children
    John, Jr, 2-11-1788, rep to QM 11 times thru 11-23-1803
    John, Jr, 1-9-1786, appt comm 16 times thru 1-19-1803
    Joseph, 12-11-1780, appt comm
    Joseph, 4-15-1782, appt comm
    Joseph, 12-09-1782, returned cert to Warrington MM for marriage with Mary Cleaver, she being deceased
    Joseph, 2-10-1783, req release from comm
    Joseph, 5-9-1785, rct Warrington to marry Rebeckah Hussey
    Joseph, 11-15-1790, appt Elder
    Joseph, 6-15-1795, released from recording Births & Deaths
    Joseph, 4-22-1802, appt to prepare memorial for Isaac Everitt, dec'd

MINUTES

GRIEST, Joseph, 9-21-1803, appt Overseer at Huntington
    Joseph, 10-23-1806, rct Virginia and Baltimore Quarter as Minister
    Joseph, 11-18-1812, rct New Jersey Mtgs with Abel Thomas
    Joseph, 8-23-1821, req cert for son Nathan to Pipe Creek MM
    Joseph, 6-19-1823, rct Miami MM, Ohio with wife Mary and 5 children
    Joseph, 5-14-1781, rep to QM 56 times thru 8-18-1831
    Joseph, 5-21-1856, rct Centre MM with mother Martha
    Joseph, 5-21-1856, rct Center MM, Centre Co, Pa with 4 children [w]
    Joseph, 8-24-1865, appt clerk
    Joseph W., 6-19-1823, rct Miami MM, Ohio
    Joseph, 3rd, 2-22-1821, appt comm
    Joseph, Jr, 4-14-1794, req marriage with Mary Wierman
    Joseph, Jr, 5-20-1807, appt Overseer
    Joseph, Jr, 11-22-1809, appt clerk
    Joseph, Jr, 1-23-1811, appt clerk
    Joseph, Jr, 8-22-1811, exempt fines: "Taken from Joseph Griest Junr in the year 1810 for two exempt fines of 5 dollar each and muster fine of 3 dollars, two cows and one heifer valued at $40. Also taken from ditto by the same collector in same year for exempt fines for the year 1809 and 1810 4 dollars each year, two steers valued at $20.00"
    Joseph, Jr, 1-22-1812, appt clerk
    Joseph, Jr, 5-18-1814, appt clerk
    Joseph, Jr, 5-17-1815, appt clerk
    Joseph, Jr, 2-20-1817, appt to represent B. Tomlinson's case in court
    Joseph, Jr, 4-24-1817, appt comm re Benjamin Tomlinson
    Joseph, Jr, 6-19-1817, appt to standing comm for care of Benj. Tomlinson
    Joseph, Jr, 4-19-1821, appt clerk
    Joseph, Jr, 8-11-1794, rep to QM 24 times thru 8-23-1821
    Joseph, Jr, 6-23-1796, appt comm 81 times thru 5-21-1823
    Joseph, Sr, 5-20-1807, rep to QM
    Joshua, 11-17-1813, appt comm
    Josiah, 4-19-1855, rocf Warrington MM
    Josiah, 7-18-1855, req membership: wife Mary Ann and daughter Ruth Elizabeth [w]
    Josiah, 7-18-1860, appt Overseer
    Josiah, 4-24-1862, appt assistant clerk
    Josiah, 7-22-1863, appt clerk
    Josiah, 8-18-1864, appt clerk
    Josiah, 8-23-1866, appt clerk
    Josiah, 6-20-1867, appt Overseer
    Josiah, 9-18-1867, appt clerk
    Josiah, 9-24-1868, appt clerk
    Josiah, 11-17-1869, appt clerk
    Josiah, 4-20-1870, appt Elder
    Josiah, 11-23-1870, appt clerk
    Josiah, 3-22-1871, appt Overseer
    Josiah, 12-20-1871, appt clerk
    Josiah, 2-19-1873, appt assistant clerk

MENALLEN MINUTES, MARRIAGES, & MISCELLANY

GRIEST, Josiah, 5-21-1873, appt Elder
    Josiah, 12-17-1873, appt Overseer
    Josiah, 2-18-1874, appt assistant clerk
    Josiah, 4-22-1874, clerk for the day 7 times thru 10-18-1882
    Josiah, 5-17-1876, appt Elder
    Josiah, 4-23-1879, appt Elder
    Josiah, 2-23-1881, appt to take care of Minute Books
    Josiah, 4-19-1882, appt Elder
    Josiah, 9-21-1882, appt to record property titles
    Josiah, 11-17-1858, rep to QM 31 times thru 11-21-1883
    Josiah, 11-18-1857, rep to MM 102 times thru 12-19-1883
    Josiah, 3-19-1856, appt comm 71 times thru 12-19-1883
    Josiah, 4-22-1885, appt Elder
    Josiah, 12-23-1885, assessed $2.50 for Yearly Meeting
    Josiah W., 8-17-1881, rep to MM
    Kezia, 3-21-1840, rct Center MM, Center Co, Pa [w]
    Lavinia, 11-20-1872, req marriage with Ziba Hibbard Moore [w]
    Leah, 10-21-1813, compl of: present at marriage out of order
    Leah, 12-25-1813, read testimony. Retained
    Leander, 4-22-1841, req membership thru mother Mary Ann and father [w]
    Leander, 5-19-1841, req membership with father Nathan and family
    Leander, 11-17-1852, rct Centre MM with father Nathan and family
    Leander, 3-19-1856, rct Center MM with father Nathan and family
    Letitia, 2-22-1871, rep to QM [w]
    Letitia B., 12-19-1861, roc
    Letitia B., 12-19-1861, rocf Penns Grove MM, Chester Co, Pa [w]
    Letitia B., 1-17-1877, appt assistant clerk [w]
    Letitia B., 6-21-1877, clerk for the day [w]
    Letitia B., 2-20-1878, appt Overseer [w]
    Letitia B., 2-20-1878, req release as Overseer [w]
    Letitia B., 4-17-1878, appt assistant clerk [w]
    Letitia B., 7-23-1884, rep to MM [w]
    Letitia B., 5-23-1888, appt Elder [w]
    Letitia B., 5-17-1865, appt comm 16 times thru 1-22-1890 [w]
    Letitia B., 2-21-1877, rep to QM 11 times thru 5-21-1890 [w]
    Levi, 6-24-1813, compl of: mou. Now living at Hopewell MM
    Lewis, 4-20-1843, rct Warrington MM with father John and family
    Lizzie M., 5-21-1862, rep to QM [w]
    Lizzie M., 5-22-1866, ack mou. Retained. Now Koser [w]
    Loreina, 4-24-1845, gct Center MM
    Louisa, 6-20-1861, appt comm [w]
    Louisa, 8-21-1862, rep to MM [w]
    Louisa, 8-18-1875, rep to QM [w]
    Louisa C., 1-23-1867, appt comm [w]
    Louisa C., 2-18-1874, rep to MM [w]
    Louisa E., 1-17-1866, rep to MM 11 times thru 11-19-1884 [w]
    Louisa E., 12-23-1885, clerk for the day [w]
    Louisa E., 4-19-1866, appt comm 9 times thru 2-22-1888 [w]
    Louisa E., 11-20-1889, appt Overseer [w]

MINUTES

GRIEST, Louisa E., 11-21-1877, rep to QM 7 times thru 11-19-1890 [w]
    Lucinda Maria, 4-19-1838, rct Warrington MM with father Uriah and family [w]
    Lucinda Maria, 3-18-1840, rocf Warrington MM with father Uriah and family
    Lucinda Maria, 4-22-1841, rct Warrington MM with father Uriah and family [w]
    Lydia Ann, 4-19-1838, rct Warrington MM with father Uriah and family [w]
    Lydia Ann, 4-23-1840, rocf Warrington MM
    Lydia Ann, 12-21-1848, req marriage with Joseph M. Spencer
    M. Alice, 12-19-1883, rep to MM [w]
    Mahlon, 4-19-1838, rct Warrington MM with father Uriah and family
    Mahlon, 3-18-1840, rocf Warrington MM with father Uriah and family
    Mahlon, 6-19-1845, rep to MM
    Malen, 12-20-1827, dis: mou
    Malon, 5-23-1827, compl of: mou
    Margaret, 7-19-1854, rocf York MM with husband Amos and 2 children [w]
    Margaret, 11-18-1857, rep to QM [w]
    Margaret, 5-22-1861, rct Penns Grove MM, Chester Co, Pa with husband Amos [w]
    Maria, 4-22-1841, rct Warrington MM with father Uriah and family
    Maria, 4-20-1843, rct Warrington MM with father John and family
    Maria E., 1-21-1863, appt comm [w]
    Maria E., 3-17-1863, req marriage with Charles J. Tyson
    Martha, 2-14-1791, rct Warrington MM
    Martha, 9-15-1794, req marriage with Isaiah John
    Martha, 8-18-1836, req membership with husband and 2 children [w]
    Martha, 7-19-1837, req membership
    Martha, 4-18-1839, req membership for daughter Eliza with husband Gideon [w]
    Martha, 1-20-1847, on comm against settling new meeting at Mechanicsville
    Martha, 1-22-1840, appt comm 9 times thru 8-23-1849 [w]
    Martha, 2-23-1839, rep to QM 9 times thru 8-24-1854 [w]
    Martha, 5-21-1856, rct Center MM, Centre Co, Pa with 4 children
    Martha, 9-18-1884, req pecuniary assistance for self & sister Ann
    Martha, 11-17-1886, req aid from MM [w]
    Martha Jane, 1-20-1858, gct Center MM, Center Co, Pa
    Martha P., 12-23-1852, appt comm [w]
    Mary, 4-19-1798, rocf Warrington MM
    Mary, 3-19-1817, appt comm
    Mary, 7-21-1819, req membership
    Mary, 6-20-1822, compl of: fornication. Daughter of Daniel
    Mary, 6-19-1823, rct Miami MM, Ohio with husband Joseph and 5 children
    Mary, 6-19-1823, rct Miami MM, Ohio with father Joseph and family
    Mary, 3-21-1827, rct Warrington MM with husband Solomon and 3 children

MENALLEN MINUTES, MARRIAGES, & MISCELLANY

GRIEST, Mary, 4-19-1838, rct Warrington MM with husband Uriah and 6 children
Mary, 3-18-1840, rocf Warrington MM with husband Uriah and 5 children
Mary, 4-22-1841, rct Warrington MM with husband Uriah and 4 children
Mary, 8-21-1862, rep to QM [w]
Mary, 10-19-1870, rep to MM [w]
Mary A., 11-18-1840, rep to QM [w]
Mary Ann, 4-18-1839, rocf Warrington MM with husband Cyrus and 6 children
Mary Ann, 4-22-1841, req membership for self and 2 children [w]
Mary Ann, 5-19-1841, req membership with husband Nathan and 2 children
Mary Ann, 7-20-1842, appt clerk [w]
Mary Ann, 10-20-1842, appt Overseer [w]
Mary Ann, 12-22-1842, req release as Overseer [w]
Mary Ann, 12-19-1844, appt assistant clerk [w]
Mary Ann, 1-22-1846, appt clerk [w]
Mary Ann, 3-18-1846, appt Overseer [w]
Mary Ann, 1-20-1847, on comm against settling new meeting at Mechanicsville
Mary Ann, 5-20-1849, appt Overseer [w]
Mary Ann, 11-21-1849, appt clerk [w]
Mary Ann, 11-20-1850, appt clerk [w]
Mary Ann, 7-23-1851, appt Elder
Mary Ann, 11-17-1852, rct Centre MM with husband Nathan and 4 children
Mary Ann, 7-19-1854, appt Elder
Mary Ann, 8-24-1854, appt Elder [w]
Mary Ann, 5-23-1855, appt clerk [w]
Mary Ann, 7-18-1855, req membership for self and dtr Ruth Elizabeth [w]
Mary Ann, 8-23-1855, req membership for daughter Ruth Elizabeth
Mary Ann, 11-21-1855, appt Elder
Mary Ann, 3-19-1856, rct Center MM with husband Nathan and 4 children
Mary Ann, 12-24-1857, appt Elder
Mary Ann, 4-21-1859, gct Philadelphia YM as Elder with husband Cyrus
Mary Ann, 4-21-1859, rct Philadelphia YM as Minister [w]
Mary Ann, 4-19-1860, appt Elder
Mary Ann, 12-21-1863, appt Elder
Mary Ann, 2-20-1867, appt Elder [w]
Mary Ann, 4-20-1870, appt Elder
Mary Ann, 5-21-1873, appt Elder
Mary Ann, 11-20-1861, appt comm 72 times thru 5-20-1874 [w]
Mary Ann, 5-17-1876, appt Elder
Mary Ann, 8-22-1839, rep to QM 49 times thru 8-23-1876 [w]
Mary Ann, 4-23-1879, appt Elder

MINUTES

GRIEST, Mary Ann, 8-21-1862, rep to MM 21 times thru 10-19-1881 [w]
Mary Ann, 4-19-1882, appt Elder
Mary Ann, 4-22-1885, appt Elder
Mary Ann S., 8-18-1859, appt Overseer [w]
Mary Ann S., 5-17-1876, appt Elder
Mary Ann S., 2-20-1878, appt Overseer [w]
Mary Ann S., 9-21-1859, appt comm 19 times thru 12-18-1878 [w]
Mary Ann S., 4-23-1879, appt Elder
Mary Ann S., 4-19-1882, appt Elder
Mary Ann S., 8-22-1883, appt Overseer [w]
Mary Ann S., 6-19-1863, rep to MM 27 times thru 10-17-1883 [w]
Mary Ann S., 4-22-1885, appt Elder [w]
Mary Ann S., 8-18-1886, appt Overseer [w]
Mary Ann S., 8-19-1868, rep to QM 18 times thru 8-17-1887 [w]
Mary Ann S., 5-23-1888, appt Elder [w]
Mary Anne, 8-18-1869, rep to QM [w]
Mary Ardella, 11-17-1852, rct Centre MM with father Nathan and family
Mary Ardella, 3-19-1856, rct Center MM with father Nathan and family
Mary E., 4-23-1884, rep to MM [w]
Mary E., 4-17-1889, appt comm [w]
Mary E., 10-23-1889, appt comm [w]
Mary E., 2-19-1890, rep to QM [w]
Mary E., 3-19-1890, hired to teach school for spring 1890
Mary E., 3-19-1890, hired as school teacher in 1890; $30.00 per month [w]
Mary Elizabeth, 8-21-1878, ack mou to J. Howard Gove in Neb. Retained [w]
Mary F., 3-22-1865, rocf Medford MM, NJ [w]
Mary Lizzie, 9-23-1874, req membership thru parents Daniel and Rose D. Griest [w]
Mary Lizzie, 8-21-1878, ack mou. Retained. Now Gove
Mary R., 3-22-1865, rocf Medford MM, NJ
Mikeja, 6-19-1823, rct Miami MM, Ohio with father Joseph and family
Miriam, 8-13-1787, rocf Warrington MM
Miriam, 2-20-1806, compl of: quarrelling with her husband; gossiping
Miriam, 9-17-1806, dis: quarrelling with husband
Miriam, 4-20-1843, rct Warrington MM with father John and family
Mordecai D., 12-18-1889, rct Genoa MM, Neb with father Daniel and family
Nathan, 8-23-1821, rct Pipe Creek MM, by father Joseph
Nathan, 3-22-1826, rocf Pipe Creek MM
Nathan, 12-23-1830, compl of: mou
Nathan, 3-23-1836, appt Trustee for Menallen and Huntington properties
Nathan, 2-21-1839, rep to QM 4 times thru 8-24-1843
Nathan, 5-19-1841, req membership with wife Mary Ann and 2 children
Nathan, 11-23-1842, appt clerk
Nathan, 6-22-1843, appt to have care of title papers of Huntington PM

MENALLEN MINUTES, MARRIAGES, & MISCELLANY

GRIEST, Nathan, 3-29-1844, appt clerk
    Nathan, 8-20-1835, rep to MM 16 times thru 2-20-1845
    Nathan, 6-19-1845, clerk for the day
    Nathan, 2-18-1836, appt comm 15 times thru 12-18-1845
    Nathan, 8-19-1847, forced to pay $1.00 Muster fine to Jacob Lerew
    Nathan, 11-17-1852, rct Centre MM with wife Mary Ann and 4 children
    Nathan, 3-19-1856, rct Center MM with wife Mary Ann and 4 children
    Owen, 6-18-1846, compl of: fornication and mou
    Owen, 8-20-1846, read testimony. Retained
    Owen, 8-21-1862, rep to QM
    Owen, 12-23-1874, appt comm
    Owen, 8-19-1868, rep to MM 22 times thru 4-18-1883
    Peter, 1-18-1832, rct Pipe Creek MM to marry Mary Edmundson
    Peter, 6-21-1832, appt comm
    Peter, 4-21-1836, rep to MM 7 times thru 7-22-1868
    Peter, 6-22-1882, req membership [w]
    Peter, 9-21-1882, gct Green Plains MM, Clark Co, Ohio
    Peter, Jr, 6-20-1867, appt Overseer
    Phebe, 2-22-1810, rocf York MM with husband Amos
    Phebe, 2-23-1826, gives up membership; joined another society; wife of Amos
    Phebe, 4-22-1841, rct Warrington MM with father Uriah and family
    Phebe Jane, 1-19-1853, gct Centre MM, Centre Co, Pa
    Phebe Malvina, 4-19-1838, rct Warrington MM with father Uriah and family
    Phebe Malvina, 3-21-1840, rocf Warrington MM with father Uriah and family [w]
    Phebe Malvina, 4-22-1841, rct Warrington MM with father Uriah and family [w]
    Philena H., 3-20-1861, rct Penns Grove MM with husband Willing C. and 1 child [w]
    Philena Jane, 4-22-1841, req membership thru mother Mary Ann and father [w]
    Philena Jane, 5-19-1841, req membership with father Nathan and family
    Philena P., 12-23-1852, gct Centre MM, Centre Co, Pa [w]
    Philene H., 5-23-1860, rocf Penns Grove MM, Chester Co, Pa
    Priscilla, 5-21-1856, rct Centre MM with mother Martha
    Priscilla, 5-21-1856, rct Center MM, Centre Co, Pa with 4 children [w]
    R. Lizzie, 7-18-1883, rep to MM [w]
    Rachel Ann, 7-19-1854, rocf York MM with father Amos and family
    Rachel Ann, 6-20-1861, rct Penns Grove MM, Chester Co, Pa [w]
    Rachel Ann, 7-17-1861, gct Penns Grove MM
    Rebecca, 7-22-1807, appt Elder
    Rebecca, 7-21-1819, req membership
    Rebecca, 4-20-1843, rct Warrington MM with father John and family
    Rebecca, 6-21-1849, appt comm [w]
    Rebecca, 9-17-1851, req marriage with William S. Cadwallader
    Rebecca, 8-20-1863, rep to QM [w]
    Rebecca, 8-24-1865, rep to QM [w]

MINUTES

GRIEST, Rebeccah, 7-19-1820, appt comm
    Rebekah, 9-12-1785, rocf Warrington MM
    Reuben, 1-19-1870, rep to MM
    Reuben, 12-21-1870, rep to MM
    Reuben, 5-19-1875, compl of: mou
    Reuben, 5-19-1875, ack mou. Retained
    Reuben, 6-22-1882, req membership [w]
    Reuben, 9-21-1882, gct Green Plains MM, Clark Co, Ohio
    Rose, 9-24-1874, req membership for 3 children
    Rose D., 9-28-1869, req membership
    Rose D., 2-21-1872, rep to QM 4 times thru 8-22-1877 [w]
    Rose D., 5-20-1874, appt comm [w]
    Rose D., 9-23-1874, req membership for children Emily and Mary Lizzie [w]
    Rose D., 6-22-1871, rep to MM 10 times thru 10-21-1874 [w]
    Rose D., 10-21-1874, appt comm [w]
    Rose D., 12-22-1875, appt comm [w]
    Rose D., 8-22-1888, absent member. Now in Kan [w]
    Rose D., 12-18-1889, rct Genoa MM, Neb with husband Daniel and 2 children
    Rose T., 11-22-1871, rep to MM [w]
    Rose T., 1-17-1872, rep to MM [w]
    Ruth, 11-22-1820, req marriage with John Russel
    Ruth Anna, 4-23-1840, compl of: mou and moving to Ohio. Now Harry [w]
    Ruth E., 5-23-1888, appt assistant clerk [w]
    Ruth E., 12-19-1888, appt comm [w]
    Ruth E., 8-21-1889, rep to QM [w]
    Ruth Elizabeth, 7-18-1855, req membership thru parents Josiah and Mary Ann [w]
    Ruth L., 6-21-1877, rep to MM [w]
    Ruth L., 11-20-1889, appt Overseer [w]
    Ruth L., 2-19-1890, rep to QM [w]
    Ruth L., 8-20-1890, rep to QM [w]
    Ruth L., 2-24-1887, appt comm 6 times thru 1-21-1891 [w]
    Ruth Lizzie, 2-19-1873, appt comm [w]
    Ruth Lizzie, 11-18-1874, rep to QM 5 times thru 8-19-1885 [w]
    Ruth Lizzie, 4-20-1881, appt assistant clerk [w]
    Ruth Lizzie, 4-19-1882, appt assistant clerk [w]
    Ruth Lizzie, 4-18-1883, appt assistant clerk [w]
    Ruth Lizzie, 4-23-1873, rep to MM 8 times thru 11-21-1883 [w]
    Ruth Lizzie, 5-18-1887, appt assistant clerk [w]
    Ruth Lizzie, 8-17-1887, appt comm [w]
    Ruth Lizzie, 12-21-1887, appt recorder of Births and Deaths [w]
    Ruth M., 11-21-1866, rep to QM [w]
    Sabilla, 11-23-1870, rep to QM [w]
    Sabilla E., 3-19-1890, hired to teach school for spring 1888
    Sabilla E., 8-20-1890, appt Elder
    Sabilla E., 1-21-1891, appt comm
    Salathiel, 3-23-1864, gct Whitewater MM, Ind

MENALLEN MINUTES, MARRIAGES, & MISCELLANY

GRIEST, Salathiel, 4-21-1869, rocf White Water MM, Ind
    Salathiel, 10-19-1870, rep to MM
    Salathiel, 6-22-1882, req membership [w]
    Samuel, 6-24-1824, compl of: mou
    Samuel Hadley, 3-20-1861, rct Penns Grove MM with parents, Willing C. and Philena
    Sarah, 6-24-1841, compl of: mou. Formerly Cook [w]
    Sarah, 6-22-1882, req membership [w]
    Sarah, 9-21-1882, gct Green Plains MM, Clark Co, Ohio
    Sarah Ann, 7-21-1847, req marriage with Edward Brooks
    Sarah G., 1-22-1851, compl of: mou. Now Woodard [w]
    Sarah T., 8-19-1847, req membership for her daughter, Alcetta Griest
    Sarathiel, 9-21-1882, gct Green Plains MM, Clark Co, Ohio
    Selathiel, 12-20-1871, rep to MM
    Sibbilla E., 10-20-1869, rocf New Garden MM, Chester Co, Pa [w]
    Sibbilla E., 1-19-1870, rep to MM 16 times thru 5-19-1886 [w]
    Sibbilla E., 8-18-1886, appt Overseer [w]
    Sibbilla E., 11-20-1889, appt Overseer [w]
    Sibbilla E., 11-20-1889, appt Overseer [w]
    Sibbilla E., 3-19-1890, hired as school teacher in 1889; $25.00 per month [w]
    Sibbilla E., 5-21-1872, rep to QM 11 times thru 5-21-1890 [w]
    Sibbilla E., 8-22-1871, appt comm 21 times thru 1-21-1891 [w]
    Sibilla E., 10-20-1869, rocf New Garden MM, Chester Co, Pa
    Sibilla E., 3-22-1871, appt comm [w]
    Sibilla E., 7-17-1871, appt comm [w]
    Sibilla E., 5-21-1872, appt comm [w]
    Sibilla E., 12-23-1885, assessed $1.00 for Yearly Meeting
    Solomon, 5-22-1822, compl of: attending muster; fornication
    Solomon, 3-19-1823, read testimony. Retained
    Solomon, 3-21-1827, rct Warrington MM with wife Mary and 3 children
    Susana, 10-23-1817, rct Warrington MM. Wife of Thomas
    Susanna, 4-21-1796, req marriage with John (of Benjamin) Wright
    Susanna, 5-20-1807, widow of John. Huntington reports she is weak
    Susanna, 4-24-1845, rct Center MM, Center Co, Pa [w]
    Tabitha, 6-22-1882, req membership [w]
    Tabitha, 9-21-1882, gct Green Plains MM, Clark Co, Ohio
    Teresa, 11-17-1852, rct Centre MM, with father Nathan and family [w]
    Teresa, 3-19-1856, rct Centre MM with father William and family [w]
    Therese, 3-19-1856, rct Center MM with father Nathan and family
    Thomas, 8-22-1799, appt Overseer at Huntington
    Thomas, 9-21-1803, released as Overseer at Huntington
    Thomas, 7-22-1807, has care of Huntington Patent Deed for 5 acres
    Thomas, 9-19-1810, compl of: mou
    Thomas, 3-21-1811, dis: mou
    Thomas, 1-19-1814, appt Overseer at Huntington
    Thomas, 1-22-1817, retained as Overseer
    Thomas, 6-19-1817, appt to standing comm for care of Benj. Tomlinson
    Thomas, 8-9-1790, rep to QM 7 times thru 8-22-1822
    Thomas, 4-9-1781, appt comm 52 times thru 12-24-1829

MINUTES

GRIEST, Thomas Elwood, 5-21-1856, rct Centre MM with mother Martha
Thomas Elwood, 5-21-1856, rct Center MM, Centre Co, Pa with 4 children [w]
Uriah, 10-23-1817, rct Warrington MM to marry Mary Vale
Uriah, 12-21-1820, appt comm 9 times thru 7-19-1837
Uriah, 8-23-1821, rep to QM 4 times thru 2-22-1838
Uriah, 1-23-1833, rep to MM 6 times thru 8-24-1837
Uriah, 4-19-1838, rct Warrington MM with wife Mary and 6 children
Uriah, 3-18-1840, rocf Warrington MM with wife Mary and 5 children
Uriah, 4-22-1841, rct Warrington MM with wife Mary and 4 children
W. H., 5-18-1887, assessed $3.00 for fuel for Ann and Martha Griest
W. H., 8-20-1890, appt Elder
W. H., 8-20-1890, rep to QM
Willaim, 3-19-1856, rct Centre MM with wife Mary Ann and 4 children [w]
William, 8-24-1820, appt comm
William, 5-23-1821, rep to QM
William, 8-23-1821, rct Miami MM, Ohio
William, 1-17-1827, compl of: mou
William, 4-22-1841, rct Warrington MM with father Uriah and family [w]
William, 5-21-1856, rct Centre MM with mother Martha
William, 11-17-1886, appt comm
William, 8-17-1887, rep to QM
William, 12-21-1887, appt recorder of Births and Deaths [w]
William E., 3-18-1840, rocf Warrington MM with father Uriah and family
William Elmer, 4-19-1838, rct Warrington MM with father Uriah and family
William H., 1-21-1891, appt Treasurer
William H., 12-23-1885, assessed $1.00 for Yearly Meeting
William H., 11-17-1886, rep to QM 6 times thru 5-21-1890
William H., 2-24-1887, appt assistant clerk
William H., 2-24-1887, appt comm 7 times thru 8-20-1890
William H., 3-21-1888, clerk for the day 8 times thru 1-21-1891
William H., 3-20-1889, appt assistant clerk
William H., 4-23-1890, appt assistant clerk
William H., 12-17-1890, clerk for the day in joint session with women
William H., 1-21-1891, clerk for the day in joint session
William H., 1-21-1891, appt Treasurer [w]
William Penn, 5-21-1856, rct Center MM, Centre Co, Pa with 4 children [w]
Willing, 1-19-1820, appt comm 4 times thru 6-23-1825
Willing, 6-21-1827, read testimony. Retained
Willing, 8-23-1827, gct Warrington MM
Willing, 7-19-1854, rocf York MM with father Amos and family
Willing C., 12-22-1859, rct Penns Grove MM, to marry Philena H. Broomell
Willing C., 3-20-1861, rct Penns Grove MM with wife Philena H. and 1 child

MENALLEN MINUTES, MARRIAGES, & MISCELLANY

GRIEST, Willing, Jr, 10-22-1794, rct Warrington MM
    Wilmore M., 9-24-1874, req membership thru parents, Daniel and Rose Griest
    Wm. Elmor Mahlon, 4-22-1841, rct Warrington MM with father Uriah and family
    Wm. H., 2-24-1887, rep to QM

GRIFFITH, Abner, 5-21-1806, req marriage with Mary Owen
    Allen, 7-17-1839, rocf Warrington MM with wife Sarah and 6 children
    Allen, 8-22-1839, rep to MM 16 times thru 3-17-1847
    Allen, 3-21-1849, compl of: "difficult case"
    Allen, 2-21-1856, gct White Water MM, Ind with wife Sarah and 1 child [w]
    Ann, 11-12-1781, req marriage with John Wright, Jr
    Elizabeth S., 6-23-1842, rct Clear Creek MM, Putnam Co, Ill [w]
    Elizabeth S., 4-23-1840, compl of: mou and moving to Ill; formerly Lundy [w]
    Henry C., 7-17-1839, rocf Warrington MM with father Allen and family
    Henry C., 8-20-1846, read testimony. Retained
    Henry C., 5-17-1848, compl of: suing at law a member of the society
    Henry C., 8-22-1850, read testimony re: mou. Comm apptd to consider
    Henry C., 7-23-1851, disowned
    Henry C., 8-21-1851, intends to appeal to Quarterly Meeting
    Huldah, 7-17-1839, rocf Warrington MM with father Allen and family
    Jesse, 1-15-1787, compl of: mou
    Jesse, 9-4-1787, dis: mou
    Maria, 7-17-1839, rocf Warrington MM with father Allen and family
    Maria E., 4-22-1847, req marriage with Thomas Pearson
    Mary, 9-17-1806, rct Dunnings Creek MM
    Mary Jane, 7-17-1839, rocf Warrington MM with father Allen and family
    Mary Jane, 6-19-1851, compl of: mou. Now Wierman [w]
    Rachel J., 2-21-1856, rct Whitewater MM, Ind with parents Allen and Sarah
    Rebecca, 6-22-1797, compl of: mou to first cousin. Formerly Blackburn
    Rebecca, 7-17-1839, rocf Warrington MM with father Allen and family
    Rebecca L., 5-23-1851, ack error. Retained [w]
    Rebecca L., 7-23-1856, rct White Water MM, Ind. Now Rebecca L. Leonard [w]
    Sarah, 5-13-1793, req membership. Daughter of John Griffith
    Sarah, 9-09-1793, req marriage with Thomas Blackburn
    Sarah, 7-17-1839, rocf Warrington MM with husband Allen and 6 children
    Sarah, 7-17-1839, rocf Warrington MM with father Allen and family
    Sarah, 11-18-1840, rep to QM 5 times thru 8-18-1853 [w]
    Sarah, 3-18-1846, appt Overseer [w]
    Sarah, 1-20-1847, on comm against settling new meeting at Mechanicsville
    Sarah, 5-18-1842, appt comm 11 times thru 10-18-1849 [w]
    Sarah, 2-21-1856, rct Whitewater MM, Ind with husband Allen and 1 child

MINUTES

GRIFFITH, Sarah, 2-21-1856, gct White Water MM, Ind with father Allen and family [w]
    Sarah, 2-21-1856, gct White Water MM, Ind with husband Allen and 1 child [w]
    Sarah A., 7-23-1856, ack mou. Retained. Now Stafford
    Sarah G., 7-23-1856, rct White Water MM, Ind. Now Sarah G. Stafford [w]
    Thomas, 4-15-1782, to marry Rachel Blackburn
    Thomas, 2-9-1789, rep to QM 8 times thru 5-23-1798
    Thomas, 5-10-1790, appt Overseer at Monallen
    Thomas, 10-13-1795, released as Overseer at Dunnings Creek
    Thomas, 7-14-1783, appt comm 35 times thru 6-24-1802
    Thomas, Jr, 3-13-1786, compl of: carnal knowledge of woman now married to
    Thomas, Jr, 4-10-1786, dis: carnal knowledge before marriage
    Thos, 3-9-1789, appt comm
    William, 10-9-1780, appt comm 29 times thru 5-13-1793
    William, 5-14-1781, rep to QM
    William, 1-14-1782, requests release as Overseer
    William, 3-11-1782, rep to QM
    William, 11-12-1792, compl of: "case of difficulty"
    William, 5-22-1799, req marriage with Sarah Owing
GRIST, Joseph, 5-12-1788, appt comm
GROUP, Amanda E., 4-19-1869, ack mou. Retained [w]
HAINES, Deborah, 8-13-1781, rocf Pipe Creek MM, with mother, Mary, and stepfather, Samuel Cookson
    Isaac, 8-13-1781, rocf Pipe Creek MM, with mother, Mary, and stepfather, Samuel Cookson
    Isaac, 12-12-1785, rct Gunpowder MM
    Samuel, 8-13-1781, rocf Pipe Creek MM, with mother, Mary, and stepfather, Samuel Cookson
HAINS, Deborah, 5-12-1783, rct East Notingham MM
    James W., 11-20-1872, rocf Miami MM, Warren Co, Ohio as minister
    Samuel, 8-11-1783, rct Notingham MM
HALLOWELL, Benjamin, 8-21-1862, appt comm [w]
    Benjamin, 3-23-1864, appt comm
    Margaret E., 8-21-1862, appt comm [w]
HALL, Rebecca K., 8-23-1882, rocf Salem MM, NJ as Minister
HAMMER, Ruth, 7-14-1783, dis: mou and unchastity
HAMMIL, Mary, 7-10-1786, compl of: mou. Now Johnston
    Mary, 9-11-1786, dis: mou. Now Johnston
HAMMON, George, 8-9-1784, req marriage with Deborah Hutton
    Nathan, 2-10-1783, rep to QM
    Nathan, 6-9-1783, appt comm
    Ruth, 5-12-1783, compl of: mou and unchastity. Formerly Hobson
HAMMOND, Ales, 7-14-1788, compl of: mou. Now Wright
    Ayles, 9-15-1788, dis: mou. Now Wright
    Benjamin, 2-19-1801, rct Redstone MM with father George and family
    Deborah, 8-9-1790, rct Warrington MM. Denied: "poor circumstances"

MENALLEN MINUTES, MARRIAGES, & MISCELLANY

HAMMOND, Deborah, 2-19-1801, rct Redstone MM with husband George and 8 children
    Deborah, 2-19-1801, rct Redstone MM with father George and family
    Elizabeth, 12-11-1780, req membership
    Elizabeth, 3-22-1815, req marriage with Eli Thomas
    George, 2-19-1801, rct Redstone MM with wife Deborah and 8 children
    James, 6-9-1794, compl of: mou
    James, 8-11-1794, dis: mou
    James, 2-19-1801, rct Redstone MM with father George and family
    James, 3-22-1820, rocf Smithfield MM
    James, 3-18-1840, removed to James Co, Ohio without certificate
    John, 6-20-1799, compl of: carnal knowledge with woman now married to
    John, 3-19-1806, sent testimony from Short Creek MM. Accepted
    Margaret, 2-19-1801, rct Redstone MM with father George and family
    Mary, 2-19-1801, rct Redstone MM with father George and family
    Mary, 4-21-1803, req marriage with Harman Wierman
    Ruth, 2-19-1801, rct Redstone MM with father George and family
    Sarah, 2-19-1801, rct Redstone MM with father George and family
    Thomas, 8-11-1794, req marriage with Ruth Wright
    Thomas, 9-19-1798, appt comm 7 times thru 6-18-1801
    Thomas, 5-20-1801, rep to QM
    Thomas, 11-18-1801, rep to QM
    Thomas, 2-18-1802, rep to QM
    William, 2-19-1801, rct Redstone MM with father George and family
HANCOCK, Benjamin, 2-9-1795, rocf Warrington MM
    Benjamin, 11-19-1800, appt comm
    Elizabeth, 2-9-1795, rocf Warrington MM, wife of James
    Elizabeth, 8-22-1799, req marriage with Isaac Fisher
    James, 2-9-1795, rocf Warrington MM
    James, 4-21-1803, rocf Warrington MM. Forwarded to Dunnings Creek MM
    Joel, 2-9-1795, rocf Warrington MM
    Joel, 2-23-1797, appt comm
    Joel, 2-23-1797, rep to QM
    Joel, 8-22-1799, req marriage with Mary Kenworthy
    John, 2-9-1795, rocf Warrington MM
    John, 12-14-1795, appt comm 4 times thru 8-23-1798
    John, 8-23-1798, rep to QM
    John, 10-23-1800, req marriage with Hannah Kenworthy
    Sarah, 2-9-1795, rocf Warrington MM
HARBOLD, Sarah, 5-23-1888, released from membership. Formerly Cook
    Sarah, 5-23-1888, dis: joined another. Daughter of Walker Cook
HARBOUGH, Sophia, 4-24-1800, req marriage with Amos Penrose
    Sophiah, 8-22-1799, req membership
HARDY, Benjamin, 12-22-1886, req membership
    Benjamin, 2-20-1889, req membership [w]
    Lewis Henry, 6-22-1876, minor child of one member. Born 5th mo 3rd 1868
    Lewis Henry, 6-22-1876, req membership. Born 5-3-1868 [w]

MINUTES

HARDY, Mary, 12-22-1869, compl of: mou. Formerly Cook [w]
    Mary, 2-23-1870, ack mou. Retained
HARLON, Joseph, 7-15-1782, a member of Nottingham MM
HARRIS, Ana Maria, 4-20-1837, rct Salem MM, Ohio with father Nathan and family
    Anna, 5-19-1802, rocf Exeter MM with father Benjamin and family
    Anna Maria, 4-21-1837, rct Salem MM, Ohio with father Nathan and family [w]
    Barbara, 5-19-1802, rocf Exeter MM with father Benjamin and family
    Benjamin, 5-19-1802, rocf Exeter MM with wife Rebecca and 6 children
    Benjamin, 5-19-1802, rocf Exeter MM with father Benjamin and family
    Benjamin, 6-21-1804, appt Guardian of Joseph Hutton (by Court)
    Benjamin, 7-22-1807, appt Elder
    Benjamin, 11-21-1821, req marriage with Jane Hutton
    Benjamin, 8-20-1835, appt Overseer
    Benjamin, 8-24-1837, appt comm in charge of graveyards
    Benjamin, 10-18-1838, appt Overseer
    Benjamin, 7-22-1840, appt Elder
    Benjamin, 7-17-1844, appt to revise, record and care for MM records
    Benjamin, 5-17-1848, appt Elder
    Benjamin, 12-23-1802, appt comm 112 times thru 12-24-1851
    Benjamin, 12-20-1832, rep to MM 42 times thru 11-22-1854
    Benjamin, 2-24-1803, rep to QM 44 times thru 11-22-1854
    Benjamin, 2-23-1881, former trustee for Samuel Hutton is now deceased
    Beulah, 5-19-1802, rocf Exeter MM with father Benjamin and family
    Bulah, 9-20-1820, req marriage with Benjamin W. Hutton
    Charles K., 1-22-1890, withdraws membership
    Charles K., 2-19-1890, req membership be discontinued [w]
    Elizabeth, 9-19-1810, req marriage with Nathan Wright
    Elizabeth, 4-20-1837, rct Salem MM, Ohio with father Nathan and family
    Ellen, 3-19-1834, rct Salem MM, Ohio with father Jacob and family
    Hanah, 3-21-1821, req membership
    Hannah, 4-20-1837, rct Salem MM, Ohio with husband Nathan and 6 children
    Hiram C., 4-20-1881, ack mou to Miriam G. Wright. Retained
    Hiram L., 2-22-1871, rep to QM
    Hiram L., 2-21-1872, rep to QM
    Jacob, 7-21-1802, rocf Exeter MM
    Jacob, 4-23-1807, req marriage with Mary Wright
    Jacob, 8-22-1811, exempt fines, "taken in 1808 by George Smyser, collector, from Jacob Harris for exempt fines of 5 dollars each for the year 1806 and 1807 eleven bushels of wheet v. at $11.00"
    Jacob, 5-19-1819, appt Overseer
    Jacob, 7-21-1819, appt Overseer
    Jacob, 3-20-1822, appt to examine record of Births & Deaths
    Jacob, 4-22-1824, req release as Overseer
    Jacob, 3-18-1829, appt for care of burying grounds
    Jacob, 2-23-1832, appt comm to list names re separation at BYM

MENALLEN MINUTES, MARRIAGES, & MISCELLANY

HARRIS, Jacob, 5-24-1832, appt Elder
    Jacob, 2-21-1833, rep to MM 5 times thru 1-22-1834
    Jacob, 5-18-1814, rep to QM 34 times thru 1-22-1834
    Jacob, 1-22-1817, appt comm 68 times thru 2-20-1834
    Jacob, 3-19-1834, rct Salem MM, Ohio with wife Mary and 7 children
    Jacob B., 3-19-1834, rct Salem MM, Ohio with father Jacob and family
    Jane, 3-23-1836, appt Overseer [w]
    Jane, 9-18-1839, appt Overseer [w]
    Jane, 7-22-1840, appt Elder
    Jane, 5-17-1848, appt Elder
    Jane, 6-20-1852, appt Overseer [w]
    Jane, 11-23-1836, appt comm 30 times thru 10-21-1868 [w]
    Jane, 5-22-1870, rep to MM [w]
    Jane, 5-20-1840, rep to QM 15 times thru 2-22-1871 [w]
    Jane W., 4-20-1837, rct Salem MM, Ohio with father Nathan and family
    Jesse, 4-20-1837, rct Salem MM, Ohio with father Nathan and family
    Joel, 3-23-1825, appt comm
    Joel, 3-23-1825, appt comm
    Joel, 6-23-1825, appt comm
    Joel G., 3-19-1834, rct Salem MM, Ohio with father Jacob and family
    John, 3-19-1834, rct Salem MM, Ohio
    John B., 9-22-1887, rct Penns Grove MM, Chester Co, Pa
    John B., 10-19-1887, ack mou. Retained [w]
    Maria, 10-23-1878, compl of: mou. Now Rakestraw [w]
    Maria L., 12-18-1878, ack mou. Retained. Now Rakestraw [w]
    Martha, 2-22-1849, rep to QM [w]
    Martha, 4-19-1849, appt comm [w]
    Martha, 3-20-1850, req marriage with Thomas Jones
    Martha, 3-21-1850, req marriage with Thomas Jones [w]
    Martha, 5-18-1887, compl of: mou to Ellis W. Cook [w]
    Martha, 6-23-1887, ack mou. Retained. Now Cook
    Mary, 5-24-1832, appt Elder
    Mary, 3-19-1834, rct Salem MM, Ohio with husband Jacob and 7 children
    Miriam G., 4-20-1881, ack mou. Retained. Formerly Wright
    Nathan, 5-19-1802, rocf Exeter MM with father Benjamin and family
    Nathan, 12-21-1820, compl of: mou
    Nathan, 1-17-1821, read testimony. Retained
    Nathan, 4-20-1837, rct Salem MM, Ohio with wife Hannah and 6 children
    Rachel, 3-19-1834, rct Salem MM, Ohio with father Jacob and family
    Rebecca, 5-19-1802, rocf Exeter MM with husband Benjamin and 6 children
    Rebecca, 7-22-1807, appt Elder
    Rebecca, 3-19-1834, rct Salem MM, Ohio with father Jacob and family
    Rebecca, 4-20-1837, rct Salem MM, Ohio with father Nathan and family
    Rebecca, 4-21-1837, rct Salem MM, Ohio with father Nathan and family [w]

MINUTES

HARRIS, Rebeckah, 2-23-1804, req marriage with Samuel Wright
    Rebeckah, 7-23-1817, appt comm
    Ruth Anna, 11-21-1838, appt assistant clerk [w]
    Ruth Anna, 8-22-1839, appt comm [w]
    Ruth Anna, 11-20-1839, appt comm [w]
    Ruth Anna, 2-20-1840, appt comm [w]
    Ruth Anna, 5-20-1840, rep to QM [w]
    Ruth Anna, 6-19-1845, rct Salem MM, Columbiana Co, Ohio [w]
    Ruthanna, 5-19-1802, rocf Exeter MM with father Benjamin and family
    Ruthanna, 1-17-1843, appt comm [w]
    Ruthanna, 7-23-1845, gct Salem MM, Ohio
    S. H., 1-18-1888, appt comm
    Samuel, 3-19-1834, rct Salem MM, Ohio
    Samuel, 8-19-1874, rep to QM 3 times thru 2-20-1889
    Samuel, 12-23-1874, appt comm
    Samuel, 1-20-1875, clerk for the day
    Samuel, 5-22-1878, appt Trustee in place of David R. McCreary, dec'd
    Samuel, 10-21-1885, appt comm
    Samuel, 12-23-1885, assessed $2.50 for Yearly Meeting
    Samuel, 5-18-1887, assessed $2.00 for fuel for Ann & Martha Griest
    Samuel E., 5-23-1888, appt Elder [w]
    Samuel H., 8-24-1848, forced to pay $1 muster fine by Daniel Plank, collector
    Samuel H., 8-23-1849, rct Warrington MM to marry Julia Kirk
    Samuel H., 3-17-1875, appt clerk
    Samuel H., 4-19-1876, appt clerk
    Samuel H., 4-19-1876, appt comm 5 times thru 1-22-1890
    Samuel H., 12-20-1876, rep to MM
    Samuel H., 3-23-1887, surviving trustee at Menallen
    Samuel H., 3-23-1887, appt Trustee for Menallen and Huntington
    Samuel H., 5-19-1875, rep to QM 8 times thru 8-21-1889
    Samuel Westly, 4-20-1837, rct Salem MM, Ohio with father Nathan and family
    Sarah, 9-23-1807, req marriage with Abner Walker
    Silas, 3-19-1834, rct Salem MM, Ohio with father Jacob and family
    Teressa, 2-21-1883, ack mou to Thomas A. Wright. Retained
    William, 3-19-1834, rct Salem MM, Ohio with father Jacob and family
HARRY, Amanda, 6-19-1834, compl of: mou. Read testimony. Retained
    Jacob, 1-23-1833, appt comm
    Lewis, 3-21-1832, req marriage with Sarah Comly
    Lewis, 4-19-1832, rocf Warrington MM
    Lewis, 7-18-1832, rocf Warrington MM with 3 children
    Lewis, 6-20-1833, appt clerk
    Lewis, 3-19-1834, appt Overseer
    Lewis, 6-19-1834, appt clerk
    Lewis, 6-18-1835, appt clerk
    Lewis, 8-22-1833, rep to QM 5 times thru 8-20-1835
    Lewis, 8-20-1835, appt Overseer
    Lewis, 9-23-1835, appt Elder [w]
    Lewis, 6-23-1836, appt clerk

MENALLEN MINUTES, MARRIAGES, & MISCELLANY

HARRY, Lewis, 12-20-1832, appt comm 14 times thru 6-22-1837
    Lewis, 8-24-1837, appt comm in charge of graveyards
    Lewis, 12-20-1832, rep to MM 13 times thru 12-21-1837
    Lewis, 6-21-1838, rct Westland MM with wife Sarah C. and 4 children
    Lewis C., 6-21-1838, rct Westland MM with father Lewis and family
    Melinda, 7-18-1832, rocf Warrington MM with father Lewis and family
    Naomi, 7-18-1832, rocf Warrington MM with father Lewis and family
    Naomi, 6-21-1838, rct Westland MM with father Lewis and family
    Ruth Anna, 4-23-1840, compl of: mou and moving to Ohio. Formerly Griest [w]
    Ruth Anna, 7-22-1840, ack error. Retained [w]
    Sarah, 8-18-1836, rep to QM [w]
    Sarah C., 6-21-1838, rct Westland MM with husband Lewis and 4 children
    Susanna, 6-21-1838, rct Westland MM with father Lewis and family
    William G., 7-18-1832, rocf Warrington MM with father Lewis and family
    William G., 6-21-1838, rct Westland MM with father Lewis and family
HAWXHURST, Townsend, 12-23-1819, rocf Westbury MM, Long Island, NY as Minister
HEICUS, Priscilla, 8-21-1862, formerly of Warrington, now removed from this area [w]
HENDREX, Elizabeth, 10-13-1788, roc
    Nathan, 12-15-1788, appt comm 7 times thru 3-15-1790
    Nathan, 8-10-1789, rep to QM
HENDRICKS, Benjamin, 5-20-1807, appt Overseer
    Hannah, 7-20-1836, appt assistant clerk [w]
    Hannah, 11-23-1836, rep to QM [w]
    James, 7-22-1807, rocf Pipe Creek MM. Compl of: mou
    Joel, 3-18-1840, removed to Fayette Co, Pa without certificate
    Joel, 10-25-1847, rct West MM, Ohio
    John, 3-23-1803, read testimony. Retained
    John, 9-19-1804, compl of: attending muster
    John, 11-21-1804, dis: mustering
    Mary, 8-9-1790, appt Elder
    Mary, 4-13-1795, appt comm
    Mary, 7-19-1820, req membership at Providence MM, Fayette Co, Pa
    Nathan, 5-15-1786, rep to QM 4 times thru 5-14-1794
    Nathan, 5-14-1787, appt Overseer at Monallen
    Nathan, 5-10-1790, released as Overseer at Monallen
    Nathan, 3-12-1787, appt comm 24 times thru 12-22-1796
    Rebecca, 5-14-1781, mou: formerly Blackburn
    Rebecca, 6-11-1781, dis: mou; formerly Blackburn
    Samuel, 9-19-1804, compl of: attending muster
    Samuel, 12-19-1839, rct Redstone MM
    Sarah, 3-19-1817, appt comm re Hanah Underwood
    Sarah, 7-19-1820, appt comm
    Sarah, 5-23-1821, req marriage with Jesse Russell
    Stephen, 9-15-1794, req marriage with Sarah Wireman
    Stephen, 2-9-1795, rep to QM

MINUTES

HENDRICKS, Stephen, 2-22-1798, rep to QM
    Stephen, 4-19-1804, proposed as Trustee for Joseph Hutton
    Stephen, 4-19-1798, appt comm 9 times thru 12-25-1813
HENDRIS, Nathan, 4-12-1790, appt comm
HENDRIX, Elizabeth, 9-15-1788, rct Pipe Creek MM
    Hannah, 10-12-1789, compl of: fornication with 1st cousin. Now Wright
    Hannah, 11-22-1837, rep to QM [w]
    Jacob, 12-20-1810, rct Redstone MM
    James, 11-23-1803, a minor, gone to live at Pipe Creek MM area
    John, 12-23-1802, compl of: attending muster
    Mary, 9-21-1803, released as Elder
    Mary, 8-22-1805, dis: falsehoods
    Nathan, 2-11-1788, appt comm 13 times thru 8-22-1799
    Nathan, 3-14-1785, rep to QM 6 times thru 8-22-1799
    Nathan, 8-24-1809, rct Pipe Creek MM
    Phebe, 11-20-1839, rct Redstone MM, Fayette Co, Pa [w]
    Samuel, 3-20-1805, dis: mustering
    Sarah, 4-23-1801, compl of: unchastity. Now Davis
    Sarah, 6-18-1801, dis: mou. Now Davis
    Stephen, 6-21-1804, appt Guardian of Joseph Hutton (by Court)
    Stephen, 12-20-1810, rct Redstone MM
    Stephen, 11-21-1798, rep to QM 10 times thru 11-18-1812
    Stephen, 2-22-1798, appt comm 14 times thru 7-20-1814
    Stephen, 6-22-1815, deceased. Replaced as trustee for Joseph Hutton
HENRICKS, Nathan, 8-13-1787, appt comm
HERRITT, Eliza, 5-18-1841, appt comm [w]
HEWET, Abel, 11-13-1786, rct Westland MM with father Jonathan and family
    Ann, 11-13-1786, rct Westland MM with husband Jonathan and 3 children
    Eliza, 5-20-1849, appt Overseer [w]
    Ellen, 3-21-1849, appt comm [w]
    Jesse, 1-17-1810, compl of: fornication with woman now his wife
    Jesse, 4-19-1810, read testimony. Retained
    John, 8-22-1805, compl of: mustering
    Jonathan, 11-13-1786, rct Westland MM with wife Ann and 3 children
    Joseph, 11-13-1786, rct Westland MM with father Jonathan and family
    Sarah, 11-13-1786, rct Westland MM with father Jonathan and family
HEWETT, George, 1-19-1842, req marriage with Ellen Wright [w]
    John, 2-20-1800, compl of: mou to Martha McGrew
    Joseph, 8-13-1787, appeals case to QM
    Joseph, 3-14-1791, rct Warrington MM for self, wife and one child
    Joseph, 10-24-1799, rocf Warrington MM with wife and 4 children
    Joseph, 10-24-1799, rocf Warrington MM with father Joseph and family
    Mary, 4-12-1790, compl of: mou. Now McGrail
    Samuel, 10-24-1799, rocf Warrington MM with father Joseph and family
    Sarah, 10-24-1799, rocf Warrington MM with father Joseph and family
    Thomas, 10-24-1799, rocf Warrington MM with father Joseph and family

MENALLEN MINUTES, MARRIAGES, & MISCELLANY

HEWITT, Edith, 6-20-1852, appt Overseer [w]
    Eliza, 3-23-1842, req membership with husband Jacob and 3 children
    Eliza, 9-19-1849, appt comm [w]
    Eliza, 10-24-1850, appt comm 6 times thru 3-23-1853 [w]
    Eliza, 5-23-1851, rep to QM [w]
    Eliza, 5-19-1852, rep to QM [w]
    Eliza, 6-20-1852, appt Overseer [w]
    Eliza, 2-23-1854, rep to QM [w]
    Eliza W., 9-21-1842, appt comm [w]
    Elizabeth, 8-21-1800, compl of: mou. Now Joice
    Elizabeth, 3-23-1842, req membership thru father Jacob and family
    Elizabeth, 6-18-1857, compl of: mou. Now Wierman [w]
    Ellen, 9-18-1850, appt comm 8 times thru 7-23-1862 [w]
    Ellen, 11-17-1852, rep to QM [w]
    Ellen, 8-23-1855, rep to QM [w]
    Ellen, 11-18-1857, rep to QM [w]
    Ellen, 12-24-1857, appt Elder
    Ellen, 4-19-1860, appt Elder
    Ellen, 9-17-1862, rep to MM [w]
    Ellen, 11-19-1862, rep to MM [w]
    Ellen, 12-21-1863, appt Elder
    Ellen, 2-20-1867, appt Elder [w]
    Ellen W., 11-21-1849, appt comm [w]
    Ellin, 1-22-1851, appt comm [w]
    Ellin, 12-24-1863, appt Elder [w]
    George, 2-24-1820, read testimony. Retained
    George, 2-23-1832, appt comm to list names re separation at BYM
    George, 8-24-1837, appt comm in charge of graveyards
    George, 10-18-1838, appt Overseer
    George, 12-23-1841, appt Overseer
    George, 1-19-1842, req marriage with Ellen Wright
    George, 1-18-1843, appt Overseer
    George, 7-17-1844, appt to record Certificates of Removal
    George, 2-20-1845, appt Elder
    George, 7-22-1846, appt Overseer
    George, 1-20-1847, on comm against settling new mtg at Mechanicsville
    George, 5-17-1848, appt Elder
    George, 5-23-1849, appt to record certificates of Removal
    George, 7-23-1851, appt Elder
    George, 8-21-1851, appt to care for burying grounds
    George, 7-19-1854, appt Elder
    George, 8-24-1854, appt Elder [w]
    George, 11-21-1855, appt Elder
    George, 12-18-1856, appt to record Certificates of Removal
    George, 12-24-1857, appt Elder
    George, 4-19-1860, appt Elder
    George, 12-21-1863, appt Elder
    George, 1-23-1828, appt comm 73 times thru 8-24-1865
    George, 2-20-1867, appt Elder [w]
    George, 4-20-1870, appt Elder

MINUTES

HEWITT, George, 2-21-1833, rep to MM 91 times thru 7-17-1872
    George, 8-18-1825, rep to QM 31 times thru 8-21-1872
    George, 5-21-1873, appt Elder
    George, 5-17-1876, appt Elder
    George, Jr, 8-19-1819, compl of: fornication. Has moved away
    George, Jr, 2-20-1834, rep to MM
    George, Jr, 2-20-1834, appt comm
    Jacob, 3-23-1842, req membership with wife and 3 children
    Jacob, 9-18-1850, appt comm
    Jacob B., 3-29-1844, appt assistant clerk
    Jacob B., 4-24-1845, appt assistant clerk
    Jacob B., 12-18-1845, appt Overseer
    Jacob B., 4-23-1846, appt clerk
    Jacob B., 4-22-1847, appt assistant clerk
    Jacob B., 1-16-1849, appt Overseer
    Jacob B., 1-21-1852, appt Overseer
    Jacob B., 5-22-1844, rep to QM 8 times thru 2-24-1853
    Jacob B., 9-21-1842, rep to MM 19 times thru 4-21-1853
    Jacob B., 3-22-1843, appt comm 25 times thru 4-21-1853
    Jane, 3-23-1842, req membership thru father Jacob and family
    Jane, 4-22-1858, compl of: illegitimate child [w]
    Jane, 2-24-1859, disowned
    Jesse, 3-18-1840, removed to Franklin Co, Pa without certificate
    John, 5-21-1800, dis: mou
    John, 10-24-1805, dis: mustering
    Joseph, 3-12-1787, compl of: disturbing meeting
    Joseph, 6-11-1787, dis: disturbing meeting
    Joseph, 4-14-1788, QM, on appeal finds charge well founded, as to his public appearances. He is acquitted of the other charge
    Joseph, Jr, 4-14-1788, req marriage with Rachel McCrery
    Louisa, 3-23-1842, req membership thru father Jacob and family
    Louisa, 6-18-1857, compl of: mou. Now Brown [w]
    Martha, 5-21-1800, dis: mou
    William, 12-20-1838, appt comm
HIBBERD, Jane, 2-23-1804, rct this area as Minister
    Job, 12-23-1874, appt comm
    Theodore, 12-23-1874, appt comm
HIBBERT, Abraham, 11-20-1822, rocf Goshen MM as Minister
    Abraham, 11-20-1822, rocf Goshen MM as Minister
HICKS, Isaac, 10-17-1883, rct visit Warrington Quarter as Minister
    James, 9-18-1805, compl of: fornication
    James, Jr, 6-20-1805, rocf Baltimore MM
    James, Jr, 2-20-1806, dis: fornication
HILTABIDLE, Mary E., 7-17-1889, ack mou to Charles T. Hiltabidle. Formerly Wright
HILTON, Titus, 4-22-1852, rocf Chesterfield MM (New Jersey). A Minor
HIRST, John, 2-11-1788, rocf Goose Creek MM as minister
HOBSON, Ruth, 5-12-1783, compl of: mou and unchastity. Now Hammon
    William, 9-4-1787, compl of: moving to Hopewell, Va; joining Methodists

MENALLEN MINUTES, MARRIAGES, & MISCELLANY

HOBSON, William, 1-14-1788, dis: moved to Hopewell without certificate; joined Methodists
HODGSON, Esther, 7-13-1789, rct Crooked Run MM
    James, 2-12-1781, rocf Hopewell MM
    James, 3-12-1781, req marriage with Rachel Wright
    James, 2-11-1782, compl of
    James, 4-15-1782, dis: carnal knowledge before marriage
    Rachel, 2-11-1782, compl of
    Rachel, 4-15-1782, dis: carnal knowledge before marriage. Formerly Wright
HOLMES, William, 8-19-1847, rocf Goose Creek MM as Minister
HOOPES, A. W., 4-17-1889, on comm requesting repairs to Warrington Meeting House
    Amanda Rhoda, 11-21-1849, rct Warrington MM with father Waln and family
    Amanda Rhoda, 8-19-1868, compl of: mou. Now Wonders [w]
    Amy, 5-23-1888, req membership. Now Nast
    Amy, 5-23-1888, ack mou. Retained. Now Kast [w]
        [note: Men's minute says that Amy Hoopes is married to Nast. Women's minute says that Amy Hoopes is married to Kast.]
    Angeline, 2-22-1888, dis: mou and joined another society. Now Dettes [w]
    Asahel, 4-17-1889, appt comm to raise money to repair Warrington Meeting House
    Elizabeth, 2-23-1865, compl of: mou. Now Moseby [w]
    Elizabeth H., 4-20-1865, ack mou. Retained. Now Mosby
    Franklin Waln, 7-18-1888, child of Waln and Sarah Ann Hoopes, now in Iowa
    Hannah, 11-21-1849, rct Warrington MM with father Waln and family
    Hannah, 4-19-1882, rep to MM [w]
    Hannah A., 12-20-1882, rep to MM [w]
    Hannah A., 8-22-1888, absent member. Now in New Carlisle, Ohio [w]
    Joseph Ellis, 11-21-1849, rct Warrington MM with father Waln and family
    Joseph Ellis, 7-18-1888, child of Waln & Sarah Ann Hoopes, now in Iowa
    Lewis, 8-21-1862, formerly of Warrington, now removed from this area [w]
    Lucinda, 2-22-1888, compl of: mou. Now Givler [w]
    Maria, 8-19-1868, compl of: mou. Now Brown [w]
    Maria L., 11-21-1849, rct Warrington MM with father Waln and family
    Mary Elizabeth, 11-21-1849, rct Warrington MM with father Waln and family
    Phebe Ann, 11-21-1849, rct Warrington MM with father Waln and family
    Phoebe Ann, 8-19-1868, compl of: mou. Now Miller [w]
    Reuben, 7-18-1888, comm reports he is deceased
    Rheuben, 11-21-1849, rct Warrington MM with father Waln and family
    Sarah Ann, 11-19-1845, rep to QM [w]

MINUTES

HOOPES, Sarah Ann, 11-21-1849, rcf Warrington MM with husband Waln and 8 children
    Sarah Ann, 8-21-1862, appt comm [w]
    Sarah Ann, 8-21-1862, rep to QM [w]
    Sarah Jane, 11-21-1849, rcf Warrington MM with father Waln and family
    Thomas L., 7-18-1888, child of Waln and Sarah Ann Hoopes, now in Iowa
    Waln, 11-21-1849, rcf Warrington MM with wife Sarah Ann and 8 children
    Waln, 8-21-1862, rep to QM
    Waln, 6-23-1864, appt Overseer

HOOPS, Hannah, 8-22-1839, rocf Warrington MM with father Waln and family
    Mary Caroline, 6-22-1876, minor child of one member. Born 4th mo 6th 1869
    Mary Caroline, 6-22-1876, req membership. Born 4-16-1860 [w]
    Pierce, 3-19-1856, rocf Birmingham MM, Chester Co, Pa with wife Sarah
    Sarah, 3-19-1856, rocf Birmingham MM, Chester Co, Pa as Minister
    Sarah, 3-19-1856, rocf Birmingham MM as Minister [w]
    Sarah Ann, 8-22-1839, rocf Warrington MM with husband Wahln and 2 children
    Sarah Ann, 8-22-1839, rocf Warrington MM with husband Waln and 2 children [w]
    Sarah Ann, 2-23-1843, rep to QM [w]
    Sarah Ann, 11-20-1844, appt comm [w]
    Sarah Jane, 8-22-1839, rocf Warrington MM with father Wahln and family
    Sarah Jane, 8-22-1839, rocf Warrington MM with father Waln and family [w]
    Wahln, 8-22-1839, rocf Warrington MM with wife Sarah Ann and 2 children
    Wahln, 1-20-1841, rep to MM
    Wahln, 4-22-1841, rep to MM
    Wahln, 6-20-1867, appt Trustee at Newberry
    Waln, 8-22-1839, rocf Warrington MM with wife Sarah Ann and 2 children [w]
    Waln, 12-19-1839, rep to MM 5 times thru 6-23-1864
    Waln, 6-19-1862, appt Overseer at Warrington
    Waln, 9-21-1871, appt comm
    Waln, 10-23-1878, appt to have charge of property title papers

HORNER, Joseph, 11-17-1847, rocf Evesham MM, NJ as Minister

HUDLES, John, 2-20-1845, rocf Baltimore MM as Minister

HUNT, Elizabeth, 2-19-1818, rocf Frankford MM as Minister
    Nathan, 7-19-1815, rocf Springfield MM, NC as Minister

HUSSEY, Abigail, 4-21-1814, rocf Warrington MM with husband Amos and 4 children
    Amos, 4-21-1814, rocf Warrington MM with wife Abigail and 4 children
    Amos, 4-21-1814, rocf Warrington MM with father Amos and family
    Amos, 8-18-1814, rep to QM

MENALLEN MINUTES, MARRIAGES, & MISCELLANY

HUSSEY, Amos, 8-22-1816, rep to QM
    Amos, 2-20-1817, rep to QM
    Amos, 12-21-1820, appt comm
    Hannah, 10-20-1814, req marriage with Joel Wierman
    Mary, 1-14-1793, rct Warrington MM
    Mary, 4-21-1814, rocf Warrington MM with father Amos and family
    Mary, 11-20-1822, req marriage with Alexander Wierman
    Miriam, 4-21-1814, rocf Warrington MM with father Amos and family
    Rebeckah, 5-9-1785, of Warrington, to marry Joseph Griest
    Stephen, 4-21-1814, rocf Warrington MM with father Amos and family
    Stephen, 11-23-1825, compl of: fornication

HUTTON, Abner, 9-15-1788, compl of: using provoking language and fighting
    Abner, 1-12-1789, dis: provoking language and fighting
    Ann, 6-23-1796, rocf Uchland MM with husband Robert and 6 children
    Benjamin, 4-12-1784, rocf Pipe Creek MM. Child of Samuel
    Benjamin, 5-14-1787, compl of: moving to Fairfax, Va; dancing
    Benjamin, 4-14-1788, compl of by Fairfax MM
    Benjamin, 9-20-1820, req marriage with Bulah Harris
    Benjamin, 11-22-1826, rct Denings Creek MM with wife Beulah and 3 children
    Benjamin W., 10-24-1822, compl of: separated from wife Beulah
    Benjamin W., 7-23-1823, read testimony. Retained
    Beulah, 10-24-1822, compl of: separated from husband Benjamin W.
    Beulah, 11-22-1826, rct Denings Creek MM with husband Benjamin, 3 children
    Beulah R., 4-24-1823, compl of: leaving husband in an unbecoming manner
    Beulah R., 7-23-1823, read testimony. Retained
    Carolina Maria, 11-22-1826, rct Denings Creek MM with father Benjamin and family
    Deborah, 8-9-1784, req marriage with George Hammon
    Deborah, 2-19-1801, rct Redstone MM with mother Rebecca and family
    Edward, 6-23-1796, rocf Uchland MM with father Robert and family
    Elija, 6-23-1796, rocf Uchland MM with father Robert and family
    George, 6-23-1796, rocf Uchland MM with father Robert and family
    George W., 11-22-1826, rct Denings Creek MM with father Benjamin and family
    Hannah, 3-14-1785, req marriage with John Morton
    James, 2-19-1801, rct Redstone MM with mother Rebecca and family
    Jane, 11-21-1821, req marriage with Benjamin Harris
    Jervis, 6-23-1796, rocf Uchland MM with father Robert and family
    Jesse, 3-23-1825, compl of: fornication
    Jesse, 11-19-1828, compl of: using profane language
    Jesse, 1-21-1829, dis: profane language
    Jesse M., 6-23-1825, read testimony. Retained
    Joel, 4-12-1784, rocf Pipe Creek MM. Child of Samuel
    Joel, 10-13-1788, compl of: dancing
    Joel, 5-23-1798, report from Redstone MM re Joel and wife
    John, 12-10-1781, mou to Sarah McGrail
    John, 2-11-1782, dis: mou by hireling teacher

MINUTES

HUTTON, John, 6-15-1789, compl of: mou to Rebeckah McGrew
  John, 2-9-1795, compl of: frequenting taverns; unchastity
  Joseph, 4-19-1804, mentally deranged. Needs guardians of his legacy
  Joseph, 10-21-1813, Plymouth MM, Ohio reports he needs care
  Levi, 11-11-1782, rocf Fairfax MM with father Samuel
  Levi, 8-11-1794, rct Indian Spring MM
  Levi, 7-20-1796, certificate to Indian Springs returned
  Levi, 8-18-1796, compl of: wagering and swearing
  Levi, 9-21-1796, req marriage with Martha Wright
  Levi, 4-10-1799, compl of: left area without settling debts (son of Samuel)
  Levi, 10-24-1799, Indian Springs MM reports he will pay debts later
  Levi, 6-19-1800, dis: left area without paying debts. Son of Samuel
  Levi, 8-20-1818, rep to QM
  Levi, 8-22-1822, rep to QM
  Levi, 5-21-1823, appt comm
  Mary, 3-10-1794, compl of: mou. Formerly McGrew
  Mary, 6-9-1794, dis: mou. Formerly McGrew. Moved away
  Nathan, 2-19-1801, rct Redstone MM with mother Rebecca and family
  Rachel, 6-23-1796, rocf Uchland MM with father Robert and family
  Rachel, 2-19-1801, rct Redstone MM with mother Rebecca and family
  Rebecca, 2-19-1801, rct Redstone MM with 6 children
  Rebeckah, 7-13-1789, compl of: had promised to marry another. Formerly McGrew
  Robert, 6-23-1796, rocf Uchland MM with wife Ann and 6 children
  Samuel, 11-11-1782, rocf Fairfax MM with 2 children
  Samuel, 2-10-1783, appt comm
  Samuel, 11-10-1783, rep to QM
  Samuel, 4-12-1784, rocf Pipe Creek MM for 2 children
  Samuel, 1-10-1785, rct Fairfax MM
  Samuel, 11-13-1786, needs of 2 orphan children, he recently deceased
  Samuel, 5-22-1844, comm reports on his condition, "We of the committee on the subject of Samuel Hutton agree to report that we have attended to the subject of our appointment as far as circumstances admit at present. We find that he is nearly forty years of age, has been deaf and dum from his infancy, that he is entirely incapable of managing his temporal concerns so as to provide for his personal comfort; we therefore propose that application be made to the court to have some suitable person duly authorized to take care of his person and property. Signed, Josiah Garretson, Nathan Wright, Nathan Griest, Jacob B. Hewitt"
  Samuel, 2-23-1881, his trustee, Benjamin Harris, is now deceased
  Sarah, 2-11-1782, dis: mou by hireling teacher. Formerly McGrail
  Solomon, 4-11-1785, rocf Warrington MM
  Solomon, 3-9-1789, rct Warrington MM
  Solomon, 11-09-1789, dis: dancing
  Susanna, 6-23-1796, rocf Uchland MM with father Robert and family
  Susanna, 2-19-1801, rct Redstone MM with mother Rebecca and family
  Thomas, 11-11-1782, rocf Fairfax MM with father Samuel

MENALLEN MINUTES, MARRIAGES, & MISCELLANY

HUTTON, Thomas, 11-23-1796, compl of: apprentice, left area indisorderly manner
    William, 11-13-1780, appt comm
    William, 2-10-1783, rep to QM
    William, 2-10-1783, appt comm re Bowen-Mickle marriage, to inquire into the young woman's clearness and inspect whether the rights of the orphant children be secured
    William, 9-15-1783, rep to QM
    William, 3-13-1786, appt comm
    William, 9-10-1787, appt comm
    William, 2-11-1788, rep to QM
    William, 2-19-1801, rct Redstone MM with mother Rebecca and family
    William Westley, 11-22-1826, rct Denings Creek MM with father Benjamin and family
ICKES, Lydia G., 1-23-1863, ack mou. Retained. Formerly Wierman
IDEN, Jesse, 12-20-1827, attended as Minister
JANNEY, Mahlon, 4-14-1788, wrote from Fairfax MM re Benjamin Hutton
    Samuel M., 8-19-1847, rocf Goose Creek MM as Minister
JANNINGS, Esther, 3-18-1784, rocf Warrington MM
    Sarah, 7-14-1788, compl of: unchastity. Had child while unmarried
    Thomas, 3-18-1784, rocf Warrington MM
    Thomas, 12-10-1787, rocf Warrington MM
JENNINGS, Esther, 5-14-1787, rct Warrington MM
    Sarah, 9-15-1788, dis: had child while unmarried
    Thomas, 2-13-1786, rct Warrington MM
    Thomas, 3-15-1790, appt comm
JINNINGS, Thomas, 6-14-1790, rct Pipe Creek MM
    Thomas, 2-19-1801, rocf Warrington MM
    Thomas, 2-19-1801, rep to QM
JOHN, Abel, 1-15-1781, rct Warrington MM son Robert, apprentice to Thomas Kirk
    Abel, 1-14-1782, appt Overseer in place of William Griffith
    Abel, 6-9-1783, released as Overseer at Monallen
    Abel, 10-9-1780, appt comm 67 times thru 9-20-1797
    Abel, 11-13-1780, rep to QM 15 times thru 8-22-1799
    Abel, 12-19-1799, requests advice re moving
    Abel, 8-21-1800, rct Westland MM with wife and 2 children
    Abel, 8-21-1800, rct Westland MM with father Joseph and family
    Able, 9-14-1789, appt comm
    Elizabeth, 12-15-1783, req marriage with Henry Mills of Hopewell MM
    Elizabeth, 8-21-1800, rct Westland MM with father Joseph and family
    Elizabeth, 2-22-1821, req membership, was disowned by Exeter MM
    Elizabeth, 12-18-1823, rct Exeter MM with husband Samuel
    Hannah, 8-21-1800, rct Westland MM with father Joseph and family
    Isaac, 6-20-1799, rct Warrington MM for self and wife
    Isaiah, 9-15-1794, req marriage with Martha Griest
    Isaiah, 8-24-1797, rocf Warrington MM for self and wife Martha
    Joseph, 5-14-1781, rct Warrington MM to marry Mary Bonine of that meeting
    Joseph, 7-11-1785, rocf Warrington MM, he a minor

MINUTES

JOHN, Joseph, 3-13-1786, rct Warrington MM
    Joseph, 7-9-1792, appt Overseer at Monallen
    Joseph, 9-9-1793, appt recorder of Marriage Certificates
    Joseph, 10-13-1795, released as Overseer at Monallin
    Joseph, 12-21-1797, appt Elder
    Joseph, 8-13-1792, rep to QM 12 times thru 2-20-1800
    Joseph, 8-21-1800, rct Westland MM with wife and 7 children
    Joseph, 8-21-1800, rct Westland MM with father Joseph and family
    Joseph, 8-21-1800, released as recorder of Marriage Certificates
    Joseph, 4-9-1781, appt comm 90 times thru 8-21-1800
    Martha, 12-15-1794, rct Warrington MM
    Martha, 8-24-1797, rocf Warrington MM for self and husband Isaiah
    Mary, 4-10-1799, req marriage with Francis Pellet
    Rachel, 8-21-1800, rct Westland MM with father Joseph and family
    Rebecca, 8-21-1800, rct Westland MM with father Joseph and family
    Robert, 1-15-1781, rct Warrington MM: put an apprentice to Thomas Kirk
    Robert, 2-10-1783, rocf Warrington MM
    Samuel, 2-22-1821, req membership, was disowned by Exeter MM
    Samuel, 4-18-1822, roc with wife
    Samuel, 12-18-1823, rct Exeter MM with wife Elizabeth
    Sarah, 8-21-1800, rct Westland MM with father Joseph and family
JOHNSTON, Joshua, 9-17-1806, rocf Crooked Run MM
    Joshua, 10-23-1806, rct Baltimore MM
    Mary, 7-10-1786, compl of: mou. Formerly Hammil
    Mary, 9-11-1786, dis: mou. Formerly Hammil
JOICE, Deborah, 8-24-1815, req membership thru mother Elizabeth
    Elizabeth, 8-21-1800, compl of: mou
    Elizabeth, 11-19-1800, read testimony. Retained
    Elizabeth, 8-24-1815, req membership for 5 children
    George, 11-23-1870, rep to QM
    George H., 5-21-1873, ack mou. Retained
    George W., 11-17-1869, rep to QM
    Joseph, 8-24-1815, req membership thru mother Elizabeth
    Joseph, 9-19-1849, rep to MM 8 times thru 5-23-1877
    Joseph, 5-21-1873, appt comm
    Joseph, 8-21-1878, rep to QM
    Margaret, 8-24-1815, req membership thru mother Elizabeth
    Margaret, 8-19-1824, req marriage with Samuel E. Cook
    Margarette, 4-24-1845, req membership [w]
    Mary, 8-24-1815, req membership thru mother Elizabeth
    Obadiah, 5-17-1837, compl of: mou
    Obadiah, 1-17-1838, dis: mou and military training
    Obediah, 8-24-1815, req membership thru mother Elizabeth
JONES, Barzilla A., 8-25-1871, rct Pipe Creek MM with father Thomas and family
    Edward, 8-22-1816, rocf Warrington MM as Minister
    Gertrude, 7-21-1886, hired to teach school
    Hannah, 2-20-1800, req membership thru father Morgan Jones
    Hannah, 2-20-1800, req membership with husband Morgan Jones

MENALLEN MINUTES, MARRIAGES, & MISCELLANY

JONES, Hiram B., 8-22-1871, rct Pipe Creek MM with father Thomas and family [w]
    Isaac, 2-20-1800, req membership thru father Morgan Jones
    Jane Edna, 8-25-1871, rct Pipe Creek MM with father Thomas and family
    John, 2-20-1800, req membership thru father Morgan Jones
    Martha, 2-21-1867, appt Elder
    Martha, 4-20-1870, appt Elder
    Martha A., 8-20-1863, rep to MM [w]
    Martha F., 5-22-1870, rep to QM [w]
    Martha H., 7-21-1852, rct Warrington MM [w]
    Martha H., 4-24-1862, appt Overseer [w]
    Martha H., 2-19-1863, rep to QM 5 times thru 11-23-1870 [w]
    Martha H., 4-20-1865, appt Overseer [w]
    Martha H., 4-20-1865, appt assistant clerk [w]
    Martha H., 2-20-1867, appt Elder [w]
    Martha H., 12-23-1868, appt Overseer [w]
    Martha H., 9-17-1862, appt comm 11 times thru 8-18-1869 [w]
    Martha H., 10-22-1863, rep to MM 22 times thru 11-17-1869 [w]
    Martha H., 4-20-1870, appt Elder [w]
    Martha H., 8-22-1870, appt assistant clerk [w]
    Martha H., 8-22-1871, rct Pipe Creek MM with husband Thomas and 3 children [w]
    Martha M., 8-19-1852, gct Warrington MM
    Morgan, 12-20-1798, rocf Warrington MM
    Morgan, 2-20-1800, req membership for 3 children
    Rachel E., 5-18-1887, ack mou. Retained. Formerly Wright [w]
    Rachel E., 12-19-1888, rct Pipe Creek MM. Formerly Wright [w]
    Thomas, 3-20-1850, req marriage with Martha Harris
    Thomas, 4-18-1850, rocf Deer Creek MM
    Thomas, 12-21-1863, appt Elder
    Thomas, 6-23-1864, appt Overseer
    Thomas, 2-20-1867, appt Elder [w]
    Thomas, 4-20-1870, appt Elder
    Thomas, 8-20-1863, rep to QM 11 times thru 8-17-1870
    Thomas, 7-23-1862, rep to MM 37 times thru 9-22-1870
    Thomas, 8-22-1871, rct Pipe Creek MM with wife Martha H. and 3 children [w]
    Thomas, 7-20-1864, appt comm 16 times thru 12-23-1874
    Thomas, 2-23-1881, to be appt trustee for Samuel Hutton
JOYCE, Joseph, 4-24-1845, read testimony. Retained
    Joseph, 11-20-1861, appt comm
    Joseph, 11-22-1871, rep to QM
    Joseph, 10-21-1841, rep to MM 15 times thru 5-19-1880
    Joseph, 8-17-1881, rep to QM
    Josiah, 8-22-1877, rep to MM
    Margaret, 6-19-1845, req membership
KAST, Amy, 5-23-1888, ack mou. Retained. Formerly Hoopes [w]
KELLEY, Sarah, 4-10-1786, compl of: mou. Formerly Oldham
KELSEY, Sarah, 8-14-1786, dis: mou. Formerly Oldham

MINUTES

KENT, Hadley, 1-18-1888, req marriage with Viola Whitson [w]
    Viola W., 1-22-1890, rct Nottingham MM, Chester Co, Pa [w]
    Viola W., 2-19-1890, rocf Nottingham MM, Chester Co, Pa
KENWORTHY, Amos, 1-13-1794, rocf Pipe Creek MM with father William and family
    Amy, 1-13-1794, rocf Pipe Creek MM with father William and family
    Amy, 3-23-1797, req marriage with William Blackburn
    Hannah, 1-13-1794, rocf Pipe Creek MM with father William and family
    Hannah, 10-23-1800, req marriage with John Hancock
    Isaac, 1-13-1794, rocf Pipe Creek MM with father William and family
    Jesse, 1-13-1794, rocf Pipe Creek MM with father William and family
    Lydia, 1-13-1794, rocf Pipe Creek MM with father William and family
    Mary, 1-13-1794, rocf Pipe Creek MM with Husband William and family
    Mary, 1-13-1794, rocf Pipe Creek MM with father William and family
    Mary, 8-22-1799, req marriage with Joel Hancock
    Mary, 8-22-1799, appt Elder at Dunnings Creek
    Phebe, 1-13-1794, rocf Pipe Creek MM with father William and family
    Ruth, 1-13-1794, rocf Pipe Creek MM with father William and family
    William, 1-13-1794, rocf Pipe Creek MM with wife Mary, 9 children, 2 nephews
    William, 10-13-1795, appt Overseer at Dunnings Creek
    William, 2-22-1798, released as Overseer at Dunnings Creek William, 11-21-1798, rep to QM
    William, 8-22-1799, rep to QM
    William, 1-13-1794, appt comm 17 times thru 11-18-1801
KENYON, Martha, 1-23-1833, has separated from Hicksites at Menallen
    Roger, 1-17-1821, req marriage with Martha Pearson
KETTLEWELL, Charles, 2-23-1815, rocf Warrington MM with wife Hanna and 2 children
    Charles, 11-20-1816, compl of: playing cards
    Charles, 2-20-1817, read testimony. Retained
    Charles, 1-22-1823, compl of: drinking, playing cards
    Charles, 7-23-1823, dis: drinking, playing cards
    Charles, 12-21-1843, read testimony. Retained
    Charles, 12-18-1845, appt Overseer
    Charles, 1-20-1847, on comm against settling new meeting at Mechanicsville
    Charles, 3-21-1849, compl of in "difficult case"
    Charles, 4-18-1850, rct Southern QM as Minister
    Charles, 9-17-1845, appt comm 17 times thru 4-18-1850
    Charles, 11-19-1845, rep to MM 14 times thru 7-17-1850
    Charles, 11-19-1845, rep to QM 8 times thru 8-22-1850
    Charles, 9-18-1850, rct Baltimore MM (Western District)
    Charles, 7-23-1851, rocf Baltimore MM (Western District)
    Hannah, 2-23-1815, rocf Warrington MM with husband Charles and 2 children
    Hannah, 5-21-1845, rep to QM [w]
    Hannah, 11-19-1845, appt comm [w]
    Hannah, 12-20-1860, rct Baltimore MM [w]

MENALLEN MINUTES, MARRIAGES, & MISCELLANY

KETTLEWELL, Hannah, 2-21-1861, gct Baltimore MM
    John, 2-23-1815, rocf Warrington MM with father Charles and family
    John, 4-24-1823, rct Baltimore MM. Son of Charles
    Mary, 2-23-1815, rocf Warrington MM with father Charles and family
    Mary, 5-18-1842, req marriage with Ephraim G. Cox
    Rebecca, 3-19-1845, compl of: mou. Now Ober at Baltimore MM [w]
    Rebecca, 1-21-1846, dis: mou. Now Ober
    Samuel, 2-23-1815, rocf Warrington MM with father Charles and family
    Samuel, 3-22-1815, rct Gunpowder MM
    Samuel, 4-20-1815, cert returned to Warrington MM
    Samuel, 7-19-1848, read testimony as to mou. Retained
    Samuel, 7-19-1848, rocf Third Haven MM, Md
    Samuel, 2-24-1853, rocf Nottingham MM dated 10th mo 5th 1852
    Samuel, 11-22-1854, rct Baltimore MM
    Thomas, 2-23-1815, rocf Warrington MM. Some objection
    Thomas, 3-22-1815, compl of: intoxication, military duty. Certificate returned
    William, 3-22-1843, compl of: fighting, profane language
    William, 8-24-1843, dis: fighting and profanity
KINIAN, Roger, 4-19-1827, compl of: left neighborhood in disorderly manner
    Rogers, 9-20-1820, req membership
KINION, Roger, 5-23-1827, dis: left area and wife in disorderly manner
KIRK, -?-, 5-23-1798, rct Warrington MM
    John, 11-9-1795, rocf Warrington MM. He is a minor
KOCH, Elizabeth, 11-19-1823, requests that her membership be restored. Approved
KOSER, A. J., 5-18-1887, assessed $3.00 for fuel for Ann and Martha Griest
    Andrew J., 10-23-1872, req membership for self and son George Wilmer
    Andrew J., 5-21-1873, rep to MM 16 times thru 8-19-1885
    Andrew J., 8-20-1873, rep to QM 10 times thru 2-20-1889
    Andrew J., 1-21-1874, appt comm 14 times thru 1-21-1891 [w]
    Elizabeth M., 5-23-1866, ack mou. Retained. Formerly Griest
    Elizabeth M., 4-20-1881, appt clerk [w]
    Elizabeth M., 4-19-1882, appt clerk [w]
    Elizabeth M., 4-18-1883, appt clerk [w]
    Elizabeth M., 4-23-1884, appt clerk [w]
    Elizabeth M., 4-22-1885, appt clerk [w]
    Elizabeth M., 12-19-1867, rep to MM 7 times thru 2-17-1886 [w]
    Elizabeth M., 4-21-1886, appt clerk [w]
    Elizabeth M., 9-17-1872, appt comm 18 times thru 2-20-1889 [w]
    Elizabeth M., 5-17-1871, rep to QM 8 times thru 11-19-1890 [w]
    G. Wilmer, 11-19-1890, rep to QM
    George W., 2-18-1885, rep to MM
    George W., 4-22-1885, rep to MM
    George W., 8-19-1885, rep to QM
    George Wilmer, 10-23-1872, req membership through father Andrew G.
    Lizzie M., 5-22-1866, ack mou. Retained. Formerly Griest [w]
    Lizzie M., 10-17-1877, appt comm [w]

MINUTES

KOSER, Lizzie M., 10-17-1877, appt comm [w]
    Lizzie M., 12-18-1889, appt comm [w]
LAFETRA, Jacob, 8-23-1838, rocf Baltimore MM, Western District as Minister [w]
    Jacob, 1-17-1843, rocf Baltimore MM as Minister [w]
LAREW, Hannah, 11-21-1862, ack mou. Retained
    Lydia Jane, 8-21-1862, formerly Warrington MM member, now removed
LEACH, Ann, 3-13-1786, rct Warrington MM
    Eli, 10-19-1842, compl of: fornication; mou
    Eli, 12-22-1842, read testimony. Retained
    Eli, 4-20-1843, compl of: drinking, abusing wife, profane language
    Eli, 5-19-1843, dis: drinking, abuse, profanity
    Ely, 5-20-1840, rocf Warrington MM with parents Thomas and Hannah [w]
    Hannah, 5-20-1840, rocf Warrington MM with husband Thomas and son Ely [w]
    Hannah, 5-20-1840, appt comm 3 times thru 12-22-1842 [w]
    Hannah, 7-22-1840, appt Elder
    Hannah, 5-18-1842, rep to QM 3 times thru 2-22-1844 [w]
    Thomas, 5-20-1840, rocf Warrington MM with wife Hannah and son Ely [w]
    Thomas, 7-22-1840, appt Elder
    Thomas, 7-22-1840, appt Elder [w]
    Thomas, 8-20-1840, rep to QM 3 times thru 11-18-1846
    Thomas, 5-19-1841, appt comm 6 times thru 8-24-1843
    Thomas, 9-23-1840, rep to MM 10 times thru 5-19-1847
LEECH, Eli, 5-20-1840, rocf Warrington MM with father Thomas and family
    Hannah, 5-20-1840, rocf Warrington MM with husband Thomas and 1 child
    Hannah, 7-22-1840, appt Elder [w]
    Hannah, 8-20-1840, rep to QM [w]
    Hannah, 4-22-1841, appt comm [w]
    Hannah, 5-18-1841, appt comm [w]
    Thomas, 3-23-1825, appt comm
    Thomas, 3-23-1825, appt comm
    Thomas, 6-23-1825, appt comm
    Thomas, 5-20-1840, rocf Warrington MM with wife Hannah and 1 child
    Thomas, 5-20-1840, rep to QM
    Thomas, 6-18-1840, rep to MM
LEFETRA, Jacob, 1-18-1843, rocf Baltimore MM as Minister
LEHMER, Leah W., 4-17-1889, on comm requesting repairs to Warrington Meeting House
LEONARD, Rebecca, 8-21-1856, gct White Water MM, Ind
    Rebecca L., 7-23-1856, ack mou. Retained
    Rebecca L., 7-23-1856, ack error. Retained [w]
    Rebecca L., 7-23-1856, rct White Water MM, Ind. Formerly Griffith [w]
LESHY, Martha M., 2-23-1860, read testimony. Retained
LIGHTNER, Isaiah, 12-23-1874, appt comm
    Isaiah, 12-23-1874, appt comm

MENALLEN MINUTES, MARRIAGES, & MISCELLANY

LINDY, Elizabeth S., 2-18-1836, rocf Burlington MM, NJ [w]
LIRUE, Hannah L., 8-21-1862, dtr of Waln Hoops, now removed from
    neighborhood [w]
    Hannah L., 11-19-1862, ack mou. Retained [w]
    Lydia Jane, 8-21-1862, formerly of Warrington, now removed from this
        area [w]
LISHY, Martha M., 2-23-1860, ack mou. Retained. Formerly Wierman [w]
LOAN, Benjamin, 3-9-1795, dis: attending muster, non-payment of debts
    Benjamin, Jr, 1-12-1795, compl of: submitted to civil law, active in
        military
    Isaac, 7-9-1787, compl of: mou
    Isaac, 1-14-1788, now lives at Patersons Creek remote from Friends
    Isaac, 2-11-1788, dis: mou. Lives in Bedford Co, Pa
    Margaret, 6-15-1795, rct Westland MM
    Margaret, 8-10-1795, roc
    Mary, 1-9-1786, compl of: mou to 1st cousin. Now Fletcher, resides in
        Bedford County, Pa
    Mary, 2-13-1786, dis: mou to 1st cousin. Now Fletcher
    Rachel, 8-13-1781, mou: dtr of Benjamin and Sarah Loan of Bedford
        Co, Pa
    Rachel, 1-14-1782, dis: mou. Now McGahey
    Sarah, 7-15-1793, dis: mou. Now Milliner
LONG, Rachel, 5-9-1791, rct Warrington MM
LONGSDORF, Elizabeth W., 2-19-1879, ack mou. Retained. Formerly Wright
    Elizabeth W., 1-20-1886, req membership for 3 children: Rebecca, Paul,
        Julia [w]
    Elizabeth W., 2-24-1887, req membership for son Hiram L.
    Elizabeth W., 2-20-1889, rep to QM [w]
    Hiram L., 2-24-1887, born 4-10-1886 req membership thru mother
        Elizabeth
    Julia Keyport, 1-20-1886, req membership thru mother Elizabeth W.
    Julia Keyport, 1-20-1886, mother req membership for, born 8th mo 31st
        1884 [w]
    Paul Wright, 1-20-1886, req membership thru mother Elizabeth W.
    Paul Wright, 1-20-1886, mother req membership for, born 10th mo 6th
        1882 [w]
    Rebecca Alice, 1-20-1886, req membership thru mother Elizabeth W.
    Rebecca Alice, 1-20-1886, mother req membership for, born 3rd mo
        25th 1881 [w]
LOVE, James, 2-13-1792, req membership thru his mother Mary Love
    James, 8-11-1794, rct Baltimore MM thru his mother Mary
    Mary, 2-13-1792, req membership for her son James Love
    Mary, 11-12-1792, rct Baltimore MM
        Mary, 8-11-1794, rct Baltimore MM for her son James
LUKENS, Hannah, 9-21-1853, rocf Fallowfield MM as Minister [w]
LUNDY, Charles, 5-17-1837, rct Putnam Co, Ill with William C. Wierman and
    family
    Charles T., 2-18-1836, rocf Burlington MM, NJ
    Elizabeth S., 2-18-1836, rocf Burlington MM, NJ

MINUTES

LUNDY, Elizabeth S., 4-23-1840, compl of: mou and moving to Ill. Now Griffith [w]
    Susannah Maria, 12-20-1832, req marriage with William C. Wierman
MAINS, Elizabeth, 10-13-1783, gct Hopewell MM
    Rebecca, 5-11-1795, rct Redstone MM. Formerly McGrew
MATHER, Lydia, 8-10-1789, compl of: mou. Formerly Bowen
    Lydia, 10-12-1789, dis: mou. Formerly Bowen
MATHERS, Lydia, 7-14-1794, read ack. Retained; rct Exeter MM. Formerly Bowen
MATTHEWS, Mary, 12-18-1845, rocf Gunpowder MM as Minister
    Thomas, 1-17-1843, rocf Baltimore MM as Minister [w]
MAURTON, Ann, 6-23-1796, rct Westland MM with mother Hanah, wife of John, Jr
    Benjamin, 6-23-1796, rct Westland MM with mother Hanah, wife of John, Jr
    Hanah, 6-23-1796, rct Westland MM with mother Hanah, wife of John, Jr
    Hannah, 6-23-1796, rct Westland MM with 5 children. Wife of John, Jr
    John, 6-23-1796, rct Westland MM with mother Hanah, wife of John, Jr
    Mary, 6-23-1796, rct Westland MM with mother Hanah, wife of John, Jr
MAXWELL, Deborah, 4-14-1794, compl of: unchastity. Formerly Wierman
    Deborah, 7-14-1794, dis: unchastity. Formerly Wierman
McCRARY, John, 6-11-1781, dis: mou; paid muster fine
McCREARY, Alice, 2-18-1836, appt comm [w]
    Benjamin, 8-18-1830, compl of: mou
    Benjamin, 4-21-1831, dis: mou
    David, 4-21-1803, req marriage with Alice Wright
    David, 8-21-1817, rep to QM
    David, 2-22-1821, appt comm
    David, 5-23-1860, rep to MM 4 times thru 12-19-1861
    David R., 3-19-1856, appt comm 7 times thru 4-23-1873
    David R., 11-21-1862, rep to QM
    David R., 2-22-1871, rep to QM
    David R., 4-23-1873, appt Trustee at Menallen
    David R., 3-22-1854, rep to MM 25 times thru 12-17-1873
    George, 12-20-1882, compl of: quarrelled with his brother William
    George, 8-22-1883, dis: quarreling with his brother William
    George H., 4-19-1849, rct Hopewell MM, Va
    George H., 7-20-1870, rocf Hopewell MM, Pa
    Jesse, 1-22-1845, compl of: mou
    Jesse, 8-21-1845, read testimony. Retained
    Jesse, 3-22-1848, compl of: drinking, non-attendance
    John, 6-18-1835, compl of: fornication
    John, 1-20-1836, read testimony. Retained
    John, 6-23-1842, dis: joined German Reformed Society
    John, 4-18-1850, compl of: profanity; non-attendance
    John, 4-24-1851, read testimony. Retained
    John, 12-20-1882, compl of: non-attendance; immoral practices
    John, 6-21-1883, comm reports he is deceased
    Lydia, 8-24-1815, req membership thru parents Thomas and Sarah

MENALLEN MINUTES, MARRIAGES, & MISCELLANY

McCREARY, Martha, 1-19-1842, compl of: joining Methodists [w]
    Martha, 4-21-1842, dis: joined Methodists
    Sarah, 8-24-1815, req membership for daughter Lydia
    Thomas, 8-24-1815, req membership for daughter Lydia
    Thomas, 11-17-1824, appt comm
    Thomas, 11-17-1824, appt comm
    Thomas, 12-20-1838, compl of: is a Justice of the Peace; administers oaths
    Thomas, 4-18-1839, dis: administering oaths
    Thomas, 5-22-1822, rep to QM 8 times thru 11-23-1842
    Thomas, 6-23-1836, rep to MM 7 times thru 7-21-1847
    Thomas A., 12-20-1849, read testimony. Not accepted
    Thomas C., 4-20-1848, compl of: dealing in lottery tickets
    William, 2-20-1845, compl of: fornication
    William, 10-25-1845, dis: fornication
McCRERY, David, 8-13-1787, req membership
    John, 3-12-1781, compl of: mou; paid muster fine
    Rachel, 7-10-1786, req membership
    Rachel, 8-13-1787, req membership
    Rachel, 4-14-1788, req marriage with Joseph Hewitt, Jr
    Robert, 2-22-1810, requests membership
    Robert, 8-23-1810, rct Dunnings Creek MM
    Thomas, 8-19-1813, req membership. Son of John
McELWEE, Ruth, 1-22-1840, compl of: mou. Formerly Wireman [w]
McGAHEY, Rachel, 1-14-1782, dis: mou. Formerly Loan
McGEE, Maria, 5-20-1818, req membership
    Maria, 7-22-1818, req marriage with Joshua Cox, Jr
McGRAIL, Elizabeth, 4-19-1804, rct Redstone MM with father John and family
    Elizabeth, 5-23-1804, rct Dunnings Creek MM
    Elizabeth, 6-21-1804, roc
    James, 12-11-1780, rep to MM
    James, 9-10-1781, rep to QM
    James, 5-12-1783, rep to QM
    James, 9-15-1783, req release as Overseer
    James, 9-13-1784, rep to QM
    James, 10-9-1780, appt comm 14 times thru 10-11-1784
    James, 8-21-1800, compl of: mou
    James, 10-23-1800, dis: mou
    James, 5-18-1803, rct Redstone MM with father James and mother
    James, 10-22-1818, req membership at Dunnings Creek MM
    John, 7-13-1795, req marriage with Mary Blackburn
    John, 1-19-1803, compl of: fighting
    John, 4-21-1803, read testimony. Retained
    John, 4-19-1804, rct Redstone MM with wife Mary and 4 children
    Martha, 7-23-1806, compl of: mou; joining Presbyterians. Now Shields
    Martha, 8-21-1806, dis: mou; joining Presbyterians. Now Shields
    Mary, 4-12-1790, compl of: mou. Formerly Hewett
    Mary, 5-10-1790, read acknowledgment
    Mary, 4-19-1804, rct Redstone MM with husband John and 4 children
    Mary, 4-19-1804, rct Redstone MM with father John and family

MINUTES

McGRAIL, Mary, 5-17-1848, req marriage with David E. Cook
    Moses, 4-19-1804, rct Redstone MM with father John and family
    Sarah, 10-9-1780, req membership
    Sarah, 11-13-1780, accepted as member
    Sarah, 2-11-1782, dis: mou by hireling teacher. Now Hutton
    Sarah, 8-21-1800, compl of: mou. Now Barkster
    Sarah, 10-23-1800, dis: mou. Now Barkster
    Sarah, 4-19-1804, rct Redstone MM with father John and family
    Sarrah, 12-10-1781, mou to John Hutton
    Thomas, 3-23-1797, req marriage with Rebekah Blackburn
    Thomas, 5-18-1803, rct Redstone MM with wife and son
    William, 4-9-1781, appt comm
    William, 8-14-1786, appt comm
McGREW, Deborah, 4-14-1794, rct Redstone MM with father James and family
    Dinah, 6-9-1783, rocf Hopewell MM with husband Finley and 8 children
    Dinah, 6-9-1783, rocf Hopewell MM with father Finley and family
    Dinah, 8-15-1785, compl of: dancing
    Dinah, 7-9-1787, rct Westland MM with husband Finly and 2 children
    Dinah, Jr, 4-10-1786, dis: dancing; raising false report about a friend
    Elizabeth, 1-10-1785, req membership
    Elizabeth, 4-14-1794, rct Redstone MM with husband James and 8 children
    Findley, 11-20-1799, appt comm 4 times thru 3-23-1825
    Findley, 4-19-1804, appt to assist in Joseph Hutton case
    Findley, 6-22-1815, appt comm to present Joseph Hutton trustees to court
    Findley, 1-23-1828, rep to QM
    Findly, 7-17-1816, appt comm
    Finely, 8-11-1788, appt comm
    Finely, 8-12-1793, appt comm
    Finely, 5-18-1803, rep to QM
    Finely, 11-23-1803, rep to QM
    Finlee, 9-10-1781, rep to QM
    Finley, 6-9-1783, rocf Hopewell MM with wife Dinah and 8 children
    Finley, 9-4-1787, rct Westland MM
    Finley, 6-10-1793, appt Overseer at Monallen
    Finley, 2-22-1798, rct Warrington MM for son Samuel as apprentice
    Finley, 4-22-1802, appt to prepare memorial for Isaac Everitt, deceased
    Finley, 8-19-1802, appt Guardian of heirs of William McGrail, deceased
    Finley, 8-23-1804, appt Overseer to QM
    Finley, 8-21-1806, appt to collect quota for YM
    Finley, 2-18-1808, rct Dunnings Creek MM thru mother Patience
    Finley, 3-23-1808, released as Overseer
    Finley, 8-24-1809, rct Redstone MM for son Samuel
    Finley, 9-15-1783, rep to QM 48 times thru 2-23-1815
    Finley, 5-21-1823, reports re Thomas Mickle (a lunitick)
    Finley, 10-14-1782, appt comm 202 times thru 4-22-1824

MENALLEN MINUTES, MARRIAGES, & MISCELLANY

McGREW, Finley, 6-18-1829, rct Salem MM, Ohio with son William
    Finley, 2-20-1845, communication re his condition rec'd from Ohio, "We the undersigned being appointed by Salem Monthly Meeting to inform you of the situation of Finley McGrews right of membership was forwarded from your meeting to this included in a certificate for his father as a minor and he at that time upwards of forty years of age which we believe to be unprecedented in the society of Friends, he being at that time and still remains, to be insane and unable to take care of himself which circumstances were unknown to the meeting at the time of the reception of his Fathers certificate, in viewing these circumstances we do not consider him properly a member of Salem Monthly Meeting and consequently not bound by any rule of discipline for his maintenance he being now destitute. You will please inform Salem Monthly Meeting of your conclusion in his case. [s] Ryeuben Griffith, Eli Thomas
    Finley, 2-20-1845, communication re his condition sent to Ohio, "To Salem Monthly Meeting, State of Ohio. Dear Friends, Finley McGrew Jun having removed with his father within the virge of your meeting this may inform that he is a member of our society as such we recommend him to your friendly care and are your friends, signed by direction of Monallen Monthly Meeting held 22nd of the 7th mo 1829 by John Wright clerk [above of copy of original certificate of removal] by which you will perceive his right of membership was not included in his father's certificate as a minor. We next inform you that he never was under such circumstances as to require the aid of our meeting but was provided for by his Father who informed our meeting that he did not intend he should be a charge to anybody or any body of people while he had the means of supporting him, this he expressed in our mo meeting when about to remove and several friends from Monallen preparative meeting well acquainted with him having removed to reside within your limits, we had every reason to believe you would be correctly informed of his situation, his father being then professed of considerable property and unimpeachable veracity and more than fifteen years having now elapsed in silence on the subject it is the conclusion of this meeting that we are not duty bound to support him according to the order of our society. Signed on behalf of Monallen Monthly Meeting held 2nd mo 20th 1845 by Nathan Griest Clerk"
  Finley, Jr, 6-18-1829, rct Salem MM, Ohio with father Finley
  Finlley, 5-20-1801, appt comm
  Finly, 6-9-1783, rocf Hopewell MM with father Finley and family
  Finly, 1-12-1784, dtr Mary ran away to Hopewell with man
  Finly, 7-12-1784, compl of: dancing
  Finly, 3-14-1785, released as Overseer at Monalin
  Finly, 7-9-1787, rct Westland MM with wife Dinah and 2 children
  Finly, 4-14-1794, rct Redstone MM with father James and family
  Finly, 5-14-1794, appt Guardian for Thomas Miccle
  Finly, 12-21-1797, released as Overseer at Monallin

MINUTES

McGREW, Finly, 6-19-1800, appt Overseer at Monallin
    Finly, 12-18-1800, appt Elder
    Finly, 5-13-1782, rep to QM 21 times thru 8-22-1816
    Finly, 2-20-1817, appt to represent B. Tomlinson's case in court
    Finly, 11-13-1780, appt comm 84 times thru 7-23-1817
    Finly, Jr, 6-9-1783, appt Overseer at Monallen
    Finly, Jr, 1-10-1785, dis: dancing
    Jacob, 6-9-1783, rocf Hopewell MM with father Finley and family
    Jacob, 7-9-1787, rct Westland MM with father Finly and family
    Jacob, 12-24-1812, appt comm
    James, 6-9-1783, rocf Hopewell MM with father Finley and family
    James, 11-10-1783, rct Hopewell for self and family
    James, 8-9-1784, compl of: leaving area without certificate, to Hopewell MM
    James, 10-10-1785, compl of: drinking, dancing. Returned from Virginia
    James, 3-13-1786, dis: drinking and dancing. Son of Finley McGrew
    James, 10-15-1787, is sorry for conduct. Son of Finly
    James, 5-11-1789, rct Warrington MM. He is son of Finley
    James, 11-15-1790, appt comm 5 times thru 12-9-1793
    James, 2-13-1792, rep to QM 3 times thru 11-11-1793
    James, 2-11-1793, req membership for children: Nathan, Jane and James
    James, 2-11-1793, req membership thru father James McGrew
    James, 4-14-1794, rct Redstone MM with wife Elizabeth and 8 children
    James, 4-14-1794, rct Redstone MM with father James and family
    James, 7-20-1796, roc
    James, 5-22-1805, membership requested by parents, Nathan and Martha
    James, 4-23-1812, rct Redstone MM
    James, Jr, 8-12-1782, rocf Warrington MM
    James, Jr, 8-9-1784, rocf Warrington MM
    Jane, 5-12-1788, req membership
    Jane, 2-11-1793, req membership thru father James McGrew
    Jane, 4-14-1794, rct Redstone MM with father James and family
    Jean, 10-15-1781, req membership
    Jean, 4-15-1782, req membership
    Joseph, 4-14-1794, rct Redstone MM with father James and family
    Margaret, 6-9-1783, rocf Hopewell MM with father Finley and family
    Margaret, 7-9-1787, rct Westland MM with father Finly and family
    Margaret, 2-18-1808, rct Dunnings Creek MM thru mother Patience
    Martha, 2-20-1800, compl of: mou to John Hewett
    Martha, 12-22-1803, rocf Warrington MM with husband Nathan
    Martha, 5-22-1805, membership requested by parents, Nathan and Martha
    Martha, 2-20-1812, rct Redstone MM with husband Nathan and son
    Mary, 6-9-1783, rocf Hopewell MM with father Finley and family
    Mary, 1-12-1784, compl of: running away with man to Hopewell MM
    Mary, 6-14-1784, dis: mou. Now Ong
    Mary, 3-17-1793, req membership. Daughter of James

MENALLEN MINUTES, MARRIAGES, & MISCELLANY

McGREW, Mary, 3-10-1794, compl of: mou. Now Hutton
    Mary, 6-9-1794, dis: mou. Now Hutton. Moved away
    Mary, 10-20-1803, req membership. Daughter of Nathan
    Mary, 6-24-1819, compl of: unchastity
    Mary, 9-22-1819, read testimony. Retained
    Mary, 7-22-1829, gct Salem MM, Ohio
    Nathan, 6-9-1783, rocf Hopewell MM with father Finley and family
    Nathan, 3-18-1784, accused of fathering child; left area
    Nathan, 7-12-1784, disowned: racing, dancing, fathering child
    Nathan, 2-11-1793, req membership thru father James McGrew
    Nathan, 4-14-1794, rct Redstone MM with father James and family
    Nathan, 12-22-1803, rocf Warrington MM with wife Martha
    Nathan, 8-22-1805, appt comm 5 times thru 5-22-1811
    Nathan, 8-21-1806, rep to QM
    Nathan, 2-20-1812, rct Redstone MM with wife Martha and son
    Nathan, 2-18-1813, compl of: fighting. Son of Peter. Now at Dunnings Creek
    Nathan, 7-21-1813, dis: fighting
    Nathan, 12-25-1813, dis: fighting. Son of Peter
    Patience, 2-18-1808, rct Dunnings Creek MM for self and 4 children
    Peter, 5-12-1783, compl of: drinking, bad language, fighting
    Peter, 8-11-1783, dis: drinking, fighting, bad language
    Peter, 2-18-1808, rct Dunnings Creek MM thru mother Patience
    Rebecca, 6-9-1783, rocf Hopewell MM with father Finley and family
    Rebecca, 5-11-1795, rct Redstone MM. Now Rebecca Mains
    Rebecca, 2-18-1808, rct Dunnings Creek MM thru mother Patience
    Rebeckah, 8-15-1785, compl of: dancing
    Rebeckah, 6-15-1789, compl of: mou to John Hutton
    Rebeckah, 7-13-1789, compl of: had promised to marry another. Now Hutton
    Rebekah, 4-10-1786, dis: dancing
    Rebekah, 9-11-1786, compl of: dancing
    Rebekah, 7-22-1829, gct Salem MM, Ohio
    Samuel, 2-22-1798, rct Warrington MM as apprentice to Willing Griest
    Samuel, 7-22-1801, rocf Warrington MM
    Samuel, 8-24-1809, rct Redstone MM thru father Finley
    Simeon, 4-14-1794, rct Redstone MM with father James and family
    Stephen, 5-22-1805, membership requested by parents, Nathan and Martha
    Stephen, 2-20-1812, rct Redstone MM with father Nathan and family
    Thomas, 4-14-1794, rct Redstone MM with father James and family
    William, 1-19-1820, appt comm
    William, 1-19-1820, appt comm
    William, 6-18-1829, rct Salem MM, Ohio with father Finley
McMILIN, Elizabeth, 4-20-1820, rct Warrington MM
McMILLAN, William, 1-14-1793, rocf Warrington MM
    William, 4-21-1796, dis: non-attendance; taking an oath
    William, Jr, 1-11-1796, compl of: non-attendance; taking oath
McMILLIN, Elizabeth, 6-21-1821, rocf Warrington MM with husband Joseph
    Elizabeth, 3-20-1822, rct Warrington MM with husband Joseph

MINUTES

McMILLIN, Enos, 3-23-1825, req marriage with Sarah Wright
    Joseph, 11-17-1819, req marriage with Elizabeth Person
    Joseph, 12-23-1819, rocf Warrington MM
    Joseph, 6-21-1821, rocf Warrington MM with wife Elizabeth
    Joseph, 3-20-1822, rct Warrington MM with wife Elizabeth
    Ruth, 8-22-1816, rocf Warrington MM as Minister
MERCER, Rachel E., 11-23-1859, dis: mou. Now at Sadsbury MM, Lancaster Co, Pa [w]
    Rachel E., 9-19-1860, ack mou. Retained
    Rachel E., 9-19-1860, case revived. Continued as a member [w]
    Rachel F., 5-18-1859, compl of: mou. Formerly Garretson [w]
METCALF, Sarah A., 6-21-1872, rep to MM [w]
    Sarah Ann, 5-17-1837, compl of: mou. Formerly Pilkington [w]
    Sarah Ann, 7-19-1837, ack mou. Retained [w]
MICCLE, Thomas, 5-14-1794, now of age, declared insane. Guardians appointed
MICHENER, Charles, 11-18-1885, rocf Abington MM, Pa [w]
    Charles, 2-17-1886, appt to Firstday School comm
    Charles, 5-18-1887, assessed $1.00 for fuel for Ann and Martha Griest
    Charles, 9-22-1887, req marriage with Florence Griest
MICKEL, Jane, 6-9-1794, compl of: mou. Now Bowen. Retained
MICKLE, Eve, 1-23-1799, rocf Warrington MM with husband Samuel
    Eve, 3-22-1820, compl of: non-attendance. Baptized elsewhere
    Evis, 5-22-1799, req membership. Child of Samuel Mickle
    Griffith, 5-22-1799, req membership. Child of Samuel Mickle
    Griffith, 12-23-1802, compl of: attending muster
    Griffith, 3-23-1803, dis: attending muster
    Jane, 5-22-1799, req membership. Child of Samuel Mickle
    Jane, 2-20-1806, compl of: dancing
    Jane, 5-21-1806, dis: dancing
    John, 5-22-1799, req membership. Child of Samuel Mickle
    John, 1-18-1809, compl of: mustering
    John, 5-17-1809, dis: mustering
    Mary, 2-20-1806, compl of: dancing
    Mary, 5-21-1806, dis: dancing
    Rebecca, 2-10-1783, req marriage with Thomas Bowen, Jr
    Robert, 2-24-1820, compl of: non-attendance, baptized at another society
    Robert, 6-22-1820, dis: joined another society
    Samuel, 1-23-1799, rocf Warrington MM with wife Eve
    Samuel, 3-20-1799, req membership for his children
    Samuel, 5-22-1799, req membership. Child of Samuel Mickle
    Samuel, 2-24-1820, compl of: non-attendance, baptized at another society
    Samuel, 6-22-1820, dis: joined another society
    Sarah, 5-22-1799, req membership. Child of Samuel Mickle
    Sarah, 2-20-1806, compl of: dancing
    Sarah, 5-21-1806, dis: dancing
    Thomas, 5-22-1799, req membership. Child of Samuel Mickle

MENALLEN MINUTES, MARRIAGES, & MISCELLANY

MICKLE, Thomas, 2-24-1820, compl of: non-attendance, baptized at another society
    Thomas, 6-22-1820, dis: joined another society
    Thomas, 5-21-1823, committee report regarding his condition: Finley McGrew and Samuel Wright informs that Thomas Mickle (a lunatick) and a member of our society who resided at Dennings Creek at the establishment of that Monthly Meeting has nearly exhausted his funds and likely to become a charge
    Thomas, 11-19-1823, report received from Dennings Creek:
    "Dear Friends, The situation of Thomas Mickle coming under the notice of our meeting and after being considered it was concluded to inform you that we do not consider it in duty bound to maintain him although he was within the virge of it at the settlement thereof as it doth not appear that this was his proper place of residence as his Estate and main support was with you and supported by it while here. It appears that he was only a sojourner here while his mother lived after her death it was requested that his estate should come here and he be maintained for term of life for his estate but it was not complied with therefore we do not consider the principal of truth binds us to administer to his necessities. Signed by direction at Dennings Creek Monthly Meeting held the 12th of the 11th mo 1823, Andrew Clever, clerk"
    Thomas, 12-22-1825, caretakers appointed for him
    Thomas, 10-18-1827, comm reports he is deceased: they forwarded accounts for nursing and funeral expense amounting to $34.24 which is directed to be raised by the preparative meetings in the usual proportion
MIFFLIN, Hannah W., 8-21-1862, ack mou to Samuel W. Mifflin. Formerly Wright [w]
MILLER, Henry S., 11-21-1877, appt to take care of Newberry property
    Jane, 11-10-1794, rocf Pipe Creek MM with husband Robert and 3 children
    Phebe Ann, 2-17-1869, compl of: mou
    Phebe Ann, 3-17-1869, dis: mou. Formerly Hoopes [w]
    Phoebe Ann, 8-19-1868, compl of: mou. Formerly Hoopes [w]
    Robert, 11-10-1794, rocf Pipe Creek MM with wife Jane and 3 children
    Ruth, 11-10-1794, rocf Pipe Creek with father Robert and family
    Samuel, 11-10-1794, rocf Pipe Creek with father Robert and family
    Sarah, 11-10-1794, rocf Pipe Creek with father Robert and family
MILLINER, Sarah, 7-15-1793, dis: mou. Formerly Loan
MILLINGER, Sarah, 5-13-1793, compl of: mou. Formerly Boen [Bowen?]
MILLOR, Robert, 2-15-1796, rep to QM
MILLS, Elizabeth, 2-9-1784, rct Hopewell MM (Va)
    Elizabeth, 5-10-1784, rec on cert
    Henry, 12-15-1783, req marriage with Elizabeth John. He of Hopewell MM
MOODY, Jean, 6-11-1787, compl of: mou. Formerly Cox
    Jean, 9-10-1787, dis: mou. Formerly Cox
MOORE, Benjamin P., 8-21-1862, appt comm [w]

MINUTES

MOORE, Harriet J., 11-17-1852, rocf Spruce Street MM, Philadelphia as Minister
    Lavinia G., 8-22-1888, absent member. Now in Oketo, Kansas [w]
    Mary G., 8-21-1862, appt comm [w]
    Thomas, Jr, 4-14-1788, wrote from Fairfax MM re Benjamin Hutton
    Ziba Hibbard, 11-20-1872, req marriage with Lavinia Griest [w]
    Ziba Hibberd, 12-23-1874, appt comm
    Ziba Hibberd, 1-20-1875, appt comm
MOOR, Jeremiah, 11-22-1837, roc as Minister
MORE, Harriet P., 11-17-1852, rocf Phila MM, Spruce St. as Minister [w]
    Rachel M., 11-17-1847, gct Baltimore MM
    Ziba Hibbard, 5-22-1872, rocf New Garden MM
    Ziba Hibbard, 11-20-1872, req marriage with Lavinia Griest
MORTHLAND, Esther, 4-24-1862, appt Overseer [w]
    Esther, 4-20-1865, appt Overseer [w]
    Esther, 2-20-1868, appt comm 13 times thru 11-21-1877 [w]
    Esther, 8-21-1877, rep to MM 34 times thru 7-19-1882 [w]
    Esther, 8-22-1870, rep to QM 18 times thru 8-19-1885 [w]
    Phebe, 4-15-1793, rct Warrington MM
    Robert, 12-10-1792, req marriage with Phebe Speakman
    Ruth, 4-21-1842, rocf Warrington MM
    Samuel, 1-21-1818, rocf Gunpowder MM
    Sarah, 1-21-1818, rocf Gunpowder MM
    Sarah, 12-21-1820, rct Baltimore MM
MORTON, Amy, 2-15-1790, dis: mou. Formerly Cox
    Eme, 8-10-1789, compl of: mou. Formerly Cox
    Hannah, 10-9-1780, compl of: carnal knowledge of husband before marriage
    Jesse, 5-11-1789, req marriage with Eamy Cox
    Jesse, 2-15-1790, dis: mou
    John, 3-14-1785, req marriage with Hannah Hutton
    John, Jr, 10-9-1780, compl of: carnal knowledge of wife before marriage
    John, Jr, 6-15-1795, compl of: rudeness to father, fighting
    John, Jr, 9-14-1795, testimony against
    Mary, 8-11-1788, req marriage with John Blackburn
    Mary, 10-13-1788, rct Warrington MM
MOSBY, Elizabeth H., 4-20-1865, ack mou. Retained. Formerly Hoopes
MOSEBY, Elizabeth, 2-23-1865, compl of: mou. Formerly Hoopes [w]
    Elizabeth, 4-20-1865, ack mou. Retained [w]
MOTT, Rachel M., 9-17-1845, rocf Baltimore MM
    Rachel M., 9-17-1845, rocf Baltimore MM, Western District [w]
    Rachel M., 1-22-1846, appt assistant clerk [w]
    Rachel M., 1-20-1847, on comm against settling new meeting at Mechanicsville
MULLINOX, Gideon, 5-22-1811, attended as Minister from Marlborough MM, NY
MYERS, Albert C., 1-23-1889, req membership thru mother Sarah. Born 12-12-1874
    Elmira Edith, 1-23-1889, req membership thru mother Sarah. Born 5-19-1885

MENALLEN MINUTES, MARRIAGES, & MISCELLANY

MYERS, Emma May, 1-23-1889, req membership thru mother Sarah. Born 11-17-1879
    Georgia, 1-23-1889, req membership thru mother Sarah. Born 11-7-1877
    Hannah, 8-21-1834, compl of: mou. Formerly Underwood. Disowned
    John, 1-23-1889, req membership for 4 children, with wife Sarah
    Sarah, 1-23-1889, req membership for 4 minor children
    Sarah A., 4-17-1878, ack mou. Retained. Formerly Cook
    Sarah A., 11-21-1888, rep to QM [w]
    Sarah A., 1-23-1889, req membership for four children [w]
    Sarah A., 2-20-1889, rep to QM [w]
    Sarah A., 4-17-1889, appt comm [w]
    Sarah A., 1-22-1890, appt comm [w]
    Sarah A., 8-20-1890, appt comm [w]
NAST, Amy, 5-23-1888, req membership. Formerly Hoopes
NEBINGER, Mary, 8-22-1844, req marriage with John B. Wright
NEEDLES, John, 2-20-1845, rocf Baltimore MM, Western District as Minister [w]
NEELY, Matilda, 6-20-1844, compl of: mou. Formerly Wierman [w]
NEWLON, Catharine, 4-9-1781, mou: formerly Wierman
    Catherine, 1-14-1782, read testimony. Retained
    Catherine, 6-10-1782, rct Warrington MM
    Catherine, 11-13-1786, rct Hopewell MM with husband
NEWPORT, Elizabeth, 2-24-1842, rocf Abington MM, Pa, as Minister
    Elizabeth, 9-21-1853, rocf Green Street MM, Phila. as Minister [w]
OATS, Sarah, 11-10-1783, compl of: mou. Formerly Squibb
    Sarah, 12-15-1783, dis: mou. Formerly Squibb
OBER, Rebecca, 3-19-1845, compl of: mou. Formerly Kettelwell [w]
    Rebecca, 11-19-1845, dis: mou [w]
    Rebecca, 1-21-1846, dis: mou. Formerly Kettlewell
OGBOURN, John, 3-23-1825, appt comm
    John, 3-23-1825, appt comm
OGBUM, John, 6-23-1825, appt comm
OLDHAM, Alice, 4-15-1782, rct Warrington MM with father Thomas and family
    Alice, 8-15-1785, rocf Warrington MM with father William and family
    John, 11-15-1784, rct Hopewell MM
    Rebecca, 4-15-1782, rct Warrington MM with husband Thomas and 2 children
    Sarah, 4-10-1786, compl of: mou. Now Kelley
    Sarah, 8-14-1786, dis: mou. Now Kelsey
    Thomas, 4-15-1782, rct Warrington MM with wife Rebecca and 2 children
    Thomas, 8-15-1785, rocf Warrington MM with father William and family
    Thomas, 10-10-1785, rep to MM
    Thomas, 8-13-1787, req marriage with Lydia Bowen, Sr
    Thomas, 12-10-1787, appt comm 8 times thru 8-20-1801
    Thomas, 8-18-1796, rep to QM 3 times thru 2-24-1803
    Thomas, 2-22-1798, appt Overseer at Dunnings Creek

MINUTES

OLDHAM, Thomas, 2-20-1800, released as Overseer at Dunnings Creek PM
    William, 4-15-1782, rct Warrington MM with father Thomas and family
    William, 9-13-1784, compl of: leaving area before end of apprenticeship
    William, 7-11-1785, rct Hopewell MM; Hopewell MM reports that he has returned and satisfied his master . . . he being but a youth it is thought best to grant his certificate
    William, 8-15-1785, rocf Warrington MM with 3 children
    William, 8-15-1785, rocf Warrington MM with father William and family
    William, 4-14-1788, rocf Hopewell MM
    William, 2-9-1789, compl of: fighting
    William, 4-13-1789, read acknowledgment
    William, 4-11-1791, compl of: moved without certificate, to Westland
    William, 11-14-1791, Westland MM reports he enlisted as soldier
    William, 12-12-1791, dis: enlisted as soldier, did not settle affairs
    William, 2-19-1801, compl of: dancing
    William, 10-22-1801, read testimony. Retained
    William, 10-22-1802, compl of: fighting
    William, 3-23-1803, read testimony. Retained
ONG, Mary, 6-14-1784, dis: mou. Formerly McGrew
    Mary, 5-14-1787, rct Hopewell MM. Has mou
OSBORN, Charles, 2-24-1820, rocf Whitewater QM, Ind, as Minister
OTMYER, Henry, 11-21-1877, appt to take care of Newberry property
    Martha, 1-18-1888, req release from membership. Formerly Garretson
OTTRIYER, Martha, 1-18-1888, dis: joined another society. Formerly Garretson [w]
OWEN, Mary, 5-21-1806, req marriage with Abner Griffith
OWENS, Mary, 10-10-1798, req membership
    Sarah, 10-10-1798, req membership
OWING, Sarah, 5-22-1799, req marriage with William Griffith
PACKER, Ann, 5-23-1883, rocf Green Plain MM, Clark Co, Ohio as Minister
    Ann, 5-23-1883, rocf Indiana YM as Minister [w]
    James, 6-23-1796, rocf Warrington MM
    James, 1-17-1798, rct Warrington MM
    Moses, 6-9-1794, rocf Warrington MM
    Moses, 2-15-1796, rct Warrington MM
PALLET, Mary, 6-20-1799, rct Warrington MM
PAUL, Abigail R., 8-23-1882, rocf Salem MM, NJ as Minister [w]
PEARSON, Amelia, 10-19-1820, dis: fornication
    Ann, 8-23-1821, compl of: fornication. Daughter of Thomas
    Ann, 5-22-1822, dis: fornication. Daughter of Thomas
    Elias, 2-12-1781, rct Warrington MM; son Thomas, apprentice to Elisha Kirk
    Elias, 7-15-1793, released as Overseer at Huntington
    Elias, 11-13-1780, rep to QM 32 times thru 8-20-1807
    Elias, 10-9-1780, appt comm 80 times thru 4-19-1810
    Elias, 11-17-1813, rct Baltimore MM. Son of Thomas
    Elias, 2-24-1814, compl of: imitating military parade, defacing sign
    Elias, 2-24-1814, read testimony. Retained
    Elias, 9-20-1815, compl of: fornication
    Elias, 2-22-1816, dis: fornication

MENALLEN MINUTES, MARRIAGES, & MISCELLANY

PEARSON, Eliza, 1-23-1833, has separated from Hicksites at Menallen
    Elizabeth, 7-23-1817, appt comm
    Elizabeth, 7-21-1819, appt Elder
    Elizabeth, 11-17-1819, req marriage with Joseph McMillin
    Elizabeth E., 3-18-1835, appt comm [w]
    Emele, 7-19-1820, compl of: fornication
    Hannah, 5-22-1816, compl of: mou. Now Studebaker
    Isaac, 11-12-1781, appt assistant clerk
    Isaac, 11-11-1782, appt assistant clerk
    Isaac, 9-15-1783, req marriage with Elizabeth Everitt
    Isaac, 9-14-1789, released as clerk
    Isaac, 7-15-1793, appt Overseer at Huntington
    Isaac, 9-9-1793, released as recorder of Marriage Certificates
    Isaac, 4-13-1795, appt Elder at Huntington
    Isaac, 6-15-1795, appt to record Births and Deaths
    Isaac, 8-24-1797, appt clerk
    Isaac, 8-22-1799, released as Overseer at Huntington
    Isaac, 6-21-1804, released as clerk
    Isaac, 5-20-1807, appt Overseer
    Isaac, 9-23-1807, appt clerk
    Isaac, 10-20-1808, appt clerk
    Isaac, 2-19-1818, req marriage with Mary Wierman
    Isaac, 7-18-1821, appt assistant clerk
    Isaac, 3-20-1822, appt to examine record of Births & Deaths
    Isaac, 7-17-1822, appt assistant clerk
    Isaac, 7-23-1823, appt assistant clerk
    Isaac, 5-14-1781, rep to QM 62 times thru 1-17-1827
    Isaac, 2-22-1827, appt clerk
    Isaac, 5-14-1781, appt comm 213 times thru 4-19-1827
    Isaac, 4-19-1827, appt to settle with Benjamin Tumbleson's trustees
    Isaac, 2-21-1828, appt clerk
    Isaac, 11-19-1828, deceased. Replaced as clerk
    Isaac, 4-19-1860, rct Prairie Grove MM, Iowa with father Edwin and
        family [w]
    Isaac E, 9-22-1830, rocf York MM
    Isaac E., 10-21-1830, compl of. Certificate returned to York MM
    Isaac E., 4-21-1831, rocf York MM
    Isaac E., 5-18-1831, cert returned to York MM. Charges cleared
    Isaac Everitt, 1-19-1820, rct York MM by his guardian, as an
        apprentice
    Isaac M., 11-21-1855, read ack. Retained
    Isaac W., 5-23-1855, compl of: mou
    Isaac W., 2-22-1866, compl of: hireling minister at child's interment
    Isaac W., 4-19-1866, dis: hireling minister at interment of his children
    Izak, 3-21-1821, appt comm
    Jane, 10-20-1853, rct White Water MM, Ind with father Thos. and
        family
    Josiah, 8-23-1827, rep to QM
    Maria E., 10-20-1853, rct Whitewater MM, Ind with husband Thomas
        and 3 children [w]

MINUTES

PEARSON, Martha, 9-23-1807, req marriage with Joel Garretson
    Martha, 1-17-1821, req marriage with Roger Kenyon
    Mary, 2-19-1829, Harman Wierman appt trustee of her estate
    Mary, 8-20-1835, rep to QM [w]
    Mary W., 3-18-1835, appt comm 4 times thru 8-24-1837 [w]
    Mary W., 7-22-1835, appt clerk [w]
    Mary W., 8-24-1837, rep to QM [w]
    Mary W., 9-20-1837, appt assistant clerk [w]
    Phebe, 6-24-1824, rct Short Creek MM, Ohio
    Phebe Anna, 10-20-1853, rct Whitewater MM, Ind with father Thomas and family [w]
    Rebecca Jane, 10-20-1853, rct Whitewater MM, Ind with father Thomas and family [w]
    Rhoda Anna, 10-20-1853, rct White Water MM, Ind with father Thomas and family
    Ruth, 4-18-1816, compl of: mou. Formerly Pilkington
    Ruth, 6-20-1816, dis: mou. Moved to reside within virge of Exeter MM
    Ruth, 8-22-1816, to appeal to QM
    Ruth, 3-19-1817, appeal to QM returned to Menallen
    Ruth, 8-21-1817, desires to appeal to QM again
    Ruth, 3-18-1818, judgement of Menallen reversed on appeal to QM
    Ruth, 5-20-1818, gct Exeter MM
    Sarah Amelia, 10-20-1853, rct Whitewater MM, Ind with father Thomas and family [w]
    Theresa, 4-19-1860, rct Prairie Grove MM, Iowa with father Edwin and family [w]
    Thomas, 2-12-1781, rct Warrington MM as apprentice to Elisha Kirk
    Thomas, 8-11-1783, rocf Warrington MM
    Thomas, 4-11-1791, req marriage with Martha Everitt
    Thomas, 8-11-1794, appt clerk
    Thomas, 7-19-1797, req release as clerk
    Thomas, 6-10-1793, appt comm 16 times thru 12-25-1809
    Thomas, 4-22-1847, req marriage with Maria E. Griffith
    Thomas, 1-22-1851, read testimony. Retained
    Thomas, 10-20-1853, rct Whitewater MM, Ind with wife Maria E. and 3 children [w]
    William, 7-18-1804, appt comm
PEGG, James, 2-24-1820, rocf Whitewater QM, Ind as Minister
PELLET, Francis, 4-10-1799, req marriage with Mary John
PENCE, Elizabeth, 5-23-1888, dis: joined another. Daughter of Walker Cook [w]
PENROSE, Abigail, 7-11-1785, rocf Warrington MM with husband Thomas and family
    Amos, 7-11-1785, rocf Warrington MM with father Thomas and family
    Amos, 4-24-1800, req marriage with Sophia Harbough
    Ann, 3-14-1785, rocf Warrington MM with husband John
    Ann, 7-11-1785, rocf Warrington MM with father Thomas and family
    Ann, 1-13-1794, rct Warrington MM
    Ann, Jr, 9-10-1787, rct York MM
    Eliakim G., 2-23-1837, rct Baltimore MM by father Josiah

MENALLEN MINUTES, MARRIAGES, & MISCELLANY

PENROSE, Elisha, 9-23-1846, req marriage with Savanna Wright
    Elisha, 12-23-1874, complaint against Hiram, Cyrus S. and Jesse W. Griest
    Elisha, 1-23-1878, requests to be released from membership
    Elisha, 1-23-1878, req membership be discontinued [w]
    Hannah, 7-11-1785, rocf Warrington MM with father Thomas and family
    Hannah, 5-19-1824, req membership
    Hannah G., 1-19-1842, appt comm [w]
    Hannah G., 7-20-1842, appt assistant clerk [w]
    Hannah G., 8-20-1846, req marriage with Charles S. Wright
    Hannah, Sr., 9-21-1836, compl of: bearing illegitimate child [w]
    Hannah, Sr., 11-23-1836, ack wrongdoing. Retained [w]
    Hulda, 6-18-1885, rep to MM [w]
    John, 3-14-1785, rocf Warrington MM with wife Ann
    John, 2-15-1790, dis: mou
    Josiah, 4-20-1815, req marriage with Rachel Garretson
    Josiah, 5-17-1815, rocf Dunnings Creek for marriage
    Josiah, 4-18-1816, rocf Dunnings Creek MM with wife Rachel
    Josiah, 2-23-1837, rct Baltimore MM for son Eliakim G.
    Josiah, 5-19-1841, compl of: non-compliance in disputed case
    Josiah, 6-24-1841, comm reports there is no basis for complaint
    Josiah, 2-20-1817, rep to QM 16 times thru 11-18-1857
    Josiah, 5-22-1833, rep to MM 28 times thru 5-19-1858
    Josiah, 12-19-1816, appt comm 23 times thru 8-19-1858
    Mary E., 8-22-1888, absent member. Now in Kansas [w]
    Rachel, 4-18-1816, rocf Dunnings Creek MM with husband Josiah
    Rachel G., 7-19-1815, rct Dunnings Creek MM
    Susanna W., 8-22-1888, absent member. Now in Kansas [w]
    Thomas, 7-11-1785, rocf Warrington with wife Abigail and 4 children
    Thomas, 5-11-1789, appt comm, to visit Bedford Co Meeting
    Thomas, 2-15-1790, appt Overseer at Monallen
    Thomas, 5-11-1795, released as Overseer at Huntington
    Thomas, 10-19-1797, appt Elder at Dunnings Creek
    Thomas, 2-22-1798, appt Elder
    Thomas, 8-20-1801, appt Overseer at Dunnings Creek PM
    Thomas, 8-11-1788, rep to QM 15 times thru 8-19-1802
    Thomas, 2-13-1786, appt comm 95 times thru 11-17-1802
    William, 5-9-1785, roc
    William, 7-11-1785, rocf Warrington MM with father Thomas and family
PENTZ, Elizabeth, 5-23-1888, released from membership
PETERS, Mary A., 7-18-1888, ack mou to Zachariah A. Peters. Formerly Tyson [w]
    Sarah, 7-22-1863, dis: mou. Formerly Wierman
PETERY, Sallie E., 1-22-1873, ack mou. Retained
PETRY, Sallie E., 1-22-1873, ack mou. Retained. Formerly Cook [w]
PHILIPS, George, 11-10-1794, rocf Warrington MM. He is a minor
    George, 11-22-1797, rct Warrington MM, by Guardians

MINUTES

PHILLIPS, Anna Wright, 2-21-1877, ack mou. Retained
    Annie M., 2-21-1877, ack mou. Retained. Formerly Wright. Now of Iowa [w]
    Annie M., 8-22-1888, living in Columbia, Pa [w]
    Hannah, 4-20-1797, rct Warrington MM
PIDGEON, Amos, 3-17-1793, rct Pipe Creek MM with father John and family
    Isaac, 3-17-1793, rct Pipe Creek MM with father John and family
    John, 4-12-1790, req marriage with Susannah Garretson
    John, 5-10-1790, rocf Pipe Creek MM
    John, 7-12-1790, appt comm
    John, 5-9-1791, rep to QM
    John, 3-17-1793, rct Pipe Creek MM with wife Susanna and 2 children
    Susanna, 3-17-1793, rct Pipe Creek MM with husband John and 2 children
PILKINGTON, Benjamin W., 12-21-1837, compl of: mou
    Benjamin W., 1-17-1838, comm reports he lives at Bloody Run, Bedford Co, Pa
    Benjamin W., 7-18-1838, dis: mou
    Levi, 3-18-1840, removed to Platte Co, Mo without certificate
    Ricard, 10-15-1787, compl of: dancing
    Richard, 2-11-1788, dis: dancing
    Richard, 2-15-1796, read acknowledgment
    Richard, 6-23-1796, rct Warrington MM for marriage with Sarah Walker
    Richard, 4-21-1808, compl of: defrauding a man
    Richard, 12-25-1809, compl of: non-payment of a just debt
    Ruth, 4-18-1816, compl of: mou. Now Pearson
    Sarah, 12-22-1796, rocf Warrington MM
    Sarah Ann, 5-17-1837, compl of: mou. Now Metcalf [w]
    Thomas, 4-14-1788, compl of: mou
    Thomas, 5-12-1788, dis: mou
    Vincent, 2-10-1783, rep to QM 3 times thru 8-11-1788
    Vincent, 12-11-1780, appt comm 24 times thru 8-10-1789
PIZEL, Michel, 8-11-1783, compl of: mou; non-attendance. Formerly Bower
    Michel, 10-13-1783, dis: mou; non-attendance
POTTS, Ann, 9-13-1784, compl of: mou. Now Graidy
    David, 5-12-1783, rep to QM
    David, 10-11-1784, compl against William Beals, for debt
    David, 5-14-1787, compl of: disturbing meeting
    David, 12-10-1787, dis: disturbing meeting
    Hannah, 3-12-1787, compl of: dancing
    Hannah, 6-11-1787, dis: dancing
    Jonathan, 9-9-1782, rct Warrington MM to marry Mary Cleaver
    Jonathan, 2-10-1783, returned certificate to Warrington MM, for marriage with Meomy Garretson with an indorsement thereon from Warrington MM expressive of their having declined their proposed marriage, but that his conduct therein sofar as has appear hath been commendable
    Jonathan, 4-12-1790, req marriage with Deborah Wright
    Jonathan, 2-18-1802, appt comm
    Jonathan, 2-18-1802, rep to QM

MENALLEN MINUTES, MARRIAGES, & MISCELLANY

POTTS, Rachel, 2-14-1791, compl of: mou. Now Adams
    Rachel, 6-13-1791, dis: mou; unchastity. Now Adams
PRICE, Ann W., 2-19-1846, rct Gunpowder MM [w]
    Ann W., 3-18-1846, rocf Gunpowder MM
    Mordica, 11-19-1884, rocf Little Falls MM
    Moses D., 10-25-1845, req marriage with Ann Wright
PRICKETT, Ella M. G., 8-17-1887, ack mou. Retained
    Ella M. G., 8-17-1887, ack mou to Josiah W. Prickett. Formerly Griest [w]
PROCTOR, Rachel, 9-20-1797, req membership
    Rachel, 8-23-1798, req marriage with John Sinclair
    Ruth, 10-24-1822, rocf Indian Spring MM
    Ruth, 7-18-1827, compl of: fornication
RAGAN, Daniel, 8-18-1808, rep to QM
    Daniel, 9-19-1804, appt comm 10 times thru 4-19-1810
    Daniel, 3-21-1811, rct York MM with wife Ruth
    Ruth, 3-21-1811, rct York MM with husband Daniel
RAGEN, Daniel, 3-23-1803, rocf York MM with wife Ruth
    Daniel, 4-21-1803, appt comm 4 times thru 10-18-1804
    Daniel, 4-19-1804, appt to assist in Joseph Hutton case
    Ruth, 3-23-1803, rocf York MM with husband Daniel
RAKESTRAW, Maria, 10-23-1878, compl of: mou. Formerly Harris [w]
    Maria, 12-19-1878, ack mou. Retained. Formerly Harris
    Maria, 1-22-1879, gct Pipe Creek MM
    Maria L., 12-18-1878, ack mou. Retained. Formerly Harris [w]
    Maria L., 12-18-1878, rct Pipe Creek MM [w]
REESE, George, 8-21-1851, rocf Little Falls MM as Minister [w]
    George, 8-21-1862, appt comm [w]
REGAN, Daniel, 5-18-1803, rep to QM
    Daniel, 11-23-1803, appt comm 16 times thru 10-18-1810
REINEHART, Anneliza, 6-22-1871, compl of: mou. Released from membership
RETZER, Alcetta B., 1-18-1860, req membership be discontinued [w]
RINEHART, Anna Eliza, 2-22-1871, compl of: mou. Formerly Cook [w]
    Anna Elizabeth, 5-17-1871, dis: mou. Formerly Cook [w]
ROBERTS, Ezekiel, 4-15-1863, rocf Short Creek MM, Ohio as Minister
    William, 4-13-1795, rct Pipe Creek MM, to make up breach with friends
    William, 3-23-1796, rocf Pipe Creek MM
    William, 10-20-1796, appt comm
    William, 5-17-1797, rep to QM
    William, 5-22-1799, rep to QM
    William, 6-18-1801, rct Pipe Creek MM
ROBINSON, Mary, 7-19-1815, rct Philadelphia MM, Northern District
    Mary, 3-20-1816, certificate to Philadelphia MM, Northern District, returned with information that she is in necessitous circumstances which being considered it appears to be the mind of this meeting that it would be best to accept the return of the certificate and . . . that she should return to reside within the virge of this meeting
    Mary, 7-17-1816, case to be considered further, committee reports that

MINUTES

    they have attended to the appointment and one of the number took a carriage in order to have her brought back but she could not be prevailed with to return to reside here and it appears that her property consists of a small matter of household furniture and a yearly income during her life arising on a small house and that at present rents at about $28 the committee is directed to furnish the amount of expenses already accruing on her account to next meeting

ROBINSON, Mary, 9-18-1816, it appears to be the judgment to write to her and also to the monthly meeting within the verge of which she resides informing them that this meeting apprehends that every requisite on our part having been performed friends here do therefore hold themselves released from any obligation to administer pecuniary relief whilst she remains absent from us

    Mary, 12-24-1818, case revived. One more try before she is disowned

    Mary, 5-19-1819, case dismissed. She is cared for by her daughter

ROGERS, Ellis, 8-13-1792, rocf Gwyned MM. Now lives at Bedford

ROUZER, Elizabeth, 4-24-1800, compl of: mou. Formerly Blackburn

    Elizabeth, 8-21-1800, dis: mou. Formerly Blackburn

RUSK, Sarah, 6-19-1817, req membership

    Sarah, 7-23-1817, accepted as member. Dis by Warrington years ago

RUSSEL, Abel H., 1-19-1842, now resides within verge of Honey Creek MM, Ind

    Abelnorth, 9-22-1819, rct Pipe Creek MM thru father Jesse

    Content, 2-20-1806, rocf Pipe Creek MM with husband Jesse and 1 child

    Hanah, 9-22-1819, rct Pipe Creek MM thru father Jesse

    Isaac, 9-22-1819, rct Pipe Creek MM thru father Jesse

    Isaac, 2-21-1839, rct Spring Borough MM, Ohio to marry Rachel Janney

    Isaac, 1-19-1842, now resides within verge of Honey Creek MM, Ind

    Jesse, 12-18-1800, req marriage with Content Garretson

    Jesse, 2-20-1806, rocf Pipe Creek MM with wife Content and 1 child

    Jesse, 11-19-1817, rep to QM 5 times thru 11-22-1820

    Jesse, 7-21-1819, appt Elder

    Jesse, 9-22-1819, rct Pipe Creek MM for his 5 children

    Jesse, 10-18-1810, appt comm 48 times thru 11-22-1837

    John, 11-22-1820, req marriage with Ruth Griest

    Jonathan, 2-20-1806, rocf Pipe Creek MM with father Jesse and mother

    Mary, 9-22-1819, rct Pipe Creek MM thru father Jesse

    Sarah, 9-22-1819, rct Pipe Creek MM thru father Jesse

RUSSELL, Abel, 3-23-1825, appt comm 3 times thru 6-23-1825

    Abel H., 12-19-1816, rocf Pipe Creek MM with father Jesse and family

    Abel H., 12-21-1837, rocf Pipe Creek MM

    Abel M., 6-23-1836, rocf Pipe Creek MM

    Abel N., 8-18-1836, compl of by Pipe Creek MM: mou

    Abel N., 3-18-1840, removed to Vigo Co, Ind without certificate

    Content, 2-19-1801, rct Pipe Creek MM

MENALLEN MINUTES, MARRIAGES, & MISCELLANY

RUSSELL, Content, 12-19-1816, rocf Pipe Creek MM with husband Jesse and 6 children
    Hanah, 12-19-1816, rocf Pipe Creek MM with father Jesse and family
    Isaac, 12-19-1816, rocf Pipe Creek MM with father Jesse and family
    Isaac, 9-23-1829, rocf Pipe Creek MM
    Isaac, 8-18-1836, compl of: attending a marriage out of order
    Isaac, 11-23-1836, produced acknowledgment. Retained
    Isaac, 1-23-1839, req membership. Denied without info re his MM
    Isaac, 3-18-1840, removed to Vigo Co, Ind without certificate
    Jesse, 12-19-1816, rocf Pipe Creek MM with wife Content and 6 children
    Jesse, 1-22-1817, appt Overseer
    Jesse, 2-20-1817, appt Guardian for Benjamin Tomlinson
    Jesse, 5-21-1817, appt Guardian by and for Benjamin Tomlinson
    Jesse, 5-23-1821, req marriage with Sarah Hendricks
    Jesse, 3-18-1829, appt for care of burying grounds
    Jesse, 2-23-1832, appt comm to list names re separation at BYM
    Jesse, 5-24-1832, appt Elder
    Jesse, 9-23-1835, appt Elder [w]
    Jesse, 1-23-1833, rep to MM 19 times thru 10-18-1838
    Jesse, 1-23-1839, appt Elder
    Jesse, 8-21-1817, rep to QM 30 times thru 5-19-1841
    Jesse, 1-22-1817, appt comm 74 times thru 5-19-1841
    Jesse, 6-23-1842, destitute; unable to provide home for self and wife
    John, 2-22-1827, rocf Pipe Creek MM with mother, Ruth
    John, 2-24-1842, rct West Branch MM thru guardian Isaac Tudor
    Jonathan, 12-19-1816, rocf Pipe Creek MM with father Jesse and family
    Joseph, 2-22-1827, rocf Pipe Creek MM with mother, Ruth
    Joseph, 2-24-1842, rct Centre MM thru guardian Isaac Tudor
    Joshua, 12-23-1874, appt comm
    Louisa A. W., 10-17-1877, rct Bald Eagle MM [w]
    Louisa A., 2-19-1873, ack mou. Retained. Formerly Wright [w]
    Louisa A. W., 11-21-1877, gct Center MM, Center Co, Pa
    Louise A. W., 2-19-1873, ack mou. Retained
    Mary, 12-19-1816, rocf Pipe Creek MM with father Jesse and family
    Ruth, 2-22-1821, rct Pipe Creek MM
    Ruth, 2-22-1827, rocf Pipe Creek MM with 2 children
    Ruth, 10-22-1835, appt Elder
    Ruth, 2-18-1836, rep to QM [w]
    Ruth, 2-22-1838, rep to QM [w]
    Ruth, 2-18-1836, appt comm 9 times thru 9-19-1838 [w]
    Ruth, 1-23-1839, appt Elder
    Ruth, 5-22-1839, req marriage with Gideon Widemire
    Ruth, 6-20-1839, comm reports rights of her children are secured
    Sarah, 12-19-1816, rocf Pipe Creek MM with father Jesse and family
    Sarah, 6-18-1835, appt comm 3 times thru 8-24-1837 [w]
    Sarah, 8-20-1835, rep to QM 4 times thru 8-23-1838 [w]
    William, 12-23-1874, appt comm
    William, 12-23-1874, appt comm

MINUTES

RUTZER, Alcetta B., 1-18-1860, dis: mou. Formerly Griest
SCHMIDT, Mary, 6-19-1863, rep to MM [w]
SCHUGH, John A., 5-17-1865, rep to QM [w]
SEAMAN, Gideon, 12-23-1819, rocf Westbury MM, Long Island, NY as Minister
    Samuel, 5-22-1811, attended as Minister from Cornwall MM, NY
SHARPLESS, Nathan, 9-20-1820, rocf Concord MM as Minister
    Sarah, 9-20-1820, rocf Chester MM as Minister
SHEARER, Mrs. L. A., 4-17-1889, on comm requesting repairs to Warrington Meeting House
SHEPHERD, Benjamin, 10-13-1783, gct Hopewell MM with father Solomon and family
    Elizabeth, 10-13-1783, gct Hopewell MM with father Solomon and family
    Jean, 10-13-1783, gct Hopewell MM with father Solomon and family
    John, 10-13-1783, gct Hopewell MM with father Solomon and family
    Joseph, 10-13-1783, gct Hopewell MM with father Solomon and family
    Joseph, 2-9-1795, rocf Warrington MM, child of William Shepherd
    Margaret, 10-13-1783, gct Hopewell MM with husband Solomon and family
    Mary, 10-13-1783, gct Hopewell MM with father Solomon and family
    Mary, 2-9-1795, rocf Warrington MM, child of William Shepherd
    Phebe, 2-9-1795, rocf Warrington MM
    Rebecca, 2-9-1795, rocf Warrington MM, child of William Shepherd
    Sarah, 10-13-1783, gct Hopewell MM with father Solomon and family
    Solomon, 10-13-1783, gct Hopewell MM with wife Margaret and 9 children
    Solomon, 10-13-1783, gct Hopewell MM with father Solomon and family
    Thomas, 10-13-1783, gct Hopewell MM with father Solomon and family
    Thomas, 2-9-1795, rocf Warrington MM, child of William Shepherd
    William, 2-9-1795, rocf Warrington MM
    Phebe, 8-20-1801, compl of: uncharitable to woman in their care
    Phebe, 5-19-1802, read testimony. Retained [see William Shepperd]
    Solomon, 12-23-1874, appt comm
    William, 8-20-1801, compl of: uncharitable to a woman in his care
    William, 5-19-1802, read testimony. Retained. "We having had a right amongst friends but for want of adhering to the dictates of truth in our own hearts which would have preserved us from error have deviated therefrom so far as to keep a woman that was put under our care who was said to be deranged in confinement in an indecent manner untill she was released by authority which has brought reproach upon the society and trouble on our friends for which transgression we are now heartily sorry and desire friends to pass it by and continue us under their care hoping to be more careful in future. s/William Shepperd, Mary Way, Phebe Shepperd"
SHIELDS, Martha, 7-23-1806, compl of: mou; joining Presbyterians. Formerly McGrail
    Martha, 8-21-1806, dis: mou; joining Presbyterians. Formerly McGrail
SHIPHERD, Rebecca D., 10-13-1783, dis: mou. Now Allen

MENALLEN MINUTES, MARRIAGES, & MISCELLANY

SHUGH, Alice, 8-19-1864, rocf Pipe Creek MM with father John A. and family [w]
 Alice F., 4-20-1870, mou; req membership be discontinued. Now Brough [w]
 Anna H., 8-19-1864, rocf Pipe Creek MM with father John A. and family [w]
 Beaulah H., 8-19-1864, rocf Pipe Creek MM [w]
 Beulah H., 9-17-1872, ack mou. Retained. Now Erb [w]
 Beulah H., 11-20-1889, gct Pipe Creek MM. Now Erb
 Beulah R., 8-18-1864, rocf Pipe Creek MM
 Bulah, 9-19-1872, ack mou. Retained
 Ezra, 8-18-1864, rocf Pipe Creek MM
 Ezra, 4-22-1868, compl of: mou, drinking, non-attendance
 Ezra, 12-23-1868, ack bad conduct. Retained
 Hannah, 3-22-1870, appt comm [w]
 John A., 8-18-1864, rocf Pipe Creek MM with wife Margaret and 2 children
 John A., 1-23-1867, appt comm 3 times thru 8-22-1867
 John A., 2-21-1867, rep to MM
 John A., 2-21-1867, rep to QM
 John A., 8-22-1867, rep to QM
 John A., 3-23-1870, rct Pipe Creek MM with wife Margaret
 Margaret, 11-18-1863, rep to QM 3 times thru 2-20-1868 [w]
 Margaret, 8-19-1864, rocf Pipe Creek MM with husband John A. and 2 children [w]
 Margaret, 11-19-1864, rep to MM 4 times thru 3-22-1870 [w]
 Margaret, 8-22-1867, appt comm [w]
 Margaret, 3-23-1870, rct Pipe Creek MM with husband John A. Shugh
 Margaret E., 8-19-1864, rocf Pipe Creek MM [w]
 Margaret Eliz., 8-18-1864, rocf Pipe Creek MM
SINCLAIR, John, 8-23-1798, req marriage with Rachel Proctor
SINCLERE, Keziah, 7-23-1800, rct Baltimore MM with mother Rachel
 Rachel, 7-23-1800, rct Baltimore MM with daughter Keziah
SMITH, Edith, 3-18-1846, rocf Dunnings Creek with husband Nathan and 2 children
 Edith, 1-20-1847, on comm against settling new meeting at Mechanicsville
 Edith, 5-20-1849, appt Overseer [w]
 Edith, 8-19-1852, rep to QM 3 times thru 2-21-1856 [w]
 Edith, 7-23-1856, appt assistant clerk [w]
 Edith, 12-24-1857, appt Elder
 Edith, 6-19-1851, appt comm 12 times thru 7-21-1858 [w]
 Gideon, 3-18-1846, rocf Dunnings Creek MM with father Nathan and family [w]
 Gideon, 10-22-1863, rep to QM 3 times thru 2-23-1865
 Gideon, 8-24-1865, ack volunteering for military duty. Retained
 Gideon, 10-24-1861, rep to MM 15 times thru 2-21-1867
 Gideon, 2-21-1867, rct Pipe Creek MM
 Gideon, 1-17-1872, req marriage with Martha Jane Cook
 Gideon, 2-21-1872, rocf Pipe Creek MM

MINUTES

SMITH, James, 9-15-1794, rocf Warrington MM with wife Mary
    James, 1-12-1795, req membership for 3 minor children
    James, 5-17-1797, read testimony. Retained
    James, 8-22-1799, req membership thru mother Mary Smith
    James, Jr, 10-22-1794, req membership
    James, Jr, 10-20-1796, compl of: quarrelling and fighting
    Jesse, 4-19-1866, rep to MM
    Jesse, 6-21-1866, rep to MM
    Jesse, 2-21-1867, rct Pipe Creek MM with parents Nathan and Mary S. Smith
    John, 2-9-1795, rocf Warrington MM
    John, 10-20-1796, compl of: mou
    John, 5-17-1797, dis: mou
    Josiah, 4-18-1861, appt assistant clerk
    Martha, 4-18-1867, gct Pipe Creek MM
    Martha J., 5-21-1873, gct Pipe Creek MM
    Martha Jane, 4-23-1873, rct Pipe Creek MM [w]
    Martha S., 2-20-1867, rct Pipe Creek MM [w]
    Mary, 9-15-1794, rocf Warrington MM with husband James
    Mary, 1-12-1795, req membership thru father James
    Mary, 8-22-1799, req membership for self and 2 children
    Mary, 11-19-1862, rep to QM [w]
    Mary, 11-21-1866, rep to MM [w]
    Mary P., 8-21-1862, rep to QM [w]
    Mary P., 12-17-1862, rep to MM [w]
    Mary S., 1-23-1861, rocf Little Britain MM, Lancaster Co, Pa
    Mary S., 4-24-1862, appt Overseer [w]
    Mary S., 4-24-1862, appt assistant clerk [w]
    Mary S., 11-19-1862, rep to MM 6 times thru 9-19-1866 [w]
    Mary S., 6-19-1863, appt clerk [w]
    Mary S., 12-24-1863, appt Elder [w]
    Mary S., 5-18-1864, appt clerk [w]
    Mary S., 5-22-1866, appt assistant clerk [w]
    Mary S., 11-20-1861, appt comm 10 times thru 6-21-1866 [w]
    Mary S., 5-22-1861, rep to QM 11 times thru 11-21-1866 [w]
    Mary S., 2-20-1867, rct Pipe Creek MM with husband Nathan and son Jesse [w]
    Mary T., 12-21-1863, appt Elder
    Mary T., 4-20-1865, appt Overseer [w]
    Mary W., 9-17-1862, appt comm
    Nathan, 5-19-1841, req marriage with Edith Griest
    Nathan, 3-18-1846, rocf Dunnings Creek MM with wife Edith and 2 children [w]
    Nathan, 1-16-1849, appt Overseer
    Nathan, 8-21-1851, appt to care for burying grounds
    Nathan, 1-21-1852, appt Overseer
    Nathan, 4-19-1855, appt Overseer
    Nathan, 12-18-1856, appt to record Marriage Certificates
    Nathan, 7-22-1857, appt Overseer
    Nathan, 4-22-1858, appt clerk

MENALLEN MINUTES, MARRIAGES, & MISCELLANY

SMITH, Nathan, 4-21-1859, appt clerk
  Nathan, 4-19-1860, appt clerk
  Nathan, 7-18-1860, appt Overseer
  Nathan, 8-23-1860, rct Little Britain MM, to marry Mary Smedley
  Nathan, 4-18-1861, appt clerk
  Nathan, 12-21-1863, appt Elder
  Nathan, 6-23-1864, appt Overseer
  Nathan, 12-21-1864, clerk for the day
  Nathan, 10-22-1846, appt comm 46 times thru 9-19-1866
  Nathan, 4-23-1846, rep to MM 89 times thru 11-21-1866
  Nathan, 8-2-0-1846, rep to QM 31 times thru 11-21-1866
  Nathan, 2-20-1867, rct Pipe Creek MM with wife Mary S. and son Jesse [w]
  Phebe Jane, 3-18-1846, rocf Dunnings Creek MM with father Nathan and family [w]
  Robert, 1-12-1795, req membership thru father James
  Sarah, 8-22-1799, req membership thru mother Mary Smith
  Susanna, 12-15-1794, req membership
  Susanna, 3-23-1797, req marriage with Thomas Bowen
  Thomas, 1-12-1795, req membership thru father James
SNYDER, John, 6-23-1796, rct Goose Creek MM
SPEAKMAN, Abenezer, 1-13-1783, req marriage with Elizabeth Cox, Jr
  Ann, 3-23-1803, rct ? with father Ebenezer and family
  Ebenezar, 9-4-1787, compl of: not paying debt to William Cox, Jr
  Ebenezer, 3-10-1788, compl of: non-payment of claim, [refuses to give up his affects; complainant is at liberty to recover the debt by Law]
  Ebenezer, 3-23-1803, rct ? with wife Elizabeth and 8 children
  Ebenezer, 3-23-1803, rct ? with father Ebenezer and family
  Elizabeth, 3-23-1803, rct ? with husband Ebenezer and 8 children
  Jacob, 3-23-1803, rct ? w father Ebenezer and family
  James, 12-9-1782, rct Warrington MM to marry Hannah Willis and settle
  Jesse, 3-23-1803, rct ? with father Ebenezer and family
  Joanna, 5-9-1785, req marriage with Robert Squibb of Warrington MM
  Joshua, 3-23-1803, rct ? with father Ebenezer and family
  Margaret, 6-24-1824, rocf London Grove MM as Minister
  Margaret, 11-23-1825, rocf London Grove MM as Minister
  Phebe, 12-10-1792, req marriage with Robert Morthland
  Phebe, 3-23-1803, rct ? with father Ebenezer and family
  Stephen, 8-12-1793, compl of: fighting. Read acknowledgment. Retained
  Stephen, 3-21-1798, compl of: mou
  Stephen, 6-21-1798, dis: mou
  Stephen, 3-23-1803, rct ? with father Ebenezer and family
  Susannah, 11-13-1786, req marriage with Jacob Cook of Warrington MM
  Thomas, 7-14-1783, rct Warrington MM as apprentice
  Thomas, 10-13-1788, rocf York MM

MINUTES

SPEAKMAN, Thomas, 4-13-1789, compl of: strong drink to excess; attending musters; gone to reside for some time within the limits of Concord MM
    Thomas, 3-23-1803, rct ? with father Ebenezer and family
    Willis, 5-19-1802, rocf Warrington MM
    Willis, 11-25-1810, compl of: mou. Now resides at Short Creek MM, Ohio
SPENCER, Joseph M., 12-21-1848, req marriage with Lydia Ann Griest
    Joseph M., 1-16-1849, rocf West Branch MM
    Lydia Ann, 4-19-1849, rct West Branch MM, Clearfield Co, Pa [w]
    Lydia Ann, 6-21-1849, gct Westbranch MM
    Susanna, 6-23-1796, rocf Hopewell MM
    Susanna, 6-23-1796, rct Warrington MM
SQUIBB, Caleb, 3-15-1790, rct Hopewell MM
    Caleb, 6-10-1793, Hopewell MM returns his cert from Monallen with information that he has not settled within the virge of that meeting but somewhere on the west of the Allegania
    Caleb, 11-11-1793, compl of: mou. Now lives in Fayette County near the Broad ford on Yough River, within virge of Redstone MM, Pa
    Caleb, 4-14-1794, dis: mou
    Joanna, 9-12-1785, rct Warrington MM
    John, 6-14-1784, rct Hopewell MM
    Lidia, 12-15-1788, compl of: moved near Hopewell and joined Methodists
    Lidia, 5-11-1789, dis: joined Methodists. Now resides at Hopewell, Va
    Lydia, 11-12-1787, compl of: attending a marriage out of unity
    Lydia, 1-14-1788, gives testimony. Retained
    Mary, 12-10-1781, mou to 1st cousin, Daniel Beals
    Mary, 1-14-1782, dis: mou. Now Beals
    Rebekah, 2-15-1790, compl of: mou to Jesse Cox
    Robert, 5-9-1785, req marriage with Joanna Speakman. He of Warrington
    Sarah, 5-14-1781, rct East Nottingham
    Sarah, 11-10-1783, compl of: mou. Now Oats
    Sarah, 12-15-1783, dis: mou. Now Oats
STABLER, Thomas P., 8-21-1862, appt comm [w]
    William, 11-19-1851, rocf Alexander MM as Minister
STAFFORD, Sarah A., 7-23-1856, ack mou. Retained. Formerly Griffith
    Sarah C., 7-23-1856, ack error. Retained [w]
    Sarah E., 8-21-1856, gct White Water MM, Ind.
    Sarah G., 7-23-1856, rct White Water MM, Ind. Formerly Griffith [w]
STEER, Louisa, 7-23-1851, rocf Fairfax MM as Minister [w]
STEPHENSON, John, 5-14-1787, req membership
STEVENSON, John, 4-12-1790, rct Hopewell MM
    John, 6-11-1792, dis: moving without settling affairs
STORER, John, 10-10-1785, visiting from Great Brittain
STRETCH, Susanna, 1-14-1793, compl of: mou. Formerly Cox
    Susanna, 3-17-1793, dis: mou. Formerly Cox
STUDEBAKER, Hannah, 5-22-1816, compl of: mou. Formerly Pearson
    Hannah, 7-17-1816, read testimony. Retained

MENALLEN MINUTES, MARRIAGES, & MISCELLANY

STUDIBECKER, Susanna, 11-23-1808, compl of: mou. Formerly Wierman
    Susanna, 12-22-1808, dis: mou. Formerly Wierman
SWAINE, Hannah, 3-23-1814, rct Philadelphia MM, Southern District
    Joshua, 9-21-1796, rct London Grove MM
SWAIN, Elizabeth, 8-23-1821, gct York MM
    Frances, 10-19-1815, rocf York MM with wife Sarah and daughter
    Hannah, 11-23-1825, rocf London Grove MM as Minister
    Jane, 10-19-1815, rocf York MM with father Frances and family
    Jesse M., 6-19-1817, req marriage with Gideon Griest
    Joshua, 6-15-1795, rocf Kennett MM
    Sarah, 10-19-1815, rocf York MM with husband Frances and daughter
    Sarah, 5-23-1827, rocf York MM
    Soosan, 7-23-1817, req marriage with Daniel Griest
SWAYNE, Francis, 2-18-1819, compl of: wagering; non-payment of debts
    Francis, 8-19-1819, dis: wagering; non-payment of debts
    Sarah, 8-19-1819, rct York MM
TALBOT, Sarah, 9-20-1820, rocf Concord MM as Minister
TALBOTT, Benjamin, 5-12-1788, rep to QM 5 times thru 11-15-1790
    Benjamin, 5-12-1788, appt comm 22 times thru 12-12-1791
    Benjamin, 5-14-1792, rct Westland MM with wife and 3 children
    Beuly, 5-14-1792, rct Westland MM with father Benjamin and family
    John, 5-14-1792, rct Westland MM with father Benjamin and family
    Mary, 5-14-1792, rct Westland MM with father Benjamin and family
TAYLOR, Thomas, 3-23-1825, appt comm
    Thomas, 6-23-1825, appt comm
THOMAS, Abel, 7-22-1801, rocf Exeter MM with wife Ellen and 3 children
    Abel, 7-22-1801, recommended as Minister, accepted
    Abel, 10-22-1802, rct the Jerseys as Minister
    Abel, 3-23-1803, rct Exeter MM for marriage with Esther Worrel
    Abel, 6-23-1803, rocf Exeter MM with father Isaac and family
    Abel, 7-18-1804, rct New England as Minister
    Abel, 7-17-1805, rct New England as Minister
    Abel, 10-23-1806, rct Virginia and Baltimore Quarter as Minister
    Abel, 1-21-1807, rocf Falmouth QM, Greenwich MM, R.I., Salem QM, NH
    Abel, 1-21-1807, rct Philadelphia QM as Minister
    Abel, 10-22-1807, rct Philadelphia YM as Minister
    Abel, 7-20-1808, rct Philadelphia and New York YMs as Minister
    Abel, 10-9-1809, rct Redstone and Ohio as Minister
    Abel, 11-18-1801, rep to QM 15 times thru 5-23-1810
    Abel, 11-25-1810, rct Virginia and North Carolina as Minister
    Abel, 1-22-1812, rct Concord, East Caln and So. QMs as Minister
    Abel, 10-22-1812, rct New Jersey Meetings as Minister
    Abel, 3-17-1813, rct Philadelphia YM, New York and Newport as Minister
    Abel, 2-23-1815, rct Pipe Creek MM thru father Isaac
    Abel, 1-20-1802, appt comm 12 times thru 9-20-1815
    Abel, 10-19-1815, rct Fairfax and Baltimore QMs as Minister
    Abel, 8-22-1816, deceased; memorial proposed
    Abel, 12-18-1817, rocf Pipe Creek MM

MINUTES

THOMAS, Abel, 3-17-1819, rct Gwynedd MM
    Abel, 5-23-1821, rct Warrington MM with mother Hannah and family
    Abel, 1-18-1826, rct York MM
    Abner, 7-22-1801, rocf Exeter MM with father Abel and family
    Abner, 6-23-1803, rocf Exeter MM with father Isaac and family
    Abner, 5-21-1806, rct Exeter MM with wife and 2 children
    Abner, 10-9-1809, rct Exeter MM with wife Esther and 3 children
    Abner, 4-18-1811, rct York MM with wife and 4 children
    Abner, 8-24-1820, compl of: mou
    Abner, 10-19-1820, read testimony. Retained
    Abner, 9-20-1826, rct Springfield MM, Ohio with wife Phebe and 4 children
    Alford, 4-19-1827, rct Springborough MM, Ohio with father Jonah and family
    Ann, 1-11-1796, rocf Warrington MM with father John and family
    Caroline, 5-23-1821, rct Warrington MM with mother Hannah and family
    Charles, 10-9-1809, rct Exeter MM with father Abner and family
    Charles Abel, 4-18-1811, rct York MM with father Abner and family
    Edward, 1-11-1796, rocf Warrington MM with father John and family
    Elel, 7-21-1819, appt comm
    Elen, 8-21-1817, rct Warrington MM with mother Elinor
    Eli, 7-22-1801, rocf Exeter MM with father Abel and family
    Eli, 3-22-1815, req marriage with Elizabeth Hammond
    Eli, 5-22-1816, rep to QM 5 times thru 11-20-1822
    Eli, 1-21-1818, appt comm 10 times thru 3-20-1822
    Eli, 9-19-1827, rct Salem MM, Ohio with wife Elizabeth and 6 children
    Elinor, 8-21-1817, rct Warrington MM with daughter Elen
    Eliza, 3-21-1855, compl of: mou. Formerly Griest [w]
    Eliza G., 4-19-1855, compl of: mou
    Eliza G., 4-19-1855, dis: mou [w]
    Elizabeth, 7-23-1817, read testimony. Retained
    Elizabeth, 10-20-1825, rct Spring Borough MM, Ohio with husband Jonah and family
    Elizabeth, 4-19-1827, rct Springborough MM, Ohio with husband Jonah and 4 children
    Elizabeth, 9-19-1827, rct Salem MM, Ohio with husband Eli and 6 children
    Ellen, 7-22-1801, rocf Exeter MM with husband Abel and 3 children
    Ellen, 2-18-1802, appt Elder for Womens meeting
    Ellen, 6-23-1803, rocf Exeter MM with father Isaac and family
    Ellen, 4-22-1824, rct York MM with father Jacob and family
    Ellin, 5-21-1806, rct Exeter MM with father Abner and family
    Ellin, 10-9-1809, rct Exeter MM with father Abner and family
    Ellin, 4-18-1811, rct York MM with father Abner and family
    Ellinor, 6-23-1803, rocf Exeter MM with husband Isaac and 6 children
    Emily, 4-19-1827, rct Springborough MM, Ohio with father Jonah and family
    Ester, 4-22-1824, rct York MM with father Jacob and family
    Ester, 9-20-1826, rct Springfield MM, Ohio with father Abner and family

MENALLEN MINUTES, MARRIAGES, & MISCELLANY

THOMAS, Esther, 11-23-1803, rocf Exeter MM. Wife of Abner
    Esther, 10-9-1809, rct Exeter MM with husband Abner and 3 children
    George, 5-21-1806, rct Exeter MM with father Abner and family
    George Worrell, 4-18-1811, rct York MM with father Abner and family
    Hammond, 9-19-1827, rct Salem MM, Ohio with father Eli and family
    Hanah, 3-21-1810, rocf Pipe Creek MM. Daughter of Isaac, Jr
    Hannah, 1-11-1796, rocf Warrington MM with father John and family
    Hannah, 5-23-1821, rct Warrington MM for self and 5 children
    Hannah, 5-19-1824, rct York MM
    Hannah, 4-19-1827, rct Springborough MM, Ohio with father Jonah and family
    Hanson, 5-23-1821, rct Warrington MM with mother Hannah and family
    Hiram, 5-23-1821, rct Warrington MM with mother Hannah and family
    Hiram A., 9-19-1827, rct Salem MM, Ohio with father Eli and family
    Ira, 4-19-1827, rct Springborough MM, Ohio with father Jonah and family
    Isaac, 6-23-1803, rocf Exeter MM with wife Ellinor and 6 children
    Isaac, 6-23-1803, rocf Exeter MM with father Isaac and family
    Isaac, 8-23-1804, appt Overseer to QM
    Isaac, 6-23-1808, appt Overseer
    Isaac, 2-23-1804, rep to QM 15 times thru 5-19-1813
    Isaac, 2-23-1815, rct Pipe Creek MM for son Abel
    Isaac, 6-18-1818, compl of: false advertisement in newspaper
    Isaac, 10-22-1818, read testimony. Retained
    Isaac, 10-20-1803, appt comm 37 times thru 4-22-1819
    Isaac, 7-21-1819, compl of: altering a receipt in his favor
    Isaac, 2-24-1820, dis: altering receipt
    Isaac, 9-20-1826, rct Springfield MM, Ohio with father Abner and family
    Isaac, 12-22-1842, rocf Warrington MM with father Mahlon Garretson
    Isaac, Jr, 9-20-1809, rct Pipe Creek MM to marry Hannah Star
    Israel, 9-19-1827, rct Salem MM, Ohio with father Eli and family
    Jacob, 1-19-1814, appt Overseer at Monallen
    Jacob, 6-22-1815, appt overseer of funerals to replace Isaac Thomas, dec'd
    Jacob, 10-24-1816, appt recorder of Certificates of Removal
    Jacob, 4-24-1817, appt comm re Benjamin Tomlinson
    Jacob, 2-21-1811, rep to QM 12 times thru 8-23-1821
    Jacob, 3-20-1822, released as recorder of Certificates of Removal
    Jacob, 3-23-1803, appt comm 48 times thru 12-19-1822
    Jacob, 4-22-1824, rct York MM with wife Margaret and 4 children
    Jacob, Jr, 7-22-1801, rocf Exeter MM with wife Margaret
    Jane, 1-11-1796, rocf Warrington MM with husband John and 7 children
    Jane, 1-11-1796, rocf Warrington MM with father John and family
    Jno, 4-24-1817, rct Warrington MM
    John, 1-11-1796, rocf Warrington MM with wife Jane and 7 children
    John, 1-11-1796, rocf Warrington MM with father John and family
    John, 2-23-1797, appt Overseer at Dunnings Creek
    John, 10-19-1797, appt Elder at Dunnings Creek

MINUTES

THOMAS, John, 2-22-1798, appt Elder
    John, 2-22-1798, rep to QM 5 times thru 2-18-1802
    John, 8-20-1801, released as Overseer at Dunnings Creek PM
    John, 6-22-1797, appt comm 16 times thru 2-18-1802
    John, 6-23-1803, rocf Exeter MM with father Isaac and family
    John, 2-20-1817, rct Warrington MM to marry Sarah Garretson
    Jonah, 1-11-1796, rocf Warrington MM with father John and family
    Jonah, 5-20-1807, compl of: fornication. Of Dunnings Creek MM
    Jonah, 11-23-1808, rocf Dunnings Creek MM
    Jonah, 4-24-1817, compl of: fornication
    Jonah, 1-19-1820, appt comm
    Jonah D., 7-23-1817, read testimony. Retained
    Jonah D., 10-20-1825, rct Spring Borough MM, Ohio with wife Elizabeth and 4 children
    Jonah D., 4-19-1827, rct Springborough MM, Ohio with wife Elizabeth and 4 children
    Jonathan, 4-22-1824, rct York MM with father Jacob and family
    Joseph, 7-22-1801, rocf Exeter MM with father Abel and family
    Joseph, 6-23-1803, rocf Exeter MM with father Isaac and family
    Joseph, 8-20-1807, compl of: fornication. Son of Isaac
    Joseph, 12-24-1807, dis: fornication. Son of Isaac
    Joseph, 11-20-1816, rep to QM
    Joseph R., 4-23-1829, compl of: left area without satisfying creditors
    Lydia, 7-19-1809, requests membership. Had been disowned at Exeter
    Margaret, 4-22-1824, rct York MM with husband Jacob and 4 children
    Maria, 9-19-1827, rct Salem MM, Ohio with father Eli and family
    Mary, 9-9-1793, rct Haverford MM
    Millards, 9-20-1826, rct Springfield MM, Ohio with father Abner and family
    Phebe, 7-21-1819, appt comm
    Phebe, 5-23-1821, rct Warrington MM with mother Hannah and family
    Phebe, 5-23-1821, req membership
    Phebe, 9-20-1826, rct Springfield MM, Ohio with husband Abner and children
    Phebe, 9-19-1827, rct Salem MM, Ohio with father Eli and family
    Rachel, 10-20-1803, req marriage with William Wright
    Rachel, 10-9-1809, rct Exeter MM with father Abner and family
    Rachel, 4-18-1811, rct York MM with father Abner and family
    Rachel, 4-22-1824, rct York MM with father Jacob and family
    Rebecca, 1-11-1796, rocf Warrington MM with father John and family
    Rebecca, 10-9-1809, req marriage with John Garretson, son of Samuel
    Rebecca H., 6-24-1858, gct Prairie Grove MM, Henry Co, Iowa
    Rebecca W., 8-20-1857, ack error. Retained [w]
    Rebecca W., 5-19-1858, rct Prairie Grove MM, Henry Co, Iowa [w]
    Sarah Ann, 9-19-1827, rct Salem MM, Ohio with father Eli and family
    Thomas, 11-25-1810, rocf Exeter MM. Son of Abner
    William, 7-22-1840, rocf Warrington MM
    William, 1-21-1846, rct Center MM
    William M, 5-23-1821, req membership

MENALLEN MINUTES, MARRIAGES, & MISCELLANY

THOMAS, William Modes, 9-20-1826, rct Springfield MM, Ohio with father Abner and family
THORNBURGH, Hannah, 5-14-1787, rocf Hopewell MM. However, she is at Warrington
    Phebe, 4-13-1795, appt comm
    Phebe, 9-20-1797, appt Elder for Women's meeting
    Thomas, 2-11-1788, rep to QM
    Thomas, 7-12-1790, appt comm 5 times thru 8-24-1797
    Thomas, 2-14-1791, rep to QM
    Thomas, 5-13-1793, compl of: unchastity with a young woman
    Thomas, 7-15-1793, read acknowledgment. Retained
    Thomas, 6-21-1804, appt Guardian of Joseph Hutton (by Court)
    Thomas, 6-22-1815, deceased. Replaced as trustee for Joseph Hutton
TODD, Ann, 11-10-1783, compl of: mou; now Vance
    Ann, 1-12-1784, dis: mou. Now Vance
    Robert, 7-15-1782, rct Nottingham MM as apprentice to Joseph Harlon
    Robert, 4-11-1785, rocf Nottingham MM
    Robert, 4-12-1790, compl of: playing cards
    Robert, 10-11-1790, dis: playing cards
TOLBERT, Benjamin, 1-14-1788, rocf Pipe Creek with wife Susannah and child
    Mary, 1-14-1788, rocf Pipe Creek with father Benjamin and family
    Susannah, 1-14-1788, rocf Pipe Creek with husband Benjamin and child
TOMLINSON, Benjamin, 5-14-1792, rocf Horsham MM with mother Elizabeth, wife of Benjamin
    Benjamin, 3-19-1806, rct Warrington MM for self with mother Elizabeth
    Benjamin, 6-23-1808, rocf Warrington MM with mother Elizabeth
    Benjamin, 2-20-1817, requires guardians, Huntington Preparative meeting informs that Benjamin Tomlinsons situation claiming the attention of this meeting he being a member of this society and heir to considerable property and so weak in mental capacity as to be incapable of taking the necessary care thereof which being considered it is thought best to nominate two friends to be appointed as trustees for him and his property
    Benjamin, 4-24-1817, comm. report re decision of Court, "Legal advice is that Benjamin Tomlinson may confer legal authority on suitable persons by himself under his hand and seal wherein their power will be as extensive & legal as though they were appointed by the court in case of a lunitick"
    Elizabeth, 5-14-1792, rocf Horsham MM for self and son Benjamin
    Elizabeth, 3-19-1806, rct Warrington MM for self and son Benjamin
    Elizabeth, 6-23-1808, rocf Warrington MM with son Benjamin
TOWNSEND, Benjamin, 11-13-1780, rep to QM 3 times thru 11-12-1781
    Benjamin, 9-10-1781, rct Concord MM
    Esther, 3-11-1782, child of Benjamin Townsend
    Hannah W., 4-22-1841, rocf New Garden MM, Chester Co, Pa
    Hannah W., 5-21-1845, rct Woodbury MM, NJ [w]
    Hannah W., 6-19-1845, gct Woodbury MM, NJ

MINUTES

TOWNSEND, James, 11-22-1843, compl of: mou on behalf of New Garden MM
    James, 3-29-1844, rocf New Garden MM
    Jessy, 3-11-1782, child of Benjamin Townsend
    John, 4-22-1841, rocf New Garden MM, Chester Co, Pa with daughter Mary Ann
    John, 4-21-1842, rep to MM
    John, 2-21-1850, gct York MM
    Liddia, 3-11-1782, child of Benjamin Townsend
    Martha B., 8-20-1884, rocf Baltimore MM as Minister [w]
    Mary, 5-21-1851, gct York MM
    Mary Ann, 4-22-1841, rocf New Garden MM, Chester Co, Pa with father John
    Mary Ann, 2-21-1850, resides within limits of York MM [w]
    Mary Ann, 4-25-1851, rct York MM [w]
    Rachel, 11-20-1861, compl of: separating from husband Warner Townsend [w]
    Rachel W., 1-19-1870, compl of: mou to John Day [w]
    Samuel, 11-18-1840, rocf Baltimore MM as Minister
    Samuel, 2-20-1845, rocf Baltimore MM as Minister
    Samuel, 2-20-1845, rocf Baltimore MM, Western District as Minister [w]
    Samuel, 8-22-1877, rocf Baltimore MM as Minister
    Sarah, 3-11-1782, child of Benjamin Townsend
    Sarah, 4-22-1841, rocf New Garden MM, Chester Co, Pa
    Sarah, 2-21-1850, resides within limits of York MM [w]
    Sarah, 4-25-1851, rct York MM [w]
    Sarah, 5-21-1851, gct York MM
    Warner, 11-22-1843, rocf New Garden MM
    Warner, 3-22-1848, compl of: mou
    Warner, 6-22-1848, read testimony. Retained
    Warner, 11-20-1861, compl of: separating from wife Rachel Townsend [w]
    Warner, 4-15-1863, compl of: unbecoming conduct. Filed for divorce
    Warner, 9-24-1863, ack wrongdoing. Retained
    Warner, 1-21-1864, dis: divorcing wife at court of law
    Warner, 2-18-1864, will appeal his case to QM
TUDOR, Elizabeth M., 9-22-1847, rocf Roaring Creek MM
    Isaac, 10-21-1819, rocf Plainfield MM, Ohio
    Isaac, 12-23-1824, rct Gunpowder MM
    Isaac, 8-18-1825, req marriage with Mary Garretson
    Isaac, 9-21-1825, rocf Gunpowder MM
    Isaac, 7-19-1826, rocf Gunpowder MM
    Isaac, 4-22-1830, appt Overseer
    Isaac, 2-23-1832, appt comm to list names re separation at BYM
    Isaac, 5-24-1832, appt Elder
    Isaac, 3-19-1834, appt Overseer
    Isaac, 8-20-1835, appt Overseer
    Isaac, 9-23-1835, appt Elder [w]
    Isaac, 10-18-1838, appt Overseer
    Isaac, 1-23-1839, appt Elder
    Isaac, 7-22-1840, appt Elder

MENALLEN MINUTES, MARRIAGES, & MISCELLANY

TUDOR, Isaac, 7-22-1840, declined appointment as Elder
    Isaac, 7-22-1840, req release as Elder [w]
    Isaac, 12-23-1841, appt Overseer
    Isaac, 2-24-1842, rct Centre MM for Joseph Russell, a minor
    Isaac, 2-24-1842, rct West Branch MM for John Russell, a minor
    Isaac, 5-18-1842, appt comm on military demands
    Isaac, 2-20-1845, appt Elder
    Isaac, 1-21-1852, appt Overseer
    Isaac, 8-20-1829, appt comm 77 times thru 3-17-1852
    Isaac, 8-20-1839, rep to QM 38 times thru 8-19-1852
    Isaac, 5-22-1833, rep to MM 61 times thru 12-23-1852
    Isaac, 2-24-1853, now deceased
    John, 8-22-1811, compl of: slaveholding; fighting
    John, 9-18-1811, complaint re slaveholding returned to Gunpowder MM
    John, 11-19-1817, req membership. Was disowned at Gunpowder MM
    John, 2-18-1819, rep to QM 3 times thru 1-17-1827
    John, 12-24-1818, appt comm 6 times thru 8-19-1824
    John, 5-24-1832, has been absent from meeting for some time
    John, Jr, 5-24-1832, has been absent from meeting for some time
    Lewis, 11-20-1850, compl of: marching with Oddfellows
    Martha, 1-23-1833, has separated from Hicksites at Menallen
    Martha, 2-19-1852, appt comm 3 times thru 11-18-1885 [w]
    Martha, 8-19-1885, rep to QM [w]
    Mary, 1-23-1839, appt Elder
    Mary, 9-18-1839, appt Overseer [w]
    Mary, 2-18-1841, appt Treasurer [w]
    Mary, 4-23-1835, appt comm 21 times thru 12-18-1851 [w]
    Mary, 5-21-1835, rep to QM 9 times thru 11-23-1853 [w]
    Phebe, 1-23-1833, has separated from Hicksites at Menallen
    Samuel, 5-24-1832, has been absent from meeting for some time
    Susan, 1-23-1833, has separated from Hicksites at Menallen
TUMBLESON, Benjamin, 6-24-1824, comm in his case report balance of $365.97 due him
    Benjamin, 8-23-1827, comm reports on settlement, "We of the committee appointed to settle with the trustees of Benjamin Tumbleson do report that we have attended to the appointment and find a balance of $247.02 of his funds remaining in the hands of Nicholas Wierman one of the trustees on the 10th day of the 5th mo last after deducting $178.60 for board and clothing for three years. Isaac Pearson, John Wright"
    Benjamin, 12-24-1829, comm apptd to examine into his situation and funds
    Benjamin, 8-18-1830, comm reports he is deceased
TYSON, C.J., 11-22-1882, appt comm
    Charles, 2-17-1886, rep to QM
    Charles, 7-20-1887, appt comm
    Charles Barclay, 4-18-1867, rct Byberry MM, Pa with father Isaac G. and family
    Charles J., 4-18-1861, rocf Philadelphia MM, Race St.
    Charles J., 3-17-1863, req marriage with Maria E. Griest

MINUTES

TYSON, Charles J., 1-22-1879, rep to MM 4 times thru 1-21-1885
    Charles J., 2-21-1883, appt to comm to plan and build new meeting house
    Charles J., 12-23-1885, assessed $3.50 for Yearly Meeting
    Charles J., 5-18-1887, assessed $3.00 for fuel for Ann and Martha Griest
    Charles J., 1-23-1878, appt comm 15 times thru 7-22-1890
    Charles J., 8-19-1875, rep to QM 11 times thru 8-20-1890
    Edwin C., 12-17-1884, appt comm
    Edwin C., 12-23-1885, assessed $1.00 for Yearly Meeting
    Edwin C., 2-17-1886, appt to Firstday School comm
    Edwin C., 2-24-1887, rct Westbury MM, NY to marry Mary W. Hawxhurst
    Edwin C., 3-23-1887, appt Trustee for Menallen and Huntington
    Edwin C., 12-17-1890, appt Treasurer
    Edwin C., 1-21-1891, declines to serve as Treasurer
    Edwin C., 1-21-1891, req release as Treasurer [w]
    Elizabeth, 9-22-1847, rct Roaring Creek MM with father William and family
    Isaac G., 11-19-1864, rocf Penns Grove MM with wife Rachel A. [w]
    Isaac G., 4-18-1867, rct Byberry MM, Pa with wife Rachel A. and 1 child
    Lewis, 6-20-1844, rocf York MM with father William and family
    Lewis, 9-22-1847, rct Roaring Creek MM with father William and family
    Maria E., 8-18-1869, appt assistant clerk [w]
    Maria E., 1-17-1877, appt clerk [w]
    Maria E., 4-17-1878, appt clerk [w]
    Maria E., 11-17-1869, rep to MM 16 times thru 2-18-1885 [w]
    Maria E., 5-17-1869, rep to QM 20 times thru 9-21-1890 [w]
    Maria E., 1-19-1870, appt comm 23 times thru 10-22-1890 [w]
    Mary A., 7-18-1888, ack mou to Zachariah A. Peters. Retained [w]
    Mary Cook, 2-19-1846, appt comm [w]
    Mary Jane, 6-20-1844, rocf York MM with husband William and 2 children
    Mary Jane, 8-22-1844, appt Minister
    Mary Jane, 8-22-1844, frequently appears as Minister [w]
    Mary Jane, 2-20-1845, rep to QM [w]
    Mary Jane, 8-22-1844, appt comm 7 times thru 2-19-1846 [w]
    Mary Jane, 9-22-1847, rct Roaring Creek MM with husband William and 3 children
    Mary W., 10-19-1887, rocf Westbury MM, NY. Formerly Hawxhurst
    Rachel A., 11-19-1864, rocf Penns Grove MM with husband Isaac G. [w]
    Rachel A., 4-18-1867, rct Byberry MM, Pa with husband Isaac G. and 1 child
    Robert, 6-20-1844, rocf York MM with father William and family
    Robert, 9-22-1847, rct Roaring Creek MM with father William and family
    William, 6-20-1844, rocf York MM with wife Mary Jane and 2 children
    William, 8-22-1844, rep to MM 3 times thru 6-24-1847
    William, 5-19-1847, appt comm
    William, 9-22-1847, rct Roaring Creek MM with wife Mary Jane and 3 children

MENALLEN MINUTES, MARRIAGES, & MISCELLANY

UNDERWOOD, Alex, 4-17-1889, appt comm to raise money to repair Warrington Meeting House
Alfred J., 9-20-1883, rocf Center MM with father Reuben L. and family
Alvina, 12-18-1834, rct Centre MM with husband William and 1 child
Amanda, 12-18-1834, rct Centre MM with father William and family
Charles, 9-21-1796, req marriage with Hannah Everitt
Edward R., 9-20-1883, rocf Center MM with father Reuben L. and family
Eli G., 9-20-1883, rocf Center MM with father Reuben L. and family
Emeline, 2-18-1885, rep to QM 4 times thru 8-18-1886 [w]
Emiline, 9-20-1883, rocf Center MM with husband Reuben L. and 7 children
Emmeline, 4-23-1884, appt comm [w]
George, 11-19-1817, rocf Warrington MM. Minor child of Chas and Hanah
Hanah, 3-19-1817, committee reports on her condition: "We the committee appointed to inspect into the circumstances of Hanah Underwood having made inspection agree to report that we find she has resided a considerable time within the verge of this meeting but says she must remove this spring from where she now is & knows not where also it appears she has no property to support her & her children within the verge of this meeting but her own labour—she expects something at York but cannot ascertain how much"
Hanah, 4-24-1817, certificate returned to Warrington MM
Hannah, 2-23-1797, rct Warrington MM
Hannah, 1-22-1817, wife of Charles Underwood req to be received
Hannah, 8-21-1834, compl of: mou. Now Myers. Disowned
Ida J., 9-20-1883, rocf Center MM with father Reuben L. and family
Isaac, 11-19-1817, rocf Warrington MM. Minor child of Chas and Hanah
John, 11-19-1817, rocf Warrington MM. Minor child of Chas and Hanah
John, 8-24-1826, compl of: mou
John, 8-21-1889, req membership
John, 10-23-1889, req membership [w]
Lydia, 5-20-1807, compl of: mou to first cousin. Formerly Beals
Martha, 10-20-1834, now Yenke. Has separated from Hicksites
Miles W., 9-20-1883, rocf Center MM with father Reuben L. and family
Owen L., 9-20-1883, rocf Center MM with father Reuben L. and family
Reuben, 4-23-1884, appt comm 3 times thru 1-20-1886
Reuben, 8-20-1884, rep to QM 5 times thru 8-18-1886
Reuben, 12-23-1885, assessed $1.00 for Yearly Meeting
Reuben, 1-20-1886, rep to MM
Reuben, 5-18-1887, assessed $1.00 for fuel for Ann and Martha Griest
Reuben L., 9-20-1883, rocf Center MM with wife Emiline and 7 children
Reuben L., 11-19-1884, appt comm
Reuben L., 11-18-1885, appt assistant clerk
Reuben L., 4-18-1888, appt comm
Susanna, 12-21-1815, rct Deer Creek MM in Md
William, 8-18-1831, rocf Warrington MM

MINUTES

UNDERWOOD, William, 4-18-1833, req marriage with Alvina Griest
    William, 1-22-1834, compl of: partiality in distribution to creditors
    William, 12-18-1834, read testimony. Retained
    William, 12-18-1834, rct Centre MM with wife Alvina and 1 child
    William A., 9-20-1883, rocf Center MM with father Reuben L. and family
UPDEGRAFF, Ambrose, 11-11-1782, req marriage with Elizabeth Cookson
    Elizabeth, 1-13-1783, rct Warrington MM
    Joseph, 4-14-1788, appt comm
    Sarah, 1-20-1819, rct Short Creek MM, Ohio
VAIL, Phebe, 3-19-1828, req marriage with Eli Cookson
VALE, Edith, 4-20-1848, rocf York MM with husband Elisha and 4 children
    Edith, 1-19-1849, appt comm 11 times thru 12-23-1852 [w]
    Edith, 11-21-1849, rep to QM 4 times thru 2-19-1857 [w]
    Elisha, 4-20-1848, rocf York MM with wife Edith and 4 children
    Elisha, 6-22-1848, rep to MM 5 times thru 4-18-1850
    Elisha, 9-20-1848, appt comm 4 times thru 4-18-1850
    Elisha, 11-21-1849, rep to QM
    Eliza, 10-18-1810, rocf Warrington MM with father Robert, Jr and family
    Eliza, 8-19-1813, rct Warrington with father Robert and family
    Emme, 8-22-1888, absent member [w]
    Gulielma, 4-20-1848, rocf York MM with father Elisha and family
    Isaac, 8-19-1813, rct Warrington with father Robert and family
    Joseph, 4-20-1848, rocf York MM with father Elisha and family
    Joshua, 7-18-1888, now in Iowa
    Josiah, 4-20-1848, rocf York MM with father Elisha and family
    Martha, 10-18-1810, rocf Warrington MM with husband Robert, Jr and 1 child
    Martha, 8-19-1813, rct Warrington with husband Robert and 3 children
    Mary G., 8-22-1888, absent member [w]
    Oliver, 7-18-1888, son of Joshua Vale. Now in Iowa
    Portia, 8-22-1888, absent member. Now in Promise City, Iowa [w]
    Rebecca, 4-20-1848, rocf York MM with father Elisha and family
    Robert, 8-19-1813, rct Warrington with wife Martha and 3 children
    Robert, Jr, 10-18-1810, rocf Warrington MM with wife Martha and 1 child
    Sarah, 11-22-1876, rep to QM [w]
    Sarah C., 8-19-1864, rep to QM [w]
    Sarah C., 1-18-1882, rep to MM [w]
    Sarah E., 1-21-1863, rep to MM 15 times thru 1-20-1886 [w]
    Sarah E., 3-22-1882, appt comm 8 times thru 10-18-1888 [w]
    Sarah E., 11-21-1877, rep to QM 8 times thru 8-21-1889 [w]
    Susanna, 8-19-1813, rct Warrington with father Robert and family
VANCE, Ann, 11-10-1783, compl of: mou. Formerly Todd
    Ann, 1-12-1784, dis: mou. Formerly Todd
VANCISE, Edwin, 10-22-1846, rep to MM
    Edwin, 4-19-1860, gct Prairie Grove MM, Iowa with father Edwin and family
    Edwin G., 6-23-1836, rep to MM 6 times thru 8-19-1853

MENALLEN MINUTES, MARRIAGES, & MISCELLANY

VANCISE, Edwin G., 2-23-1837, req marriage with Maria M. Garretson
    Edwin G., 8-24-1837, rep to QM 3 times thru 8-23-1855
    Edwin G., 2-21-1839, clerk for the day
    Edwin G., 10-19-1842, appt comm
    Edwin G., 5-23-1849, appt to record Marriage Certificates
    Edwin G., 4-21-1853, appt comm
    Edwin G., 4-19-1860, gct Prairie Grove MM, Iowa with wife Maria and 6 children
    Edwin Griest, 7-22-1835, req membership
    Elizabeth G., 5-23-1860, gct Prairie Grove MM, Iowa
    Isaac Pearson, 4-19-1860, gct Prairie Grove MM, Iowa with father Edwin and family
    Joel G., 4-19-1860, gct Prairie Grove MM, Iowa with father Edwin and family
    Lavinia, 5-23-1860, gct Prairie Grove MM, Iowa
    Maria, 4-19-1860, gct Prairie Grove MM, Iowa with husband Edwin and 6 children
    Maria Louisa, 4-19-1860, gct Prairie Grove MM, Iowa with father Edwin and family
    Orson Fowler, 4-19-1860, gct Prairie Grove MM, Iowa with father Edwin and family
    Teresa Emma, 4-19-1860, gct Prairie Grove MM, Iowa with father Edwin and family
VANSCYOC, Benjamin W., 10-25-1845, req marriage with Priscilla Allen
    Benjamin W., 9-23-1846, rct Baltimore MM with wife Priscilla
    Benjamin W., 3-17-1847, rocf Baltimore MM with family
    Priscilla, 9-23-1846, rct Baltimore MM with husband Benjamin W.
    Susan, 11-18-1846, gct Baltimore MM with father Benjamin J. and mother
VANSHRYOC, Hepsibah, 8-19-1858, rep to QM [w]
VOAR, Benjamin, 6-12-1786, rct Warrington MM with father Peter and family
    Bettee, 6-12-1786, rct Warrington MM with husband Peter and 2 children
    Betty, 8-11-1783, rocf Warrington MM with husband Peter
    Gideon, 1-15-1787, rocf Warrington MM with father Jesse and mother
    Gideon, 1-15-1787, gct York MM with father Jesse and mother
    Jesse, 1-15-1787, rocf Warrington MM with wife Lidia and 1 child
    Jesse, 1-15-1787, gct York MM with wife Lidia and son Gideon
    Joseph, 6-12-1786, rct Warrington MM with father Peter and family
    Lidia, 1-15-1787, rocf Warrington MM with husband Jesse and 1 child
    Lidia, 1-15-1787, gct York MM with husband Jesse and son Gideon
    Peter, 8-11-1783, rocf Warrington MM with wife Betty
    Peter, 6-12-1786, rct Warrington MM with wife Bettee and 2 children
VORE, Hannah, 6-9-1794, rocf Warrington MM with father Jesse and family
    Jesse, 6-9-1794, rocf Warrington MM with wife Lydia and 4 children
    Jesse, 6-9-1794, rocf Warrington MM with father Jesse and family
    Josiah, 6-9-1794, rocf Warrington MM with father Jesse and family
    Lydia, 6-9-1794, rocf Warrington MM with husband Jesse and 4 children
    Thomas, 6-9-1794, rocf Warrington MM with father Jesse and family

MINUTES

WAHLEY, Charlotte V., 6-22-1876, req membership. Born 5-23-1873 [w]
WALHAY, Mary G., 5-21-1890, req membership be discontinued [w]
    Rachel, 11-21-1866, ack mou. Retained. Formerly Wright [w]
    Rachel, 5-21-1890, req membership be discontinued [w]
    Rachel T., 11-21-1866, ack mou. Retained. Formerly Wright
WALHEY, Charlotte J., 6-22-1876, minor child of one member. Born 5th mo 23rd 1873
    Emma G., 6-22-1876, minor child of one member. Born 11th mo 11th 1869
    Emma G., 6-22-1876, req membership. Born 10-11-1869 [w]
    Mary G., 6-22-1876, minor child of one member. Born 8th mo 22nd 1867
WALHEY, Mary G., 6-22-1876, req membership. Born 8-22-1867 [w]
WALKER, Abel, 2-19-1824, req membership
    Abel, 7-21-1824, req membership for two minor children
    Abel, 2-22-1827, appt Overseer
    Abel, 12-18-1828, appt assistant clerk
    Abel, 2-19-1835, rep to MM 9 times thru 1-17-1838
    Abel, 6-24-1824, appt comm 20 times thru 1-17-1838
    Abel, 2-24-1825, rep to QM 15 times thru 2-22-1844
    Abel, 2-18-1874, rct Baltimore MM, Western District
    Abner, 9-23-1807, req marriage with Sarah Harris
    Anna, 7-20-1825, rocf Warrington MM with mother Sarah and family
    Anna, 5-23-1827, rct Dennings Creek MM with mother and family
    Arnold, 7-21-1824, req membership thru parents Abel and Margaret
    Arnold, 7-20-1842, compl of: military training
    Arnold B., 4-20-1843, dis: military training to avoid fine
    Asahel, 8-18-1864, rep to MM 3 times thru 5-17-1871
    Barbara H., 7-20-1825, rocf Warrington MM with mother Sarah and family
    Barbara H., 5-23-1827, rct Dennings Creek MM with mother and family
    Benjamin, 4-14-1788, appt comm
    Benjamin, 4-19-1821, rocf Warrington MM. Son of Abel
    Benjamin, 9-20-1826, roc. Son of Abner
    Benjamin H., 5-23-1827, rct Dennings Creek MM with mother and family
    Beulah, 5-23-1827, rct Dennings Creek MM with mother and family
    Bulah, 7-20-1825, rocf Warrington MM with mother Sarah and family
    Edward S., 2-22-1866, compl of: joined Methodists
    Edward S., 4-19-1866, dis: joined Methodists
    Elizabeth, 11-22-1815, rocf Warrington MM with mother Mary
    Elizabeth, 1-21-1818, rct Warrington MM thru mother Mary
    Elizabeth G., 3-20-1850, read testimony. Retained
    Elizabeth J., 3-18-1874, rct Baltimore MM [w]
    Elizabeth J., 4-22-1874, gct Baltimore MM
    Elizabeth Jane, 3-21-1850, ack error. Retained [w]
    Isaac, 11-22-1815, rocf Warrington MM with mother Mary
    Isaac, 1-21-1818, rct Warrington MM thru mother Mary
    Isaac, 2-20-1840, rocf Warrington MM. Too much time has passed

MENALLEN MINUTES, MARRIAGES, & MISCELLANY

WALKER, Isaac, 8-21-1862, formerly of Warrington, now removed from this area [w]
    Joshua, 8-21-1862, formerly of Warrington, now removed from this area [w]
    Louisa, 3-18-1874, rct Baltimore MM [w]
    Louise, 4-22-1874, gct Baltimore MM
    Margaret, 4-22-1824, req membership
    Margaret, 7-21-1824, req membership for two minor children
    Margaret, 3-22-1837, appt comm [w]
    Margaret, 8-24-1837, rep to QM [w]
    Margaret Ann, 2-22-1866, compl of: non-attendance; joining another society [w]
    Mary, 11-22-1815, rocf Warrington MM with 2 children
    Mary, 1-21-1818, rct Warrington MM for self and 2 children
    Rebecca H., 7-20-1825, rocf Warrington MM with mother Sarah and family
    Rebekah H., 5-23-1827, rct Dennings Creek MM with mother and family
    Ruth, 5-23-1827, rct Dennings Creek MM with mother and family
    Ruthanna, 7-20-1825, rocf Warrington MM with mother Sarah and family
    Sarah, 7-20-1825, rocf Warrington MM with 6 children
    Sarah, 7-20-1825, rocf Warrington MM with mother Sarah and family
    Sarah, 5-23-1827, rct Dennings Creek MM with 7 children
    Sarah, 5-23-1827, rct Dennings Creek MM with mother and family
    William, 7-21-1824, req membership thru parents Abel and Margaret
    William, 12-23-1847, rep to QM
    William J., 2-24-1848, rep to QM
    William J., 12-21-1848, rep to MM
    William J., 2-22-1849, rep to MM
    William J., 9-19-1849, read testimony. Retained
    William J., 12-20-1849, rep to MM
WALTON, Emma, 8-22-1888, absent member. Now in Oketo, Kan [w]
    Mary, 2-19-1818, rocf Byberry MM as Minister
WAR, Samuel, 5-17-1797, appt comm
WATSON, James, 3-11-1782, rep to QM 4 times thru 3-18-1784
    James, 4-9-1781, appt comm 23 times thru 1-10-1785
    James, 1-9-1792, rct Exeter MM for self and wife
WAY, Alice, 1-20-1819, rct Short Creek MM, Ohio
    David, 6-9-1794, rocf Warrington MM with father Samuel and family
    Hannah, 6-9-1794, rocf Warrington MM with husband Samuel and 5 children
    Hannah, 6-9-1794, rocf Warrington MM with father Samuel and family
    James, 6-9-1794, rocf Warrington MM with father Samuel and family
    Mary, 11-10-1794, rocf Warrington MM
    Mary, 8-20-1801, compl of: uncharitable to woman in their care
    Mary, 6-23-1803, read testimony. Retained
    Robert, 6-9-1794, rocf Warrington MM with father Samuel and family
    Samuel, 6-9-1794, rocf Warrington MM with wife Hannah and 5 children

MINUTES

WAY, Samuel, 6-9-1794, rocf Warrington MM with father Samuel and family
    Samuel, 5-17-1797, appt comm 5 times thru 6-24-1802
    Samuel, 2-20-1800, rep to QM
    Samuel, 10-22-1818, req marriage with Alice Blackburn
WEBB, Leah, 2-21-1850, compl of: mou and removing to Salem; formerly Wright [w]
    Leah, 8-19-1850, ack error. Retained as member of Salem MM [w]
    Leah, 10-24-1850, gct Salem MM, Ohio
WELSH, Julia, 12-20-1832, compl of: mou. Formerly Everitt
WHITE, Nathaniel, Jr, 11-12-1787, asst clerk at Hopewell MM
WHITSON, Jane, 5-17-1882, rep to QM [w]
    Jane C., 5-18-1881, rep to MM 6 times thru 11-11-1882 [w]
    Jane C., 5-18-1881, rep to QM [w]
    Jane C., 2-22-1882, rep to QM [w]
    Jane C., 2-22-1882, appt comm 3 times thru 1-17-1883 [w]
    Viola, 8-17-1881, rocf Sadsbury MM, Lancaster Co with father William [w]
    Viola, 1-18-1888, req marriage with Hadley Kent [w]
    W., 11-22-1882, appt comm
    W., 6-18-1885, rep to MM
    W., 2-24-1887, rep to QM
    William, 9-21-1876, req marriage with Jane C. Wright
    William, 9-21-1876, req membership with Jane C. Wright [w]
    William, 10-18-1876, rocf Sadsbury MM, Lancaster Co, Pa
    William, 8-17-1881, rocf Sadsbury MM with daughter Viola
    William, 8-17-1881, rocf Sadsbury MM, Bart, Lancaster Co with daughter Viola [w]
    William, 2-22-1882, appt Overseer
    William, 2-21-1883, appt to comm to plan and build new meeting house
    William, 12-17-1884, appt Overseer
    William, 12-23-1885, assessed $2.50 for Yearly Meeting
    William, 5-17-1882, rep to MM 27 times thru 5-19-1886
    William, 11-17-1886, appt comm to aid Ann and Martha Griest
    William, 5-18-1887, assessed $2.00 for fuel for Ann and Martha Griest
    William, 5-23-1888, appt Elder [w]
    William, 2-22-1882, rep to QM 13 times thru 5-21-1890
    William, 6-19-1890, clerk for the day
    William, 7-22-1890, appt Overseer
    William, 3-22-1882, appt comm 22 times thru 8-20-1890
WICKERSHAM, Josiah, 4-22-1852, rocf Warrington MM with wife Lydia and 1 child
    Lydia, 4-22-1852, rocf Warrington MM with husband Josiah and 1 child [w]
    Mary, 8-21-1862, rep to MM 3 times thru 12-21-1864 [w]
    Mary Ann, 4-21-1864, appt comm [w]
    Robert, 8-23-1882, rep to QM
    Robert, 8-23-1882, appt comm
    Robert A., 4-22-1852, rocf Warrington MM with parents Josiah and Lydia [w]

MENALLEN MINUTES, MARRIAGES, & MISCELLANY

WICKERSHAM, Robert A., 9-24-1885, req marriage with Mary R. Walker
    Robert A., 9-24-1885, gct Hopewell MM, Frederick Co, Va to marry M. Walker
    Robert A., 12-23-1885, assessed $3.50 for Yearly Meeting
    Thomas, 9-22-1841, rocf Briddleton MM, Ohio as Minister
    Thomas, 9-22-1841, rocf Beaver Falls MM, Ohio as Minister [w]
WIDEMIER, Ruth, 9-18-1839, rct West Branch MM, Clearfield Co, Pa [w]
    Gideon, 5-22-1839, req marriage with Ruth Russell
    Gideon, 6-20-1839, rocf West Branch MM
WIERMAN, Adaliza, 5-21-1856, compl of: illegitimate child [w]
    Adaliza, 6-19-1856, ack error. Retained [w]
    Adaliza S., 6-19-1856, ack breach of discipline. Retained
    Alexander, 11-20-1822, req marriage with Mary Hussey
    Alfred A., 2-23-1860, read testimony. Retained
    Amy, 6-22-1837, roc
    Catherine, 4-9-1781, mou: now Newlon
    Daniel, 10-18-1821, compl of: non-attendance; refuses to settle dispute
    Daniel, 12-23-1830, compl of: mou
    Daniel, 8-18-1831, disowned
    Deborah, 4-14-1794, compl of: unchastity. Now Maxwell
    Deborah, 7-14-1794, dis: unchastity. Now Maxwell
    Eliza, 6-22-1837, roc
    Eliza, 12-18-1851, req membership [w]
    Eliza, 2-19-1852, req membership
    Elizabeth, 6-18-1857, compl of: mou. Formerly Hewitt [w]
    Emma, 6-11-1787, compl of: marrying 1st cousin, Joseph Cox
    Esther Mira, 5-17-1837, rct Putnam Co, Ill with father William C. and family
    Gartrude, 8-15-1785, compl of: dancing
    Gartrude, 6-11-1787, dis: dancing
    George, 5-22-1850, appt comm
    H., 1-20-1847, read testimony. Retained
    Hannah, 6-14-1790, appt Elder
    Hannah, 3-22-1815, req marriage with Daniel Gibbons
    Hannah, 6-20-1833, now Bonen, reports she has separated from Hicksite
    Hannah, 10-20-1842, compl of: mou. Now Gitt [w]
    Hannah M., 12-23-1858, gct Clear Creek MM, Putman Co, Ill
    Harman, 4-21-1803, req marriage with Mary Hammond
    Harman, 1-21-1818, appt comm 8 times thru 3-21-1832
    Harman, 2-18-1819, rep to QM 6 times thru 11-17-1830
    Harman, 11-21-1821, compl of: mou
    Harman, 2-21-1822, read testimony. Retained
    Harman, 12-18-1823, appt Trustee for deeds and property at Menallen and Huntington
    Harman, 2-19-1829, appt Trustee of Mary Pearson's Estate, she being incapable of taking care of herself
    Harman, 6-21-1838, has title papers for Huntington in his care
    Harman, 12-20-1838, compl of: wagering
    Harman, 1-23-1839, read testimony. Retained

MINUTES

WIERMAN, Harman, 11-18-1846, compl of: drinking, non-attendance at meeting
Henry, 2-12-1781, appt comm 9 times thru 6-13-1785
Henry, 5-14-1781, rep to QM 3 times thru 11-12-1781
Henry, 7-15-1782, appt Overseer at Huntington to replace John Garretson
Henry, 9-12-1785, released as Overseer at Huntington
Henry, 10-11-1790, compl of: non-attendance; muster; drinking to excess
Henry, Jr, 11-13-1780, appt comm 3 times thru 3-12-1787
Henry, Jr, 1-10-1791, dis: non-attendance; drinking to excess
Henry, Sr, 10-9-1780, compl of
Henry, Sr, 11-13-1780, disowned: "Whereas Henry Wierman has had a Right of Membership amongst us the People called Quakers, but for want of attention to that which would preserve from erring gave way so far as to be guilty of uncharitable conduct to people passing through his land to dig a grave in a time of deep snow; and in the 8th month last he took a woman into his house to whom he said he was married in the 3rd month and he produced two papers signed by him and the Woman, expressive of taking each other for husband and wife but neither of the papers witnessed; and he said that some time after they for some reasons went to a Minister and got their marriage confirmed; for which reproachful conduct we disown him the said Henry Wierman from being any longer a member of our Religious Society untill he is favoured with a True sense of his outgoing and condemn the same which is desired on his behalf"
Isaac, 1-20-1802, compl of: quarrelling and fighting
Isaac, 2-18-1802, read testimony. Retained
Isaac, 2-20-1806, req marriage with Susanna Comley
Isaac, 1-19-1820, appt comm
Isaac, 2-24-1820, rep to QM
Isaac, 1-22-1851, compl of: improper intercourse with Jane Plowden
Isaac, 2-20-1851, dis: improper conduct
Isaac Everitt, 5-24-1832, has been absent from meeting for some time
J. W., 12-20-1882, rep to MM
Jacob B., 7-20-1853, rep to MM
Jane, 6-23-1796, rocf Warrington MM
Jesse, 12-22-1853, rep to MM
Joel, 10-20-1814, req marriage with Hannah Hussey
Joel, 12-23-1830, rct Burlington MM, NJ to marry Lydia S. Lundy
Joel, 3-23-1836, appt Trustee for Menallen and Huntington properties
Joel, 3-21-1849, compl of in difficult case
Joel, 7-18-1849, accuses another member of lying and cheating
Joel, 1-21-1818, appt comm 23 times thru 1-17-1855
Joel, 2-20-1823, rep to QM 12 times thru 11-19-1856
Joel, 3-20-1833, rep to MM 39 times thru 2-19-1857
Joel, 5-22-1857, rct Sadsbury MM, Lancaster Co, Pa with wife Lydia S.
John, 5-17-1809, compl of: mou
John, 7-19-1809, dis: mou

MENALLEN MINUTES, MARRIAGES, & MISCELLANY

WIERMAN, John, 1-22-1823, compl of: mou
    John, 6-19-1823, read testimony. Retained
    John, 3-18-1840, removed to Stark Co, Ohio without certificate
    John W., 4-19-1882, rep to MM 16 times thru 3-18-1885
    Jos., 12-20-1860, rep to MM
    Joseph, 8-24-1820, compl of: non-attendance; attending muster
    Joseph, 1-17-1821, read testimony. Retained
    Joseph, 8-23-1827, compl of: mou
    Joseph, 10-18-1827, read testimony. Retained
    Joseph, 5-19-1853, appt Overseer in place of Isaac Tudor, deceased
    Joseph, 8-19-1853, rep to QM 6 times thru 2-23-1860
    Joseph, 3-22-1854, appt comm 4 times thru 7-20-1864
    Joseph, 4-19-1855, appt Overseer
    Joseph, 7-22-1857, appt Overseer
    Joseph, 7-18-1860, appt Overseer
    Joseph, 1-18-1854, rep to MM 35 times thru 10-23-1862
    Joseph, 6-23-1864, appt Overseer
    Lucretia M., 12-23-1858, gct Clear Creek MM, Putman Co, Ill
    Lydia, 1-23-1833, has separated from Hicksites at Menallen
    Lydia, 1-22-1845, rct Md & Va slave holders as Minister [w]
    Lydia, 1-20-1847, on comm against settling new meeting at Mechanicsville
    Lydia, 4-19-1855, appt comm [w]
    Lydia G., 1-23-1863, ack mou. Retained. Now Ickes
    Lydia S., 9-22-1852, named Minister [w]
    Lydia S., 9-21-1836, appt comm 29 times 6-19-1856 [w]
    Lydia S., 11-18-1840, rep to QM 13 times thru 11-21-1856 [w]
    Lydia S., 5-22-1857, rct Sadsbury MM, Lancaster Co, Pa with husband Joel
    Martha M., 2-23-1860, ack mou. Retained. Now Lishy [w]
    Mary, 4-14-1794, req marriage with Joseph Griest, Jr
    Mary, 2-19-1818, req marriage with Isaac Pearson
    Mary, 3-17-1824, req marriage with William Wilson
    Mary, 2-23-1826, compl of: fornication
    Mary, 4-24-1834, compl of: became mother of illegitimate child
    Mary Jane, 1-22-1851, compl of: attended a marriage out of order [w]
    Mary Jane, 6-19-1851, compl of: mou. Formerly Griffith [w]
    Mary Jane, 7-23-1851, ack error. Retained [w]
    Mary Jane, 5-18-1853, rct White Water MM, Richmond, Ind [w]
    Mary Jane, 6-25-1853, gct Whitewater MM, Ind
    Matilda, 6-20-1844, compl of: mou. Now Neely [w]
    Nicholas, 10-13-1795, rct Warrington MM for marriage with Jane Underwood
    Nicholas, 8-22-1816, rep to QM
    Nicholas, 5-21-1817, appt Guardian by and for Benjamin Tomlinson
    Nicholas, 2-22-1821, rep to QM
    Nicholas, 9-10-1787, appt comm 10 times thru 10-23-1823
    Nicholas, 5-24-1832, has been absent from meeting for some time
    Nicholas, 4-18-1850, compl of: mou; non-attendance
    Nicholas, 8-22-1850, dis: has joined Orthodox Friends

MINUTES

WIERMAN, Nicholas, Jr, 5-24-1832, has been absent from meeting for some time
    Phebe, 10-23-1817, req marriage with William Wright
    Phebe, 7-22-1829, compl of: mou. Now Phebe Day
    Phebe, 1-23-1833, has separated from Hicksites at Menallen
    Phebe, 12-23-1858, gct Clear Creek MM, Putman Co, Ill
    Priscilla, 9-19-1798, dis: unchastity, bore child in unmarried state
    Priscilla, 6-21-1798, compl of: unchastity; bore child in unmarried state
    Sarah, 8-22-1816, compl of: mou. Now Cox
    Sarah, 8-21-1817, appt Elder
    Sarah, 2-18-1836, rep to QM 3 times thru 8-23-1849 [w]
    Sarah, 6-22-1837, roc
    Sarah, 1-22-1845, req membership thru foster parents Jesse Cook and wife [w]
    Sarah, 5-21-1863, compl of: mou. Now Peters
    Sarah, 7-22-1863, dis: mou. Now Peters
    Sarah C., 1-22-1845, req membership thru guardians, Jesse and Rebecca Cook
    Sarah Catherine, 5-17-1837, rct Putnam Co, Ill with father William C. and family
    Sarah, Jr, 6-22-1837, roc
    Stephen, 4-18-1850, compl of: mou; non-attendance
    Susanna, 11-23-1808, compl of: mou. Now Studibecker
    Susanna, 12-22-1808, dis: mou. Now Studibecker
    Susanna, 1-23-1839, appt Elder
    Susanna, 10-20-1842, appt Overseer [w]
    Susanna M., 5-17-1837, rct Putnam Co, Ill with husband William C. and 3 children
    Susannah, 3-23-1808, req marriage with Samuel Comley
    Susannah, 1-23-1833, has separated from Hicksites at Menallen
    Susannah, 11-22-1842, rep to QM [w]
    Susannah, 8-24-1843, rep to QM [w]
    Thomas, 11-17-1819, compl of: mou
    Thomas, 2-24-1820, read testimony. Retained
    Thomas, 7-19-1820, read testimony. Retained
    Thomas, 5-18-1825, compl of: mou
    Thomas, 3-18-1840, removed to Delaware Co, Ind without certificate
    Thomas T., 12-24-1840, compl of: mou
    Thomas T., 6-23-1842, disowned
    William, 10-15-1787, appt Overseer at Huntington
    William, 11-12-1787, appt Elder at Huntington
    William, 5-12-1788, rct Fairfax to accompany Isaac Everitt
    William, 7-14-1788, returned cert endorsed by Westland MM and Fairfax QM
    William, 4-12-1790, dis: mou and attending muster. Son of Henry
    William, 3-23-1797, released as Elder and Overseer at Monallin
    William, 4-22-1802, appt to prepare memorial for Isaac Everitt, deceased
    William, 1-19-1803, compl of: attending muster. Son of Henry
    William, 2-24-1803, appt Overseer at Huntington

MENALLEN MINUTES, MARRIAGES, & MISCELLANY

WIERMAN, William, 3-23-1803, read testimony. Retained
    William, 11-23-1803, compl of: non-attendance; dancing; aiding elopement
    William, 4-19-1804, dis: non-attendance; dancing; aiding elopement
    William, 7-18-1804, appt clerk
    William, 1-19-1814, appt Overseer at Huntington
    William, 6-23-1814, appt overseer of Burials at Huntington
    William, 1-22-1817, retained as Overseer
    William, 8-21-1817, appt Elder
    William, 9-18-1822, appt Overseer
    William, 11-19-1823, appt to have care of Huntington PM books
    William, 8-18-1825, appt Overseer
    William, 12-22-1825, appt caretaker for Thomas Mickle
    William, 11-13-1780, appt comm 227 times thru 2-23-1832
    William, 11-13-1780, rep to QM 43 times thru 8-21-1834
    William, 2-19-1835, rep to MM 4 times thru 12-22-1836
    William, 3-18-1840, removed to Stark Co, Ohio without certificate
    William, 7-20-1842, compl of: military training
    William C., 12-20-1832, req marriage with Susanna Maria Lundy
    William C., 8-22-1833, rep to MM 3 times thru 10-20-1836
    William C., 5-17-1837, rct Putnam Co, Ill with wife Susanna M. and 3 children
    William H., 10-19-1842, read testimony. Retained
    William, Jr, 5-15-1786, rep to QM 9 times thru 2-23-1815
    William, Jr, 4-19-1821, appt Overseer in place of Jesse Russell
    William, Sr, 12-13-1784, appt comm 15 times thru 11-13-1786
    William, Sr, 12-11-1786, appt Guardian of Samuel Hutton's orphan children
WILKES, Lydia, 11-22-1820, rct Warrington MM
WILLIAMS, Israel, 5-14-1787, rocf Warrington MM
    Israel, 12-10-1787, compl of: fornication
    Israel, 2-11-1788, dis: fornication
    Jane, 6-9-1788, rct Pipe Creek MM
    Ruth, 11-9-1795, rocf Warrington MM
    Ruth, 8-23-1798, compl of: mou. Now Adams
    Ruth, 11-21-1798, dis: mou. Now Adams
WILLIAMSON, Mary, 6-14-1784, compl of: mou to 1st cousin; unchastity. Formerly Delap
    Mary, 7-12-1784, dis: mou to 1st cousin; unchastity. Formerly Delap
WILLSON, Benjamin, 5-14-1794, appt comm
    George, 4-19-1798, req marriage with Sarah Wright
WILSON, Alice, 9-19-1804, req marriage with John Wright, son of John
    Benjamin, 5-13-1793, rep to QM 3 times thru 11-9-1795
    Benjamin, 10-13-1795, appt Overseer at Monallin
    Benjamin, 4-10-1799, released as Overseer at Monallin
    Benjamin, 5-10-1790, appt comm 37 times thru 6-18-1801
    Benjamin, 8-19-1802, appt Guardian of heirs of William McGrail, deceased
    Benjamin, 5-24-1832, has been absent from meeting for some time
    George, 6-22-1815, appt Trustee for Joseph Hutton

MINUTES

WILSON, George, 7-19-1815, appt recorder of Marriage Certificates
    George, 1-22-1817, appt Overseer
    George, 3-19-1817, appt comm re Hanah Underwood
    George, 6-19-1817, appt clerk
    George, 8-21-1817, appt Elder
    George, 10-23-1817, appt Elder
    George, 6-18-1818, appt clerk
    George, 5-19-1819, appt Overseer
    George, 7-21-1819, appt clerk
    George, 4-20-1820, rct Centre MM as Minister, with Ruth McMilin
    George, 7-19-1820, appt clerk
    George, 12-18-1823, appt Trustee of deeds and property at Menallen
        and Huntington
    George, 8-22-1811, rep to QM 18 times thru 11-23-1825
    George, 4-19-1827, appt to settle with Benjamin Tumbleson's trustees
    George, 4-9-1781, appt comm 89 times thru 5-23-1827
    George, 5-24-1832, has been absent from meeting for some time
    John, 6-23-1796, rocf Hopewell MM with wife Margaret and 1 child
    John, 6-23-1796, rct Warrington MM with wife Margaret and 1 child
    John, 5-24-1832, has been absent from meeting for some time
    Margaret, 9-15-1783, rct Warrington MM
    Margaret, 2-9-1784, lost cert
    Margaret, 6-23-1796, rocf Hopewell MM with husband John and 1 child
    Margaret, 6-23-1796, rct Warrington MM with husband John and 1
        child
    Mary, 1-22-1812, compl of: fornication
    Mary, 4-23-1812, dis: fornication
    Mary, 7-21-1819, read testimony. Retained
    Mary, 1-23-1833, has separated from Hicksites at Menallen
    Mary, Sr, 1-23-1833, has separated from Hicksites at Menallen
    Ruth, 2-10-1794, compl of: unchastity, had child in unmarried state
    Ruth, 4-14-1794, dis: unchastity, bore child in unmarried state
    Ruth, 1-23-1833, has separated from Hicksites at Menallen
    Sarah, 7-21-1819, appt Elder
    Sarah, 7-19-1820, appt comm
    Susannah, 1-23-1833, has separated from Hicksites at Menallen
    Tamer, 6-23-1796, rocf Hopewell MM with father John and family
    Tamer, 6-23-1796, rct Warrington MM with father John and family
    William, 3-17-1824, req marriage with Mary Wierman
    William, 5-24-1832, has been absent from meeting for some time
    William B., 9-19-1827, appt comm
WIRECARVER, Elizabeth, 6-9-1794, compl of: mou. Formerly Blackburn
WIREMAN, Amy, 5-17-1837, rct Putnam Co, Ill [w]
    Eliza, 5-17-1837, rct Putnam Co, Ill [w]
    Emy, 11-15-1784, rocf Cain Creek with husband William and family
    Esther Mira, 5-17-1837, rct Ill with father William C. and family [w]
    Gartrude, 1-12-1787, compl of: dancing
    Henry, 9-9-1782, rep to QM 4 times thru 3-18-1784
    Henry, 5-14-1781, appt comm 11 times thru 9-13-1784
    John, 8-11-1783, compl of: mou to Ruth Cox

MENALLEN MINUTES, MARRIAGES, & MISCELLANY

WIREMAN, John, 10-13-1783, disowned: mou to Ruth Cox
    L. S., 2-22-1838, rep to QM [w]
    Lydia, 6-21-1838, appt comm [w]
    Lydia S., 11-23-1836, rep to QM 5 times thru 11-21-1849 [w]
    Lydia S., 4-21-1836, appt comm 10 times thru 9-18-1844 [w]
    Mary, 11-15-1784, rocf Cain Creek with father William and family
    Nicholas, 10-13-1783, appt comm
    Nicholas, 10-11-1784, appt comm
    Ruth, 10-13-1783, disowned: mou to John Wireman
    Ruth, 1-22-1840, compl of: mou. Now McElwee [w]
    Sarah, 9-15-1794, req marriage with Stephen Hendricks
    Sarah, 5-17-1837, rct Putnam Co, Ill [w]
    Sarah Catherine, 5-17-1837, rct Ill with father William C. and family [w]
    Sarah, Jr, 5-17-1837, rct Putnam Co, Ill [w]
    Susan, 5-17-1837, rct Ill with husband William C. and 2 children [w]
    Susanna, 1-23-1839, appt Elder [w]
    Susannah, 9-23-1835, appt Elder [w]
    William, 11-15-1784, rocf Cain Creek with wife Emy and 3 children
    William, 11-15-1784, rocf Cain Creek with father William and family
    William, 3-12-1787, appt comm
    William C., 5-17-1837, rct Ill with wife Susan and 2 children [w]
    William, Jr, 6-14-1790, rct Warrington MM to marry Sarah Cleaver
WISECARVER, Elizabeth, 8-11-1794, dis: mou. Formerly Blackburn
WONDERS, Amanda Rhoda, 8-19-1868, compl of: mou. Formerly Hoopes [w]
    Amanda Rhoda, 2-17-1869, compl of: mou
    Amanda Rhoda, 3-17-1869, dis: mou. Formerly Hoopes [w]
WOOD, James, 11-20-1872, rocf Little Briten MM as Elder
    Jane, 11-20-1872, rocf Little Brittan MM as Minister [w]
    Pemberton, 12-23-1874, appt comm
    Shepperd, 12-23-1874, appt comm
WOODARD, Sarah G., 1-22-1851, compl of: mou. Formerly Griest [w]
    Sarah G., 6-19-1851, ack error. Retained at Kennet MM [w]
    Sarah G., 8-21-1851, rct London Grove MM, Chester Co, Pa [w]
WOODWARD, Sarah G., 6-19-1851, report from Kennet MM. Recommends membership
    Sarah G., 9-17-1851, gct London Grove MM
WORRALL, George, 11-25-1810, rocf Exeter MM
WRIGHT, Aaron, 7-20-1814, rct Miami MM, Ohio with father Jonathan and family
    Abel C., 10-20-1853, appt comm
    Abel C., 5-17-1854, rep to QM
    Abel E., 3-22-1854, rep to MM
    Abel G., 3-23-1853, appt comm
    Abel G., 11-23-1853, appt comm
    Abel G., 3-17-1863, rep to MM
    Abel S., 8-20-1863, rep to QM
    Abel T., 4-24-1845, appt clerk
    Abel T., 4-23-1846, appt clerk
    Abel T., 4-22-1847, appt clerk
    Abel T., 8-24-1848, clerk for the day 6 times thru 10-21-1866

MINUTES

WRIGHT, Abel T., 5-23-1849, appt to record Births and Deaths
    Abel T., 3-22-1854, appt clerk
    Abel T., 9-20-1854, req marriage with Jane C. Griest
    Abel T., 4-19-1855, appt clerk
    Abel T., 4-24-1856, appt clerk
    Abel T., 12-18-1856, appt to record Births and Deaths
    Abel T., 4-25-1857, appt clerk
    Abel T., 4-24-1862, appt clerk
    Abel T., 6-23-1864, appt Overseer
    Abel T., 2-22-1866, appt to care for Warrington MM records
    Abel T., 2-20-1867, appt Elder [w]
    Abel T., 8-19-1868, appt correspondent
    Abel T., 11-17-1841, rep to MM 36 times thru 9-24-1868
    Abel T., 12-22-1842, appt comm 65 times thru 2-17-1869
    Abel T., 1-23-1833, rep to QM 24 times thru 2-17-1869
    Abel T., 8-17-1870, an Elder, died 11 of 9th mo 1869
    Adella J., 12-21-1887, ack mou. Retained. Formerly Griest [w]
    Albert S., 2-22-1871, ack mou. Retained
    Albert Stewart, 2-19-1852, req membership thru father Thomas H.
        Wright [w]
    Ales, 7-14-1788, compl of: mou. Formerly Hammond
    Alice, 4-21-1803, req marriage with David McCreary
    Alice, 9-19-1849, appt comm [w]
    Alice, 7-23-1862, appt comm [w]
    Alice, 8-21-1862, rep to QM [w]
    Alice, 12-23-1885, assessed $2.00 for Yearly Meeting
    Alice, 5-18-1887, assessed $2.00 for fuel for Ann and Martha Griest
    Alice Anna, 5-17-1865, rct Warsanonoc MM, Iowa with father George W.
        and family
    Alice C., 6-21-1877, rep to MM [w]
    Alice G., 8-24-1843, rocf Warrington MM
    Alice G., 11-18-1863, rep to MM 20 times thru 2-17-1886 [w]
    Alice G., 9-17-1862, appt comm 24 times thru 10-23-1889 [w]
    Alice G., 11-22-1843, rep to QM 13 times thru 2-19-1890 [w]
    Alice S., 9-20-1865, appt comm [w]
    Ann, 9-20-1826, rct Dennings Creek MM with father Samuel and
        family
    Ann, 5-17-1843, rep to QM [w]
    Ann, 10-25-1845, req marriage with Moses D. Price
    Anna, 3-22-1820, req membership with husband Thomas and 6
        children
    Anna, 9-19-1849, rct Salem MM, Ohio with 3 children
    Anna, 9-19-1849, rct Salem MM, Ohio for self and 3 children [w]
    Anna, 9-19-1849, rct Salem MM, Ohio thru mother Anna [w]
    Anna, Jr, 10-18-1849, gct Salem MM, Ohio
    Anne, 8-23-1866, rep to QM [w]
    Annie, 2-24-1859, appt comm [w]
    Annie, 6-21-1866, rep to MM [w]
    Annie, 7-22-1869, rep to MM [w]
    Annie M., 2-21-1877, ack mou to Joseph B. Phillips of Iowa. Retained
        [w]

MENALLEN MINUTES, MARRIAGES, & MISCELLANY

WRIGHT, Annie M., 3-18-1885, rep to MM [w]
    Ayles, 9-15-1788, dis: mou. Formerly Hammond
    B., 2-9-1795, rep to QM
    Barbary, 9-20-1826, rct Dennings Creek MM with father Samuel and family
    Benjamin, 2-10-1783, req release from comm
    Benjamin, 11-15-1784, compl of: fighting
    Benjamin, 12-13-1784, read testimony. Retained
    Benjamin, 5-14-1794, appt Guardian for Thomas Miccle
    Benjamin, 10-20-1796, rct York MM: son Benjamin apprentice to John Love
    Benjamin, 4-10-1799, appt Overseer at Monallin
    Benjamin, 4-22-1802, appt to prepare memorial for Isaac Everitt, deceased
    Benjamin, 4-19-1804, proposed as Trustee for Joseph Hutton
    Benjamin, 10-9-1780, appt comm 144 times thru 4-21-1808
    Benjamin, 11-12-1781, rep to QM 34 times thru 5-18-1808
    Benjamin H., 9-19-1849, rct Salem MM, Ohio
    Charles S., 8-20-1846, req marriage with Hannah G. Penrose
    Charles S., 3-22-1854, appt comm 8 times thru 3-21-1866
    Charles S., 9-19-1855, rep to MM 6 times thru 3-20-1872
    Charles S., 4-24-1856, appt assistant clerk
    Charles S., 8-22-1861, rep to QM
    Charles S., 11-22-1865, rep to QM
    Charles T., 4-15-1863, appt comm
    Cyrus T., 4-15-1863, appt comm
    Cyrus T., 5-21-1863, appt comm
    Deborah, 4-12-1790, req marriage with Jonathan Potts
    E. Belle Griest, 8-20-1884, rep to QM [w]
    Elijah, 2-24-1842, rct Warrington MM to marry Mary A. Hoops
    Elijah, 5-18-1842, appt comm on military demands
    Elijah, 8-20-1846, forced to pay $1.00 muster fine
    Elijah, 8-19-1847, forced to pay $1.00 muster fine to Daniel Plank, collector
    Elijah, 4-19-1871, appt Elder
    Elijah, 5-21-1873, appt Elder
    Elijah, 5-17-1876, appt Elder
    Elijah, 11-22-1854, rep to QM 12 times thru 2-21-1877
    Elijah, 10-20-1853, appt comm 26 times thru 8-22-1877
    Elijah, 9-22-1858, rep to MM 50 times thru 11-21-1877
    Eliza R., 12-23-1874, req marriage with Amos W. Griest
    Elizabeth, 1-11-1796, compl of: mou. Now Cook
    Elizabeth, 10-19-1797, rct Gunpowder MM with father Jonathan and family
    Elizabeth, 5-20-1818, req membership. Wife of Samuel Wright
    Elizabeth, 9-23-1835, appt Elder [w]
    Elizabeth, 3-23-1836, appt Overseer [w]
    Elizabeth, 1-23-1839, appt Elder
    Elizabeth, 5-21-1835, rep to QM 8 times thru 8-24-1843 [w]
    Elizabeth, 2-18-1836, appt comm 10 times thru 3-19-1845 [w]

MINUTES

WRIGHT, Elizabeth, 1-23-1850, gct Warrington MM with father John B. and family
    Elizabeth, 2-19-1879, ack mou. Retained. Now Longsdorf
    Elizabeth L., 9-21-1836, appt comm [w]
    Elizabeth M., 8-24-1837, rep to QM [w]
    Elizabeth S., 9-18-1839, appt Overseer [w]
    Elizabeth S., 10-20-1842, appt Overseer [w]
    Elizabeth S., 12-19-1844, appt Treasurer [w]
    Elizabeth S., 7-22-1835, appt comm 8 times thru 3-18-1846 [w]
    Elizabeth S., 11-18-1835, rep to QM 11 times thru 5-28-1850 [w]
    Ellen, 1-19-1842, req marriage with George Hewitt
    Emilie, 5-17-1869, rep to QM [w]
    Emilie W., 1-17-1872, ack mou. Retained. Now Black [w]
    G. Ed., 5-18-1887, assessed $1.00 for fuel for Ann and Martha Griest
    G. Edward, 12-23-1885, assessed $1.50 for Yearly Meeting
    George, 8-22-1833, compl of: attending a marriage out of order
    George, 10-24-1833, read testimony. Retained
    George, 2-22-1838, req marriage with Lucy Wright
    George, 9-19-1849, appt comm
    George, 5-17-1865, rct Wapsanonoc MM, Iowa with wife Lucy A. and 4 children [w]
    George, 3-20-1889, rocf Wapsenonoc MM, Iowa with wife Lucy A.
    George E., 3-23-1881, ack marriage to Jane G. Wright without approval

MENALLEN MINUTES, MARRIAGES, & MISCELLANY

WRIGHT, George Edward, 3-23-1887, appt Trustee for Menallen and
    Huntington
    George M., 9-22-1852, rep to MM
    George W., 11-19-1851, rep to MM 3 times thru 12-22-1853
    George W., 4-22-1852, appt assistant clerk
    George W., 4-21-1853, appt assistant clerk
    George W., 3-22-1854, clerk for the day
    George W., 5-17-1865, rct Warsanonoc MM, Muscatine Co, Iowa with
        wife Lucy
    George W., 3-20-1889, rocf Wapasnooc MM, Cedar Co, Iowa [w]
    H.G., 4-24-1862, appt clerk [w]
    Hannah, 4-12-1784, compl of: with child by brother-in-law
    Hannah, 5-10-1784, dis: unchastity
    Hannah, 10-12-1789, compl of: fornication with 1st cousin. Formerly
        Hendrix
    Hannah, 4-19-1804, offered testimony to condemn her misconduct
    Hannah, 7-20-1814, rct Miami MM, Ohio with father Jonathan and
        family
    Hannah, 4-22-1841, appt comm [w]
    Hannah, 4-24-1845, appt comm [w]
    Hannah, 11-20-1850, rep to QM [w]
    Hannah, 12-23-1868, rep to MM [w]
    Hannah G., 4-25-1851, appt treasurer [w]
    Hannah G., 5-17-1854, appt assistant clerk [w]
    Hannah G., 3-19-1856, appt Overseer
    Hannah G., 8-18-1859, appt Overseer [w]
    Hannah G., 3-20-1861, appt assistant clerk [w]
    Hannah G., 4-24-1862, appt Overseer [w]
    Hannah G., 4-20-1865, appt Overseer [w]
    Hannah G., 6-21-1866, clerk for the day [w]
    Hannah G., 12-23-1868, appt Overseer [w]
    Hannah G., 4-19-1871, appt Elder
    Hannah G., 4-19-1871, appt Overseer [w]
    Hannah G., 5-21-1873, appt Elder
    Hannah G., 6-18-1874, appt Overseer [w]
    Hannah G., 5-17-1876, appt Elder
    Hannah G., 2-21-1877, clerk for the day [w]
    Hannah G., 4-23-1879, appt Elder
    Hannah G., 4-19-1882, appt Elder
    Hannah G., 4-22-1885, appt Elder
    Hannah G., 12-23-1885, assessed $1.00 for Yearly Meeting
    Hannah G., 2-19-1863, rep to MM 38 times thru 3-17-1886 [w]
    Hannah G., 5-18-1887, assessed $2.00 for fuel for Ann and Martha
        Griest
    Hannah G., 5-23-1888, appt Elder [w]
    Hannah G., 9-17-1862, appt comm 60 times thru 7-23-1890 [w]
    Hannah G., 8-18-1859, rep to QM 29 times thru 8-20-1890 [w]
    Hannah H., 8-21-1862, ack mou. Retained. Now married to Samuel F.
        Mifflin
    Hannah S., 11-21-1866, rep to MM [w]

MINUTES

WRIGHT, Hannah S., 7-18-1877, clerk for the day [w]
    Hannah T., 12-22-1875, appt comm [w]
    Hannah W., 8-21-1862, ack mou to Samuel W. Mifflin. Retained
    Hansen T., 9-19-1849, rct Salem MM, Ohio
    Hanson, 3-22-1820, req membership thru father Thomas and family
    Harris, 3-22-1820, req membership thru father Thomas and family
    Hiram, 11-23-1831, rep to QM
    Hiram G., 12-17-1862, rep to MM
    Hiram S., 4-20-1843, rct Warrington MM to marry Alice Garretson
    Hiram S., 12-17-1873, appt Overseer
    Hiram S., 3-18-1874, appt to record Certificates of Removal
    Hiram S., 7-19-1876, appt Overseer
    Hiram S., 5-22-1878, appt Trustee in place of David R. McCreary, deceased
    Hiram S., 3-18-1857, appt comm 25 times, thru 4-20-1881
    Hiram S., 2-22-1882, appt Overseer
    Hiram S., 4-19-1882, appt Elder
    Hiram S., 5-21-1863, rep to QM 11 times thru 5-17-1882
    Hiram S., 4-25-1857, rep to MM 67 times thru 10-18-1882
    Hiram T., 4-15-1863, rep to MM
    Howard L., 1-21-1885, ack wrongdoing. Retained
    Isaac, 12-22-1842, rct Warrington MM to marry Sarah Garretson
    Isaac, 8-24-1848, forced to pay $1 muster fine by Daniel Plank, collector
    Isaac, 2-21-1863, rep to MM
    Isaac, 4-23-1879, appt Elder
    Isaac G., 9-23-1875, rep to MM
    Isaac G., 12-23-1885, assessed $3.50 for Yearly Meeting
    Isaac J., 8-20-1846, forced to pay $1.00 muster fine
    Isaac J., 8-19-1847, forced to pay $1.00 muster fine to Daniel Plank, collector
    Isaac J., 1-17-1866, rep to MM 6 times thru 8-23-1882
    Isaac J., 8-17-1870, rep to QM 5 times thru 8-23-1882
    Isaac J., 1-20-1875, appt comm 3 times thru 8-23-1882
    Isaac N., 9-19-1849, rct Salem MM, Ohio thru mother Anna [w]
    Isaac T., 2-21-1863, rep to QM
    Isaac T., 10-22-1863, appt comm
    Isaac T., 1-21-1864, rep to MM
    Isaac T., 5-18-1864, appt comm
    Israel, 3-22-1820, req membership thru father Thomas and family
    Israel, 5-17-1865, rct Wapsanonoc MM, Iowa with father George and family [w]
    Israel P., 3-22-1848, compl of: mou; moving to Salem MM, Ohio with no certificate
    Israel P., 8-24-1848, report from Salem MM he condemned action. Retained
    Israel P., 5-17-1865, rct Warsanonoc MM, Iowa with father George W. and family
    Jacob, 9-19-1827, rct Dennings Creek MM
    James C., 8-20-1884, ack mou. Retained
    James C., 12-23-1885, assessed $1.00 for Yearly Meeting

MENALLEN MINUTES, MARRIAGES, & MISCELLANY

WRIGHT, Jane, 5-20-1835, rocf Warrington MM
    Jane, 6-23-1836, appt comm 27 times thru 7-18-1855 [w]
    Jane, 2-22-1838, rep to QM 13 times thru 11-21-1856 [w]
    Jane, 5-17-1865, rct Wapsanonoc MM, Iowa with father George and family [w]
    Jane A., 8-23-1860, rep to QM [w]
    Jane C., 9-23-1857, appt assistant clerk [w]
    Jane C., 8-19-1858, appt assistant clerk [w]
    Jane C., 10-20-1859, appt assistant clerk [w]
    Jane C., 3-20-1861, appt clerk [w]
    Jane C., 4-20-1865, appt clerk [w]
    Jane C., 5-22-1866, appt clerk [w]
    Jane C., 4-19-1871, appt Overseer [w]
    Jane C., 8-22-1871, appt clerk [w]
    Jane C., 10-23-1872, appt clerk [w]
    Jane C., 12-17-1873, appt clerk [w]
    Jane C., 6-18-1874, appt Overseer [w]
    Jane C., 12-23-1874, appt clerk [w]
    Jane C., 1-19-1876, appt clerk [w]
    Jane C., 8-23-1855, rep to QM 23 times thru 2-23-1876 [w]
    Jane C., 2-20-1868, appt comm 27 times thru 4-22-1876 [w]
    Jane C., 3-17-1869, rep to MM 14 times thru 7-19-1876 [w]
    Jane C., 9-21-1876, req marriage with William Whitson
    Jane E., 8-22-1870, appt clerk [w]
    Jane E., 2-21-1872, rep to QM [w]
    Jane F., 5-23-1855, appt assistant clerk [w]
    Jane F., 7-23-1856, appt clerk [w]
    Jane F., 9-23-1857, appt clerk [w]
    Jane F., 8-19-1858, appt clerk [w]
    Jane F., 10-20-1859, appt clerk [w]
    Jane F., 6-19-1863, appt assistant clerk [w]
    Jane F., 5-18-1864, appt assistant clerk [w]
    Jane F., 6-20-1867, appt clerk [w]
    Jane F., 8-19-1868, appt clerk [w]
    Jane F., 8-18-1869, appt clerk [w]
    Jane F., 4-19-1871, appt Overseer [w]
    Jane F., 8-22-1871, appt assistant clerk [w]
    Jane F., 10-23-1872, appt assistant clerk [w]
    Jane F., 5-21-1873, appt Elder
    Jane F., 12-17-1873, appt assistant clerk [w]
    Jane F., 6-18-1874, appt Overseer [w]
    Jane F., 12-23-1874, appt assistant clerk [w]
    Jane F., 1-19-1876, appt assistant clerk [w]
    Jane F., 5-17-1876, appt Elder
    Jane F., 8-22-1877, clerk for the day [w]
    Jane F., 2-20-1878, appt Overseer [w]
    Jane F., 4-23-1879, appt Elder
    Jane F., 4-23-1879, appt clerk [w]
    Jane F., 4-19-1882, appt Elder
    Jane F., 8-22-1883, appt Overseer [w]

MINUTES

WRIGHT, Jane F., 4-22-1885, appt Elder
    Jane F., 10-23-1862, rep to MM 25 times thru 4-22-1885 [w]
    Jane F., 12-23-1885, clerk for the day [w]
    Jane F., 8-18-1886, appt Overseer [w]
    Jane F., 5-18-1887, assessed $1.00 for fuel for Ann and Martha Griest
    Jane F., 5-23-1888, appt Elder [w]
    Jane F., 5-21-1856, rep to QM 26 times thru 2-20-1889 [w]
    Jane F., 1-20-1858, appt comm 26 times thru 4-23-1890 [w]
    Jane G., 3-23-1881, ack marriage to George W. Wright without approval
    Jane G., 3-23-1881, ack mou to George E. Wright. Retained [w]
    Jane Mary, 5-17-1865, rct Warsanonoc MM, Iowa with father George W. and family
    Jas, 5-18-1887, assessed $ .25 for fuel for Ann and Martha Griest
    Jesse, 5-17-1797, compl of: lottery
    Jesse, 6-22-1797, read testimony. Retained
    Jesse, 1-23-1799, compl of: playing cards
    Jesse, 4-10-1799, dis: playing cards for a wager
    Jesse, 7-20-1814, rct Miami MM, Ohio with father Jonathan and family
    Jesse, 3-23-1853, appt comm
    Jno, 8-13-1787, rep to QM
    Jno, Jr, 1-22-1817, appt comm
    Jno, Jr, 4-24-1817, appt comm
    Joel, 4-13-1795, rct Pipe Creek with father Jonathan and family
    Joel, 10-19-1797, rct Gunpowder MM with father Jonathan and family
    Joel, 8-24-1837, appt comm in charge of graveyards
    Joel, 5-18-1842, appt comm on military demands
    Joel, 11-17-1841, rep to MM 37 times thru 10-21-1866
    Joel, 11-17-1841, appt comm 23 times thru 5-22-1867
    Joel, 5-23-1838, rep to QM 26 times thru 8-22-1867
    Joel T., 10-22-1863, appt comm
    John, 9-15-1783, appt Overseer in place of James McGrail
    John, 6-15-1789, released as Overseer at Monallen
    John, 10-19-1791, rct Pipe Creek MM. Son of Benjamin
    John, 9-15-1794, rocf Pipe Creek MM. Son of Benjamin Wright
    John, 4-21-1796, req marriage with Susanna Griest
    John, 12-22-1796, rct Hopewell MM with wife Susannah
    John, 6-19-1800, released as Overseer at Monallin
    John, 9-19-1804, req marriage with Alice Wilson
    John, 9-18-1805, released as recorder of Removals
    John, 11-17-1813, rep to QM. Son of Samuel
    John, 8-18-1825, appt Overseer
    John, 2-22-1827, appt assistant clerk
    John, 2-21-1828, appt assistant clerk
    John, 11-18-1835, clerk for the day 5 times thru 11-21-1838
    John, 6-21-1838, has title papers for Menallen in his care
    John, 1-23-1839, appt Elder
    John, 7-23-1851, appt Elder
    John, 8-21-1851, appt to care for burying grounds
    John, 5-14-1781, rep to QM 42 times thru 11-17-1852

MENALLEN MINUTES, MARRIAGES, & MISCELLANY

WRIGHT, John, 5-14-1781, appt comm 146 times thru 4-21-1853
    John, 7-19-1854, appt Elder
    John, 8-24-1854, appt Elder [w]
    John, 12-20-1832, rep to MM 50 times thru 7-18-1855
    John, 11-21-1855, appt Elder
    John, 12-24-1857, appt Elder
    John, 4-19-1860, appt Elder
    John (of Samuel), 7-20-1814, appt comm
    John B., 8-22-1844, req marriage with Mary Nebinger (she not a member)
    John B., 8-20-1846, forced to pay $1.00 muster fine
    John B., 8-19-1847, forced to pay $1.00 muster fine to Daniel Plank, collector
    John B., 1-23-1850, gct Warrington MM with wife Mary N. and 2 children
    John B., 6-19-1862, appt Overseer at Newberry
    John B., 6-23-1864, appt Overseer
    John B., 4-23-1873, appt Trustee at Menallen
    John B., 12-23-1874, clerk for the day
    John B., 7-19-1876, appt Overseer
    John B., 9-17-1862, appt comm 25 times thru 4-23-1879
    John B., 8-21-1862, rep to MM 20 times thru 1-19-1881
    John B., 8-21-1862, rep to QM 12 times thru 2-23-1881
    John G., 1-23-1863, rep to MM
    John (of Samuel), 9-18-1816, appt comm
    John (of Samuel), 8-20-1818, appt comm
    John, Jr, 11-12-1781, req marriage with Ann Griffith
    John, Jr, 12-21-1797, appt Overseer at Monallin
    John, Jr, 3-21-1798, appt to record Certificates
    John, Jr, 8-22-1811, exempt fines, "Taken from John Wright Junior in the year 1809 by George Smiser collector for two years exempt fines of five dollars each one watch, and one heifer valued as $21.50."
    John, Jr, 6-22-1815, appt Trustee for Joseph Hutton
    John, Jr, 6-19-1817, appt to standing comm for care of Benj. Tomlinson
    John, Jr, 7-21-1819, appt assistant clerk
    John, Jr, 7-19-1820, appt assistant clerk
    John, Jr, 4-19-1821, appt Overseer in place of George Wilson
    John, Jr, 6-21-1821, appt clerk
    John, Jr, 1-23-1822, appt comm
    John, Jr, 7-17-1822, appt clerk
    John, Jr, 7-23-1823, appt clerk
    John, Jr, 12-18-1823, appt Trustee for deeds and property at Menallen and Huntington
    John, Jr, 4-22-1824, req release as Overseer
    John, Jr, 5-19-1824, appt Overseer
    John, Jr, 5-19-1824, appt Overseer
    John, Jr, 11-23-1825, appt assistant clerk
    John, Jr, 12-22-1825, appt caretaker for Thomas Mickle

MINUTES

WRIGHT, John, Jr, 4-19-1827, appt to settle with Benjamin Tumbleson's trustees
    John, Jr, 12-18-1828, appt clerk
    John, Jr, 2-23-1797, rep to QM 16 times thru 1-20-1830
    John, Jr, 7-14-1794, appt comm 57 times thru 8-23-1832
    John, Sr, 11-21-1798, rep to QM
    John, Sr, 11-22-1815, rep to QM
    Jonathan, 10-09-1780, appt clerk for first Monthly Meeting at Monallin
    Jonathan, 11-13-1780, appt Elder
    Jonathan, 3-12-1781, appt Elder
    Jonathan, 11-12-1781, appt clerk
    Jonathan, 11-11-1782, appt clerk
    Jonathan, 12-11-1786, appt Guardian of Samuel Hutton's orphan children
    Jonathan, 5-11-1789, appt comm to visit Bedford Co Meeting
    Jonathan, 6-15-1789, appt Overseer at Monallen in place of John Wright
    Jonathan, 9-14-1789, appt clerk in place of Isaac Pearson
    Jonathan, 5-10-1790, rct to York MM for his son Thomas
    Jonathan, 6-10-1793, released as Overseer at Monallen
    Jonathan, 4-14-1794, appt comm
    Jonathan, 8-11-1794, released as clerk
    Jonathan, 4-13-1795, rct Pipe Creek with wife Susana and 5 children
    Jonathan, 4-13-1795, rct Pipe Creek with father Jonathan and family
    Jonathan, 6-15-1795, released from recording Births & Deaths
    Jonathan, 2-15-1796, rocf Pipe Creek MM with wife
    Jonathan, 8-18-1796, appt Elder
    Jonathan, 10-19-1797, rct Gunpowder MM with wife Susanna and 7 children
    Jonathan, 10-19-1797, rct Gunpowder MM with father Jonathan and family
    Jonathan, 12-21-1797, released as Elder, removed
    Jonathan, 2-20-1806, req marriage with Mary Bateman. Son of Joel
    Jonathan, 3-19-1806, rocf Baltimore MM. Son of Joel
    Jonathan, 1-20-1813, appt clerk
    Jonathan, 10-9-1780, appt comm 164 times thru 10-21-1813
    Jonathan, 1-19-1814, appt clerk
    Jonathan, 11-13-1780, rep to QM 28 times thru 2-24-1814
    Jonathan, 4-21-1814, req release as clerk
    Jonathan, 7-20-1814, rct Miami MM, Ohio with wife Mary and 5 children
    Josiah, 7-20-1814, rct Miami MM, Ohio with father Jonathan and family
    Julia, 9-19-1849, rct Salem MM, Ohio thru mother Anna [w]
    Julia A., 10-18-1849, gct Salem MM, Ohio
    Julia A., 5-17-1865, rct Warsanonoc MM, Iowa with father George W. and family
    Leah, 3-22-1820, req membership thru father Thomas and family
    Leah, 2-21-1850, compl of: mou and removing to Salem. Now Web
    Louisa A., 2-19-1873, ack mou. Retained. Now Russell [w]

MENALLEN MINUTES, MARRIAGES, & MISCELLANY

WRIGHT, Lucy, 3-22-1820, req membership thru father Thomas and family
    Lucy, 2-22-1838, req marriage with George Wright
    Lucy A., 5-17-1865, rct Wapsanonoc MM, Iowa with husband George and 4 children [w]
    Lucy A., 3-20-1889, rocf Wapsenonoc MM, Iowa with husband George
    Lydia, 3-22-1820, req membership thru father Thomas and family
    M. Alice, 8-17-1881, rep to QM 3 times thru 8-20-1890 [w]
    M. Alice, 5-17-1882, rep to MM 5 times thru 1-20-1886 [w]
    M. Alice, 12-23-1885, clerk for the day [w]
    M. Alice, 5-22-1889, appt assistant clerk [w]
    M. Alice, 5-21-1890, appt assistant clerk [w]
    M. Alice, 2-21-1883, appt comm 10 times thru 10-22-1890 [w]
    Mahlon, 7-20-1814, rct Miami MM, Ohio with father Jonathan and family
    Malinda Ann, 9-20-1826, rct Dennings Creek MM with father Samuel and family
    Maria, 7-22-1835, appt assistant clerk [w]
    Maria, 1-19-1842, appt comm 5 times thru 7-23-1845 [w]
    Martha, 9-21-1796, req marriage with Levi Hutton
    Martha, 2-20-1845, rep to QM [w]
    Mary, 4-13-1795, rct Pipe Creek with father Jonathan and family
    Mary, 10-19-1797, rct Gunpowder MM with father Jonathan and family
    Mary, 4-23-1807, req marriage with Jacob Harris
    Mary, 7-20-1814, rct Miami MM, Ohio with husband Jonathan and 5 children
    Mary, 1-23-1850, gct Warrington MM with husband John B. and 2 children [w]
    Mary, 5-17-1865, rct Wapsanonoc MM, Iowa with father George and family [w]
    Mary A., 6-22-1843, rocf Warrington MM
    Mary A., 4-19-1871, appt Elder
    Mary A., 5-21-1873, appt Elder
    Mary A., 9-17-1862, appt comm 20 times thru 11-19-1873 [w]
    Mary A., 5-17-1876, appt Elder
    Mary A., 4-23-1879, appt Elder
    Mary A., 11-21-1849, rep to QM 27 times thru 8-19-1885 [w]
    Mary A., 11-19-1862, rep to MM 30 times thru 11-18-1885 [w]
    Mary A., 12-23-1885, assessed $1.00 for Yearly Meeting
    Mary Alice, 9-20-1882, rep to MM [w]
    Mary Alice, 8-20-1884, rep to QM [w]
    Mary E., 7-17-1889, ack mou to Charles T. Hiltabidle. Retained
    Mary G., 8-22-1883, rep to QM [w]
    Mary M., 9-20-1826, rct Dennings Creek MM with father Samuel and family
    Mary N., 1-23-1850, gct Warrington MM with husband John B. and 2 children
    Mary N., 8-21-1862, appt comm [w]
    Mary N., 8-21-1862, rep to QM [w]
    Mary T., 5-18-1853, rep to QM [w]
    Miriam G., 4-20-1881, ack mou. Retained. Now Harris [w]

MINUTES

WRIGHT, Nathan, 9-19-1810, req marriage with Elizabeth Harris
    Nathan, 3-20-1822, appt recorder of Certificates of Removals
    Nathan, 3-19-1834, appt Overseer
    Nathan, 8-20-1835, appt Overseer
    Nathan, 8-24-1820, rep to QM 34 times thru 5-19-1847
    Nathan, 1-17-1816, appt comm 54 times thru 4-18-1850
    Nathan, 7-17-1833, rep to MM 33 times thru 7-21-1852
    Nathan H., 9-20-1826, rct Dennings Creek MM with father Samuel and family
    Phebe, 10-20-1842, appt Overseer [w]
    Phebe, 3-19-1856, appt Overseer [w]
    Phebe, 7-22-1835, appt comm 37 times thru 5-23-1860 [w]
    Phebe, 8-20-1835, rep to QM 24 times thru 2-21-1861 [w]
    Pheby, 10-19-1797, rct Gunpowder MM with father Jonathan and family
    Rachel, 3-12-1781, req marriage with James Hodgson
    Rachel, 4-15-1782, dis: carnal knowledge before marriage. Now Hodgson
    Rachel, 4-14-1794, req marriage with Benjamin Farquer
    Rachel, 9-20-1815, compl of: mou. Now Farquhar
    Rachel, 1-17-1816, dis: mou. Now Farquhar
    Rachel, 7-21-1819, appt comm
    Rachel, 5-24-1832, appt Elder
    Rachel, 8-19-1842, appt comm [w]
    Rachel, 2-19-1852, req membership thru father Thomas H. Wright [w]
    Rachel, 11-21-1866, ack mou. Retained. Now Walhay [w]
    Rachel A., 7-19-1876, req release from membership
    Rachel E., 5-18-1887, ack mou. Retained. Now Jones [w]
    Rachel E., 12-19-1888, rct Pipe Creek MM. Now Jones [w]
    Rachel T., 11-21-1866, ack mou. Retained. Now Walhay
    Rachie A., 7-19-1876, req membership be discontinued [w]
    Reb, 7-19-1865, rep to MM [w]
    Rebecca, 4-13-1795, rct Pipe Creek with father Jonathan and family
    Rebecca, 10-19-1797, rct Gunpowder MM with father Jonathan and family
    Rebecca, 2-22-1849, appt comm [w]
    Rebecca, 2-19-1852, appt comm [w]
    Rebecca, 3-17-1852, appt assistant clerk [w]
    Rebecca, 11-21-1855, rep to QM [w]
    Rebecka, 9-20-1826, rct Dennings Creek MM with husband Samuel and 8 children
    Rebkah, 9-20-1826, rct Dennings Creek MM with father Samuel and family
    Richard M., 12-21-1887, ack wrongdoing. Retained
    Robert N., 11-22-1882, ack mou. Retained
    Robert N., 1-23-1850, gct Warrington MM with father John B. and family
    Ruth, 8-11-1794, req marriage with Thomas Hammond
    Ruth, 8-24-1843, appt assistant clerk [w]
    Ruth, 5-17-1854, rep to QM [w]

MENALLEN MINUTES, MARRIAGES, & MISCELLANY

WRIGHT, Ruth, 7-22-1868, rep to MM [w]
    Ruth Ann, 3-21-1860, appt comm [w]
    Ruth Anna, 12-24-1840, appt comm [w]
    Ruth Anna, 8-18-1859, rep to QM 3 times thru 8-18-1869 [w]
    Ruth Anna, 3-18-1868, rep to MM 3 times thru 12-22-1869 [w]
    Ruth F., 4-20-1870, rep to MM [w]
    Ruth H., 7-20-1870, appt comm [w]
    Ruth M, 9-20-1865, appt comm [w]
    Ruth M., 11-20-1850, appt assistant clerk [w]
    Ruth M., 11-19-1862, rep to QM [w]
    Ruth M., 11-17-1875, rep to QM [w]
    Ruth M., 12-19-1867, rep to MM 15 times thru 10-17-1877 [w]
    Ruth M., 6-24-1858, appt comm 11 times thru 10-17-1877 [w]
    Ruthanna, 9-20-1826, rct Dennings Creek MM with father Samuel and family
    Ruthanna, 2-21-1856, appt comm [w]
    Ruthanna, 8-24-1865, rep to QM [w]
    S. J., 3-22-1876, appt comm
    Samuel, 2-23-1804, req marriage with Rebeckah Harris. Son of John
    Samuel, 11-22-1809, compl of: mou. Son of Benjamin
    Samuel, 1-17-1810, read testimony. Retained
    Samuel, 4-23-1818, req membership for son William Harry Wright
    Samuel, 5-20-1818, wife Elizabeth requests membership
    Samuel, 8-20-1818, rep to QM 7 times thru 5-18-1825
    Samuel, 5-21-1823, reports re Thomas Mickle (a lunitick)
    Samuel, 12-22-1825, appt caretaker for Thomas Mickle
    Samuel, 9-20-1826, rct Dennings Creek MM with wife Rebecka and 8 children
    Samuel, 7-23-1817, appt comm 24 times thru 1-22-1834
    Samuel B., 5-19-1824, appt Overseer
    Samuel B., 5-19-1824, appt Overseer
    Samuel B., 8-18-1825, appt Overseer
    Samuel B., 3-18-1829, appt for care of burying grounds
    Samuel B., 3-17-1830, appt clerk for the day
    Samuel B., 5-19-1824, rep to QM 8 times thru 1-22-1834
    Samuel B., 3-19-1834, appt Overseer
    Samuel B., 3-17-1824, appt comm 19 times thru 5-21-1834
    Samuel B., 3-20-1833, rep to MM 8 times thru 2-19-1835
    Samuel, Jr, 8-19-1819, rep to QM
    Samuel, Jr, 5-23-1821, rep to QM
    Samuel, Jr, 12-24-1818, appt comm 18 times thru 6-24-1824
    Sarah, 4-19-1798, req marriage with George Willson
    Sarah, 3-23-1825, req marriage with Enos McMillin
    Sarah, 6-19-1863, rep to MM [w]
    Sarah, 12-24-1863, rep to MM [w]
    Sarah G., 6-22-1843, rocf Warrington MM
    Sarah G., 11-20-1861, appt comm 4 times thru 1-20-1875 [w]
    Sarah G., 4-24-1862, appt Overseer [w]
    Sarah G., 11-19-1862, rep to MM 4 times thru 8-19-1868 [w]
    Sarah G., 2-19-1863, rep to QM 5 times thru 2-18-1875 [w]

MINUTES

WRIGHT, Sarah P., 12-17-1862, appt comm [w]
    Sarah T., 2-19-1879, rep to QM [w]
    Savanna, 9-23-1846, req marriage with Elisha Penrose
    Susana, 4-13-1795, rct Pipe Creek with husband Jonathan and 5 children
    Susanna, 4-13-1795, rct Pipe Creek with father Jonathan and family
    Susanna, 10-19-1797, rct Gunpowder MM with husband Jonathan and 7 children
    Susannah, 10-15-1787, appt Elder at Monallin
    Susannah, 12-22-1796, rct Hopewell MM with husband John
    Susannah, 10-19-1797, rct Gunpowder MM with father Jonathan and family
    Terressa Harris, 2-21-1883, ack mou to Thomas A. Wright. Formerly Harris
    Thomas, 5-10-1790, rct to York MM by his father Jonathan
    Thomas, 10-24-1792, rocf York MM
    Thomas, 8-11-1794, rep to QM 3 times thru 2-21-1822
    Thomas, 1-12-1795, appt comm 4 times thru 5-22-1833
    Thomas, 4-20-1797, rct Indian Spring MM
    Thomas, 8-22-1805, compl of: attending review. Son of John
    Thomas, 10-24-1805, dis: mustering
    Thomas, 5-18-1808, rct Hopewell MM. Son of Benjamin
    Thomas, 11-22-1809, rocf Hopewell MM
    Thomas, 7-22-1812, compl of: mou. Now lives at Hopewell MM
    Thomas, 7-21-1813, dis: mou
    Thomas, 3-22-1820, read testimony. Retained
    Thomas, 3-22-1820, req membership with wife Anna and 6 children
    Thomas, 9-18-1833, rep to MM
    Thomas, 12-23-1885, assessed $1.00 for Yearly Meeting
    Thomas A., 2-21-1883, ack mou to Terressa Harris. Retained
    Thomas G., 9-20-1826, rct Dennings Creek MM with father Samuel and family
    Thomas H., 2-23-1843, compl of: mou
    Thomas H., 3-22-1843, read testimony. Retained
    Thomas H., 2-19-1852, req membership for 2 children: Rachel and Albert S. [w]
    Thomas H., 5-22-1857, rep to QM
    Thomas H., 2-24-1859, appt comm
    Thomas H., 3-21-1860, rep to MM 4 times thru 1-17-1872
    Thomas H., 11-21-1860, rep to QM
    Thomas R., 9-17-1856, read ack. Retained
    Thomas S., 12-20-1860, rep to MM
    William, 1-10-1791, compl of: non-attendance and mou
    William, 3-14-1791, dis: non-attendance and mou
    William, 10-20-1803, req marriage with Rachel Thomas
    William, 9-18-1805, appt recorder of Certificates of Removal
    William, 1-19-1814, appt Overseer at Monallen
    William, 5-22-1816, appt clerk
    William, 10-24-1816, released as recorder of Certificates of Removal
    William, 10-23-1817, req marriage with Phebe Wierman

MENALLEN MINUTES, MARRIAGES, & MISCELLANY

WRIGHT, William, 7-21-1819, appt Elder
    William, 5-24-1832, appt Elder
    William, 4-24-1834, compl of: being father of illegitimate child
    William, 8-21-1834, disowned: illegitimate child
    William, 9-23-1835, appt Elder [w]
    William, 1-23-1839, appt Elder
    William, 7-22-1840, appt Elder
    William, 2-20-1845, appt Elder
    William, 5-17-1848, appt Elder
    William, 2-23-1809, appt comm 104 times thru 6-19-1851
    William, 7-23-1851, appt Elder
    William, 11-12-1781, rep to QM 50 times thru 11-19-1851
    William, 8-22-1833, rep to MM 29 times thru 3-17-1852
    William B., 1-17-1844, rep to MM
    William H., 2-20-1834, rct Warrington MM to marry Jane Cook
    William H., 12-24-1840, clerk for the day
    William H., 8-19-1841, appt assistant clerk
    William H., 12-23-1841, appt Overseer
    William H., 5-18-1842, appt comm on military demands
    William H., 11-23-1842, appt assistant clerk
    William H., 1-18-1843, appt Overseer
    William H., 9-18-1844, clerk for the day
    William H., 4-20-1848, appt assistant clerk
    William H., 4-19-1849, appt assistant clerk
    William H., 4-24-1851, appt assistant clerk
    William H., 8-21-1851, appt to care for burying grounds
    William H., 4-19-1855, appt Overseer
    William H., 11-20-1833, rep to QM 17 times thru 2-21-1856
    William H., 9-17-1834, appt comm 52 times thru 3-19-1856
    William H., 10-20-1834, rep to MM 48 times thru 2-19-1857
    William H., 11-22-1865, rct Wapsononock MM, Muscatine Co, Iowa
    William H., 2-22-1866, comm reports he and wife are separated
    William H., 7-19-1871, rct Wapsononock MM, West Liberty, Muscatine Co, Iowa
    William Harry, 4-23-1818, req membership thru father Samuel
    William M., 12-22-1836, rep to MM
    William T., 10-23-1862, rep to MM
    William W., 4-19-1860, rep to MM
    William W., 8-23-1866, rep to QM
    William W., 7-22-1868, rep to MM
    William W., 7-22-1868, appt comm
    William, Jr, 12-18-1823, appt Trustee for deeds and property at Menallen and Huntington
    William, Jr, 8-22-1833, rep to QM
    William, Jr, 3-17-1819, appt comm 10 times thru 12-19-1833
    William, Sr, 3-13-1786, appt comm
WYDEMYER, Gideon, 5-22-1839, req marriage with Ruth Russell [w]
YENKE, Martha, 10-20-1834, formerly Underwood. Has separated from Hicksites

BURIALS

A., I., d.1792; bur. Newberry
AENESOON, Jean, d.3-21-1842; bur. Warrington
B., I.; bur. Newberry
B., J.; bur. Newberry
B., M.; bur. Newberry
B., O.; bur. Newberry
B., P.; bur. Newberry
B., T.; d.1805; bur. Newberry
B., W.; bur. Newberry
BARRY, Belle, d.1902; bur. Redlands
    Burrell H., b.1899, d.1979; bur. Redlands
BEALES, Caleb, d.8-31-1850, aged 66 yr 23 da; bur. Huntington
    Charlotte, d.1865, aged 54 yr 5 mo 24 da; wife of David Beales; bur. Huntington
    David, d.7-19-1880, aged 84 yr 6 mo 11 da; bur. Huntington
    Evaline M., d.1-19-1866, aged 63 yr 4 mo 3 da; bur. Huntington
BEALS, Beth, d.1800; bur. Huntington
    Jacob; bur. Huntington

MENALLEN, MARRIAGES AND MISCELLANY

BECK, Rachel Wright, b.7-20-1847, d.4-10-1915, daughter of Charles S. Beck and Hannah G. Wright; bur. Menallen
BEIDLER, Infant, d.2-16-1940; son of J. Willis and Martha G.; bur. Menallen
BELL, Ebbenezer, d.8-31-1834; bur. Warrington
BELL, Mary, d.7-30-1829; bur. Warrington
BENTZ, Mrs., d.1827 [Michael Bentz's wife]; bur. Warrington
BIRKHOLDER, David, d.1838; bur. Warrington
BLACK, Alice Luella, b.10-27-1881, d.10-6-1967; bur. Menallen
    Anna M., b.8-19-1875, d.10-25-1970; bur. Menallen
    Emilie Wright, b.6-20-1849, d.5-26-1914; bur. Menallen
    Mabel Elma, b.1-22-1873, d.10-9-1947; bur. Menallen
    Susan Edith, b.1-6-1884, d.4-25-1937; bur. Menallen
    William Hugh, b.10-10-1842, d.2-28-1921; bur. Menallen
BLACKFORD, Joseph, d.1-1-1832; bur. Warrington
BLAIR, Johannah, d.9-12-1824; bur. Warrington
BOYER, John, b.3-9-1838, d.6-21-1891; bur. Redlands
BRINTON, John, d.1-14-1825; bur. Newberry
    Lydia, d.1-7-1835; bur. Newberry
BURKHOLDER, Mary, d.1838; bur. Warrington
CADWALADER, child, d.8-23-1823 [William's child]; bur. Warrington
    Rebecca; bur. Old Griest
    David, d.3-19-1843; bur. Warrington
    David, d.1846; bur. Warrington
CARDELL, Margaret K., b.9-25-1896, d.10-27-1972; bur. Menallen
CARWALETER, Sarah, d.1839; bur. Warrington
CHALFANT, George, d.4-12-1878, aged 38 yr 4 mo 28 da; bur. York
    Hannah U., d.6-10-1861, aged 18 yr 6 mo 15 da; bur. York
    James, d.11-29-1842, aged 40 yr 9 mo 18 da; bur. York
    Mary Ann, d.9-21-1876, aged 77 yr 8 mo 12 da; wife of James Chalfant; bur. York
    Susan M.; bur. York
CLEAVER, child, d.8-9-1823 [Peter Cleaver's child]; bur. Warrington
    Mrs., d.7-12-1823 [Peter Cleaver's mother]; bur. Warrington
CLEVER, John, Sr, d.5-3-1823; bur. Warrington
COMFORT, child, d.7-31-1823 [Jacob Comfort's child]; bur. Warrington
    Mrs., d.1835 [Jacob Comfort's wife]; bur. Warrington
COOK, Alisha, d.2-1-1846; bur. Warrington
    Amos G., d.7-1-1897, aged 52 yr 5 mo 12 da; bur. Menallen
    Arthur E., b.1880, d.1970, aged 90; bur. Menallen
    Charles D., b.12-9-1838, d.9-28-1911; bur. Menallen
    child, d.4-1-1846 [Alisha Cook's child]; bur. Warrington
    David J., d.9-20-1897, aged 64 yr 5 mo 27 da; bur. Menallen
    Ellis W., b.7-22-1846, d.1-2-1910; bur. Menallen
    Elmira J., b.10-9-1839, d.9-12-1914 [daughter of Ruth M. and Jessie Cook. Wife of C. D. Cook]; bur. Menallen
    Esther Ella, b.5-28-1887, d.11-1-1905; bur. Menallen
    Frances A., b.7-15-1847, d.2-5-1917; bur. Menallen
    Francis M., b.4-8-1862, aged 1 [son of D. & M. Cook]; bur. Menallen
    Geo. H., b.9-7-1835, d.8-5-1898; bur. Menallen
    Harris W., b.2-2-1862, d.5-1-1941; bur. Menallen

BURIALS

COOK, Harry A., d.7-22-1910 [aged 34 yr 5 mo 3 da]; bur. Menallen
    Henry, b.3-18-1843, d.3-28-1904; bur. Menallen
    Henry, d.4-10-1835; bur. Warrington
    Hezekiah, d.11-20-1833; bur. Warrington
    I. Elmer, MD, b.1-27-1843, d.1-13-1900; bur. Menallen
    Infant, b.2-26-1895, d.2-27-1895 [day old son of Ellis W. & Martha H. Cook]; bur. Menallen
    Isaac, d.1-1-1830; bur. Warrington
    J. Kersey, d.7-16-1865 [son of Jesse and Ruth Cook. Aged 27 yr 9 mo 2 da]; bur. Menallen
    J. Wilbert, b.1872, d.1942; bur. Menallen
    Jennie M., b.9-8-1871, d.8-20-1903; bur. Menallen
    Jesse, d.11-21-1855, aged 51 yr 5 mo 12 da; bur. Menallen
    Jesse, d.2-10-1880, aged 84; bur. Huntington
    John B., b.5-28-1889, d.3-13-1949; bur. Menallen
    John W., b.1804, d.3-28-1855 [aged 50 yr 5 mo 12 days]; bur. Friends Gr
    Josiah, d.10-21-1880, aged 75 yr 9 mo 2 da; bur. Menallen
    Julian, d.6-6-1857, aged 17 yr 9 mo 16 da; bur. Huntington
    Juliet T., d.8-17-1871, aged 29 yr 3 mo 6 da [wife of C. G. Cook]; bur. Menallen
    Lewis H., d.11-08-1861, aged 19 yr 6 mo [son of Jesse & Ruth]; bur. Menallen
    Lola M., b.4-4-1885, d.7-11-1910; bur. Menallen
    Margarett, d.8-24-1871, aged 68 yr 6 mo 26 da; bur. Menallen
    Maria, d.7-27-1890, aged 68 yr [wife of Wm. W. Cook and daughter of Abner Wickersham]; bur. Menallen
    Maria K., b.1849, d.1925; bur. Menallen
    Martha Ann, d.6-4-1861, aged 11 yr 9 mo 2 da [daughter of ? and M. G. Cook]; bur. Menallen
    Martha H., b.8-27-1853, d.3-1-1895; bur. Menallen
    Mary, d.9-24-1907, aged 61 yr 3 mo 23 da [wife of Josiah Cook]; bur. Menallen
    Mary, d.1830; bur. Warrington
    Mary, d.10-17-1833; bur. Warrington
    Mary, d.1835; bur. Warrington
    Mary A., d.1-10-1898, aged 71 yr 1 mo 24 da [wife of David J. Cook]; bur. Menallen
    Mary E. Lupp, b.1873, d.1960; bur. Menallen
    Mary G., b.5-28-1880, d.5-14-1899; bur. Menallen
    Mary T., d.11-26-1890, aged 86; bur. Menallen
    Mattie E., d.3-26-1964, aged 82 yr 1 mo 2 da; bur. Menallen
    May Bowker, b.1879, d.1951; bur. Menallen
    Melvin Jesse, b.1877, d.1960; bur. Menallen
    Milton W., d.1-8-1877, aged 2 yr 8 mo 16 da [son of C. D. & E. J. Cook]; bur. Menallen
    [Doctor Cook's mother in law], d.10-09-1823; bur. Warrington
    Mrs., d.12-03-1824 [John Cook's mother]; bur. Warrington
    Mrs., d.8-16-1835 [Josiah Cook's mother]; bur. Warrington
    Nora Hartman, b.1886, d.1980; bur. Menallen

MENALLEN, MARRIAGES AND MISCELLANY

COOK, Peter Bennett, b.1960, d.1986; bur. Menallen
    Rebecca, d.10-3-1857, aged 66 [wife of Jesse Cook]; bur. Huntington
    Ruth M., d.3-23-1887, aged 70 yr 20 da; bur. Menallen
    Samuel E., b.7-14-1797, d.4-24-1888; bur. Menallen
    Seymour E., d.4-4-1909, aged 1 yr 7 mo 26 da; bur. Menallen
    Susannah, Sr., d.4-12-1823; bur. Warrington
    T. Elwood, b.1-16-1869, d.2-11-1954; bur. Menallen
    Thomas E., d.12-22-1878, aged 67 yr 7 mo; bur. Menallen
    William W., d.12-2-1864, aged 58; bur. Friends Gr
COOKSON, [John Cookson's child], d.11-20-1833; bur. Warrington
    [John Cookson's child], d.1838; bur. Warrington
    E. Franklin, b.3-19-1829, d.4-4-1913; bur. Menallen
    Elizabeth, d.11-27-1839; bur. Warrington
    Sarah, Sr., d.9-9-1823; bur. Warrington
COX, Aaron, d.4-7-1862, aged 63 yr 6 mo 22 da; bur. Huntington
    Amanda, d.1859; bur. Huntington
    Elizabeth, d.2-5-1852, aged 7 yr 10 mo 10 da [daughter of Aaron & Sarah Cox]; bur. Huntington
    Jacob S., b.1853, d.1916; bur. Huntington
    John, b.11-30-1846, d.3-22-1894; bur. Huntington
    Mary Abigail; bur. Huntington
    Sarah Sticker, d.12-4-1887, aged 75 yr 10 mo 19 da [wife of Aaron Cox]; bur. Huntington
    Sarah W., d.11-9-1822, aged 37; bur. Huntington
CRUM, Margaret, b.1835, d.1893, aged 58 [mother of William Crum]; bur. Menallen
    Wm. H., d.3-16-1882, aged 17 yr 8 mo 1 da; bur. Menallen
DAVIS, Mary Wright, b.8-2-1790, d.10-1-1844; bur. Friends Gr
    Phineas [the inventor of the locomotive B & O RR buried to the N.W. just under the big elm in the east side], bur. York
DAY, John, d.2-4-1874, aged 70 yr 1 mo; bur. Huntington
    Phebe T., d.8-10-1863, aged 56 yr 9 mo 1 da; bur. Huntington
    Samuel, b.1-23-1756, d.2-14-1803; bur. Newberry
    Stephen, b.4-8-1837, d.1-5-1860, aged 22 yr 8 mo 27 da; bur. Huntington
    Susan, d.9-24-1835, aged 1 yr 21 da [daughter of John and Phebe Day]; bur. Huntington
DEAN, Rodger, b.1946, d.1947; bur. Huntington
DEMSTON, [Michael Demston's daughter], d.10-4-1823; bur. Warrington
DENISTON, Margaret, d.1830; bur. Warrington
DERBY, Sarah J., b.1828, d.1909; bur. Menallen
DUGAN, Francis Kenneth, b.12-27-1893, d.1-12-1919 [Q.M.C., U.S.A]; bur. Menallen
E., H., d.1774; bur. Newberry
E., N., d.4-24-1804; bur. Newberry
E., R., bur. Newberry
E., S., d.1816; bur. Newberry
ELCOCK, William, d.1846; bur. Warrington
ELLIS, Elizabeth, d.12-21-1853, aged 67 [wife of William Ellis]; bur. Menallen
    Mary Ann, b.1823, d.1904; bur. Menallen

BURIALS

ELLIS, William, d.2-14-1870, aged 71; bur. Menallen
EVANS, Oprah Jane, d.11-6-1893, aged 57 yr 8 mo 3 da; bur. Menallen
EVERITT, Isaac, d.8-1-1801, aged 64; bur. Huntington
    Martha, d.8-1-1851, aged 92; bur. Huntington
EYLER, Rebecca Jordan, b.5-4-1987, d.5-21-1987; bur. Menallen
F., H., bur. Newberry
F., L., d.1774; bur. Newberry
F., M., bur. Newberry
F., N., d.4-24-1804; bur. Newberry
FAUSS, John C., d.7-9-1822, aged 12 yr 2 da; bur. Huntington
FELIX, Mrs., d.1831 [Jacob Felix's wife]; bur. Warrington
FIELD, Joseph, d.12-27-1830, aged 35 yr 6 mo; bur. Newberry
FISHER, Joel, d.1857, aged 62; bur. Menallen
FRANKEBARG, Eliza, d.2-1-1866, aged 77; bur. Redlands
FRAZER, Alexander, b.8-13-1770, d.12-14-1816; bur. Newberry
    Alexander, d.1-2-1881, aged 44 yr 6 mo 15 da [son of John & Phebe Frazer]; bur. Redlands
    Charlotte A., d.11-20-1876, aged 38 yr 8 mo 13 da [wife of Julius, daughter of John & Phebe Frazer]; bur. Redlands
    Esther, d.7-1-1873, aged 14 yr 11 mo [daughter of John & Phebe Frazer]; bur. Redlands
    Jane, d.3-11-1882, aged 10 [daughter of John & Phebe Frazer]; bur. Redlands
    Mr., d.2-22-1879, aged 82 yr 1 mo 12 da; bur. Redlands
    Susan, d.4-17-1871, aged 40 yr 8 mo 3 da [daughter of John & Phebe Frazer]; bur. Redlands
G., A., bur. Newberry
G., I., bur. Newberry
G., J., bur. Newberry
G., K., bur. Newberry
G., S., bur. Newberry
G., T., d.1802; bur. Newberry
G., T., d.1804; bur. Newberry
G., T., d.1760; bur. Friends Gr
GARDNER, Robert Lewis, b.1931, d.1961; bur. Huntington
GARRETSON, A. B.; bur. Redlands
    Alice P., b.11-5-1865, d.12-9-1866 [daughter of Joel V. & Hannah A. Garretson]; bur. Menallen
    B., bur. Redlands
    Chester W., b.10-8-1908, d.12-31-1982 [TSGT US Army World War II]; bur. Menallen
    Donald F., b.11-18-1904, d.1-3-1969; bur. Menallen
    Eli B. d.4-10-1859, aged 28 yr 7 mo 10 da; bur. Redlands
    Eliza, d.2-18-1892, aged 46 yr 2 mo; bur. Redlands
    Eliza Jane, d.4-11-1818, aged 22 yr 4 mo 19 da [daughter of Thomas & Jane Garretson]; bur. Redlands
    Elizabeth, b.12-28-1861, d.1-12-1931; bur. Menallen
    Elizabeth, b.1813, d.1818; bur. Huntington
    Elizabeth, d.5-7-1849, aged 82 yr 5 mo 13 da [former wife of Israel Meredith]; bur. Newberry

MENALLEN, MARRIAGES AND MISCELLANY

GARRETSON, Elizabeth B., b.3-5-1794, d.2-13-1862; bur. Redlands
    Ezra, b.1-25-1834, d.11-14-1915 [son of Benjamin & Oprah Garretson]; bur. Menallen
    Franklin, b.1-14-1830, d.10-14-1842; bur. Redlands
    Hannah, d.4-11-1864, aged 89 yr 9 mo 24 da; bur. Menallen
    Infants [infant son and daughter of Jacob & Eliza Garretson], bur. Redlands
    Isaac P., b.8-15-1810, d.6-28-1854; bur. Huntington
    Israel, d.10-13-1894, aged 64 yr 2 mo 18 da; bur. Menallen
    Israel, d.6-20-1880, aged 82 yr 1 mo 13 da; bur. Redlands
    J. Blair, d.3-5-1944, aged 80 yr 10 mo 8 da; bur. Menallen
    Jacob, bur. Newberry
    Jacob, bur. Redlands
    James, bur. Newberry
    Jane, d.4-27-1859, aged 68 yr 11 mo 10 da [wife of Thomas Garretson]; bur. Redlands
    Josiah, d.5-20-1853, aged 72 yr 11 mo; bur. Huntington
    Lillie M., d.4-12-1882 [daughter of Jacob & E. Garretson]; bur. Redlands
    Lizzie M., d.1-2-1918, aged 55 yr 5 mo 27 da [wife of J. Blair Garretson]; bur. Menallen
    Louisa, b.3-11-1820, d.8-16-1864; bur. Redlands
    Martha, b.1784, d.1820; bur. Huntington
    Mary, b.9-20-1825, d.3-28-1904; bur. Menallen
    Mary, bur. Newberry
    Mary C., b.1881, d.1931; bur. Menallen
    Minnie M., b.4-18-1882, d.8-15-1882 [daughter of Jacob & E. Garretson]; bur. Redlands
    O., bur. Redlands
    Oliver, d.9-29-1854, aged 40 yr 4 mo; bur. Huntington
    Phebe, d.9-8-1823, aged 12 yr 6 mo; bur. Huntington
    Rachel, d.1-26-1902, aged 74 yr 4 mo 8 da; bur. Menallen
    Rebecca F., b.5-27-1876, d.2-2-1952; bur. Menallen
    Rhoda H., d.10-10-1880, aged 83 yr 5 mo; bur. Menallen
    Robert, b.1867, d.1953; bur. Menallen
    Robert N., d.4-3-1841; bur. Redlands
    Ruth, d.2-6-1880, aged 75 yr 1 mo 12 da; bur. Redlands
    Ruth Mildrid, b.1-25-1907, d.12-15-1937; bur. Menallen
    Ruth R., d.6-4-1878 [infant daughter of Jacob & Eliza Garretson]; bur. Redlands
    son, d.8-14-1817, aged 14 yr 1 mo 1 da; bur. Redlands
    Susan, b.12-12-1823, d.2-23-1852 [daughter of Thomas & Jane Garretson]; bur. Redlands
    Thomas, d.1-25-1862, aged 71 yr 5 da; bur. Redlands
    Willie H., b.3-26-1864, d.10-30-1864; bur. Redlands
    Alice F., b.11-05-1865, d.12-09-1866; bur. Menallen
    Franklin G., b.11-15-1857, d 1947 ["Uncle Frank"]; bur. Menallen
    Hannah A., b.7-22-1832, d.2-29-1899; bur. Menallen
    Joel V., b.3-1-1833, d.4-22-1912; bur. Menallen
GITT, Daniel D., b.3-20-1820, d.2-1-1891; bur. Menallen

BURIALS

GITT, Hannah W., d.5-3-1857, aged 70 yr 5 mo 24 da [wife of Daniel D. Gitt, daughter of Isaac & Susannah Wierman]; bur. Menallen
  Infant, d.2-1-1856 [infant son of Daniel D.]; bur. Menallen
GIVEN, David, d.9-2-1888, aged 66 yr 2 mo 7 da; bur. Redlands
  Elizabeth, d.2-10-1843, aged 49; bur. Redlands
  James E., d.2-22-1854, aged 27; bur. Redlands
  Meria, d.7-23-1870, aged 39 yr 7 mo 23 da; bur. Redlands
GLANCY, Martha, bur. Newberry
GLASS, child, d.1832 [William Glass' child]; bur. Warrington
GLAT, Daniel, d.5-1-1839; bur. Warrington
GOLD, Joseph, d.12-27-1830, aged 35 yr 6 mo; bur. Newberry
GOVE, Mary E., b.1853, d.1943 [wife of J. Howard Gove. Daughter of Hiram and Louisa Griest]; bur. Menallen
GRAT, child, d.2-4-1823 [Jesse Grat's child]; bur. Warrington
GRATZ, Mrs., d.5-2-1834 [Jesse Gratz's wife]; bur. Warrington
GRAY, child, d.5-1-1824 [Jesse Gray's child]; bur. Warrington
  Mrs., d.1-30-1823 [Isaac Gray's mother]; bur. Warrington
GRIEST, Amos, d.11-30-1865, aged 79 yr 5 mo 11 da; bur. Huntington
  Amos Willing, b.1848, d.1930; bur. Menallen
  Anne M., b.11-20-1832, d.11-14-1900 [daughter of Cyrus & Mary Ann Griest]; bur. Menallen
  C. Arthur, b.8-25-1878, d.9-15-1962; bur. Menallen
  C. G., bur. Old Griest
  Charles E., d.9-16-1866, aged 2 mo 6 da [son of J. W. and M. H. Griest]; bur. Menallen
  child, d.9-15-1823 [Jonathan Griest's child]; bur. Warrington
  Content, d.1-29-1880, aged 74 yr 1 mo 4 da; bur. Huntington
  Cyrus, b.5-29-1803, d.11-3-1869; bur. Menallen
  Cyrus S., b.3-1-1835, d.8-5-1918 [son of C. & M. A. Griest]; bur. Menallen
  daughter, d.8-16-1852, aged 6 yr 9 mo 2 da [daughter of Amos & Margaret Griest]; bur. Huntington
  E. Clyde, b.6-1-1895, d.7-14-1896 [son of Eli L. & Maria J. Griest]; bur. Menallen
  Edith, bur. Menallen
  Eleanor Pricket, b.5-29-1897, d.1-9-1974; bur. Menallen
  Eliza R., b.1852, d.1928; bur. Menallen
  Elizabeth, b.7-18-1868, d.7-5-1935 [daughter of C. S. & L. B. Griest]; bur. Menallen
  Elizabeth, bur. Old Griest
  Ellis, d.11-22-1860, aged 9 yr 22 da [son of H. & L. E. Griest]; bur. Menallen
  Elmira, bur. Old Griest
  Frederic E., b.3-4-1883, d.5-17-1976; bur. Menallen
  George, bur. Old Griest
  George G., b.4-21-1873, d.8-25-1933; bur. Menallen
  George M., d.1853; bur. Menallen
  George W., d.11-30-1861, aged 1 yr 4 mo 4 da [son of J. S. & M. A. Griest]; bur. Menallen
  Gideon, bur. Old Griest

MENALLEN, MARRIAGES AND MISCELLANY

GRIEST, Harold W., b.3-1-1903, d.4-11-1905; bur. Menallen
Harriette, b.6-5-1879, d.8-5-1955; bur. Menallen
Hiram, b.12-9-1827, d.6-27-1919, aged 92 yr 6 mo 16 da; bur. Menallen
I. G., d.1791; bur. Old Griest
Infant son, d.8-15-1876 [son of A. W. and E. R. Griest]; bur. Menallen
Isaac, bur. Old Griest
J. G., d.1841; bur. Old Griest
Jacob, d.6-28-1857, aged 58 yr 9 mo 20 da; bur. Huntington
Jane, bur. Old Griest
Jesse W., d.3-20-1885, aged 47 yr 9 mo; bur. Menallen
Josiah, d.11-11-1885, aged 73 yr 1 mo 18 da; bur. Menallen
Letitia B., b.8-2-1837, d.5-1-1898 [wife of Cyrus S. Griest. Daughter of John Broomell]; bur. Menallen
Letitia G., b.3-7-1909, d.2-1-1979; bur. Menallen
Levi, d.7-15-1864, aged 84; bur. Friends Gr
Lola W., b.8-22-1877, d.5-9-1961; bur. Menallen
Louisa E., b.6-12-1825, d.10-16-1903, aged 78 yr 4 mo 4 da [wife of Hiram Griest]; bur. Menallen
Lydia, bur. Old Griest
Margaret, d.8-1-1879, aged 68 yr 9 mo [wife of Amos Griest]; bur. Huntington
Marian Marshal, b.9-14-1888, d.10-04-1916; bur. Menallen
Mary, bur. Old Griest
Mary, bur. Old Griest
Mary, bur. Old Griest
Mary, d.6-10-1825; bur. Friends Gr
Mary Alice, b.7-14-1858, d.1-19-1929; bur. Menallen
Mary Ann, b.2-10-1884, aged 78 yr 2 mo 28 da; bur. Menallen
Mary Ann, b.11-19-1817, d.4-15-1900; bur. Menallen
Mary E., b.5-21-1864, d.2-17-1937 [daughter of C. S. & L. B. Griest]; bur. Menallen
Mary H., d.7-10-1866, aged 26 yr 6 mo 15 da [wife of Jesse W. Griest]; bur. Menallen
Miriam, bur. Old Griest
Miriam, d.8-20-1817, aged 80 yr 5 da [daughter of Peter Cleaver]; bur. Redlands
Mrs., d.1829 [Amos Griest's wife]; bur. Warrington
N. G., bur. Old Griest
Owen, b.1818, d.1907; bur. Menallen
Peter, bur. Old Griest
Rachel, bur. Old Griest
Rose C., b.6-19-1862, d.11-25-1944 [wife of William H. Griest]; bur. Menallen
Ruth Eliza, b.6-9-1854, d.12-16-1918; bur. Menallen
Sibilla E., b.12-27-1835, d.8-24-1904 [wife of Jesse W. Griest]; bur. Menallen
Solomon, bur. Old Griest
Susanna A., d.11-6-1861, aged 6 yr 1 mo 28 da [daughter of J. S. & M. A. Griest]; bur. Menallen
Virginia, d.11-20-1860, aged 11 yr 7 da [daughter of H. and L. E.

BURIALS

    Griest]; bur. Menallen
GRIEST, William H., b.4-14-1860, d.9-17-1930; bur. Menallen
GRIFFITH, Abraham, d.6-20-1841; bur. Warrington
    child, d.7-17-1823 [Amos Griffith's child]; bur. Warrington
    child, d.8-13-1823 [Abraham Griffith's child]; bur. Warrington
    daughter, d.1827 [Amos Griffith's daughter]; bur. Warrington
    Deborah, d.2-22-1845; bur. Warrington
    Elmer, d.1838; bur. Warrington
    Mitchel, d.1834; bur. Warrington
    son, d.8-11-1823 [Abraham Griffith's son]; bur. Warrington
GRIFFITHS, child, d.9-26-1823 [Geoy Griffith's child]; bur. Warrington
    child, d.1-2-1826 [Abraham Griffith's child]; bur. Warrington
    child, d.1829 [Abraham Griffith Jr's child]; bur. Warrington
    child, d.2-18-1834 [Aba Griffith's child]; bur. Warrington
    child, d.1836 [Mitchell Griffith's child]; bur. Warrington
    Mrs., d.8-20-1835 [Joseph Griffith's wife]; bur. Warrington
GRIGGS, Clarisa A., d.8-01-1845, aged 14 yr 2 mo 18 da; bur. Redlands
GRINDER, Jeffrey L., b.2-5-1952, d.9-5-1976; bur. Redlands
GRIST, Isaac, d.4-21-1842; bur. Warrington
    Solomon, d.2-27-1844; bur. Warrington
    Willen, d.1832; bur. Warrington
H., A., bur. Newberry
H., D., d.1812; bur. Newberry
H., D. A., d.1824; bur. Newberry
H., I., bur. Newberry
H., I. A., d.1818; bur. Newberry
H., M., bur. Newberry
H., M., bur. Friends Gr
H., N., d.1750; bur. Newberry
H., S. B., d.1810; bur. Newberry
H., T., d.1753; bur. Newberry
H., W., bur. Newberry
HACKNEY, Robert H., d.6-19-1862, aged 18 yr 11 mo 19 da [son of Aaron H. &
    Sarah H. Hackney]; bur. Menallen
HALL, G. W., d.6-18-1830, aged 17; bur. Newberry
HAMERLY, Robert, bur. Newberry
HAMILG, child, d.6-20-1845 [William Hamilg's child]; bur. Warrington
HARDY, Benj. B., d.12-23-1903, aged 68 yr 2 mo 13 da; bur. Menallen
    Mary B., d.10-4-1906, aged 73 yr 9 mo 11 da; bur. Menallen
HARLAN, Sam'l, d.4-23-1859, aged 81 yr 8 mo 14 da; bur. Friends Gr
HARLON, Sarah, b.5-22-1793, d.7-11-1873; bur. Friends Gr
HARMON, child, d.1-10-1834 [Bia -?- Harmon's child]; bur. Warrington
HARRIS, Annie G., b.10-07-1865, d.3-25-1926; bur. Menallen
    B., d.1-11-1881, aged 87 yr 4 mo 7 da; bur. Friends Gr
    Beula E., b.5-14-1881, d.4-30-1934; bur. Menallen
    Charles K., b.1850, d.1922; bur. Menallen
    Hiram L., b.5-20-1836, d.3-9-1882; bur. Menallen
    Jane, d.2-20-1880, aged 81 yr 4 mo 20 da; bur. Friends Gr
    Julia K., d.3-13-1885, aged 64 yr 2 mo 24 da [wife of Samuel H. Harris];
        bur. Menallen

MENALLEN, MARRIAGES AND MISCELLANY

HARRIS, Matilda J., d.8-28-1841, aged 7 yr 5 mo 5 da; bur. Friends Gr
    Matilda Wierman, b.1841, d.1911; bur. Menallen
    Miriam C., b.3-5-1846, d.9-22-1922; bur. Menallen
    Samuel H., b.7-27-1824, d.4-15-1908; bur. Menallen
HART, Elizabeth, d.8-9-1876, aged 77 yr 4 mo 14 da [wife of Joseph Hart];
        bur. Redlands
    Isaac, b.9-3-1788, d.10-4-1839; bur. Newberry
    Jacob, d.9-9-1811, aged 9; bur. Newberry
    James, d.9-6-1820; bur. Newberry
    Jane, d.12-10-1824, aged 16 yr 7 mo 14 da; bur. Newberry
    Mary, d.2-25-1833, aged 29 yr 4 mo [wife of Joseph Hart]; bur.
        Newberry
    Michael, d.9-12-1811, aged 12; bur. Newberry
    Robert L., d.12-2-1851, aged 16 yr 6 mo 6 da [son of Isaac & Elizabeth
        Hart]; bur. Redlands
    Sarah, aged 61 yr 27 da; bur. Newberry
HAYWARD, child, d.1828 [Doctor Hayward's child]; bur. Warrington
    child, d.1829 [Doctor Hayward's child]; bur. Warrington
HEATHCOTE, wife, aged 47 yr [wife of Lulec Heathcote. A native of Stayley
        Wood, Cheshire, England]; bur. Redlands
    Rachel, d.6-18-1869, aged 71 yr 10 mo 20 da [wife of Lulec Heathcote];
        bur. Redlands
HEWITT, Ellen W., d.2-10-1883 [wife of Geo Hewitt]; bur. Menallen
    Geo., d.1-26-1879, aged 87; bur. Menallen
    Mary, aged 74; bur. Friends Gr
HIT, Mr., d.8-16-1823 [Sarah Hit's (?) husband]; bur. Warrington
HOFFMAN, Abram T., b.5-7-1870, d.8-8-1903; bur. Menallen
    Annie F. C., b.9-7-1873, d.8-5-1940; bur. Menallen
    Dora A., b.1898, d.1984; bur. Menallen
HOLLABAUGH, Howard F., b.1884, d.1949; bur. Menallen
    J. Esther, b.1889, d.1973; bur. Menallen
HOLLAND, Henry, d.5-9-1823; bur. Warrington
    Mary, d.6-25-1822; bur. Warrington
HOLLY, child, d.4-3-1824 [widow Holly's child]; bur. Warrington
    widow, d.4-8-1824; bur. Warrington
HOLTZ, John, Jr. d.9-12-1823; bur. Warrington
HOOPES, Daniel, d.5-9-1875, aged 71 yr 7 mo 9 da; bur. Redlands
    Jacob, d.1816; bur. Newberry
    Lydia, d.12-7-1860; bur. Menallen
    Lydia, d.1824 [Lydia Hoopes & daughter]; bur. Newberry
    Mary, d.8-5-1877, aged 56 yr 1 mo 15 da [daughter of Jacob B. Hoopes];
        bur. Redlands
    Mary, d.12-15-1884, aged 77 yr 2 mo 18 da [wife of Daniel Hoopes]; bur.
        Redlands
    William Henry, b.11-27-1842, d.10-31-1845 [son of Jacob B. & Mary
        Hoopes]; bur. Redlands
HOOPS, Job, d.10-12-1847, aged 52 yr 8 mo 29 da; bur. Redlands
    Phebe, d.4-6-1857, aged 82; bur. Redlands
    William, d.1-6-1816, aged 27 yr 5 mo; bur. Redlands
    Wilmer, b.9-30-1768, d.9-15-1843; bur. Redlands

BURIALS

HOWEL, Jose, d.2-14-1872, aged 78; bur. Huntington
HOWELL, Elizabeth, b.8-13-1790, d.8-24-1879; bur. Huntington
HUSSEY, child, d.11-5-1822 [Judiah Hussey's child]; bur. Warrington
    Judiah, d.9-1-1828; bur. Warrington
    Judiah, Sr. d.10-7-1823; bur. Warrington
HUSSYS, child, d.9-25-1825 [Judiah Hussy's child]; bur. Warrington
HUTTEN, daughter, d.2-12-1823 [Simeon Hutten's daughter]; bur. Warrington
HUTTON, Levi, d.2-22-1844, aged 86 yr 22 da; bur. Friends Gr
    Levi, d.10-1-1838, aged 2; bur. Friends Gr
    Martha, d.4-3-1827, aged 60; bur. Friends Gr
    Rhubeon, d.1-31-1843; bur. Warrington
    Simeon, d.7-24-1836; bur. Warrington
HYMES, David, d.8-19-1861, aged 99; bur. Redlands
I., R., bur. Newberry
J., S., d.1770; bur. Newberry
JAMES, Amanda, d.11-20-1862, aged 2 yr 6 mo; bur. Redlands
JESSOP, Edward, d.5-31-1878, aged 68 yr 4 mo 7 da; bur. York
    Francis, bur. York
    William, d.5-25-1861; bur. York
JOHN, Joseph, d.3-10-1844; bur. Warrington
JOHNS, Sarah, d.3-01-1837 [Samuel Johns' wife]; bur. Warrington
JOHNSON, James, bur. Newberry
JOLIN, Mrs., d.11-1-1829 [John Joseph Jolin's wife]; bur. Warrington
JONES, Barzillai, d.5-19-1939; bur. Menallen
    child, d.1830 [Benjamin Jones' child]; bur. Warrington
    John, d.1830; bur. Warrington
    Mrs., d.9-6-1830 [John Jones' mother]; bur. Warrington
    Rachel E., b.8-13-1856, d.7-26-1948; bur. Menallen
    Samuel, aged 68 yr 11 mo 25 da; bur. Newberry
JOYCE, Alice Virginia, b.6-30-1878, d.4-2-1948; bur. Menallen
    Elizabeth, d.3-22-1861, aged 12 yr 10 mo 14 da [daughter of Joseph & M. Joyce]; bur. Menallen
    Ellen Harriet, d.3-17-1872, aged 17 yr 9 mo 22 da [daughter of Joseph & M. Joyce]; bur. Menallen
    Frankline, aged 7 mo 16 da [son of G. H. and Jennie Joyce]; bur. Menallen
    George Hewitt, b.5-9-1851, d.9-3-1919; bur. Menallen
    Joel, d.3-20-1855, aged 66; bur. Menallen
    Joseph, d.3-28-1882, aged 90; bur. Menallen
    Margaret, b.7-25-1811, d.4-10-1891; bur. Menallen
    Phillip Amos, b.10-19-1892, d.7-25-1904 [son of E. H. and S. A. V. Joyce]; bur. Menallen
    S. A. Virginia, d.4-27-1901, aged 50 yr 8 mo 15 da [wife of George H. Joyce]; bur. Menallen
K., D., bur. Newberry
K., J., d.1832; bur. Newberry
K., M., bur. Newberry
KEEFER, Clarence E., b.1891, d.1964; bur. Menallen
KERR, Arabella G., b.3-5-1858, d.11-22-1915; bur. Menallen
    Dr. Robert, b.2-1-1857, d.8-3-1917; bur. Menallen

MENALLEN, MARRIAGES AND MISCELLANY

KETTLEWELL, Charles, d.5-27-1851, aged 71; bur. Huntington
    Samuel, d.2-14-1853; bur. Huntington
KIRK, Eliza, bur. Redlands
    Hannah, d.6-4-1824 [wife of Jacob Kirk and Daughter of Je and Ann Wickersham]; bur. Newberry
    Hannah, d.11-15-1884, aged 82 yr 5 mo; bur. Redlands
    Jacob, d.9-17-1782, aged 15 yr 2 mo; bur. Redlands
KITTLEWELL, Mary, d.9-21-1823; bur. Warrington
KNISSLY, Lavinia, d.9-20-1861, aged 49 yr 7 mo 25 da [wife of John Knissly]; bur. Redlands
KOHR, Eliza, b.2-9-1833, d.8-11-1882; bur. Redlands
    Hattie May, d.3-11-1882, aged 3 [daughter of Daniel W. & Mary E. Kohr]; bur. Redlands
    Reuben, b.8-30-1832, d.5-12-1906; bur. Redlands
KOSER, Andrew J., b.7-25-1843, d.7-27-1909; bur. Menallen
    Eleanor Richard, b.12-15-1867, d.6-28-1960; bur. Menallen
    Elizabeth, b.7-18-1870, d.3-12-1906; bur. Menallen
    George Wilmer, b.6-13-1869, d.7-5-1949; bur. Menallen
KRIEGER, Elizabeth, d.1832; bur. Newberry
    George, b.12-25-1838, d.12-25-1839; bur. Newberry
    Jacob, d.1815; bur. Newberry
    Ludwig, bur. Newberry
LAUGHMAN, Daniel, b.9-1-1763, d.3-5-1836; bur. Newberry
    Elizabeth, b.3-20-1772, d.9-5-1820 [wife of Daniel Laughman]; bur. Newberry
LEACE, Ann, d.1846; bur. Warrington
    Margret, d.1846; bur. Warrington
LEECH, child, d.1831 [Joseph Leech's 2 children]; bur. Warrington
    Mrs., d.10-25-1822 [Thomas Leech's mother]; bur. Warrington
LEONARD, Sarah Alma, d.7-13-1869; bur. Menallen
LEWIS, bur. Newberry
    Harvey P., b.8-28-1882, d.2-1-1928; bur. Menallen
    Robert N., b.7-30-1799, d.3-16-1846; bur. Redlands
    Webster, b.3-19-1779, d.5-16-1830; bur. Redlands
LONGSDORF, Alice, bur. Menallen
    C. S., b.1881, d.1957; bur. Menallen
    Charles L., b.6-15-1851, d.8-4-1931; bur. Menallen
    Elizabeth, b.1-23-1853, d.9-13-1917; bur. Menallen
    Hiram Starr, d.7-27-1889, aged 3 yr 3 mo 17 da [C. L. & E. W.]; bur. Menallen
LOVE, Anna, d.12-13-1877; bur. York
    Mary, d.6-6-1844; bur. York
M., A., bur. Newberry
MAHLEN, George, d.9-22-1828; bur. Warrington
MAHLON, child, d.3-5-1823 [John Mahlon's child]; bur. Warrington
    Mrs., d.5-25-1822 [George Mahlon's wife]; bur. Warrington
MALLENCE, Mrs., d.10-2-1822 [Jarret Mallence's wife]; bur. Warrington
MARILL [?], Elwood, d.2-15-1846, aged 4 yr 2 mo 25 da; bur. Redlands
MAY, David, d.1-30-1855, aged 35 yr 11 mo 29 da; bur. Redlands
    Eliza, d.2-6-1862, aged 38 [wife of David May]; bur. Redlands

BURIALS

MAY, Jacob R., d.3-18-1845, aged 3 [son of David & Lisa May]; bur. Redlands
MAYRES, Mrs., d.10-15-1823 [Peter Mayres' wife]; bur. Warrington
McCREARY, Alice, d.2-6-1855, aged 75 yr 11 mo 21 da; bur. Friends Gr
    Cyrus Lamar, d.3-3-1861, aged 6 weeks 5 days [son of Thomas & Sarah McCreary]; bur. Menallen
    David, d.3-25-1828, aged 69; bur. Friends Gr
    David R., b.1826, d.1874; bur. Friends Gr
    Deborah H., b.1814, d.1892; bur. Friends Gr
    George H., b.1822, d.1893; bur. Friends Gr
    John, d.12-12-1821, aged 32; bur. Friends Gr
    John H., b.1824, d.1882; bur. Friends Gr
    Lydia, b.10-7-1850, d.1-26-1851 [daughter of Samuel McCreary]; bur. Redlands
    Lydia Elverda, d.11-17-1864, aged 6 weeks 5 da [daughter of Thomas & Sarah A. McCreary]; bur. Menallen
    Lydia H., b.1812, d.1890; bur. Friends Gr
    Mary, d.1830; bur. Warrington
    Mary, d.1-29-1822, aged 5 yr 5 da; bur. Friends Gr
    Sarah, bur. Friends Gr
    Thomas, d.3-8-1865, aged 88 yr 3 mo 8 da; bur. Friends Gr
    Thos, d.7-9-1829; bur. Warrington
    William H., b.1816, d.1884; bur. Friends Gr
McCRERY, Julias, b.2-16-1832, d.2-22-1839; bur. Newberry
McELLEE, Samuel, d.9-1-1823; bur. Warrington
    Sarah, d.10-7-1823; bur. Warrington
McKONLY, Abbie, d.1718 [son of I. & S. McKonly]; bur. Friends Gr
    David W., aged 20 days [son of I. & S. A. McKonly]; bur. Friends Gr
    George F., d. 9-5-1870, aged 2 mo 10 days [son of I. & S. A. McKonly]; bur. Friends Gr
    Levi C., d.5-11-1863, aged 3 yrs 9 da [son of I. & S. A. McKonly]; bur. Friends Gr
    Sarah A., d.10-15-1873 [wife of Isaac McKonly]; bur. Friends Gr
McMILAN, Jacob, d.1832; bur. Warrington
    Jorge, d.1846; bur. Warrington
McMILLAN, child, d.1834 [Amos McMillan's child]; bur. Warrington
    Joseph, d.3-29-1826; bur. Warrington
McMILLEN, Mrs., d.1829 [Jacob McMillen's wife]; bur. Warrington
McMILLIAN, child, d.1828 [George McMillian's child]; bur. Warrington
    Mrs., d.10-7-1823 [Joseph McMillian's wife]; bur. Warrington
MELONE, Ann, d.3-10-1844; bur. Warrington
MEREDITH, E., bur. York
    Eliza, d.3-19-1852, aged 19 yr 2 mo 18 da [daughter of Jesse & Jane Meredith]; bur. Redlands
    Elizabeth, bur. York
    Israel, d.6-28-1814, aged 47 yr 1 mo 14 da; bur. Newberry
    Jesse, d.1-26-1870, aged 63 yr 2 mo 4 da; bur. Redlands
    Jules [Prin. Mus. Co. B 2 IOWA INF Marker: GAR 1861–1865], bur. Redlands
    Mary S., b.11-1-1839, d.9-1-1925; bur. Redlands
    Sidney, bur. York

MENALLEN, MARRIAGES AND MISCELLANY

METCALFE, Mary, d.11-26-1840, aged 52 yr 1 mo 14 da [wife of John P. Metcalfe]; bur. Huntington
    Matilda P., d.9-20-1839, aged 2 [daughter of D. Metcalfe]; bur. Huntington
    Nathan B., d.11-11-1859, aged 16 yr 1 mo 3 da [son of J. P. & M. J. Metcalfe-Illinois]; bur. Huntington
MICHENER, Anna M., b.4-10-1893, d.1-9-1961; bur. Menallen
    C. Raymond, b.3-5-1895, d.3-18-1966; bur. Menallen
    Charles, b.2-28-1854, d.2-27-1911; bur. Menallen
    Cyrus G., d.1-27-1893, aged 4 yr 3 mo 20 da [son of C. M. & F. G. Michener]; bur. Menallen
    Florence G., b.5-3-1866, d.1-1-1935 [wife of Charles Michener]; bur. Menallen
    Sybil S. J., b.3-12-1888, d.2-8-1975; bur. Menallen
MICKLE, Eve, d.2-11-1814; bur. Friends Gr
    Samuel, d.3-26-1819, aged 63; bur. Friends Gr
    Samuel, d.7-30-1797, aged 9 yr; bur. Friends Gr
    Thomas, d.4-4-1826, aged 34; bur. Friends Gr
MILLER, Charlie, d.1-7-1877, aged 1 yr 11 mo 24 da [son of William & ? Miller]; bur. Redlands
    Henry S., b.4-6-1817, d.12-27-1897; bur. Redlands
    Jerome, b.1858, d.1926; bur. Redlands
    Jesse B., b.1842, d.1927 [Co. L. Pa. Cav.]; bur. Redlands
    John, d.4-9-1802, aged 35 [of Cumberland County]; bur. Newberry
    John, bur. Newberry
    Malinda E., b.1856, d.1944; bur. Redlands
    Mary Ann, b.10-11-1818, d.1-9-1887 [wife of Henry S. Miller]; bur. Redlands
    Peter, d.6-19-1823; bur. Warrington
MOORE, Flora Tilton, b.1867, d.1949; bur. Menallen
    Isaac, b.2-28-1819, d.3-30-1836 [son of Mordecai and Elizabeth Moore]; bur. Newberry
    Sarah, d.1-12-1842, aged 72 yr 19 da [wife of John Moore]; bur. Redlands
MORE, Betsey, d.7-14-1809; bur. Newberry
    John, b.10-14-1774, d.11-20-1851; bur. Redlands
MORRIS, child, d.4-12-1823 [Nehemiah Morris's child]; bur. Warrington
    Mr., d.10-9-1823 [Nehemiah Morris's father]; bur. Warrington
    Mrs., d.1830 [Charles Morris's Mother]; bur. Warrington
    Robert, d.1846; bur. Warrington
MORTHLAND, child, d.4-21-1823 [Hugh Morthland's child]; bur. Warrington
    child, d.1827 [Hugh Morthland's child]; bur. Warrington
    child, d.8-15-1836 [Hugh Morthland's child]; bur. Warrington
    Esther, d.1-31-1892, aged 89 yr 11 mo 9 da; bur. Menallen
    Mrs., d.6-14-1822 [Hugh Morthland's Mother]; bur. Warrington
    Mrs., d.8-20-1837 [Hugh Morthland's wife]; bur. Warrington
    Mrs., d.5-23-1841 [Hugh Morthland's wife]; bur. Warrington
    Phebe, d.1-20-1850, aged 28 [daughter of John & Phebe Tudor]; bur. Huntington
    Phebe, d.7-1-1838; bur. Warrington

BURIALS

MORTHLAND, Robert, d.10-25-1822; bur. Warrington
    Walter, d.2-1-1836; bur. Warrington
    William, d.9-22-1823 [got killed]; bur. Warrington
MOSBY, infant son [of L. E. & I. H. Mosby], bur. Menallen
    Lizzie H., d.3-28-1868, aged 29 [wife of Andrew F. Mosby]; bur. Menallen
MUELLER, E. [a seamstress], bur. York
MYER, daughter, d.3-1-1831 [Peter Myer's daughter]; bur. Warrington
MYRES, Jacob, d.10-7-1826; bur. Warrington
NAV?, David; bur. Newberry
NEBINGER, Ann, d.6-10-1827; bur. Newberry
    George, d.12-07-1796 [by their son Robert Nebinger]; bur. Newberry
NEELY, Huldah Wierman, b.1829, d.1910; bur. Huntington
NELSON, child, d.3-8-1823 [Daniel Nelson's child]; bur. Warrington
    child, d.1842 [William Nelson's child]; bur. Warrington
    Daniel, d.12-7-1838; bur. Warrington
    Esther, d.10-18-1823 [Wm. Nelson's daughter]; bur. Warrington
    John, d.10-28-1834; bur. Warrington
    Margaret, d.1830; bur. Warrington
    Robert, d.2-11-1823; bur. Warrington
    Wm, d.1835; bur. Warrington
NESBET, Nancy, d.8-25-1832; bur. Warrington
NESBIT, James, d.1830; bur. Warrington
NICHOLS, Elizabeth, d.1-3-1836, aged 65 yr 3 da; bur. Newberry
NOBLEMAN, Polish [A Polish Nobleman died after the Revolution and is buried in the W. part. buttons. No stone], bur. York
NORIS, Charles, d.12-25-1845 [Christmas]; bur. Warrington
NORRIS, Elizabeth, d.8-3-1828, aged 9 mo 28 da [daughter of Richard & Eliza Norris of Baltimore]; bur. Huntington
    Mrs., d.6-23-1829 [Nehemiah Norris' wife]; bur. Warrington
NORTIN, Isaac, bur. Warrington
OCKER, John C., d.8-25-1834, aged 22 yr 2 mo 21 da [son of Benj. and Mary Ocker]; bur. Huntington
OWENS, A. [Abraham Owens], bur. York
    M. [Abraham's wife], bur. York
P., d.2-29-1825; bur. Newberry
P. A., bur. Newberry
PACANO, Maria, b.9-18-1837, d.9-9-1921; bur. Menallen
PARMER, Ardella Cook, b.1870, d.1956; bur. Menallen
    Howard E., b.1905, d.1913; bur. Menallen
    W. Clyde, b.1908, d.1943; bur. Menallen
    William H., b.1864, d.1945; bur. Menallen
PARRY, James E., b.8-21-1899, d.2-13-1988; bur. Menallen
PARSONS, Muriel Tyson, b.3-3-1889, d.9-27-1970; bur. Menallen
PEARSON, Charles Godfrey, b.9-20-1859, aged 11 mo 21 da [son of I. W. & Mary C. Pearson]; bur. Huntington
    Francis Wiesley, d.10-8-1865, aged 1 yr 7 mo 14 da [son of I. W. & M. Pearson]; bur. Huntington
    Martha, d.10-11-1818, aged 73 yr 1 mo 15 da [wife of Thomas Pearson]; bur. Huntington

MENALLEN, MARRIAGES AND MISCELLANY

PEARSON, Phebe, d.7-23-1860, aged 61 yr 20 da; bur. Huntington
    Thomas, d.3-31-1811, aged 52 yr 3 mo 29 da; bur. Huntington
PENROSE, Hulda S., b.1-12-1820, d.5-16-1908; bur. Menallen
    Josiah, d.1-7-1860, aged 69 yr 9 mo 10 da; bur. Menallen
    Rachel C., d.12-25-1824, aged 36 yr 17 da; bur. Huntington
    William, d.2-12-1815, aged 16 yr 26 da; bur. Redlands
PETERS, Elizabeth, b.6-28-1896, d.12-30-1896 [daughter of Z. J. & M. A. T.
    Peters]; bur. Menallen
    Mary Tyson, b.8-1-1866, d.8-16-1931; bur. Menallen
    Zachariah, b.4-22-1859, d.7-9-1936; bur. Menallen
PETREY, Sara E., b.10-26-1842, d.7-2-1914; bur. Menallen
PHILLIPS, Thomas, d.3-13-1842; bur. Warrington
PILKINGTON, Richard, d.11-13-1819, aged 52 yr 15 da; bur. Huntington
    Sarah, d.8-4-1852, aged 81 yr 4 mo 17 da [wife of Richard]; bur.
    Huntington
    Vincent, d.12-14-1819, aged 20 yr 8 mo 29 da [son of Richard & Sarah
    Pilkington]; bur. Huntington
POTTS, Ann, d.3-12-1856; bur. Redlands
    Anna, d.2-20-1840, aged 18 mo; bur. Redlands
    George, d.8-7-1845, aged 37 yr 4 mo 4 da; bur. Redlands
    Harriet, d.3-3-1840, aged 10; bur. Redlands
    Jane, d.3-24-1852, aged 9 yr 3 da [daughter of George & Mary Potts];
    bur. Redlands
PRICKETT, Chester C., b.8-12-1895, d.7-15-1896 [son of J. W. & E. M. G.
    Prickett]; bur. Menallen
    Ella M. Griest, b.1868, d.1941; bur. Menallen
    Jesse C., b.3-19-1889, d.4-12-1894 [son of J. W. and E. M. G. Prickett];
    bur. Menallen
    Josiah W., b.1857, d.1924; bur. Menallen
PROWELL, Edgar -?-wood, b.3-29-1849, d.11-13-1856; bur. Redlands
    Jane, b.12-25-1809, d.1-5-1886; bur. Redlands
QUIGLEY, James, d.6-3-1817, aged 22 yr 2 mo 18 da; bur. Newberry
    Sarah, d.9-22-1845, aged 47 yr 11 mo 3 da [wife of James Quigley]; bur.
    Newberry
R., R., bur. Newberry
RAMSEY, Ann, d.1838; bur. Warrington
READ, child, d.1838 [David Read's child]; bur. Warrington
REED, child, d.8-4-1822 [David Reed's child]; bur. Warrington
    child, d.5-1-1830 [David Reed's child]; bur. Warrington
    Deborah, aged 74; bur. Menallen
    Henry, aged 68; bur. Menallen
    Sarah, d.1830 [Zacharies Reed's Daughter]; bur. Warrington
    son, d.1831 [Zacharies Reed's son]; bur. Warrington
    William W., b.7-22-1804, d.6-2-1880; bur. York
REXROTH, Sarah M., b.1908, d.1962; bur. Menallen
RIGHT, James, d.12-1-1838; bur. Warrington
    Mrs., d.1838 [James Right's wife]; bur. Warrington
ROBBENS, child, d.9-2-1824 [James Robbens' child]; bur. Warrington
ROBINSON, Harriet, b.3-1-1822, d.1-28-1882; bur. Redlands
    Joseph, b.6-10-1824, d.3-16-1904; bur. Redlands

BURIALS

ROBINSON, Margaret, d.9-15-1853, aged 64 yr 7 mo 5 da [wife of Solomon Robinson]; bur. Redlands
    Solomon, b.2-19-1789, d.9-18-1876; bur. Redlands
ROBISON, Ty Burtrus, d.2-16-1861, aged 10 mo 1 da [son of H. & R. Robison]; bur. Redlands
ROSBERRY, Ellannen, d.5-11-1830; bur. Warrington
ROSS, Benjamin, d.1830; bur. Warrington
    child, d.5-3-1830 [William Ross' child]; bur. Warrington
    child, d.1833 [James Ross' child]; bur. Warrington
    Cthe, d.9-13-1823; bur. Warrington
    Margaret, d.7-25-1829; bur. Warrington
    Mrs., d.8-3-1830 [Benjamin Ross' mother]; bur. Warrington
RUSH, Jemima E., b.1-12-1805, d.07-09-1890; bur. Huntington
SHAFER, Naomi W., b.1-30-1817, d.8-18-1833 [daughter of Daniel & Naomi Shafer]; bur. Huntington
SICKLY, Eliza, d.12-25-1821, aged 17; bur. Newberry
    William, d.2-12-1822, aged 3 mo; bur. Newberry
SMITH, David I. W., d.10-31-1831, aged 12 days; bur. Friends Gr
    Edith, bur. Old Griest
    Emily, bur. Old Griest
    Lydia, d.10-29-1821; bur. Newberry
    Phebe Jane, bur. Old Griest
    Rebecca, bur. Old Griest
    Wm Reily, bur. Old Griest
SPEAKMAN, Eliza, d.9-14-1867, aged 56 yr 7 mo 22 da [Consort of John A. Speakman]; bur. Huntington
    Jacob, d.4-15-1829, aged 61 yr 2 da; bur. Newberry
    John A., d.5-29-1862, aged 51 yr 6 mo 22 da; bur. Huntington
    Lydia, d.12-3-1831, aged 2; bur. Newberry
    Mary, d.5-8-1836, aged 66 yr 6 mo 20 da; bur. Newberry
SPENCE, Esther, d.9-1-1825, aged 26 yr 2 mo 16 da; bur. Newberry
    Isaac, b.9-22-1786, d.9-6-1819; bur. Newberry
    John, b.3-29-1762, d.3-18-1833; bur. Newberry
    Mary, d.8-26-1823, aged 60 yr 4 mo 28 da; bur. Newberry
SQUIB, Jorge, d.1830; bur. Warrington
SQUIBB, Joanna A., aged 72 [wife of Robert Squibb]; bur. Huntington
    Robert, d.5-12-1823, aged 69 yr 10 mo 12 da [son of Robert & Joanna Squibb]; bur. Huntington
    Susannah, d.11-23-1857, aged 66 yr 23 da; bur. Menallen
    William, bur. Huntington
    William, d.1-6-1826; bur. Warrington
    Wm, d.1830; bur. Warrington
STARR, Charles B., d.7-12-1861, aged 8 yr 10 mo 9 da [son of Hiram & Eliza Starr]; bur. Redlands
    Clayton N., d.4-6-1850, aged 1 mo 11 da [son of Joseph & Susan Starr]; bur. Redlands
    Hiram, d.1-7-1870, aged 73 yr 5 mo 24 da; bur. Redlands
    John K., d.8-29-1862, aged 22 yr 4 mo 16 da; bur. Redlands
    Morris W., d.2-5-1851, aged 11 mo 10 da [son of Joseph & Susan Starr]; bur. Redlands

MENALLEN, MARRIAGES AND MISCELLANY

STARR, Morris W., d.12-4-1855, aged 27 yr 2 mo 6 da; bur. Redlands
    Rebecca, d.7-13-1860, aged 60 yr 9 mo 10 da; bur. Redlands
    Samuel E., d.2-3-1851, aged 15 da [son of Joseph & Susan Starr]; bur. Redlands
    Willie, d.4-28-1866, aged 14 yr 6 mo 7 da [son of R. T. & E. Starr]; bur. Redlands
STREATH, Ruth, d.3-9-1843; bur. Warrington
STRETCH, child, d.10-29-1823 [Richard Stretch's child]; bur. Warrington
    Ritchard, d.4-29-1845; bur. Warrington
STUBBS, Esther P., b.1899, d.1972; bur. Menallen
    Joseph I., b.1932, d.1978; bur. Menallen
    Joseph I., b.1897, d.1938; bur. Menallen
SWEEZY, Florence K., b.2-14-1908, d.2-2-1973; bur. Menallen
SYFORD, L—tner, b.2-18-1821, d.1-19-1854; bur. Redlands
T., Ann, bur. Newberry
T., I., d.1763; bur. Newberry
T., R., bur. Newberry
TAYLER, Benj'n, b.1-6-1803, d.1-24-1873; bur. Redlands
TAYLOR, Ann, bur. Newberry
    Anne, b.11-09-1811, d.12-26-1861 [wife of Isaac Taylor]; bur. Redlands
    E., d.1822; bur. Newberry
    Eve, d.1823; bur. Newberry
    Geo., bur. Newberry
    Isaac, b.5-20-1805, d.9-20-1880; bur. Redlands
    John, b.9-14-1794, d.4-10-1838; bur. Newberry
    John, d.1834; bur. Newberry
    Joseph, bur. Newberry
    Libni, b.1-19-1790, d.11-04-1868; bur. Redlands
    Margaret, b.1-17-1832, d.10-24-1839; bur. Newberry
    Mary, b.7-23-1795, d.9-12-1872 [wife of Libni Taylor]; bur. Redlands
    Mrs., d.9-4-1823 [Joseph Taylor's mother]; bur. Warrington
    Mrs., d.9-28-1825 [Joshua Taylor's wife]; bur. Warrington
    Phebe, b.2-20-1811 d.1-25-1844 [wife of Isaac Taylor]; bur. Redlands
    Sarah, d.1814; bur. Newberry
THOMAS, Hannah, d.7-21-1871, aged 76 yr 7 mo 16 da; bur. Redlands
TILTON, Charles B., b.10-11-1902, d.4-10-1986 [Maj. US Army World War II]; bur. Menallen
TOMY, Henry, d.1832; bur. Warrington
TOWNSEND, Hannah W., d.1-16-1884; bur. York
TREAZURE, Mrs., d.1826 [John Treazure's mother]; bur. Warrington
TRESCOTT, Ruthanna, d.12-1-1879, aged 88 yr 7 mo 26 da; bur. Menallen
TUDOR, David White, d.9-19-1862, aged 1 yr 2 mo 22 da [son of Isaac E. & Susan W. Tudor]; bur. Huntington
    Isaac, d.1-30-1853, aged 64 yr 4 mo 29 da; bur. Huntington
    Isaac F., d.8-31-1897, aged 72 yr 4 mo 5 da; bur. Huntington
    John, b.1853, d.1911; bur. Huntington
    John, d.1-21-1857; bur. Huntington
    John Stewart, d.12-16-1862, aged 1 yr 11 mo 26 da [son of Wm. A. & Charlotte Tudor]; bur. Huntington
    Martha A., d.9-15-1889, aged 59 yr 1 mo; bur. Menallen

BURIALS

TUDOR, Mary, d.9-30-1881, aged 95 yr 3 mo 5 da; bur. Menallen
    Phebe, d.11-4-1859; bur. Huntington
    Sarah M., d.7-12-1875 [daughter of J. & P. Tudor]; bur. Huntington
    Susan W., d.5-12-1863 [wife of Isaac F. Tudor]; bur. Huntington
    Susie, d.3-26-1883, aged 20 yr 11 da [daughter of Isaac F. & Susan Tudor]; bur. Huntington
TYRELL, Dr. T., aged 54; bur. York
TYSON, Bertha H., b.9-24-1881, d.6-1-1973; bur. Menallen
    Charles J., b.9-5-1838, d.12-22-1906; bur. Menallen
    Chester J., b.9-4-1877, d.6-18-1938; bur. Menallen
    Chester J., Jr., b.9-22-1912, d.6-12-1972; bur. Menallen
    Donald Charles, b.1-19-1902, d.11-16-1980; bur. Menallen
    E. Philip, b.7-28-1909, d.2-17-1973 [Pa.T.SGT US Army World War II]; bur. Menallen
    Edna Kerr, b.4-28-1888, d.1-21-1953; bur. Menallen
    Edwin Comly, b.8-28-1864, d.11-21-1945; bur. Menallen
    Frederick, b.2-9-1908, d.6-25-1974; bur. Menallen
    Irene Kenyon, b.1-15-1905, d.8-4-1968; bur. Menallen
    Maria E., b.3-7-1840, d.3-11-1927; bur. Menallen
    Mary Willis, b.9-27-1862, d.7-3-1941 [Mary Willis Daughter of Marianna Hawxhurst, Westbury L.I.]; bur. Menallen
    William C., b.9-24-1879, d.6-10-1953; bur. Menallen
UNDERWOOD, Alexandrea, d.1846; bur. Warrington
    Amos, d.1834 [Amos Underwood's son]; bur. Warrington
    daughter, d.9-29-1823 [Amos Underwood's daughter]; bur. Warrington
    Isaac, d.8-30-1823 [Amos Underwood's son]; bur. Warrington
    Mary Ann, d.5-3-1830; bur. Warrington
    Samuel, d.1835; bur. Warrington
    Solomon, d.1846; bur. Warrington
UNKNOWN, Anne Margaret, bur. Menallen
    Mary [Grandmother], bur. Huntington
UPDEGRAFF, Harman, b.1-8-1821, d.3-16-1835; bur. Newberry
VALE, daughter, d.8-9-1823 [Robert Vale's daughter]; bur. Warrington
    Elizabeth, b.4-10-1757, d.2-11-1841; bur. Redlands
    Josue, d.1829; bur. Warrington
    Peter, d.8-14-1834; bur. Warrington
    Robert, d.8-20-1823; bur. Warrington
    Sarah E., d.9-28-1889, aged 66 yr 10 mo 28 da; bur. Menallen
    Wm, d.1838; bur. Warrington
VANOSDAL, Sarah, d.1832 [Sarah Vanosdal's daughter Sarah]; bur. Warrington
VARNON, Tecy, b.9-27-1763, d.9-1-1839; bur. Newberry
VROMAN, A. Clark, b.1856, d.1916; bur. Menallen
    Esther H., b.1865, d.1894 [daughter of J. W. & M. H. Griest]; bur. Menallen
W., E., d.1829; bur. Huntington
W., I., bur. Newberry
W., J., bur. Newberry
W., J., bur. Redlands
W., P., d.1891; bur. Huntington

MENALLEN, MARRIAGES AND MISCELLANY

WALES, Mary, d.1827 [William Wales' wife Mary]; bur. Warrington
WALHAY, Eliekim, d.2-26-1907, aged 63 yr 2 mo 14 da; bur. Menallen
    Infant son, b.2-1-1875, d.2-18-1875 [infant son of E. and R. Walhay]; bur. Menallen
    Rachel, d.10-24-1910, aged 67 yr 5 mo 29 da; bur. Menallen
WALKER, Alethe J., d.3-20-1888, aged 41 yr 11 mo 26 da; bur. Huntington
    child, d.2-14-1824 [Joseph Walker's child]; bur. Warrington
    child, d.1-1-1834 [Isaac C. Walker's child]; bur. Warrington
    child, d.1837 [Isaac Walker's child]; bur. Warrington
    Elizabeth, b.1-25-1828, d.6-19-1913; bur. Menallen
    Mary Ann, bur. Huntington
    Mrs., d.4-5-1823 [Joel Walker's mother]; bur. Warrington
    Mrs., d.4-20-1827 [Asahel Walker's wife]; bur. Warrington
    William, b.11-29-1821, d.11-10-1862; bur. Menallen
WALLS, Mary, d.1-31-1845; bur. Warrington
    William, d.1839; bur. Warrington
WALMER, Gerald R., b.5-31-1926, d.12-7-1967 [Pennsylvania S Sgt Co H 187 Glider Inf World War II]; bur. Menallen
WALN, Hannah, d.7-12-1863, aged 56 yr 4 mo 27 da [wife of Nathan Waln]; bur. Redlands
    Nathan, d.7-21-1859, aged 50 yr 1 mo 21 da; bur. Redlands
WARNER (?), unknown; bur. Newberry
WARREN, Mary, d.1822; bur. Newberry
WARTIN, Mrs., d.7-8-1875, aged 78 yr 8 mo 14 da; bur. Redlands
WATTS, Andrew, d.1-23-1871, aged 72 yr 11 mo 18 da [wife of Andrew Watts]; bur. Redlands
WAY, David, b.5-17-1768, d.2-7-1770; bur. Newberry
WELCH, Eleanor, d.1-21-1836; bur. Huntington
    Sidney, bur. York
WELLS, child, d.9-11-1824 [Abraham Wells' child]; bur. Warrington
    Hannah, d.6-20-1847; bur. Warrington
WHITSON, Jane C., d.9-14-1899; bur. Menallen
WICKERSHAM, Abner, b.9-11-1788, d.2-9-1853; bur. Redlands
    Annie, d.4-25-1863, aged 66 yr 11 mo 18 da; bur. Redlands
    J., bur. Newberry
    James, d.1815; bur. Newberry
    Jesse, b.2-22-1776, d.3-11-1820; bur. Newberry
    John, b.12-29-1780, d.2-20-1853; bur. Redlands
    Josiah, d.2-19-1882, aged 56 yr 9 mo 6 da; bur. Menallen
    Lydia, d.4-12-1893, aged 64 yr 8 da [wife of Josiah Wickersham]; bur. Menallen
    Maria Edith, b.1858, d.1934; bur. Menallen
    Mary Ann, d.3-16-1906, aged 74 yr 10 mo [Daughter of Abner & Annie Wickersham]; bur. Menallen
    Rebecca, b.8-6-1791, d.11-25-1873 [wife of John Wickersham]; bur. Redlands
    Rebecca, b.1843, d.1845; bur. Redlands
    Robert A., b.1850, d.1933; bur. Menallen
    Ruth Anna, b.1822, d.1919; bur. Menallen

BURIALS

WICKERSHAM, William, b.1852, d.1853 [children of Joseph & H. C. Wickersham]; bur. Redlands
WIERMAN, Adliza S., b.2-16-1829, d.8-19-1857; bur. Huntington
    Alexander, d.1-14-1824; bur. Huntington
    B. F., b.1823, d.1891; bur. Huntington
    Hannah, d.8-15-1836, aged 88; bur. Huntington
    Isaac, b.10-13-1781, d.12-26-1853; bur. Menallen
    James, b.8-22-1791, d.7-31-1832; bur. Huntington
    John, b.8-9-1759, d.2-25-1851 [This monument was dedicated by his only child & daughter Naomi Shafer]; bur. Huntington
    John Howard, b.1825, d.1908; bur. Huntington
    Joseph, d.12-11-1822, aged 82 yr 11 mo; bur. Huntington
    Lydia, d.6-7-1850, aged 92 [wife of Nicholas Wierman]; bur. Huntington
    Mary, b.1813, d.1895 ["Aunt Polly"]; bur. Huntington
    Nicholas, d.10-12-1839, aged 84; bur. Huntington
    Ruth, d.1-19-1827, aged 79 yr 3 mo 29 da; bur. Huntington
    Sarah C., b.9-10-1811, d.1-18-1855; bur. Menallen
    Sidney, d.11-14-1834, aged 22 yr 8 mo 2 da; bur. Friends Gr
    Susan, bur. Huntington
    Thomas, d.9-11-1832, aged 71 yr 15 da; bur. Huntington
    Westly Edger, b.11-24-1854, d.11-28-1857 [Grandson of Joseph Wierman]; bur. Huntington
    William, d.4-6-1824; bur. Huntington
WILLIS, Mary, d.1804; bur. Newberry
WILLS, John, d.6-13-1872, aged 64 yr 8 mo 22 da; bur. Redlands
    Lydia, d.6-23-1862, aged 44 yr 2 mo 24 da [wife of John Wills]; bur. Redlands
    Rebecca, d.11-27-1874, aged 44 yr 8 mo 18 da [wife of John Wills]; bur. Redlands
    Reuben, d.4-27-1866, aged 20 yr 7 mo [son of John & Lydia Wills]; bur. Redlands
    William, d.10-17-1865, aged 23 yr 4 mo 7 da [son of John & Lydia Wills]; bur. Redlands
WILSON, Elizabeth, b.12-26-1843, d.1-14-1924; bur. Menallen
WILY, child, d.12-1-1838 [John Wily's child]; bur. Warrington
WIREMAN, Susannah, b.4-13-1781, d.7-6-1873; bur. Menallen
WORLEY, Albert C., d.10-23-1863, aged 19 days; bur. Huntington
    Alice Elmira, b.10-31-1847, d.10-11-1852 [daughter of Isaac D. & Caroline G. Worley]; bur. Huntington
    Caroline G., d.1-16-1892, aged 66 yr 4 mo 15 da [wife of Isaac D. Worley]; bur. Huntington
    Chester B., b.1890, d.1981; bur. Huntington
    Elizabeth, d.1-9-1855, aged 3 mo [daughter of Isaac D. & Caroline G. Worley]; bur. Huntington
    Grace A., b.1856, d.1940; bur. Huntington
    Harry H., d.11-8-1861, aged 6 yr 6 mo 8 da; bur. Huntington
    Hermie M., b.1889, d.1978; bur. Huntington
    Isaac D., d.9-7-1904, aged 81 yr 11 mo 27 da; bur. Huntington
    Isaac W., d.8-1-1851, aged 1 mo 15 da [son of Isaac D. & Caroline G. Worley]; bur. Huntington

MENALLEN, MARRIAGES AND MISCELLANY

WORLEY, Joseph E., d.10-15-1863, aged 1 yr 3 mo 18 da [son of Isaac D. & Caroline G. Worley]; bur. Huntington
    Mary C., b.1851, d.1937; bur. Huntington
    Ruth Tudor, b.1-19-1913, d.3-21-1988; bur. Huntington
WOTTS, Mary, d.1842; bur. Warrington
WRIGHT, Abel T., b.9-21-1810, d.9-11-1869; bur. Menallen
    Alice, d.8-12-1881; bur. Friends Gr
    Alice Garretson, b.1-11-1823, d.1-23-1901 [wife of Hiram S. Wright]; bur. Menallen
    Annie Clark, b.1865, d.1929; bur. Menallen
    Ardella J., d.8-20-1895, aged 31 yr 10 mo 28 da [wife of Richard M. Wright. Daughter of H. L. E. Griest]; bur. Menallen
    Chapman A., b.1853, d.1928; bur. Menallen
    Charles S., b.10-6-1816, d.11-16-1872; bur. Menallen
    Charlotte, d.8-18-1882, aged 71 yr 3 mo 15 da; bur. Menallen
    Chester S., d.1-29-1904, aged 9 yr 8 mo 27 da; bur. Menallen
    Clark H., b.9-24-1886, d.4-21-1905; bur. Menallen
    Elijah, d.2-8-1878, aged 64 yr 11 mo 14 da; bur. Menallen
    Elizabeth, d.9-8-1839, aged 85 yr 5 mo 2 da; bur. Friends Gr
    Elizabeth, d.8-11-1861, aged 52 yr 9 mo 6 da; bur. Friends Gr
    Elsie, d.7-27-1886, aged 1 yr 7 mo 8 da [daughter of R. M. and A. J. Wright]; bur. Menallen
    Ethel, b.4-11-1889, d.4-1-1985; bur. Menallen
    Eve, d.10-17-1842, aged 64; bur. Friends Gr
    Gen. Wm. Wierman, b.7-27-1824, d.3-9-1882; bur. Huntington
    Geo. Edward, b.8-19-1855, d.7-17-1937; bur. Menallen
    George H., d.11-28-1888, aged 2 yr 8 mo 19 da; bur. Menallen
    Hanna J., d.8-21-1853, aged 6 [daughter of J. & M. Wright]; bur. Friends Gr
    Hannah G., b.3-4-1824, d.4-21-1908; bur. Menallen
    Hiram S., b.1-3-1815, d.3-8-1883; bur. Menallen
    Ida Olive, b.1885, d.1953; bur. Menallen
    Infant son [of Albert S. and Sally M. Wright], bur. Menallen
    Isaac, d.10-6-1850, aged 21 yr 10 mo [son of William and Phebe Wright]; bur. Huntington
    Isaac J., b.7-9-1813, d.7-6-1892; bur. Menallen
    James C., b.6-14-1850, d.6-5-1913; bur. Menallen
    Jane F., d.4-15-1898, aged 76 yr 1 mo 12 da; bur. Friends Gr
    Jane G., b.12-27-1853, d.3-3-1928; bur. Menallen
    Joel, aged 5 yr 11 mo 16 da; bur. Friends Gr
    John, d.8-30-1830, aged 10 yr 2 mo 7 da [son of William and Phebe Wright]; bur. Huntington
    John, d.12-8-1860, aged 78 yr 7 mo 22 da; bur. Friends Gr
    Joseph, d.6-21-1854, aged 11 yr 6 mo 2 da [son of E. & M. A. Wright]; bur. Friends Gr
    Leander R., d.7-24-1849, aged 2 yr 1 mo 25 da [son of E. & M. A. Wright]; bur. Friends Gr
    Lewes G., d.9-1-1853, aged 1 yr 4 mo 23 da [son of I. & ? Wright]; bur. Friends Gr
    Lloyd D., d.12-7-1896, aged 9 yr 11 mo 2 da; bur. Menallen

BURIALS

WRIGHT, Lydia, d.8-1-1853, aged 81 yr 5 mo 21 da; bur. Friends Gr
    Maria L., d.9-1-1852, aged 40 yr 11 mo 13 da; bur. Friends Gr
    Mary A., d.11-6-1886, aged 65 yr 10 mo 27 da; bur. Menallen
    Mary Olive [daughter of Isaac J. and Sarah G. Wright]; bur. Menallen
    Myrtle, b.1878, d.1947; bur. Menallen
    Nathan, d.12-1-1853; bur. Friends Gr
    Nellie Wilson, b.10-5-1883, d.3-7-1976; bur. Menallen
    Owen William, b.4-25-1942, d.1-3-1944 [son of W. & R. Wright]; bur. Menallen
    Phebe, b.2-8-1790, d.7-30-1873; bur. Huntington
    Rachel, d.4-19-1836, aged 38 yr 1 mo 11 da; bur. Friends Gr
    Ruth Anna, d.4-3-1852, aged 54 yr 9 mo 22 da; bur. Friends Gr
    Ruth M., aged 64 yr 4 mo 7 da; bur. Friends Gr
    Ryland H., b.10-11-1881, d.11-28-1969; bur. Menallen
    S. I., d.3-27-1816, aged 8 yr 1 mo 25 da; bur. Friends Gr
    Samuel, b.3-4-1835, d.9-11-1859; bur. Friends Gr
    Samuel D., d.12-27-1843, aged 21 yr 10 mo 23 da; bur. Friends Gr
    Sarah G., b.10-21-1820, d.12-31-1909; bur. Menallen
    Theresa H., b.1855, d.1921; bur. Menallen
    Thomas, d.6-18-1845, aged 60 yr 10 mo 12 da; bur. Friends Gr
    Thomas A., b.1848, d.1929; bur. Menallen
    Thomas F., b.1865, d.1944; bur. Menallen
    Thomas H., d.7-8-1882, aged 75 yr 9 mo 8 da; bur. Menallen
    William, d.10-25-1865, aged 78 yr 10 mo 5 da; bur. Huntington
    William, d.3-8-1853, aged 74 yr 5 mo 21 da; bur. Friends Gr
    William E., d.9-21-1865, aged 14 yr 14 da [son of Isaac J. and Sarah G. Wright]; bur. Menallen
    Willis N., d.4-27-1851, aged 3 yr 10 mo 23 da [son of H. S. & A. G. Wright]; bur. Friends Gr
WRITEE, Jesse, b.4-26-1849, d.10-1-1924; bur. Redlands
YARMAN, Jenne M., d.4-11-1920, aged 62 yr 1 mo 15 da; bur. Menallen

MARRIAGES

#1 13th of 6th mo 1781   JAMES HODGSON-RACHEL WRIGHT
James Hodgson of Monalin Township County of York and Province of Pensylvania son of John and Martha Hodgson of Beckley County, Virginia, and Rachel Wright of the Township, County and Province afforesaid Daughter of Samuel Wright Deceased and Gartrude His Wife . . . this thirteenth day of the Sixth Month in the Year of our Lord One thousand Seven Hundred and Eighty One . . . at Monalin.

		James Hodgson
		<u>Rachel Hodgson</u>
Elizabeth McGrail	Eve Griffith	Gartrude Wright
James McGrail	Sarah Hewitt	William Wright
John Morton	Isabel John	John Wright
John Yawger	Benjamin Townsend	Jonathan Wright
Mary Scoggan	Elizabeth Wireman	Nicholas Wireman
Jesse Wright	Finley McGrew	Benjamin Wright
Joseph Griest	William Wireman	Alise Henderson
John Wireman	Nehemiah -?-	

MENALLEN MINUTES, MARRIAGES, & MISCELLANY

#2 12th of 12th mo 1781   JOHN WRIGHT-ANN GRIFFITH
Whereas John Wright, Son of Samuel Wright deceased and Gartrude his wife of Monalin Township in the County of York and Province of Pensylvania; and Ann Griffith Daughter of Thomas Griffith, Deceased and Eve his wife of the Township County and Province aforesaid . . . this Twelfth day of the twelfth Month in the Year of our Lord One Thousand Seven Hundred and Eighty One . . . at Monalin Meeting-House.

		John Wright
		Ann Wright
Rachel Blackburn	Thomas Wright	Gertrude Wright
Alice Blackburn	Benjamin Wright	Eve Griffith
Finley McGrew	Jane Wright	Benjamin Wright
Mary McGrew	Elizabeth Wright	Jonathan Wright
Elizabeth McGrew	Rebekah Mickle	William Wright
William Hutton	Benjamin Townsend	Thomas Griffith
John Wireman	James Watson	Hannah Wright
Joseph Hewitt	Anthony Blackburn	John Wright

#3 22nd of 5th mo 1782   THOMAS GRIFFITH-RACHEL BLACKBURN
Whereas Thomas Griffith, son of Thomas Griffith Deceased & Eve, his wife of Monalin Township County of York and Province of Pennsylvania and Rachel Blackburn, Daughter of Thomas Blackburn and Alice his wife of the Township County and Province aforesaid . . . this Twenty Second day of the Fifth Month in the Year of our Lord One Thousand Seven Hundred and Eighty Two . . . at Monalin Meeting-House.

		Thomas Griffith
		Rachel Griffith
Thomas Blackburn	William Griffith	Thomas Blackburn
Jonathan Wright	William Wright	Eve Griffith
James McGrew	John Wright	Isabel Blackburn
James McGrail	Joseph Hewitt	Alice Blackburn
William Colmary	Finley McGrew	Elizabeth Blackburn
John Colmary	Thomas Hewitt	Thomas Blackburn
Mary McGrew	James Watson	John Blackburn
Rebekah Oldham	George Wilson	Rebekah Mickle
Hannah Wright	Thomas Oldham	Susanna Wright
	Thomas Bowen	Jane Wright
	Nathan Hammond	Ann Wright

#4 18th of 12th mo 1782   AMBROSE UPDEGRAFF-ELIZABETH COOKSON
Whereas Ambrose Updegraff of York Town in the County of York in Pensylvania son of Joseph Updegraff and Susanna his wife Deceased and Elizabeth Cookson of Monalin Township in the County aforesaid Daughter of Samuel Cookson and Jane his wife Deceased . . . this Eighteenth day of the Twelfth Month in the Year One thousand Seven Hundred and Eighty two . . . at Monalin.

		Ambrose Updegraff
		Elizabeth Updegraff
Samuel Cookson Jr	Joseph Hewit	Joseph Updegraff
James McGrew	William Wright	Mary Updegraff

MARRIAGES

Elizabeth Wright	Jonathan Wright	Samuel Cookson
Jane Wright	Finley McGrew Jr	Nathan Updegraff
Susanna Wright	Peter McGrew	Hannah Haines
Mary Watson	Jacob Worley	Edith Updegraff
Hannah Hutton	James McGrail	Ann Updegraff
Ann Rotts	James McGrew	James Love
William Haines	John Wright	Joseph Dodds Jr
Deborah Hutton	James Watson	Mary Updegraff
John Mitchel	Robert Hempton	Finley McGrew
Hannah Bryan	William Wright	Jacob Updegraff

#5 20th of 2nd mo 1783 — EBENEZER SPEAKMAN-ELIZABETH COX

Whereas Ebenezer Speakman of the Township of Huntington in the County of York in Pennsylvania Son of Joshua Speakman and Ann his wife Deceased and Elizabeth Cox of the township of Warrington and County of York aforesaid Daughter of Nathaniel Cox Deceased and Elizabeth his wife . . . at Huntington in the County of York . . . the twentieth day of the second month in the Year of our Lord One thousand Seven Hundred and Eighty three.

Ebenezer Speakman
<u>Elizabeth Speakman</u>

		Joshua Speakman
Rebecca Pilkington	William Cox	Elizabeth Cox
Ann Pearson	Robert Squibb	James -?-
Martha Everitt	Jacob Jones	Hannah Speakman
Ann Griest	Timothy Vanscoyoc	Susanna Speakman
Sarah Wierman	Susanna Malaun	Benjamin Speakman
Hannah Wierman	John Malaun	Hannah -?-
Jacob Cook	John Cox	Jean Cox
Eme Cox	Nicholas Wierman Jr	Thomas Speakman
Ruth Cox	Richard Pilkington	Stephen Speakman
Susanna Cox	John Garretson	John Cox
William Cox	Ann Griest	-?- Cox
Ann Cox	Thomas Griest	Elias Pearson
Nicholas Wierman	Isaac Everitt	Thomas Pilkington
Henry Wierman Jr	Vincent Pilkington	

#6 12th of 3rd mo 1783 — THOMAS BOWEN-REBECCA MICKLE

Whereas Thomas Bowen of Monallen Township in the County of York in Pensylvania Son of Thomas Bowen and Jane his wife and Rebecca Mickle Daughter of Thomas Griffith deceased and Eve his wife of the County aforesaid . . . this twelfth day of the third month in the Year of our lord One thousand Seven Hundred and Eighty three . . . at Monallin.

Thomas Bowen
<u>Rebecca Bowen</u>

Elizabeth Wright	Mary McGrew	Thomas Bowen
Rebecca Griffith	Rachel Long	Jean Bowen
Deborah Hutton	Elizabeth McGrew	James Watson
Jonathan Wright	Alice Blackburn	Jean Bowen
Samuel Hutton	Jane Wright	Lidia Bowen
Isaac Garretson	Deborah Cox	John Bowen

MENALLEN MINUTES, MARRIAGES, & MISCELLANY

William Hutton	Rebecca Pilkington	Thomas Griffith
Thomas Blackburn	Susanna Garretson	Amos Edwards
John Wright	Hannah Long	Finley McGrew
George Hammond	William Wright	James McGrew
Thomas Long		Isaac Everitt

#7 22nd of 5th mo 1783   JACOB BEALS-ELIZABETH BLACKBURN
Whereas Jacob Beals of the township of Huntington and County of York in Pennsylvania son of Jacob Beals and Elizabeth his wife and Elizabeth Blackburn of the Place aforesaid, Daughter of John Blackburn and Rebecca his wife, (Both deceased) . . . at Huntington in the Co of York aforesaid . . . the twenty Second day of the fifth month in the Year of our lord One thousand seven Hundred and eighty three.

Jacob Beals
Elizabeth Beals

Joseph Griest	Susanna Everitt	Solomon Beals
John Griest	Lydia Wierman	Rebecca Beals
Isaac Garretson	Isabella -?-	Mary Beals
Thos Pearson	Phebe Thornburgh	Jacob Beals
John Griest	Emey Kenworthy	Samuel Blackburn
Jacob Griest	Hannah Thomson	Mary Garretson
Richard Pilkington	Rebecca Pilkington	Martha Everett
Henry Wierman	Ann Pearson	Hannah Wierman
William Wierman	Susanna Garretson	Elizabeth Everitt
Thos Thornburgh	Martha Griest	-?- Speakman
Susanna Griest	Isaac Everitt	Elias Pearson
William Cox Sr		

#8 13th of 10th mo 1783   ISAAC PEARSON-ELIZABETH EVERITT
Whereas Isaac Pearson of the Township of Huntington County of York in Pennsylvania son of Elias Pearson and Ann his wife And Elizabeth Everitt of the Township and County aforesaid Daughter of Isaac Everitt and Martha his wife . . . at Huntington in the County of York . . . this thirteenth day of the tenth month in the year of our lord One Thousand Seven Hundred and eighty three.

Isaac Pearson
Elizabeth Pearson

Richard Pilkington	Susanna Garretson	Elias Pearson
Vincent Pilkington	Daniel Griest	Isaac Everitt
Nicholas Wierman	Ann Griest	Martha Everitt
Sarah Wierman	Joseph Griest	Ann Pearson
Isaac Garretson	Ann Thomson	Thomas Pearson
Daniel Griest Jr	Susanna Griest	Susanna Everitt
Finley McGrew	Rebecca Pilkington	William Wisely
Henry Wierman Jr	Phebe Thornburgh	John Everitt
Thomas Pilkington	Mary Whittear	Nicholas Wierman Jr
Thomas Griffith	John Garretson	Lydia Wierman
William Wierman	Robert Squibb	

MARRIAGES

#9 14th of 5th mo 1784   HENRY MILLS-ELIZABETH JOHN
Whereas Henry Mills of Middle Creek in Berkley County in Virginia and Elizabeth John of the Township of Monallin in the County of York in Pennsylvania . . . this fourteenth day of the fifth month in the Year One thousand Seven Hundred and Eighty four . . . at Monallin.

		Henry Mills
		Elizabeth Mills
James McGrew	Mary McGrew	Mary John
John Hutton	Susanna Wright	Joseph John
	Elizabeth Wright	Jonathan Pilkington
	Rachel Long	Joseph Hewitt
	Hannah Wright	Jonathan Hewitt
	Mary Mickle	Jonathan Wright
		Finley McGrew
		William McGrew
		William Hutton
		Anna Edmondton
		Samuel Hutton

#10 18th of 8th mo 1784   SAMUEL GARRETSON-ALICE BLACKBURN
Whereas Samuel Garretson son of John Garretson of Newberry Township in the County of York in Pennsylvania and Jean his wife deceased; and Alice Blackburn daughter of Thomas Blackburn of Monallen Township in said County and Alice his wife . . . this Eighteenth day of the Eighth Month in the year of our Lord one thousand Seven Hundred and Eighty Four . . . at Monallen.

		Samuel Garretson
		Alice Garretson
William Hutton	James McGrew	John Garretson
John Colmery	Jacob Garretson	Joseph Garretson
Samuel Love	Jesse Gibson	John Garretson Jr
William Colmery	Rachel Griffith	Thomas Blackburn Jr
John Garretson	Thomas Oldham	John Blackburn
John Wright	Rebecca Oldham	Joseph Hewett
John Griest	Thomas Griffith	Edward Jones
Finley McGrew	Jonathan Bowing	Elizabeth McGrail
Jonathan Wright	Thomas Hammond	Isabel Blackburn
Susanna Wright	James Hammond	Alice Hammond
James McGrew	Ludia Bonin	
Alice Hendrix	Martha Griste	
Mary McGrew	Margaret Wilson	
Jane Wright	George McMillan	
Rachel Long	William Hobson	

#11 15th of 9th mo 1784   GEORGE HAMMOND-DEBORAH HUTTON
Whereas George Hammond of Monallin Township in the County of York in Pennsylvania son of James Hammond and Alice his wife deceased And Deborah Hutton of Monallen Township in the County aforesaid Daughter of William Hutton and Deborah his wife . . . this fifteenth day of the ninth

MENALLEN MINUTES, MARRIAGES, & MISCELLANY

month in the Year of our Lord One thousand seven Hundred and Eighty four . . . at Monallen Meeting House.

		George Hammond
		Deborah Hammond
John Morton	Susanna Wright	James Hammond
George Hewett	Mary McGrew	William Hutton
Lydia Bowen	Mary Morton	George Wilson
Benjamin Wilson	Joseph Hewett	Abner Hutton
John Hutton	Jesse Morton	Deborah Hutton
Elizabeth McGrail	John Morton	Sarah Risk
Lydia Bonin	Deborah Hewett	John Hammond
Henry Wierman	John Griffith	Jonathan Wright
	Elisha Gready	Levi Hutton

#12 20th of 10th mo 1784   JOHN CLEAVER-SUSANNA EVERITT

Whereas John Cleaver son of Peter and Miriam Cleaver of the Township of Warrington and County of York in Pennsylvania and Susanna Everitt Daughter of Isaac and Martha Everitt of Huntington Township in the County of York . . . this twentieth day of the tenth month in the Year of our Lord one thousand Seven Hundred and Eighty four . . . at Huntington.

		John Cleaver
		Susanna Cleaver
Mary Garretson	Benjamin Underwood	Peter Cleaver
Martha Griest	Willing Underwood	Isaac Everitt
Rebecca Pilkington	Susanna Griest	Martha Everitt
Elizabeth Garretson	Nicholas Wierman Jr	Peter Cleaver Jr
Vincent Pilkington	Lydia Wierman	Elizabeth Pearson
John Garretson	Susanna Garretson	Isaac Pearson
Richard Pilkington	Phebe Thornburgh	Sarah Cleaver
John Garretson Jr	Elizabeth Beals	Joshua Vail
Joseph Griest	Ann Pearson	Elizabeth Vale
Hannah Wierman	Finley McGrew	Miriam Cleaver Jr
William Nevitt	Thomas Pilkington	Neomy Garretson
Nicholas Wierman	Thomas Thornburgh	Isaac Garretson
Elias Pearson	Thomas Pearson	Nathan Sharpless
	Thomas -?-	Daniel Griest

#13 13th of 4th mo 1785   JOHN MORTON-HANNAH HUTTON

Whereas John Morton of Monallin Township York County in Pennsylvania Son of John Morton and Mary his wife and Hannah Hutton daughter of John Hutton and Ann, his wife, deceased, of Monallin Township in the County aforesaid . . . the thirteenth day of the fourth Month in the year of our Lord one thousand seven hundred and eighty five . . . at Monallen.

		John Morton
		Hannah Morton
William Dewoody	Ann Hutton	John Morton
George Hewett	Mary McGrew	William Hutton
Solomon Hutton	Rachel Long	Jesse Morton
Jonathan Wright	Elizabeth Farquhar	Joseph Hewett
John Wright	Ludia Bowen	Abner Hutton

MARRIAGES

Jean Wright
Susanna Wright
Deborah Hewett
Mary Morton

George Wilson
Finley McGrew
George Hammond

#14 23rd of 6th mo 1785   ROBERT SQUIBB-JOANNA SPEAKMAN

Whereas Robert Squibb of Warrington Township in the County of York and State of Pennsylvania son of William Squibb and Joanna Speakman of Huntington Township in the County of York aforesaid Daughter of Joshua Speakman . . . at Huntington this twenty third day of the sixth month One thousand Seven hundred eighty five.

Robert Squibb
Joanna Squibb

Susanna Garretson	Daniel Griest	William Squibb
Willing Griest	Nicholas Wierman	Joshua Speakman
John Griest	Martha Everitt	Sarah Squibb
Hannah Wierman	Elizabeth Pearson	Susanna Speakman
Susanna Cleaver	Mary Garretson	William Squibb
Jacob Jones	William Wierman	Thomas Speakman
John Griest Jr	Robert Morthland	Stephen Speakman
Jacob Griest	Allin Robinet	Phebe Speakman
Thomas Pilkington	John Cleaver	Rebecca Squibb
Henry Wierman Jr	Esther Foulk	Elizabeth Speakman
Susanna Fickes	Margaret Foulk	Ebenezer Speakman
Isaac Cook	Martha Griest	Isaac Everitt
	Sarah Cox	

#15 14th of 12th mo 1786   JACOB COOK-SUSANNA SPEAKMAN

Whereas Jacob Cook of Warrington Township York Co and State of Pennsylvania son of Thomas Cook and Mary his wife of the Township, County and State aforesaid and Susanna Speakman Daughter of Joshua Speakman and Ann his wife of Huntington Township York County and state aforesaid . . . this fourteenth day of twelfth month One Thousand Seven hundred and eighty six . . . at Huntington.

Jacob Cook
Susanna Cook

Emey Wierman	Henry Wierman Jr	Thomas Speakman
Elizabeth Cox	Elias Pearson	Stephen Speakman
Martha Everitt	William Wierman	Phebe Speakman
Abigail Penrose	Finley McGrew	Thomas Pilkington
Martha Griest	Isaac Pearson	Richard Pilkington
Eme Cox	William Wierman ye 3rd	John Way
Emey Wierman	Thomas Penrose	Joseph Pilkington
Jean Williams	Thomas Pearson	Vincent Pilkington
Hannah Wierman	John Griest	Isaac Everitt
Mary Garretson		Nicholas Wierman
		Daniel Griest

MENALLEN MINUTES, MARRIAGES, & MISCELLANY

#16 14th of 5th mo 1788   JOSEPH HEWETT-RACHEL McCRERY
Whereas Joseph Hewett son of Joseph Hewett and Sarah his wife of the township of Monallen County of York and State of Pennsylvania and Rachel McCrery daughter of Thomas McCrery deceased and Sarah his widow of the Township of Mount Pleasant County and State aforesaid . . . this fourteenth of fifth month one thousand seven hundred eighty eight . . . at Monallen aforesaid.

Joseph Hewett
Rachel Hewett

Jane McCrery	John Hewett	George Hewett
Mary Hewett	Deborah Hewett	David McCrery
Rachel Griffith	George Wilson	Jesse Morton
Hannah Long	Thomas Blackburn	Abner Hutton
John Wright	Benjamin Talbot	John Hutton
Abel John	Finley McGrew	James McGrew
Mary John	Rebecca McGrew	William Hutton
Lydia Bowen	Sarah Glasgow	Sollomon Hutton
Jane Long	Margaret Elgar	John Stevanson
	Mary John	Thomas Bowen

#17 17th of 9th mo 1788   JOHN BLACKBURN-MARY MORTON
Whereas John Blackburn son of Thomas and Alice Blackburn of Monallen Township in the County of York and State of Pennsylvania and Mary Morton Daughter of John and Mary Morton of the Township, County and State aforesaid . . . this seventeenth day of the ninth month one thousand seven hundred and eighty eight . . . at Monallen.

John Blackburn
Mary (her X mark) Blackburn

John Wierman	Thomas Braken	Thomas Blackburn
John Glasgow	Thomas Hammond	Jesse Morton
Benjamin Talbott	Joseph Hewett	John Morton
Susanna Talbott	Martha Bracken	George Hewett
Solomon Hutton	John Hewett	Finley McGrew
Ann Bowen	George Hammond	Abner Hutton
Rachel Griffith	Deborah Hammond	Levi Hutton
Elizabeth McGrail	Joseph Hewett	John Hutton
-?- Blackburn	Rachel Hewett	Thomas Oldham
John McGrail	Jean Glasgow	Lydia Oldham
Deborah Hewett	Esther Hodgson	Robert Todd
	William King	Thomas Hammond
	Sarah Glasgow	

#18 20th of 5th mo 1790   JOHN PIDGION-SUSANNA GARRETSON
Whereas John Pidgion of Warrington Township York County and State of Pennsylvania son of William Pidgion and Rachel his wife of Bedford County in Virginia and Susanna Garretson Daughter of John Garretson and Mary his wife of Warrington Township aforesaid . . . this twentieth day of the fifth month one thousand seven hundred and ninety . . . at Huntington.

John Pidgion
Susanna Pidgion

MARRIAGES

Thomas Penrose	Daniel Griest	John Garretson
Abigail Penrose	Isaac Griest	Mary Garretson
Sarah Wierman Jr	Joseph Griest	Isaac Garretson
Joseph Griest	Elizabeth Pearson	Cornelius Garretson
Ann Griest	Mary Hussey	Isaac Everett
Ann Penrose	John Everett	Willing Griest
Rebecca Garretson	Nicholas Wierman	William Wierman 3rd
John Griest Jr	Martha Everett Jr	John Garretson
Jacob Garretson	John Griest	John Garretson Jr
Isaac Pearson	Nicholas Wierman Jr	Content Garretson
Thomas Griest	Lydia Wierman	Susanna Griest
		Martha Everett
		Ann Griest

#19 12th of 5th mo 1790   JONATHAN POTS-DEBORAH WRIGHT

Whereas Jonathan Pots son of David and Alice Pots of the township and County of Bedford and State of Pennsylvania and Deborah Wright Daughter of John and Elizabeth Wright of the Township of Monalon County of York and State aforesaid . . . this twelfth day of the fifth month one thousand seven hundred and ninety . . . at the Meeting House in Monalon.

Jonathan Potts
Deborah Potts

Finly McGrew	Samuel Wright	Hannah Potts
James McGrew	John Wright	John Wright
Thomas Blackburn	Abner Hutton	Elizabeth Wright
Joel Hutton	Ezekel Vance	Benjamin Wright
Rosey Walker	Margaret Elgar	Wm Wright
Nancy Stewart	Martha Wright	Jonathan Wright
Joseph Elgar	Mary Hendricks	Alice Hendricks
Benjamin Talbott	Benj Farquar	Able John
John Wright	Steven Hendricks	Mary John
Benj Wilson	Rachel Griffith	
Jesse Wright	Rachel Wright	
John Carson		

#20 13th of 5th mo 1791   THOMAS PEARSON-MARTHA EVERITT

To all People to whome these presents Shall come, Know ye that Thomas Pearson (son of Elias Pearson and Ann his wife) and Martha Everitt (Daughter of Isaac Everitt and Martha his wife) both of the Township of Huntington County of York and State of Pennsylvania . . . this thirteenth day of the fifth month one thousand seven hundred ninety one . . . at Huntington.

Thomas Pearson
Martha Pearson

Elias Pearson	John Griest	Thomas Griest
Ann Pearson	Mary Love	Ann Griest
Isaac Everitt	Miriam Griest	Susanna Wierman
Martha Everitt	Joseph Griest	John Wierman
Isaac Pearson	Nicholas Wierman Jr	Content Garretson
Elizabeth Pearson	Lydia Wierman	Griffith John
John Everett	David Griest	John Cox Jr

MENALLEN MINUTES, MARRIAGES, & MISCELLANY

Hannah Everitt	Isaac Griest	Caleb Beals
Joseph Griest	John Garretson	Lydia Beals
-?- Wierman	Mary Garretson	Isaac Everitt Jr
John Garretson Jr	Thomas Thornburgh	Thomas Penrose
William Beals	Phebe Thornburgh	Abigail Penrose
-?-	Mary Hussey	Nicholas Wierman Sr
-?-	John Griest	Rachel Beals
	James Wierman Jr	Sarah Wierman Sr

#21 17th of 1st mo 1793   ROBERT MORTHLAND-PHEBE SPEAKMAN

Whereas Robert Morthland of Warrington Township County of York State of Pennsylvania son of Wm Morthland and Ruth his wife Deceased and Phebe Speakman of Huntington Township County aforesaid Daughter of Joshua Speakman and Ann his wife . . . at Huntington the seventeenth of first month one thousand seven hundred ninety three.

		Robert Morthland
Thomas Penrose	Isaac Everett	Phebe Morthland
Abigail Penrose	Martha Everett	Joshua Speakman
John Pigion	William Wireman	Stephen Speakman
Wm Wireman Jr	Jacob Comly	Alexander Underwood
Nicholas Wireman	Sarah Comly	Susanna Cook
Thomas Grist	Mary Garretson	Robert Morthland
Richard Pilkington	Isaac Pearson	Wm Marsh
John Grist	John Grist Jr	Vincent Pilkington
Miriam Grist	Joseph Grist	Elenor Welch
John Garretson Jr	Elihu Underwood	Jane Jones
Samuel Underwood	Sarah Morthland	William Squibb
Jane Underwood	Henry Jones	Charles Underwood

#22 22nd of 5th mo 1794   JOSEPH GRIEST-MARY WIREMAN

Be it Remembered that Joseph Griest son of Daniel Griest deceased and Ann his wife of the Township of Monahan in the County of York and State of Pennsylvania and Mary Wireman Daughter of Wm Wireman and Emy his wife of the Township of Huntington in the County and State aforesaid . . . at Huntington . . . the twenty second day of the fifth month in the year of our Lord one thousand seven hundred Ninety four.

		Joseph Griest
Thomas Pearson	Content Garetson	Mary Griest
Martha Pearson	Hannah Garetson	Emey Wireman
Isaac Pearson	John Wireman	Ann Griest
Elizabeth Pearson	Samuel Comly	Nicholas Wireman
Martha Everitt	Jacob Comly	Wm Wireman
John Clever	Thos Penrose	Sarah Wireman
Susanna Clever	Abigail Penrose	Daniel Griest
Wm Farqueor	John Grist	John Garitson
John Everitt	Susanna Griest	-?- Griest
		David Griest

MARRIAGES

Mary Beals   Thos Griest   John Griest
Sarah Comly   Ann Griest   Miriam Griest
Hannah Everett   Thos Thornburgh

#23 16th of 10th mo 1793   THOMAS BLACKBURN-SARAH GRIFFITH
Whereas Thomas Blackburn son of Thomas Blackburn and Alice his wife of the Township of Monalon County of York and State of Pennsylvania and Sarah Griffith Daughter of John Griffith and Lidia his wife of the Township County and State aforesaid . . . this sixteenth day of the tenth month one thousand seven hundred and ninety three . . . at Menalon.

                                                Thomas Blackburn
                                                <u>Sarah Blackburn</u>

Thomas Bowen   Rachel Griffith   John Griffith
Elizabeth Wright   Ann Bowen   John Blackburn
-?- Oldham   Isabel Blackburn   Samuel Garriston
Thomas Hammond   Benjamin Wright   Alice Garetson
Thomas Hammond   George Hammond   Sally Johnston
James Hammond   John Blackburn   Mary McGrew
Sarah Rusk   Thomas Wright   Martha McGrew
Reachal Wright   John Bowen   Finly McGrew
Ruth Wilson   Ruth Wright   Joel Hutton
John McGrail   Steven Hendriks   George Wilson

#24 12th of 2nd mo 1794   JAMES ALISON-SARAH BOWEN
Whereas James Alison son of James Alison and Elizabeth his wife deceased of the Township of Bedford in the County of Bedford and State of Pennsylvania and Sarah Bowen daughter of Jonathan Bowen and Ann his wife of the same place . . . this twelfth day of the second month One thousand seven hundred ninety four . . . at Meeting House in Monalon.

                                                James Alison
                                          <u>Sarah (her X mark) Alison</u>
                                                Jonathan Bowen

Mary John   Benjamin Wilson
Mary Hutton   Joel Hutton
Marget Hutton   Thomas Wright
Sarah Rusk   John Baldwin
Susana Wright   Charles McGrew
Ann Wright   Mary Hammond
Rachel Davis   Sarah Wilson
Elizabeth Wright   Deborah Potts
Lydia Oldham   Isbel Blackburn

#25 14th of 5th mo 1794   BENJAMIN FARQUHAR-REACHEL WRIGHT
Benjamin Farquhar son of Alen Farquhar of Frederick County and State of Maryland and Phebe his wife and Reachel Wright daughter of Jonathan Wright of York County State of Pennsylvania and Susanna his wife . . . this fourteenth day of the fifth month One thousand seven hundred ninety four . . . at Monalon.

                                                Benjamin Farquhar
                                                <u>Reachel Farquhar</u>

MENALLEN MINUTES, MARRIAGES, & MISCELLANY

Elizabeth Wright	Joseph Elgar	Alen Farquhar
John Wright Sr	Margaret Elgar	Jonathan Wright
Samuel Mickle	Joseph Elgar Jr	Susanna Wright
John Wright	Finly McGrew	Joel Wright
Moses Wright	Benjamin Wright	Thomas Wright
Jese Wright	John Wright Jr	Wm Farquhar
Martha Wright	Wm Wright	Alen Farquhar Jr
Elizabeth Wright	Mary John	Hannah Farquhar
Ruth Wright	Ann Wright	Caleb Farquhar
Aron Hibberd	Stephen Hendricks	Jane Hibberd
Jane Wright		Alice Hendricks

#26 26th of 5th mo 1796   JOHN WRIGHT-SUSANNA GRIST
Whereas John Wright of Monalon Township York County and State of Pennsylvania son of Benjamin Wright and Jane his wife and Susanna Grist daughter of Daniel Grist Monoghan Township County and State aforesaid and Ann his wife (the former deceased) . . . this twenty sixth day of the fifth month in the Year of our Lord one thousand seven hundred ninety six . . . at Meeting House in Huntington.

		John Wright
		Susanna Wright
Thomas Griest	Daniel Grist	Ann Griest
Jese Wright	Wm Wireman	John Griest
John Griest	Abigail Comly	Hannah Everitt
Joseph Griest	Thomas Pearson	Elizabeth Wright
David Griest	Isaac Everitt	Martha Pearson
Phebe Thornburgh	Wm Wireman	Phebe Wright
Steven Hendricks	Joseph Grist	Miriam Griest
Jonathan Wright	Thomas McCreary	Hannah Gariston
Nicholas Wireman Jr	Isaac Griest	Jane Wireman
Levi Grist	John Underwood	Mary Marsh
Josiah Garetson	John Everitt	Mary McCreary
John Wireman	Samuel Comly	Isaac Pearson

#27 14th of 5th mo 1794   AMOS FARQUHAR-MARY ELGAR
Amos Farquhar son of Allon Farquhar of Frederick County and State of Maryland and Phebe his wife and Mary Elgar daughter of Joseph Elgar of York County and State of Pennsylvania and Margaret his wife . . . this fourteenth day of fifth month one thousand seven hundred ninety four . . . and the Meeting house at Monalon.

		Amos Farquhar
		Mary Farquhar
Jonathan Wright	Moses Wright	Joseph Elgar
Susana Wright	Benjamin Wright	Allen Farquhar
Joel Wright	Jese Wright	Margaret Elgar
Thomas Wright	John Wright	Joseph Elgar Jr
Stephen Hendricks	Martha Wright	Wm Farquhar

MARRIAGES

Samuel Mickle	Sarah Hendricks	Allen Farquhar Jr
Jane Wright	Jane Hibberd	Hannah Farquhar
Alice Hendricks	Aron Hibberd	Caleb Farquhar
	Finly McGrew	Ann Wright

#28 24th of 9th mo 1794   THOMAS HAMMOND-RUTH WRIGHT

Whereas Thomas Hammond of Tirone Township York County and State of Pennsylvania son of James Hammond and Mary his wife and Ruth Wright daughter of John Wright of Monalon Township county and state aforesaid . . . this twenty fourth day of the ninth month one thousand seven hundred ninety four . . . at Monalon.

		Thomas Hammond
		<u>Ruth Hammond</u>
George Hammond	Jesse Wright	John Wright
Thomas Blackburn	Benjamin Wright	Mary Hammond
Finly McGrew	Benj Wilson	Elizabeth Wright
Stephen Hendricks	Wm Wright	Jane Wright
John Wright	Mary McGrew	Sarah Wright
Wm Roberts	Mary Hendricks	Phebe Wright
John Hutton	Elizabeth McGrail	Mary John
John McGrail	Able Wright	Sarah Burkholder
Samuel Wright	David Bonine	Hannah Wright

#29 30th of 10th mo 1794   STEPHEN HENDRICKS-SARAH WIREMAN

Stephen Hendricks son of Samuel Hendricks and Alice his wife (the former deceased) of Monalon Township York County and State of Pennsylvania and Sarah Wireman daughter of William Wireman Jr and Hannah his wife of Huntington Township County and State aforesaid . . . this thirtieth day of the tenth month one thousand seven hundred ninety four . . . at their meeting house in Huntington.

		Stephen Hendricks
		<u>Sarah Hendricks</u>
Jacob Comly	John Grist	William Wireman
Sarah Comly	Miriam Grist	Hannah Wireman
Thomas Pearson	Jonathan Wright	Nicholas Wireman
Thos Thornburgh	Thomas Wright	Susana Wireman
Phebe Thornburgh	William Roberts	Isaac Everitt
John Gariston	Amos Penrose	Martha Everitt
		Hannah Everitt

#30 6th of 11th mo 1794   ISAIAH JOHN-MARTHA GRIST

Whereas Isaiah John son of Joshua John of Newbury Township in the County of York in Pennsylvania and Reachel his wife and Martha Grist daughter of Willen Grist of Monahan Township in said County and Ann his wife . . . this sixth day of the eleventh month one thousand seven hundred ninety four . . . at Huntington.

		Isaiah John
		<u>Martha John</u>
John Grist	William Griest	Hannah Everitt
Jacob Griest	Ann Griest	Robert Squibb

MENALLEN MINUTES, MARRIAGES, & MISCELLANY

Isaac Griest	Robert Davis	John Garretson Jr
Content Griest	Elizabeth Davis	Rebeckah Griest
Samuel Gariston	Isaac Everitt	Joseph Griest
John Garetson	Martha Everitt	Ann Penrose
Mary Garretson	Stephen Hendricks	Thomas Penrose
Willing Griest	Sarah Hendricks	Hannah Wireman
Sarah John	Amos Penrose	Jacob Comly
Ann More	Mary Griffith	David Griest
Abigail Comly	Thomas Kirk	
Phebe Thornburgh	Elizabeth Kirk	

#31 27th of 10th mo 1796   DAVID GRIEST-MARY BEALS

David Griest of the Township of Huntington County of York and State of Pennsylvania son of Daniel Griest deceased and Ann his widow and Mary Beals daughter of Solomon Beals of the place aforesaid and Rebecca his wife . . . this twenty seventh day of the tenth month One thousand seven hundred ninety six . . . in the Meeting House at Huntington.

David Griest
<u>Mary Griest</u>

Ann Griest	Nathan Griffith	Thomas Griest
Daniel Griest	Nicholas Wireman	Ann Griest
Joseph Griest	Sarah Wireman	Nicholas Wireman
Mary Griest	Jacob Comly	Lidia Wireman
John Wright	Elias Pearson	Thomas Thornburgh
Susana Wright	Isaac Pearson	Phebe Thornburgh
Nathan Beals	Elizabeth Pearson	Charles Underwood
Mary Beals	Joseph Griest	Susana Wireman
Levy Griest	Rebeccah Griest	Caleb Beals
Caleb Beals	Samuel Comly	Mary Cox
Stephen Beals	David Beals	Hannah Gariston
Isaac Everitt	Mary Gareston	Hannah Wireman

#32 2nd of 11th mo 1796   LEVY HUTTON-MARTHA WRIGHT

Levy Hutton of Monalon Township York County and State of Pennsylvania son of William Hutton and Deborah his wife (the latter deceased) and Martha Wright daughter of Benjamin Wright and Jane his wife of the Township, County and State aforesaid . . . this second day of the seventh month One thousand seven hundred ninety six . . . at the Meeting House at Monalon.

Levy Hutton
<u>Martha Hutton</u>

William Hutton	Mary Wright	Thomas Blackburn
Benjamin Wright	Mary John	Jesse Morton
Jane Wright	Priscilla Wireman	John Hammond
Elizabeth Wright	Samuel Wright	Mary Maxwell
Phebe Wright	William -?-	Thomas Wright
Benjamin Wright	Charles Stewart	John Wright
John -?-	David Stewart	Ann Gilbreath
Alice Wright	John Stewart	Christian Lehman
Sally Wright	Hannah Wright	Margaret Gilbreath

MARRIAGES

Thomas Wright   Finly McGrew   John Gilbreath
Wm Wright   Benjamin Wilson   Nancy Lehman
John Blackburn   Harman Wireman

#33 12th of 8th mo 1795   JOHN McGRAIL-MARY BLACKBURN

Whereas John McGrail son of James McGrail deceased and Elizabeth his wife of the Township of Monalen and County of York and State of Pennsylvania and Mary Blackburn daughter of Moses Blackburn and Mary his wife of the Township, County and State aforesaid . . . this twelfth day of the fifth month One thousand seven hundred ninety five . . . at their Meeting house at Monalen.

                                                         John McGrail
                                                         Mary McGrail
John Wright   Elizabeth McGrail   John Blackburn
John Hammond   Isabel Blackburn   Thomas McGrail
Finly McGrew   Rebekah Blackburn   Thomas Blackburn
Benj Wright   Sally Wright   Thomas Hammond
Benj Wilson   Mary John   Finly Blackburn
Finly McGrew 2nd   Elizabeth Wright   Thomas Wright
Peggy Davis   Sarah Blackburn   Samuel Hendricks
Sally Burkholder   Jane Wright   John Hutton
                         Sarah Hendricks   George Wilson

#34 3rd of 11th mo 1796   CHARLES UNDERWOOD-HANNAH EVERITT

Whereas Charles Underwood of Warrington Township in the County of York and State of Pennsylvania son of John Underwood deceased and Mary his wife and Hannah Everitt of Huntington Township in the County and State aforesaid daughter of Isaac Everitt and Martha his wife . . . at Huntington . . . third day of eleventh month One thousand seven hundred ninety six.

                                                         Charles Underwood
                                                         Hannah Underwood
Thomas Thornburgh   Abigail Comly   Isaac Everitt
Samuel Comly   Mary Beals   Martha Everitt
Nicholas Wireman   Ann Griest   Benj Underwood
Jacob Comly   Sarah Wireman   John Everitt
Robert Long   Ruth Ragin   Susana Everitt
John Cox   Rebecka Long   Samuel Underwood
John Gariston   Hannah Underwood   Isaac Pearson
Robert Morthland   Sarah Hendricks   Elizabeth Pearson
Abraham Underwood   Phebe Thornburgh   John Clever
Elias Pearson   Susana Wireman   Susanna Clever
Stephen Hendricks   Elizabeth Deardorff   Solomon Beals
                         Mary Marsh   Rebekah Beals

#35 26th of 4th mo 1797   THOMAS McGRAIL-REBECCA BLACKBURN

Thomas McGrail son of James McGrail deceased and Elizabeth his wife of Monalon Township York County and State of Pennsylvania and Rebecca Blackburn daughter of Moses Blackburn and Mary his wife of the Township County and State aforesaid . . . this twenty sixth day of the fourth month One thousand seven hundred ninety seven . . . in this Meeting House in Monalon.

MENALLEN MINUTES, MARRIAGES, & MISCELLANY

		Thomas McGrail
		Rebecca McGrail
John Wright	Mary Hendricks	Moses Blackburn
Finly McGrew	Sarah Hendricks	Nathan Hendricks
Archibald McGrew	Phebe Wright	Thomas Blackburn
Jonathan Wright	Deborah Blackburn	Benjamin Wright
Moses Blackburn Jr	Mary John Jr	Samuel Hendricks
John Davis	Sarah Wright	Finley McGrew
		William Wright

#36 20th of 9th mo 1798   JOHN SINCLAIR-REACHEL PROCTER

John Sinclair of Berkly County State of Virginia son of Job Sinclair of the State of Kentucky and Elizabeth his wife deceased and Reachel Prockter Daughter of John Procter of York County and Sarah his wife . . . this twentieth day of the ninth month One thousand seven hundred ninety eight . . . in Meeting House in Huntington.

		John Sinclair
		Rachel Sinclair
Nicholas Wireman	Elizabeth Pearson	Hermon Cox
Amy Wireman	Hannah Wireman	Thomas Wireman
Elias Pearson	Rachel Hutton	Sarah Owen
Jesse Wright	Hannah Garretson	Mary Owen
William Wright	John Griest	Elizabeth Wright
Francis Swayne	Miriam Griest	Eliza Wright
Thomas Pearson	Sarah Wireman	Phebe Thornburgh
John Garretson	Susanna Wireman	Rebecca Pilkington
	Joseph Griest	Edward Hutton

#37 26th of 4th mo 1797   THOMAS BOWEN-SUSANNA SMITH

Whereas Thomas Bowen son of William Bowen deceased and Lidia his wife of Sinclair Township in the County of Bedford and State of Pennsylvania and Susanna Smith daughter of James Smith and Mary his wife of the Township County and State aforesaid . . . this twenty sixth of the fourth month One thousand seven hundred ninety seven . . . at their Meeting place at Dennens creek.

		Thomas Bowen
		Susanna Bowen
Mary Smith	John Bowen	Thomas Blackburn
Hannah Penrose	Jacob Williams	James Smith
Anne Penrose	John Hancock	Lydia Oldham
Jean Bowen	Wm Blackburn	Mary Smith
Mary -?-	Obadiah Adams	Jonathan Bowen
	Mordacai Adams	Thomas Bowen
	Susanna Adams	Thomas Griffith
	Dinah Adams	Elijah Adams
	Jane Thomas	Thomas Blackburn
	Mary Kenworthy	James Smith Jr
	Lidia Thomas	Anthony Blackburn
	Rachel Griffith	John Smith

MARRIAGES

                Ann Bowen   Amos Edwards
                                        Amos Penrose

#38 3rd of 5th mo 1797 — WILLIAM BLACKBURN-AMY KENWORTHY

William Blackburn son of Thomas Blackburn and Elizabeth his wife of Bedford County in the Commonwealth of Pennsylvania and Amy Kenworthy daughter of William and Mary Kenworthy of the same place . . . third day of the fifth month One thousand seven hundred ninety seven . . . at Meeting house of Dunnigs Creek in Bedford County aforesaid.

                                                                    William Blackburn
                                                                    Amy Blackburn

Jonathan Bowen	Abigail Penrose	Thomas Blackburn
Ann Bowen	Elizabeth Hancok	William Kenworthy
Mordicai Adams	Thomas Bowen	Elizabeth Blackburn
Hannah Adams	John Smith	Mary Kenworthy
Adam Bowman	William Griffith	Anthony Blackburn
Isaac Kenworthy	James Adams	Hannah Kenworthy
Lidia Kenworthy	William Shepperd	Jesse Kenworthy
Ruth Kenworthy	Susanna Adams	Thomas Griffith
	James Smith	Thomas Adams

#39 30th of 5th mo 1798 — GEORGE WILSON-SARAH WRIGHT

Whereas George Wilson son of Benjamin Wilson and Sarah his wife of the township of Monalon County of York and State of Pennsylvania and Sarah Wright daughter of John Wright and Elizabeth his wife of the same place . . . thirtieth day of the fifth month seventeen hundred ninety eight . . . at their meeting house at Monalon.

                                                                    George Wilson
                                                                    Sarah Wilson

Thos Thornburgh	Mary Wright	Benj Wilson
Mary Hammond	Eliza Wright	John Wright
Finly McGrew	Jesse Wright	Elizabeth Wright
Henry Wireman	Mary Hammond	William Wright
Jacob Cocks	Mary John Jr	John Wright
Stephen Hendricks	Sarah Hendricks	Thomas Griffith
Sarah Hendricks	Mary John	Benj Wright
Levy Hutton	Sarah Risk	George Hammond
Martha Hutton	Thomas Hammond	Jane Bowen
Zechariah Ferris	Simon Hadly	Rebekah Cox
		David Minicheel

#40 23rd of 5th mo 1799 — FRANCIS PELLETT-MARY JOHN

Whereas Francis Pellett of Warrington Township York Co and State of Pennsylvania and Mary John daughter of Abel John and Mary His wife of Monalin Township and County aforesaid . . . this twenty third day of the fifth month seventeen hundred ninety nine . . . at their meeting house at Monalin.

                                                                      Francis Pellett
                                                                    Mary Pellett

William Griffith	Finly McGrew	Mary John
Nathan Wright	Benj Wilson	Joseph John

MENALLEN MINUTES, MARRIAGES, & MISCELLANY

Isabel Blackburn	Elizabeth McGrail	Elizabeth John
Charles Kettlewell	Elizabeth Wright	Isaac Fisher
William Cook	Benjamin Wright	Alice Fisher
Hannah Nevitt	Stephen Hendricks	Sarah Hendricks
		Eliza Wright
		Alice Wright

#41 26th of 6th mo 1799   WILLIAM GRIFFITH-SARAH OWEN
Whereas William Griffith son of William Griffith and Sarah his wife of Bedford Township in the County of Bedford and State of Pennsylvania and Sarah Owen daughter of John Owen and Sarah his wife of Tyrone Township in the County of York and State aforesaid . . . the twenty sixth day of the sixth month seventeen hundred ninety nine . . . at Meeting House at Monallen.

William Griffith
Sarah Griffith

Benjamin Wilson	Eliza Wright	John Owen
William Wright	Mary Owen	Jesse Griffith
Stephen Hendricks	Sarah Wilson	John Wright
George Wilson	Jane Mickle	Benjamin Wright
John Wright	Sarah Hendricks	John Morton
Samuel Wright	Mary Wright	John Wright Jr
Benjamin Wright Jr	Sarah Hendricks	Finly McGrew
	Mary Harr	Nathan Hendricks
	Alice Wright	Nathan Wright

#42 30th of 10th mo 1799   ISAAC FISHER-ELIZABETH HANCOCK
Whereas Isaac Fisher of St. Clair Township in the County of Bedford and State of Pennsylvania son of James Fisher and Alice his wife of Monallen Township in the County and State aforesaid and Elizabeth Hancock of St. Clair aforesaid Daughter of James Hancock and Elizabeth his wife of St. Clair Township in the County of Bedford aforesaid . . . this thirtieth day of the tenth month seventeen hundred ninety nine at Dennings Creek in St. Clair aforesaid.

Isaac Fisher
Elizabeth Fisher

Jesse Vore	John Sweezy	Elizabeth Hancock
Lydia Vore	Ruth Williams	Benjamin Hancock
Hannah Penrose	Mary Gordon	Sarah Hancock
Lydia Thomas	Eve Blackburn	Joel Hancock
Ann Penrose	Margaret Blackburn	Wm Kenworthy
Thos Penrose	George Berkbeck	Mary Kenworthy
Mary Brown	Susanna Bowen	Thos Griffith
Hannah Kenworthy	Ann Bowen	Sam'l Way
Lydia Kenworthy	Thos Oldham	Hannah Way
Mary Kenworthy	Lydia Oldham	Thos Bowen Jr
Jonnathan Bowen	Thos Bowen	James Smith Sr
Thos Blackburn	Wm Blackburn	Joseph Everitt
John Everitt	Robert Miller	Mordecai Adams
Wm Griffith	Jane Miller	Amos Penrose

MARRIAGES

#43 30th of 10th mo 1799   THOMAS JENNINGS-ISABEL BLACKBURN
Whereas Thomas Jennings of Sinclair Township in the County of Bedford and State of Pennsylvania son of Thomas Jennings and Hannah his wife deceased of the County of York and State aforesaid and Isabel Blackburn Daughter of Thomas Blackburn Deceased and Alice his wife of the County of York . . . this thirtieth day of the tenth month seventeen hundred ninety nine . . . in their Meeting House at Dunnings Creek.

		Thomas Jennings
		Isabel Jennings
Thomas Bowen	Susanna Bowen	Jonathan Bowen
William Griffith	Mary Smith	Mary Kenworthy
Thomas Bowen	Joseph Everitt	Hannah Kenworthy
Thomas Griffith	Benjamin Bowen	Mary Brown
Thomas Oldham	Benjamin Hancock	Hanna Penrose
Thomas Blackburn	John Everitt	Anne Penrose
William Blackburn	Lydia Thomas	Amos Penrose
Samuel Way	Mordicai Adams	James McGrail
John Smith	Robert Miller	John Harbaugh
Hannah Way	Jane Miller	Lydia Vore
William Penrose	Alex McGregor Jr	Alice Oldham
Sopiah Habough	Thomas Mickle	Thomas Penrose Jr
Alice Bowen	Elizabeth Bowen	Thomas Penrose Sr
James Smith Sr	Thomas Oldham	Abigail Penrose
	Hannah Vore	

#44 6th of 11th mo 1799   JOEL HANCOCK-MARY KENWORTHY
Whereas Joel Hancock of St. Clair Township in the County of Bedford and State of Pennsylvania Son of James Hancock of St. Clair aforesaid Deceased and Elizabeth his wife and Mary Kenworthy Daughter of William Kenworthy of the Township and County aforesaid and Mary his wife . . . this sixth day of the eleventh month seventeen hundred ninety nine . . . at Dunnings Creek.

		Joel Hancock
		Mary Hancock
Abigail Penrose	Hennay Way	Wm Kenworthy
Amos Penrose	Jon Thomas	Mary Kenworthy
Lydia Thomas	Jane Thomas	Elizabeth Hancock
Robert Miller	Sophia Harbough	Wm Blackburn
Jacob Williams	Hannah Penrose	Elizabeth Fisher
Anthony Blackburn	Enos Blackburn	Isaac Fisher
Samuel Way	Mary Fisher	Jm Hancock
Thos Bowen	John Sweezy	Sarah Hancock
Susanna Bowen	Isaac Bonfall	Benjamin Hancock
Thos Jennings	Sarah Lundy	Jesse Kenworthy
Isabel Jennings	Elizabeth Brotherton	Ruth Kenworthy
Thos Bowen	Nathan Sharpless	Jonathan Bowen
Thos Oldham	Penrose Wily	Ann Bowen
Jonathan Potts	Thomas Griffith	

MENALLEN MINUTES, MARRIAGES, & MISCELLANY

#45 4th of 6th mo 1800   AMOS PENROSE-SOPHIA HARBOUGH
Whereas Amos Penrose son of Thomas Penrose and Abigail his wife of the Township of St. Clair in the County of Bedford and Province of Pennsylvania and Sophia Harbough of the same place daughter of Peter Harbough and Sophia his wife late of the County of York . . . this fourth day of the sixth month Eighteen Hundred . . . at Dennings Creek in the County of Bedford aforesaid.

		Amos Penrose
		Sophia Penrose
John Thomas	William Penrose	Thos Penrose
Jane Thomas	Thomas Griffith	Abigail Penrose
Lydia Thomas	Jesse Vore	Hannah Penrose
John Harbaugh	Lydia Vore	Anne Penrose
Hannah Vore	Jesse Griffith	Edward Thomas
Eve Blackburn	Thomas Jinnings	Alice Oldham
Margaret Blackburn	Isabel Jinnings	Alice Bowen
Eve Blackburn	Thomas Oldham	Thomas Smith
Ruth Williams	Thomas Bowen Jr	Hannah Addams
Hannah Blare	Susanna Bowen	Nathan Hammond
Dianah Adams	Jesse Blackburn	William Blackburn
Mary Smith	William Blair	Emy Blackburn

#46 3rd of 12th mo 1800   JOHN HANCOCK-HANNAH KENWORTHY
Whereas John Hancock son of James Hancock deceased and Elizabeth his wife of Bedford County in the Commonwealth of Pennsylvania and Hannah Kenworthy Daughter of William Kenworthy and Mary his wife of the same place . . . this third day of the twelfth month Eighteen hundred . . . at their Meeting House at Denning Creek in Bedford County.

		John Hancock
		Hannah Hancock
John Thomas	Ruth Kenworthy	Wm Kenworthy
Thomas Bowen Sr	Isaac Kenworthy	Mary Kenworthy
Thomas Bowen Jr	Amos Kenworthy	Elizabeth Hancock
Susanna Bowen	Thomas Jinnings	Benjamin Hancock
James Smith Sr	Isabel Jinnings	Lydia Kenworthy
Thomas Blackburn	Thomas Penrose	James Hancock
Robert Miller	Abigail Penrose	Elizabeth Fisher
Samuel Way	John Thomas	William Blackburn
Amos Penrose	Jane Thomas	Joel Hancock
Thomas Blackburn	John Wisegaver	Mary Hancock
Hannah Penrose	John Sweze	Amy Blackburn
Anna Penrose	Susanna Easter	Jesse Kenworthy
-?- Matthews		
Phebe Matthews		

#47 22nd of 1st mo 1801   JESSE RUSSELL-CONTENT GARRETSON
Whereas Jesse Russell of Frederick County and State of Maryland son of John Russell and Hannah his wife and Content Garretson of Adams County and

MARRIAGES

State of Pennsylvania daughter of John Garretson and Mary his wife . . . this twenty second day of the first month Eighteen hundred One . . . at Huntington in the County of Addams.

                                                              <u>Jesse Russell</u>
                                                             <u>Content Russell</u>

John Garretson	Isaac Everitt	Benj Griest
Mary Garretson	Jacob Comly	Hannah Jones
Thomas Russell	Richard Roberts	Nicholas Wierman Jr
John Garretson Jr	Joel Garretson	Rebecah Pilkington
Sarah Russell	Wm Farquhar	Ann Griest
Zachariah Roberts	Hannah Wierman	Rachel Sinclair
Hannah Garretson	David Griest	Mary Griest
Amos Garretson	Ann Griest	John Griest
Mary Russell	Thos Wierman	Joseph Griest
Abel Russell	Susanna Wierman	Phebe Thornburgh
Mary Garretson Jr	Susanna Comly	Thomas Griest
Josiah Garretson	Saml Comly	Ann Griest
Martha Pearson	Isaac Wierman	Rachel Garretson

#48 2nd of 12th mo 1801   THOMAS BLACKBURN-ELIZABETH BOWEN

Whereas Thomas Blackburn of St Clair Township Bedford County and State of Pennsylvania son of Anthony Blackburn of the same place and Mary his wife and Elizabeth Bowen daughter of Jonathan Bowen of the Township County and State aforesaid and Anne his wife . . . this second day of the twelfth month Eighteen hundred One . . . in their meeting house at Dunnings Creek.

                                                              Thomas Blackburn
                                                             <u>Elizabeth Blackburn</u>

Anthony Blackburn	Nathan Hammond	Eve Griffith
Jonathan Bowen	Hannah Penrose	Lydia Kenworthy
Mary Blackburn	Anne Penrose	Mary Fisher
Jesse Griffith	Hannah Addams	Thomas Penrose Jr
Alice Bowen	William Garretson	Robert Miller
Thomas Bowen Jr	John Harbaugh	George Gordon
Margaret Blackburn	Peter Rouzer	Isable Bowen
Susanna Bowen	Sarah Hancock	Wm Blackburn
Wm Griffith	Sophia Penrose	Amos Edwards
Jesse Blackburn	Amos Penrose	John Thomas
Benjamin Bowen	Lydia Thomas	Jane Thomas
Thomas Bowen	Ruth Kenworthy	Thomas Griffith

#49 20th of 5th mo 1803   DAVID McCREERY-ALICE WRIGHT

Whereas David McCreery son of Thomas McCreery and Sarah his wife both deceased of Conoughstoga Township in the County of Adams and State of Pennsylvania and Alice Wright daughter of Benjamin Wright and Jane his wife of Monallen Township in County and State aforesaid . . . this twentieth day of the fifth month Eighteen hundred Three . . . at Monallen.

                                                              David McCreery
                                                             <u>Alice McCreery</u>

George Willson	Nathan Wright	Benjamin Wright
Daniel Ragen	Rebekah Bateman	Jane Wright

MENALLEN MINUTES, MARRIAGES, & MISCELLANY

Thomas Penrose	Alice Wilson	Eliza Wright
Mary McGrew	William Wierman	Levi Hutton
Ann McGrew	John Bateman	Samuel Wright
Thomas Griffith	Hannah Bateman	John Wright
Thomas McGrail	Henry Wierman	Thos Wright
Jonathan Wright	Susanna Wierman	Mary Wright
Richard Ridgeway	Naomi Wierman	Deborah Yarnell
Benjamin Harris	Abner Thomas	Finly McGrew
Rebechah Harris	Esther Thomas	Abel Thomas
William Wright	Samuel Wright	Allin Thomas
Mary Cochran	Stephen Hendricks	Ruth Ragen

#50 25th of 5th mo 1803   HARMON WIERMAN-MARY HAMMOND

Whereas Harmon Wierman son of Henry Wierman and Susannah his wife of the Township of Monallen County of Adams and State of Pennsylvania and Mary Hammond daughter of James Hammond and Mary his wife of Tyrone Township County and State aforesaid . . . this twenty fifth day of the fifth month Eighteen hundred three . . . at the Meeting House at Monallen.

Harmon Wierman
Mary Wierman

George Wilson	Rebechah Bateman	Elizabeth Wright
John Bateman	Abel Thomas	Levi Hutton
Hannah Bateman	Ellin Thomas	Wm Wierman
Richard Ridgeway	Mary Willson	Susanna Wierman
Jonathan Wright	Eliza Wright	Henry Wierman
Thomas Penrose	Alice Willson	Benjamin Wright
John McGrail	Deborah Worrel	Samuel Wright
Benjamin Harris	Nicholas Wierman	Stephen Hendricks
Thomas Johns Jr	Naomi Wierman	Nathan Wright
Sarah Wilson	Jacob Harris	Wm Wright
Finly McGrew	Elizabeth Cook	John Wright
James McGrail	Elizabeth Hammond	Samuel Wright
Mary McGrail	Abner Thomas	Rachel Bateman
Jacob Thomas	Esther Thomas	
Margaret Thomas		
Eli Thomas		

#51 30th of 11th mo 1803   WILLIAM WRIGHT-RACHEL THOMAS

Whereas William Wright son of John and Elizabeth Wright of Monallen Township Adams County and State of Pennsylvania and Rachel Thomas daughter of Abel and Ellen Thomas of the Township County and State aforesaid . . . this thirtieth day of the eleventh month Eighteen hundred three . . . at Monallen Meeting House.

William Wright
Rachel Wright

John Bateman	Nathan Wright	John Wright
Hannah Bateman	Eli Thomas	Abel Thomas
Jacob R. Thomas	Mary Wright	Ellin Thomas
Samuel Wright	Elizabeth McGrail	Isaac Thomas
Thomas Wright	Mary Wilson	Jacob Thomas

MARRIAGES

Elizabeth Thomas	Casandra Cochran	Margaret Thomas
Rebekah Harris	Isaa Thomas	Esther Thomas
Rebekah Thomas	Mary Bateman	Ruth Hammond
Anne Harris	Barbara Harris	George Wilson
Joseph Thomas	Finley McGrew	Benjamin Harris
Jacob Bateman	Daniel Ragen	Joseph Thomas
Jacob Harris	Benjamin Wilson	Rebekah Harris
Francis Rusk	Nathan McGrew	John Wright
Stephen Hendricks	Elizabeth Harris	
	Sarah Hendricks	

#52 28th of 3rd mo 1804   SAMUEL WRIGHT-REBEKAH HARRIS

Whereas Samuel Wright son of John and Ann Wright of Monallen Township Adams County in the State of Pennsylvania and Rebekah Harris Daughter of Benjamin Harris and Rebekah Harris of the Township County and State aforesaid . . . this twenty eighth day of the third month Eighteen hundred four . . . at Monallen.

		Samuel Wright
		<u>Rebekah Wright</u>
Jane Mickle	Levi Hutton	John Wright
Eliza Wright	Ruth Hammond	Ann Wright
Eli Thomas	Isaac Thomas	Benjamin Harris
William Wright	Isaac Thomas Jr	Rebecca Harris
Anna Harris	Nathan McGrew	Jacob Harris
Elizabeth McGrail	Jane Bateman	Mary Wright
William Bateman	Rebekah Bateman	Elizabeth Harris
Nathan Wright	Rachel Bateman	Sarah Harris
Joseph Thomas	Mary Bateman	Barbara Harris
Jacob Bateman	Stephen Hendricks	Abel Thomas
Nathan Harris	Sarah Hendricks	Ellin Thomas
Abel Thomas	Ruth Regin	John Wright
Sarah Mickle	Daniel Ragin	Benjamin Wright
Samuel Wright	Rebekah Thomas	Finly McGrew
William Wright	John Owen	Abner Thomas
	Thomas Wright	Benjamin Harris Jr

#53 24th of 10th mo 1804   JOHN WRIGHT-ALICE WILSON

Whereas John Wright son of John and Elizabeth Wright of Monallen Township Adams County in the State of Pennsylvania and Alice Wilson daughter of Benjamin and Sarah Wilson of the Township, County and State aforesaid . . . this twenty fourth day of the tenth month Eighteen hundred four . . . at Monallen Meeting House.

		John Wright
		<u>Alice Wright</u>
Jacob Thomas	Finly McGrew	John Wright
Eli Thomas	Daniel Ragen	Benjamin Wilson
Ellin Thomas	Mary Wright	Elizabeth Wright
Benjamin Harris	Jacob Hock	Nathan Wright
Rebekah Harris	Rebekah Bateman	William Wright
Jacob Bateman	Abner Thomas	Rachel Wright

MENALLEN MINUTES, MARRIAGES, & MISCELLANY

Mary Wright	Isaac Wierman	Mary Wilson
Mary Bateman	Elizabeth Thomas	George Wilson
Jacob Harris	Rachel Bateman	Abel Thomas
Barbara Harris		Ellin Thomas

#54 19th of 3rd mo 1806   JONATHAN WRIGHT-MARY BATEMAN

Jonathan Wright son of Joel Wright of Frederick County and State of Maryland and Elizabeth his wife (the latter deceased) and Mary Bateman daughter of William Bateman of Adams County and Commonwealth of Pennsylvania and Elizabeth his wife . . . this nineteenth day of the third month Eighteen hundred six . . . in the Meeting house at Monallen.

                                                                                         Jonathan Wright
                                                                                          Mary Wright

Alice Wright	Abel Thomas	Joel Wright
Nathan Wright	Ellen Thomas	William Bateman
Mary Wright	Isaac Thomas	Elizabeth Bateman
Isaiah Thomas	Elener Thomas	Allen Wright
Mary Wilson	Stephen Hendricks	Elizabeth Wright
Thomas Wright	Sarah Hendricks	Rebekah Bateman
Hannah Garretson	Wm Wright	Jacob Bateman
Martha -?- Jr	Rachel Wright	Rachel Bateman
Amos Garretson	Ruth Hammond	Elizabeth Bateman
Daniel Ragin	Jacob Thomas	John Bateman
Rebekah Harris	Samuel Colber	Phebe Wright
Sarah Pilkington	Joel Garretson	Alice Hendricks
Hepzibah Walker	John Garretson Jr	Israel Wright
Azel Walker	Eli Thomas	Rebekah Thomas
	Elias Pearson Jr	Sarah Harris
	John Wright	Samuel Wright

#55 27th of 3rd mo 1806   ISAAC WIERMAN-SUSANNA COMLEY

Isaac Wierman son of William Wierman of the Township of Huntington, County of Adams and State of Pennsylvania and Hannah his wife and Susanna Comley, daughter of Jacob Comley and Sarah his wife of the Township County and State aforesaid . . . this twenty seventh day of the third month Eighteen hundred six . . . at their meeting house at Huntington. Isaac Wierman

                                                                                         Susanna Wierman

Samuel Comly	Stephen Hendricks	Jacob Comly
Jesse Comly	Sarah Hendricks	Hannah Wierman
Thomas Wierman	Susanna Wierman	Thomas Thornburgh
John Wierman	Hannah Wierman Jr	Phebe Thornburgh
Jesse Russell	Phebe Wierman	Amy Wierman
Robert Bond	John Everitt	Joel Wierman
Hannah Burkholder	Susanna Everitt	John Garretson Jr
Mary Lyrch	Levi Griest	Hannah Garretson
Christian Deardorff	Ann Griest	Elias Pearson
Eliza Wright	Amos Garretson	Joseph Griest
Benjamin Blackford	Mary Garretson	Rebekah Griest
Daniel Shaffer	Isaac Everitt	William Wierman

MARRIAGES

Lydia Worley	Rebekah Everitt	Abel Thomas
Francis Worley	Amos Griest	Joseph Griest Jr
Samuel Wright	Uriah Griest	Mary Griest
Isaac W. Woodland	Richard Pilkington	Nicholas Wierman
Josiah Garretson	Sarah Pilkington	Jane Wierman
William Wierman	Joel Garretson	Isaac Pearson
Nicholas Wierman	Rachel Garretson	Thos Pearson
	Ruth Griest	Martha Pearson
		Martha Pearson Jr
		Elias Pearson Jr

#56 25th of 6th mo 1806 ABNER GRIFFITH-MARY OWEN

Whereas Abner Griffith son of William Griffith and Sarah his wife of Bedford Township in the County of Bedford and State of Pennsylvania and Mary Owen daughter of John Owen and Sarah his wife of Tyrone Township Adams County and State aforesaid . . . this twenty fifth day of the sixth month eighteen hundred six . . . at Monallen.

		Abner Griffith
		Mary Griffith
Catharine McKnight	Elizabeth Bateman	John Owen
Ann McGrew	John Bateman	Sarah Owen
Nancy McElhinney	Wm Wright	Elizabeth Wright
Victor McElhinney	Mary McGrew	Mary Wright
Nancy King	Rebekah Thomas	Nathan McGrew
Nancy Elliott	Benjamin Wright	Jacob Bateman
Mary McGrew	Rebekah -?-	Robert McIlhenny
Mary Kirk	John McKnight	Finley McGrew
Amos Boen		Griffith Mickel
		Sarah Rusk
		Jane Mickel

#57 27th of 5th mo 1807 JOHN GARRETSON-REBEKAH BATEMAN

Whereas John Garretson of Adams County and State of Pennsylvania son of John Garretson of the same place and Mary his wife, and Rebekah Bateman daughter of William Bateman of the County and State aforesaid and Elizabeth his wife . . . this twenty seventh day of the fifth month Eighteen hundred seven . . . at Monallen.

		John Garretson
		Rebekah Garretson
Nathan Harris	Abel Russell	John Garretson Sen
Eli Thomas	Elizabeth Thomas	Mary Garretson
Thomas Wright	Isaac Thomas	William Bateman
Anne Wright	Joseph Thomas	Elizabeth Bateman
Martin Mackey	Rebekah Thomas	Amos Garretson
Samuel Wright	Lydia Thomas	Mary Garretson
Rebekah Wright	Amos Griest	John Bateman
William Wright	Phebe Wierman	Hannah Bateman
Rachel Wright	Martha Pearson	Jonathan Wright
John Wright	Abel Thomas	Mary Wright
Ann Wright	Ellin Thomas	Josiah Garretson

MENALLEN MINUTES, MARRIAGES, & MISCELLANY

John Wright Jr	Isaac Thomas	Joel Garretson
Benjamin Wright	Benjamin Harris	Hannah Garretson
Samuel Wright	Rebecca Harris	Mary Garretson Jr
Mary Wright	Sarah Harris	Rachel Garretson
Ruth Hammon	Jacob Harris	Rachel Bateman
David Cox	Mary Harris	Elizabeth Bateman
Sarah Wilson	Elizabeth Harris	Stephen Hendricks
George Wilson	Barbarah Harris	Sarah Hendricks
Mary Wilson	Nathan McGrew	Finley McGrew
Sarah Wilson Jr	Elizabeth Wright	
	Mary Dodds	

#58 27th of 5th mo 1807   JACOB HARRIS-MARY WRIGHT
Whereas Jacob Harris son of Benjamin Harris of Monallen Township Adams County in the State of Pennsylvania and Mary Wright Daughter of John Wright and Ann Wright of the Township County and State aforesaid . . . this twenty seventh day of the fifth month Eighteen hundred seven . . . at Monallen.

Jacob Harris
Mary Harris

Elizabeth Bateman	Benj Wright	John Wright
Elizabeth Thomas	Jane Wright	Ann Wright
Isaac Thomas Jr	John Wright	Benjamin Harris
Abel Russell	Elizabeth Wright	Rebecca Harris
Lydia Thomas	Wm Wright	Sam'l Wright
Rebekah Thomas	Rachel Wright	Rebecca Wright
Eli Thomas	Abel Thomas	Jacob Wright
Joseph Thomas	Ellin Thomas	Thomas Wright
Martin Machey	Isaac Thomas	Anna Wright
Mary Wilson	William Bateman	William Wright
Sarah Wilson	John Garretson	Sarah Harris
George Wilson	Rebekah Garretson	Elizabeth Harris
Mary McGrew	Amos Garretson	Barbara Harris
Mary McGrew	Josiah Garretson	Nathan Harris
Ruth Hammond	Joel Garretson	Benjamin Harris Jr
Eliza Wright	John Bateman	John Wright
Daniel Reagon	Hannah Bateman	Rachel Wright
Ruth Reagon	Hannah Garretson	Sarah Mickle
Finley McGrew	Rachel Bateman	Samuel Wright
Nathan McGrew	Amos Griest	
Stephen Hendricks	Mary Wright	
Sarah Hendricks		

#59 28th of 10th mo 1807   ABNER WALKER-SARAH HARRIS
Whereas Abner Walker of Warrington Township York County and State of Pennsylvania son of Benjamin Walker of the Township aforesaid and Ruth his wife and Sarah Harris daughter of Benjamin Harris of Monallin Township and County of Adams and State aforesaid and Rebekah his wife . . . this twenty eighth day of the tenth month Eighteen hundred seven . . . at Monallen.

MARRIAGES

		Abner Walker
		Sarah Walker
Elizabeth Thomas	Elizabeth Walker Jr	Benjamin Walker
Mary Wright	Nathan Harris	Benjamin Harris
Elizabeth Bateman	Nathan Wright	Rebekah Harris
Mary Wright	Ely Thomas	James Thomas
Elizabeth Harris	William Bateman	Samuel Wright
Barbara Harris	Jno Bateman	Rebecca Wright
Ann Wright	Ann Bateman	Isaac Thomas
Daniel Ragen	Jonathan Wright	Daniel Richards
Ruth Ragen	John Wright	Lydia Richards
Martin Mackey	Stephen Hendricks	Ellen Thomas
	Jacob Thomas	Hephzibah Walker
	Benj'n Wright	Jacob Harris
	Sam'l Wright	Mary Harris
	Finley McGrew	Thomas Wright
	John Wright	Anna Wright
	Joseph Thomas	Richard Pilkington
		Sarah Pilkington

#60 29th of 10th mo 1807   JOEL GARRETSON-MARTHA PEARSON

Whereas Joel Garretson son of John Garretson and Mary his wife and Martha Pearson daughter of Isaac Pearson and Elizabeth his wife all of the County of Adams and State of Pennsylvania . . . this twenty ninth day of the tenth month Eighteen hundred seven . . . at Huntington.

		Joel Garretson
		Martha Garretson
John Griest	Rachel Garretson	John Garretson
Elias Pearson Jun	Isaac Everitt	Mary Garretson
Joel Wireman	Rebekah Everitt	Isaac Pearson
Susanna Wireman	Hannah Wireman	Elizabeth Pearson
Phebe Wireman	Isaac Pearson	Elias Pearson
A. Gilbert	William Wireman	John Garretson Jr
Isaac Thomas Jr	Hannah Wireman Sr	Rebekah Garretson
William Wireman	Phebe Thornburgh	Jesse Russel
Thomas Griest	John Everitt	Content Russel
Ann Griest	Susanna Everitt	Amos Garretson
Aaron Griest	Jacob Comly	Mary Garretson
Ann Griest	Allen Robinet	Josiah Garretson
Thomas Pearson	Sarah Hendricks	Mary Garretson Jr
Martha Pearson	Thos Wireman	
Hannah Pearson	Uriah Griest	
	George Robinett	
	Joseph Griest Jr	

#61 28th of 4th mo 1808   SAMUEL COMLEY-SUSANNA WIERMAN

Whereas Samuel Comley son of Jacob Comley and Sarah his wife (the latter deceased) and Susanna Wierman daughter of William Wierman and Hannah his wife all of Latimore Township Adams County and State of Pennsylvania

MENALLEN MINUTES, MARRIAGES, & MISCELLANY

... this twenty eighth day of the fourth month Eighteen hundred eight ... at Huntington.

		Samuel Comly
		Susanna Comly
William Wierman	Thos Wierman	Jacob Comly
Josiah Garretson	Levi Griest	William Wierman
Jonathan Cox	John Garretson Jr	Hannah Wierman
Isaac Pearson	Joseph Griest Jr	Jesse Comly
Elizabeth Pearson	Amos Garretson	Stephen Hendricks
Thomas Pearson	Mary Garretson	Sarah Hendricks
Martha Pearson	Isaac Thomas	Nicholas Wierman
Elias Pearson Jr	Susan Wierman	Isaac Wierman
A. Robenet	Ruth Griest	Susanna Wierman
Geo. Robenet	John Kenworthy	Joel Wierman
Jacob -?-	Joseph Griest	Hannah Wierman
John Griest	Rebekah Griest	Phebe Wierman
Charles Godfrey	Martha Everitt	Thomas Griest
John Tolan	Phebe Thornburgh	Ann Griest
	Mary Garretson Sr	Lydia Wierman
	Joel Garretson	Mary Wierman
	Martha Garretson	
	Mary Garretson Jr	
	Rachel Garretson	
	Ann Griest	
	E. Bowman	

#62 29th of 11th mo 1809   JOHN GARRETSON-REBEKAH THOMAS

Whereas John Garretson of Newbury Township in the County of York and State of Pennsylvania son of Samuel Garretson of the same place and Jane his late wife deceased and Rebekah Thomas daughter of Isaac Thomas of Monallen Township in the County of Adams and State aforesaid and Eleanor his wife deceased ... this twenty ninth day of the eleventh month Eighteen hundred nine ... at Monallen.

		John Garretson
		Rebekah Garretson
Samuel Garretson	Elin Thomas	Stephen Hendricks
Isaac Thomas	Abner Thomas	Sarah Hendricks
Elinor Thomas	Jacob Bateman	Elias Pearson
Isaac Thomas Jr	Eli Thomas	Ruth Ragan
Hannah Thomas	Joseph Thomas	Mary Wright
Joseph McMillan	Mary Wright	Abner Thomas
Rebecah McMillan	Elizabeth Bateman Jr	Jacob R. Thomas
Alice Garretson	Elin Thomas	John Bateman
Isaac Cleaver	Elizabeth Bateman	Hannah Bateman
Thomas Garretson	Rebekah Harris	Finley McGrew
Elizabeth Thomas	Jacob Harris	Daniel Ragan
Isaac Kirk	Mary Harris	Samuel Wright
Elizabeth Hammond	George Wilson	Elizabeth Wright
John Thomas	John Wright	Benj Wright
Abel Thomas	Ruth Hammond	Wm Wright

MARRIAGES

Lydia Thomas	Benj'n Harris Jr	Hannah Wierman
Joseph Thomas	Joel Wierman	Phebe Wierman

#63 24th of 10th mo 1810   NATHAN WRIGHT-ELIZABETH HARRIS

Whereas Nathan Wright of Menallen Township in the County of Adams in Pennsylvania son of John Wright of the Township County and State aforesaid and Elizabeth his wife and Elizabeth Harris daughter of Benjamin Harris of the place aforesaid and Rebekah his wife . . . this twenty fourth day of the tenth month Eighteen hundred ten . . . at Monallen.

		Nathan Wright
		Elizabeth Wright
Elizabeth Bateman Jr	Ruth Hammond	John Wright
Barbara Harris	Ellin Wright	Elizabeth Wright
Elizabeth Hammond	Wm Wright	Benj'n Harris
Mary Wright	Jonathan Wright	Rebekah Harris
Ruth Cook	George Wright	Benj'n Harris
Eli Thomas	Mary Hobson	Samuel Wright
Nathan Harris	Abner Thomas	Abel Thomas
Joseph Thomas	Daniel Ragen	Ellin Thomas
Mary McGrew	Finley McGrew	George Wilson
Ann Wright	Jacob Bateman	Harman Wierman
Abner Walker	Isaac Thomas	John Hammond
Sarah Walker	Lydia Thomas	Beulah Harris
J. R. Thomas	Margaret Thomas	Benj'n Wright
	Isaac Thomas Jr	John Wright
	Esther C. Starr	Alice Wright
	Anne Bateman	Jacob Harris
		Sarah Wilson

#64 1st of 12th mo 1814   JOEL WIERMAN-HANNAH HUSSEY

Whereas Joel Wierman son of William Wierman and Hannah his wife of Latimore Township in the County of Adams and State of Pennsylvania and Hannah Hussey daughter of Amos Hussey and Abigail his wife of the Township of Franklin, County of York and State aforesaid . . . this first day of the twelfth month Eighteen hundred fourteen . . . at Huntington.

		Joel Wierman
		Hannah Wierman
Amos Griest	Thomas Wierman	Amos Hussey
Phebe Griest	Thomas Wierman Jr	Abigail Hussey
Allen Robinet	John Marsh	Phebe Thornburgh
Mary Cox	Hannah Marsh	Elizabeth Pearson
Anne Griest	Eliza Marsh	Nicholas Wierman
William Penrose	Rhoda M. Bartlett	Isaac Wierman
Jacob Jones	Susan Wierman	Mary Hussey
Thos Pilkington	Phebe Wierman	Samuel Comly
Margaret Gray	Samuel Hendricks	Susanna Comly
Joseph Griest Jr	Charles Godfrey	Stephen Hussey
Uriah Griest	Mord'i Matthews	John Wierman
Eli Griest	Ruth Matthews	Hannah Wierman
Mary Pearson	Ruth Griest	Lydia Wierman

MENALLEN MINUTES, MARRIAGES, & MISCELLANY

Gideon Griest	Thomas Griest	Mary Wierman
Rachel Matthews	John Garretson	Betsy Pearson
David Griest	Rebekah Garretson	Steven Hendrix
David Griest Jr	Josiah Garretson	Joseph Griest
William Wright	Elizabeth Garretson	Rebekah Griest
Joel Garretson	Daniel Griest	Nicholas Wierman
Martha Garretson	John Griest	Hannah Hendricks
	Elias Pearson	Alexander Wierman
		Daniel Gibbons
		William Wierman
		Isaac Pearson

#65 26th of 4th mo 1815   ELI THOMAS-ELIZABETH HAMMOND

Whereas Eli Thomas of Monallen Township in the County of Adams and State of Pennsylvania son of Abel Thomas of Monallen and Ellen his wife and Elizabeth Hammond daughter of Thomas Hammond of Tyrone Township in the County and State aforesaid deceased and Ruth his wife . . . this twenty sixth day of the fourth month Eighteen hundred fifteen . . . at Monallen.

<pre>   Eli Thomas
                                                              Elizabeth Thomas</pre>

Jonah Thomas	Finly McGrew	Abel Thomas
Nathan Harris	Henry Bender	Elen Thomas
Hiram Starr	Lydia Thomas	Ruth Hammond
Ruth Hock	Samuel Wright	Margaret Thomas
Beulah Harris	Levi Hutton	William Wright
Henry Bender Jr	Martha Hutton	Rachel Wright
Elizabeth Thomas	John F. Frieve	Abner Thomas
Abner Thomas	Simon Baker	Esther Thomas
John Thomas	Harmat Lutes	John Wright
Abraham Studebaker	Sarah Rusk	Alice Wright
	Jane Hutton	Isaac Thomas Sr
	Effe Mickle	Hannah Thomas
	Merna Hopkie	George Wilson
	Ann Bateman	Benj'n Harris
	Henrietta Baker	Mary Wright
	William Wright	

#66 4th of 5th mo 1815   DANIEL GIBBONS-HANNAH WIERMAN

Whereas Daniel Gibbons of Lampeter Township in the County of Lancaster and State of Pennsylvania son of James Gibbons dec'd of the same place and Deborah, his wife and Hannah Wierman daughter of William Wierman of Latimore Township Adams County and state of Pennsylvania aforesaid and Hannah his wife . . . this fourth day of the fifth month Eighteen hundred fifteen . . . at Huntington.

<pre>   Daniel Gibbons
                                                                Hannah Gibbons</pre>

Samuel Comly	Phebe Wierman	William Wierman
Susanna Comly	Phebe Thornburgh	Hannah Wierman
Lydia Wierman	Joel Wierman	Sam'l Gibbons
Mary Wierman	Hannah Wierman	William Daniel

MARRIAGES

Hannah Hendricks	Nicholas Wierman	Rachal Daniel
Massey Gibbons	Jane Wierman	Peter Griest
Lydia Gibbons	John Tudor	John Sadler
Mary Hussey	Phebe Tudor	Joshua Cox
Ruth Griest	John Garretson	David Griest Jr
Rebekah Peart	Rebekah Garretson	Phebe Pearson
William Wright	Joseph Griest Jr	John Griest
Elizabeth Pearson Jr	Mary Ocker	Isaac Pearson
Abraham Gibbons	Elizabeth Pearson	Wm Wierman
A. Gilbert	Amos Griest	Benj'n Wright
Mary Garretson	Phebe Griest	Uriah Griest
Elias Pearson	Thos Wierman	Thos Griest
Eli Griest	Rachel Garretson	Ann Griest
Stephen Hussey	Anne Griest	David Griest
Thomas Wierman	Mary Cox	Content Griest
Sam Hendricks	Wm Griest	John Everitt
	Daniel Griest	Susanna Everitt
	Anna Godfrey	Gideon Griest
	Mary Moorhead	John Wierman
	Alexander Wierman	Nicholas Mullen

#67 18th of 5th mo 1815   JOSIAH PENROSE-RACHEL GARRETSON
Whereas Josiah Penrose of Sinclair Township in the County of Bedford in the State of Pennsylvania son of Thomas Penrose of the Township County and State aforesaid and Abigail his wife and Rachel Garretson of Latimore Township in the County of Adams and State aforesaid daughter of John Garretson dec'd and Mary his wife . . . this eighteenth day of the fifth month Eighteen hundred fifteen . . . at Huntington.

Josiah Penrose
Rachel G. Penrose

David Griest Jr	Mary Wierman	Mary Garretson
Peter Griest	Uriah Griest	John Garretson
Abraham Smith	Joshua Cox Jr	Rebekah Garretson
Maria Clark	Nicholas Wierman Jr	Thos Penrose Jr
John Griest	Sally Wierman	Wm Wierman
Elias Pearson	Mary Pearson	Hannah Wierman
Thomas Wierman	Ruth Griest	Hannah Garretson
Lydia Wierman	Eli Griest	Mary Garretson
Susan Wierman	John Tudor	Ann Penrose
Mary Cox	Phebe Tudor	Josiah Garretson
Sam'l Comly	Elizabeth Pearson	William Penrose
Susanna Comly	Joseph Griest Jr	Joel Garretson
William Griest	Mary Griest	Elizabeth Pearson Jr
William Wierman	Sam'l Cox	Phebe T. Wierman
	Amy Wierman	William Wierman Jr

#68 31st of 7th mo 1817   GIDEON GRIEST-JANE M. SWAYNE
Whereas Gideon Griest son of Joseph Griest of Latimore Township County of Adams and State of Pennsylvania and Rebecca his wife and Jane M. Swayne daughter of Francis Swayne of Washington Township County of York and

MENALLEN MINUTES, MARRIAGES, & MISCELLANY

State aforesaid and Sarah his wife . . . this thirty first day of the seventh month eighteen hundred seventeen . . . at Huntington.

Gideon Griest
<u>Jane M. Griest</u>

Joseph Griest - Rebecca Griest - Francis Swayne - Sarah Swayne - William Wierman - Hannah Wierman - Uriah Griest - Eli Griest - Thomas Griest - Ann Griest - Hannah B. Swayne - Daniel Griest - Rachal Owen - Ruth Griest - Susan Swain - Amos Griest - Phebe Griest - Stephen Hussey - Mi-?- Hussey - Mary Hussey - Phebe Wierman - Lydia Wierman - Mary Wierman - Susanna Bower - Elizabeth Pearson - Mary Garretson - Maria McGee - Susanna Comly - Josiah Garretson - Phebe T. Wierman - Susan Wierman - Joel Garretson - Martha Garretson - Joel Wierman - William Wright - Isaac Memus - Petter Griest - William Griest - Mary Pearson - Ann Pearson - David Griest Jr - Alex'r Wierman - Elizabeth Pearson Jr - Anne Griest - Rebecca Griest - Miriam Griest - John G. Garretson - Alice Garretson - Maryann Garretson - Mary Wierman - Hannah Wierman - Thos Wierman - Malon Griest - Maria Clark - Thomas Cox - Isaac Tudor - Elias Pearson - Isaac Pearson - Samuel Cox - Wm Wierman Jr - Cornelius Smith - Enoch Vanscoyoc - Josiah Cox Jr - Mary F. Beals - Louisa Ross - Margaretta Gray - Mary Griest - Amy Wierman - Mary Wierman - Nathan Griest

#69 28th of 8th mo 1817   DANIEL GRIEST-SUSAN SWAIN

Whereas Daniel Griest son of Joseph Griest and Mary his wife of Huntington Township in the County of Adams and State of Pennsylvania and Susan Swain daughter of James Swain and Hanah his wife of the Township of New Garden County of Chester and State aforesaid (deceased) . . . this twenty eighth day of the eighth month eighteen hundred seventeen . . . at Huntington.

Daniel Griest
<u>Susan Griest</u>

Joseph Griest	Mary Griest	William Griest
Joseph Griest	Isaac Altemus	Hanah B. Altemus
Anne Griest	Elizabeth Pearson Jr	William Wierman
Sarah Wierman	Elizabeth Griest	Amy Wierman
Mary Wierman	Wm Wierman Jr	Thomas Cox
Samuel Cox	Amos Griest	David Griest Jr
Peter Griest	Isaac Pearson	Isaac Tudor
Mary Pearson	Ann Pearson	John Griest
Mary Griest	Rebecca Griest	Susan Griest
Miriam Griest	Joshua Cox Jr	Lydia Wierman
Maria McGee	Maria Clark	Mary Wierman
Hannah Hendricks	Sam'l Comly	Joel Garretson
Martha Garretson		Josiah Garretson
Content Griest Jr		Susan Wierman
Phebe G. Wierman		Susanna Cox
Mary Cox	Leah Sholl	John Griest Jr
Isaac Griest		

#70 27th of 11th mo 1817   WILLIAM WRIGHT-PHEBE WIERMAN

Whereas William Wright of Monalen Township in the County of Adams in Pennsylvania son of John Wright of the Township County and State aforesaid

MARRIAGES

and Ann his wife and Phebe Wierman daughter of William Wierman of Latimore Township in the County and State aforesaid and Hanah his wife . . . this twenty seventh day of the eleventh month eighteen hundred seventeen . . . at Huntington.

William Wright
Phebe Wright

John Wright - Ann Wright - William Wright - Hannah Wierman - Phebe Thornburg - Nicholas Wierman - Jane Wierman - Thomas Griest - Ann Griest - Sam'l Comly - Susanna Comly - Joel Wierman - Daniel Gibbons - Hanah W. Gibbons - Isaac Wierman - Sarah Hendricks - Lydia Wierman - Mary Wierman - Mary Wierman - Elizabeth Pearson - Ann Pearson - Jesse Russell - Content Russell - Mary Garretson - Alex'r Wierman - Susan Wierman - Samuel Hendricks - William Penrose - Abel Thomas - Hiram Starr - Phebe T. Wierman - Rachel Rakestraw - Mary Hussy - Miriam Hussey - Thomas Shepherd - William Wierman - Joseph Griest - Mary Griest - Harman Wierman - Daniel Griest - Susan Griest - Susanna Everit - Catherine Deardorf - Josiah Garretson - Wm Griest - Joseph Griest Jr - Phebe Tudor - Jacob Comly - Mary Griest - Rebecca Griest - Amos Griest - Miriam Griest Jr - Content Griest Jr - Phebe Griest - Ann Pearson - John Griest Jr - Nicholas Wierman Jr - Robert R. Lowry - Isaac Pearson - Thomas Cox - Samuel Cox - Wm Wierman Jr - John Everitt Jr - Peter Griest - David Griest Jr - Josiah Penrose - John Cleaver - Louisa Ross - Amelia Pearson - Phebe Pearson - Mary Day - Maria Clark - Hannah Hussy - Joel Garretson - Martha Garretson - Elizabeth Pearson Jr

<u>#71 26th of 3rd mo 1818</u>   ISAAC PEARSON-MARY WIERMAN
Whereas Isaac Pearson of Huntington Township in the County of Adams in Pennsylvania son of Isaac Pearson Deceased Late of the Township County and State aforesaid and Elizabeth his wife and Mary Wierman Daughter of William Wierman of the Township County and State aforesaid and Sarah his wife . . . this twenty sixth day of the third month eighteen hundred eighteen . . . at Huntington.

Isaac Pearson
Mary W. Pearson

Elizabeth Pearson - William Wierman - Sarah Wierman - Joel Garretson - Martha Garretson - Elias Pearson - Elizabeth Pearson Jr - Amy Wierman - Mary Pearson - Wm C. Wierman - Sarah Wierman - Joseph Griest - Mary Griest - David Griest - Susan Griest - William Griest - Joseph Garretson Jr - Lydia Wierman - Mary Cox - Anne Griest - Thomas Cox - Samuel Cox - Peter Griest - Joshua Cox - David Griest Jr - Sam'l Comly - Susanna Comly - Josiah Garretson - John Griest - Hanah Underwood - Miriam Wierman - Miriam Griest Jr - Eliza Wierman - Mary Wierman - Hanah Wierman - Ruth Griest - Susanna Cox - Amy Cox - John Everet Jr - Stephen Hussey - Benjamin Funke - Mariah McGee - Mary Griest - Rebeka Griest - Content Griest Jr - Phebe Griest - John Griest Jr - Nicholas Wierman Jr - Joel Wierman - Uriah Griest - Mary V. Griest - Eli Griest - John Wierman - Ruth Wierman - Eliz Moorhead - Sarah Smith - Phebe Pearson - Mary Hussey - Wm Penrose - Moses V Scoyoc - Thos Wierman - Isaac Tudor - Josiah Penrose - Rachel G. Penrose - Jesse Russel

MENALLEN MINUTES, MARRIAGES, & MISCELLANY

#72 3rd of 9th mo 1818   JOSHUA COX JR-MARIA McGEE
Whereas Joshua Cox Jr of Latimore Township in the County of Adams in the State of Pennsylvania son of Joshua Cox and Amy his wife of the same place and Maria McGee of the Township County and State aforesaid (whose parents are both deceased) . . . this third day of the ninth month eighteen hundred eighteen . . . at Huntington.

Joshua Cox
Maria Cox

William Cox - Ruth G. Cox - Thomas Cox - Samuel Cox - Mary Cox - Amy Cox - Susanna Cox - William Wierman - Sarah Wierman - Thomas Griest - Ann Griest - Benjamin Cox - Mary Garretson - Joseph Griest - Mary Griest - William Griest - Joseph Griest Jr - Anne Griest - Phebe G. Wierman - Louisa Ross - Susan Wierman - Phebe Pearson - Amy Wierman - Elizabeth Swayne - Sarah Wierman - Hannah Russell - Jesse Russell - Content Russell - Peter Griest - Josiah Penrose - Rachel G. Penrose - Mary Griest - Rebecca Griest - Isaac Tudor - William Wierman - Mary Garretson Sr - Joel Wierman - Miriam Griest Jr - Content Griest Jr - John Griest Jr - Abel Russell - James Platts - Isaac Griest - Willing Griest - Isaac Pearson - Mary W. Pearson - Josiah Garretson - Elizabeth Garretson - Sam'l Comly - Susanna Comly - Joel Garretson - Joseph Griest - Rebecca Griest - Phebe Thornburgh - Elizabeth Pearson - Phebe Tudor - Mary Wierman - Ann Pearson - Eli Griest - Elizabeth Pearson Jr - Ruth Griest - Uriah Griest

#73 19th of 11th mo 1818   SAMUEL WAY-ALICE BLACKBURN
Whereas Samuel Way of St. Clair Township in the County of Bedford and State of Pennsylvania son of Samuel Way and Hanah his wife of the same place and Alice Blackburn of Monalin Township Adams County and State aforesaid daughter of John Blackburn (deceased) and Mary his wife of the same place . . . this nineteenth day of the eleventh month eighteen hundred eighteen . . . at Monalin.

Samuel Way Jr
Alice Way

Mary Blackburn - James Way - James Blackburn - Thomas Way - Mary Hewitt - Jesse Blackburn - Ruth Wilson - Ellin Wright - Barbara Harris - Ester G. Stair - Hannah Hendricks - Hannah Rife - Christian Rife - Ruthanna Harris - Jacob Harris - John Wilson - Eli -?- - Elizabeth Thomas - Nathan Harris - Benj'n Harris - Jane Hutton - Mary Wright - Beulah K. Harris - Elizabeth Thomas - Matilda Wierman - Finley McGrew - Sam'l Wright Jr - Rebecca Wright - Jacob Thomas - Margaret Thomas - Hannah Thomas - Jacob Bender - John Wright - Sarah Wright - Martha Hutton - Sarah Wilson - George Wilson - Samuel Wright - Elizabeth Wright - Benjamin Hutton - Jonah D. Thomas - Isaac Thomas - Joseph R. Thomas

#74 30th of 12th mo 1819   JOSEPH McMILLAN-ELIZABETH PEARSON
Whereas Joseph McMillan of Warrinton Township, York County Pennsylvania son of Thomas McMillan of the place aforesaid and Ruth his wife and Elizabeth Pearson daughter of Isaac Pearson deceased late of Huntington Township Adams County Pennsylvania and Elizabeth his wife . . . this thirtieth day of the twelfth month eighteen hundred nineteen . . . at Huntington.

MARRIAGES

                                        Joseph McMillan
                                        Elizabeth McMillan
Thomas McMillan - Ruth McMillan - Elizabeth Pearson - Isaac Pearson - Mary W. Pearson - Jacob P. McMillan - Mahlon McMillan - Mary Pearson - Joseph Taylor - Ann Pearson - Mary Wierman - Lydia Wierman - Amy Wierman - Lucy Ann Godfrey - Joel Wireman - Eli Griest - Joseph Griest - Rebecca Griest - Wm Wierman - Sarah Wireman - Sam'l Comly - Wm Griest - Wm C. Wireman - David Griest - Thomas Cox - Josiah Garretson - Elizabeth Wireman - Isaac Tudor - Malon Griest - Mary Wierman - Louisa Ross - Thomas G-?- - Abraham Cox - Joseph Griest - John Tudor - John Griest - Martha Tudor - Henry Bittinger - Alex Wireman - Nathan Griest - Benjamin Cox - Thomas Wickersham

#75 25th of 10th mo 1820   BENJAMIN W. HUTTON-BULAH R. HARRIS
Whereas Benjamin W. Hutton son of Levi and Martha Hutton of Monallen Township Adams County and State of Pennsylvania and Bulah R. Harris daughter of Benjamin and Rebecca Harris (dec'd) of the Township County and State aforesaid . . . this twenty fifth day of the tenth month eighteen hundred twenty . . . at Monallin.

                                        Benjamin W. Hutton
                                        Bulah R. Hutton

Findly McGrew	Rebecca Ann McGrew	W. B. Wilson
Eli Thomas	Hanah Rife	Jacob Harris
Elizabeth Thomas	Eli Griest	Mary Harris
Jacob Thomas	Nathan Wright	Ruth Wilson
Margaret Thomas	Sarah Hendricks	Ruth Hammond
Rebecca McGrew	Levi Hutton	Jane Wright
Abner Thomas	Martha Hutton	John Harris
Phebe Thomas	Sarah Walker	Abel Thomas
Lydia Thomas	Jane Hutton	Hanah Thomas
Mary Wright	Ruthann Harris	Jonathan Thomas
Isaac Boone	Barbarah Harris	Jacob Wright
Jos. R. Thomas	John Wright	John Wright Jr
Sam'l Hendricks	Sam'l Hutton	George Wright
J. D. Thomas	Jesse Hutton	Wm Wright
Elizabeth Thomas	Nathan Harris	Thos H. Wright
Isaac Thomas	Alex Wierman	Samuel Wright Jr
Hanah Thomas	Ellin Wright	Rebecca Wright
Ann Wright	Phebe T. Hendricks	George Wilson
Wm. C. Wierman	Sarah Wright	

#76 22nd of 12th mo 1820   JOHN RUSSELL-RUTH GRIEST
Whereas John Russell of Bush Creek in the County of Frederick in the State of Maryland son of John Russell of the same place and Hanah his wife (the former now deceased) and Ruth Griest daughter of Joseph Griest of Huntington in the County of Adams in the State of Pennsylvania and Rebekah his wife . . . this twenty second day of the twelfth month eighteen hundred twenty . . . at Huntington.

                                        John Russell
                                        Ruth Russell

MENALLEN MINUTES, MARRIAGES, & MISCELLANY

Rebecca Griest - Amos Griest - Joseph Griest - Jesse Russell - Usiah Griest - Mary Griest - Gideon Griest - Jane M. Griest - Eli Griest - Malon Griest - Nathan Griest - George Hughes - Amos Hussey - Elizabeth Swayne - Susanna Bower - Susannah Russell - Mary Hussey - Lydia Hughs - Mira Hussey - Samuel Comly - Susanna Comly - Hannah W. Hendrix - Phebe T. Hendrix - Mary Wierman - Hannah Wierman - Abraham Cook - Rosanna Zinn - Phebe Tudor - Ruth Wilson - Lydia Wierman - Thomas Griest - Ann Griest - Wm Wierman - John Griest - Josiah Garretson - Elizabeth Garretson - Susan Wierman - Isaac Pearson - Mary W. Pearson - William Griest - Joseph Griest Jr - Anne Griest - Rebecca Griest - Phebe Wright - Julia Ann Everitt - Lavinia Garretson - Susan White - James G. Oliver - Stephen Hussey - Rogers Kenyon - Evelina Godfrey - Mary M. Herr - Susanna Everitt - B. F. Wilson - Thompson T. Bonner - John Everitt Jr - Sam'l Hendrick - Joel Garretson - Joel Wierman - Elizabeth McMillan - Ann Pearson - Margaret Bonner

#77 1st of 3rd mo 1821   ROGERS KENYON-MARTHA PEARSON
Whereas Rogers Kenyon of Huntington Township Adams County in the State of Pennsylvania and Martha Pearson (widow of Thomas Pearson) of the Township of Huntington aforesaid . . . this first day of the third month eighteen hundred twenty one . . . at Huntington.

Rogers Kenyon
Martha Kenyon

Elizabeth Pearson - Robert Vale - Martha Vale - Mary Griffith - Elizabeth Everitt - Sarah Smith - Hepsibah Van Scyoc - Nathan Cleaver - Isaac P. Garretson - Martha Tudor - Charlotte Ockes - Daniel Griest - James Blake - Isaac E. Wierman - William Jones - John Everitt Jr - Phineas Kenyon - Wm. Boner - Enoch Vanscyoc - Joel Funk - Lucy Ann Godfrey - Martha Everitt - Ann Pearson - Joel Bower - Wm C. Wierman - Joel Wierman - Susan Wierman - Jacob Abel - John Day - Danial Funk Jr - Nicholas Wierman Jr - James Robinette - John Welch - Geo. Robinette - Wm Moorhead - Rebecca Ann McGrew - Mira Hussey - Margaret Smith - Jane Van Scyoc - Jane Jones - Mary Hussey - Harriet McGrew - Mary Wierman - Mary Day - Jane Thompson - Nancy Jones - Eveline Godfrey - Mary Foch - Ruth Wilson - Jane Foulk - Stephen Hussey - Jasly Oliver - George Deardorff - C. Smith - B. Funk - Conrad Wierman - William Griest - Abraham Cook - William Gardner - Benjamin Walker Jr - Malen Griest - Gibson Agnew - Jacob Ziegler - Joseph Griest Jr - Thomas Wikersham - Thomas Speakman - Abraham How - Benjamin Cox - Jonathan Cox

#78 27th of 6th mo 1821   JESSE RUSSELL-SARAH HENDRICKS
Whereas Jesse Russell of Latimore Township in the County of Adams in the State of Pennsylvania son of John Russell deceased late of Frederick County in the State of Maryland and Hanah his wife and Sarah Hendricks of Menalin Township in the County of Adams and State of Pennsylvania daughter of William Wierman of Latimore Township in the same County and State and Hannah his wife . . . this twenty seventh day of the sixth month eighteen hundred twenty one . . . at Menalen.

Jesse Russell
Sarah Russell

MARRIAGES

William Wierman - Samuel Comly - Susanna Comly - William Wright - Phebe Wright - Isaac Wierman - Susanna Wierman - Lydia Wierman - Mary Wierman - Sam'l Hendricks - Hannah W. Hendricks - Phebe T. Hendricks - Hannah Russell Jr - Joel Wierman - Mary Wierman - Alex'r Wierman - Joel Garretson - Wm C. Wierman - W. B. Wilson - B. Z. Wilson - George Wilson - Sarah Wilson - Ann Pearson - Ruth Wilson - Eli Griest - Jane Hutton - Susan Wierman - Wm Wright - Rachel Wright - John Wright - Nathan Wright - Elizabeth Thomas - Mary Wright - Moses Jenkins - Mary Fleming - Elizabeth Thomas - Esther C. Boone - Phebe Thomas - Martha Hutton - Jane Wright - Mary Harris - Elizabeth Wright - Jacob Harris - Samuel Wright - Jacob Thomas

#79 26th of 12th mo 1821   BENJAMIN HARRIS-JANE HUTTON
Whereas Benjamin Harris of Menallen Township in the County of Adams and State of Pennsylvania son of Benjamin Harris of the same place and Rebecca his wife dec'd and Jane Hutton daughter of Levi Hutton of the same place and Martha his wife . . . this twenty sixth day of the twelfth month eighteen hundred twenty one . . . at Menallen.

                                                                Benj'n Harris
                                                                Jane Harris
                                            Elizabeth Hoch Jr
Finley McGrew   Martha Hutton
Isaac Boone   Elizabeth John   Jacob Harris
Esther C. Boone   Phebe Thomas   Ruth A. Harris
W. B. Wilson   Jacob Griest   Sam'l Wright Jr
Ruth Hammond   Maris Myers   Benj'n W. Hutton
Phebe T. Hendrix   Margaret Galbreath   Beulah F. Hutton
Rebecca Ann McGrew   Jacob Thomas   Sam'l Wright
John Wright Jr   Margaret Thomas   Nathan Wright
Ruth Wilson   Jesse Russell   Elizabeth Wright
Mary Wright   Abel Thomas
George Wilson   Nathan Harris
Joseph R. Thomas   Hannah Harris
Barbara Harris   Samuel Hendricks
Moses Jenkins   Eli Thomas
Jacob Wright   John B. Hutton
Jesse Hutton   Sarah Russell
Thomas Wright
Ann Wright

#80 26th of 12th mo 1822   ALEXANDER WIERMAN-MARY HUSSEY
Whereas Alexander Wierman of Latimore Township in the County of Adams and State of Pennsylvania son of Nicholas and Jane Wierman of the Township County and State aforesaid and Mary Hussey daughter of Amos Hussey (deceased) and Abigail his wife of Franklin Township York County and State aforesaid . . . this twenty sixth day of the twelfth month eighteen hundred twenty two . . . at Huntington.
                                                            Alexander Wierman
                                                            Mary H. Wierman
Nicholas Wierman - Jane Wierman - Abigail Hussey - Miriam Hussey - Mary Wierman - Stephen Hussey - Wm C. Wierman - Thomas Wierman - Rachel S. Matthews - Mary Wierman - John Wierman - Jane Wierman - Amos Hussey -

MENALLEN MINUTES, MARRIAGES, & MISCELLANY

Joel Wierman - Lucy Ann Godfrey - Hannah W. Hendricks - Hannah Wierman - Phebe T. Hendricks - William Wright - Phebe Wright - Esther Moorhead - Julia A. Everitt - Mary Ann Dehl - A. J. Kenyon - William Gardner - Sam'l Comly - Jane Thompson - Eliza A. Warren - Evelina Godfrey - Anna Godfrey - Mary M. Herr - Eliza S. Thompson - Josiah Penrose - Joseph Griest - Rebecca Griest - Sidney Dimon - Charles Underwood - John Everitt Jr - Mordecai Matthews Jr - Susana Wierman - Phebe T. Wierman - Jane M. Griest - Phebe Tudor - Margaret Boner - Isaac E. Wierman - William Jones - Rogers Kenyon - Martha Kenyon - Rebecca Griest Jr - Content Griest Jr - Ann Pearson - Phebe Pearson - Jane Brandon - Mary Brandon - Rebecca Everitt - Elizabeth Everitt - Sarah Brandon - Sarah Neely - Mary Brandon - Mary Garretson - Amy Wierman - Susan Wierman - Mary Day - George W. Everitt - Josiah Garretson - Henry Bushong - Isaac Tudor - Wm Wierman - Sarah Wierman - Thompson T. Boner - Jacob Weaver - James J. Oliver - Benjamin P. Junkin - Temp'n Brandon - Joshua Reynold - Maria Arnold - Sarah McCreary - Abraham Colo - Robert McIlhenny - Geo Robinette - James Dixon - Geo W. Brandon - J. S. Neely - Isaac Pearson - Mary W. Pearson - Samuel Hendricks - Nathan Griest - Abel Thomas - Hanah Thomas - Malon Griest - Eli Griest

#81 6th of 5th mo 1824   WILLIAM B. WILSON-MARY WIERMAN
Whereas William B. Wilson of Menallin Township in the County of Adams in the State of Pennsylvania son of George Wilson and Sarah Wilson of Monallin aforesaid and Mary Wierman daughter of Nicholas and Jane Wierman of Latimore Township and County and State aforesaid . . . this sixth day of the fifth month eighteen hundred twenty four . . . at Huntington.

		William B. Wilson
		Mary Wilson
George Wilson	Hanah Wierman	Bonine F. Gardner
Sarah Wilson	Ruth Wilson	Isaac E. Wierman
Nicholas Wierman	Stephen Hussey	W. C. Wierman
Jane Wierman	John Wierman	John Everitt Jr
Thos Wierman	Phebe T. Wierman	John Moorhead
Harriet Wierman	Susan Wierman	Thomas Wierman
Susanna Comly	William Wright	Elizabeth Moorhead
Julia A. Everitt	Phebe Wright	Samuel E. Cook
Susan Wierman	Evelina M. Godfrey	John Cook
Jesse W. Cook M.D.	Mary Wierman	John Griest Jr
Joel Wierman	Martha Everitt	Isaac Everitt
Miriam Wierman	B. F. Wilson	Nathan Griest
Amy Wierman	Aron Cox	T. T. Bonner
Sarah Wierman	John McCreary	Jo'n Neely
Lavinia Garretson	Zeba Griest	Julian Sheffer
Wm Wierman	Isaac -?-	Jane R. Thompson
Hanah Wierman	Lidia Wierman	Mary M. Kerr
Susanna M. Tudor	Mary Garretson	Eliza Cook
		Mary Day

#82 29th of 6th mo 1824   SAMUEL E. COOK-MARGARET JOYCE
Whereas Samuel E. Cook of Huntington Township in the County of Adams State of Pennsylvania son of Isaac and Sidney Cook (the latter deceased) of

MARRIAGES

Warrington Township York County and State aforesaid and Margaret Joyce daughter of George and Elizabeth (the former deceased) of Menallen Township Adams County . . . this twenty ninth of the sixth month eighteen hundred twenty four . . . at Menallen.

                                                                          Samuel E. Cook
                                                                          Margaret Cook

Jesse Cook	Susannah House	John Smith
Elizabeth Joyce	Catherine Hewitt	Abner -?-
Samuel House	W. B. Wilson	John W. Cook
B. F. Wilson	Mary Wilson	David Cook
Jesse W. Cook	Mary Cook	William Joyce
Elizabeth T. Cook	Mary McGrail	Ann Cook
Jane Harris	Martha Hutton	Phebe T. Hendrix
Ruth Wilson	Sarah Wilson	Sarah W. Wright
John Wright Jr	Ellin Wright	Jesse Cook Jr
Mary Ann Cook	Eliza Cook	Mary Cook
Mary Joyce	Sarah Cook	Findley McGrew
Joseph Joyce	Samuel Wright	George Hewett
John Joyce	Sam'l B. Wright	Elizabeth Wright
Obadiah Joyce	Nathan Wright	Elizabeth Wright

#83 27th of 4th mo 1825   ENOS McMILLAN-SARAH WRIGHT

Whereas Enos McMillan of Washington Township in the County of York and State of Pennsylvania son of Jacob and Ruth McMillan of the place aforesaid and Sarah Wright daughter of John and Alice Wright of Menallen Township Adams County Pennsylvania . . . this twenty seventh day of the fourth month eighteen hundred twenty five . . . at Menallen.

                                                                         Enos McMillan
                                                                         Sarah McMillan

George Wilson	Findley McGrew	Jacob McMillan
Jesse Russell	Samuel Wright Jr	Ruth McMillan
Sarah Russell	Rebecca Wright	John Wright
Esther C. Boon	Hannah Wierman	Alice Wright
Catherine Hewett	Phebe T. Wierman	Nathan Wright
Levi Hutton	Mary Wilson	Elizabeth Wright
George Wright	Nathan Harris	Amos Griest
Jane Harris	Martha Hutton	Ruth Wilson
Rachel Wright	Mary McGrew	Ann McMillan
Beulah Hutton	John Hartzel	Ellin Wright
Thos G. Wright	David Kenny	Cyrus McMillan
Samuel B. Wright	Rebecca McGrail	Nathan Cleaver
Abel T. Wright	Thos. H. Wright	Jehu Wilson
Ruth Ann Harris		

#84 29th of 9th mo 1825   ISAAC TUDOR-MARY GARRETSON

Whereas Isaac Tudor of the County of Baltimore in the State of Maryland son of William and Martha Tudor deceased late of Muskingum County in the State of Ohio and Mary Garretson daughter of John and Mary Garretson the former dec'd of the County of Adams in the State of Pennsylvania . . . this twenty ninth day of the ninth month eighteen hundred twenty five . . . at Huntington.

MENALLEN MINUTES, MARRIAGES, & MISCELLANY

Isaac Tudor
<u>Mary Tudor</u>

Josiah Garretson - Joel Garretson - Josiah Penrose - Hanah Garretson - Lavinia Garretson - Elizabeth Everett - Samuel Comly - Susanah Comly - Isaiah Price - John Everitt - Rebecca Price - Isaac G. Garretson - Elisha R. Penrose - Eliakim G. Penrose - Joel Wierman - Wm Wright - Phebe Wright - Martha Albert - Margaret Albert - Hanah Godfrey - Isaac E. Wierman - Joseph Wierman - Susannah Everett - John Harris - George D. Hamilton - John Griest - John Griest Jr - Isaac Pearson - Mary W. Pearson - Eveline M. Godfrey - Susan Wierman - Phebe T. Wierman - Mirah Hussey - Wm C. Wierman - Hanah Wierman - Julian Everett - Isaac Griest - Rebecca Griest - Rebecca R. Garretson - Mary Griest - Solomon Griest - Jesse Cook - Mary Cook - Miriam Griest - Phebe G. Hendrix - Eliza Wierman - Sarah Wierman - Sarah Comly - Charles F. Bonen - David Cox - Peter Griest - Abel Walker - Samuel Cook - Sarah Wierman

#85 27th of 7th mo 1826   <u>JOEL GARRETSON-ELIZABETH EVERETT</u>
Whereas Joel Garretson of Latimore Township in the County of Adams and State of Pennsylvania son of John and Mary Garretson (the former dec'd) and Elizabeth Everett of the Township County and State aforesaid daughter of Isaac and Rebecca Everitt . . . this twenty seventh day of the seventh month eighteen hundred twenty six . . . at Huntington.

Joel Garretson
<u>Elizabeth Garretson</u>

Rebecca Everitt - John Everitt - Susana Everitt - Josiah Garretson - Hanah Garretson - Josiah Penrose - John Everitt Jr - Margaret Bonnen - Frances Bonnen - Julia A. Everitt - Lavinia Garretson - Isaac P. Garretson - Maria M. Garretson - Isaac Tudor - Mary Tudor - Martha Everitt - Eliza Mullinu - Jesse Russell - Obadiah Joyce - Hamilton Everett - George W. Everett - Ann Pearson - Malinda Everett - Isaac Pearson - Mary W. Pearson - Job Hoops - Rhoda Hoops - Thos Wierman - Harriet Wierman - Rebecca Bonnen - Samuel Comly - Susanna Comly - Susan Wierman - Sidney McGrew - Sarah A. Bunan - Rebecca Wierman - Isaac E. Wierman - James L. McGrew - Eveline M. Godfrey - Hanah Gadfrey - Esther Beaty - Mary Harry - Jane Braden - Henry Bushong - Sarah Bushong - Abraham Cook - Peter Griest - Nathan Griest - Jacob Gardner Jr - Mary Cook - Martha Kenyon - Lydia Pearson - Rebecca K. Garretson - Elizabeth Bonnen - Henry Beals - Lidia Wierman - Henry Cook - F. Gardner - Isaac Griest - D. Fahnestock - Mary M. Neely - Andrew Johnston - Amos Hussey - Joshua F. Cox - George Harman - David Cox - Wm Wright - Samuel Harris - Jane R. Thomson - Maria Cleaveland - Elizabeth Diehl - Mary Kettlewell - Thomas Grange - Joel Wierman - Rebecca Ann Blish - Phebe T. Wierman - Eliza Wierman - Mary Wierman - Amy Wierman - John Griest - Wm Wierman

#86 1st of 5th mo 1828   <u>ELI COOKSON-PHEBE VALE</u>
Whereas Eli Cookson of Warrington Township York County and State of Pennsylvania son of Daniel Cookson and Sarah his wife of the same place and Phebe Vale of Latimore Township Adams County and State aforesaid daughter of William Vale of Washington Township York County and State aforesaid and

MARRIAGES

Ann his wife . . . this first day of fifth month eighteen hundred twenty eight . . . at Huntington.

Josiah Cook
John Griest
Lydia W. Pearson
Lynn Bushong
Wm Wierman
Sam'l Comly
Susanna Comly
Ruth Russell
Susan Wireman
Sarah Brandon
Jane Cook
Hephzibah Walker
Jesse Cook
Agnes McGrew
Rebecca Wierman
Isaac Griest
Wm Kettlewell

Mary Harris
Martha Tudor
Eli McMillan
Susan M. Tudor
Nathan Griest
Sarah Vale
Eli Griest
Ruth Cookson
Nathan Hussey
Sarah Brewster
Jesse Walker
Sam'l M. Tudor
G. E. Pearson
David H. Mellinger
Peter Griest
Henry Bittinger
William Vale

Eli Cookson
Phebe Cookson
John Cookson
Jediah Hussey
Mary C. Hussey
Mary Griest
Josiah Garretson
Isaac P. Garretson
J. Tudor
John Bushong
Rebecca Griest
Hannah Wierman
Josiah Penrose

#87 28th of 4th mo 1831   HAMILTON EVERITT-REBECCA K. GARRETSON
Whereas Hamilton Everitt of Huntington Township in the County of Adams and State of Pennsylvania son of Isaac and Rebecca Everitt and Rebecca K. Garretson daughter of Josiah and Elizabeth Garretson of Washington Township in the County of York and State aforesaid . . . this twenty eighth day of the fourth month eighteen hundred thirty one . . . at Huntington.

Hamilton Everitt
Rebecca K. Everitt

Josiah Garretson - Elizabeth Garretson - Rebecca Everitt - Susanna Everitt - John Everitt Jr - Hanah M. Garretson - Joel Garretson - Elizabeth Garretson - Martha Everitt - Margaret Boner - Oliver Garretson - Rachel Eliza Garretson - Isaac P. Garretson - Isaac Russell - Sam'l Comly - Rebecca Bonner - William Wright - Isaac E. Wierman - W. C. Wierman - Isaac Tudor - Hannah Garretson - Phebe T. Wierman - Rebecca Griest - Huldah S. Penrose - Hanah G. Penrose - Mariah M. Garretson - Elisha Penrose - Josiah Penrose - Mary Kettlewell - Jane Wierman - Leah Faus - Miriam Griest - Matilda Pilkington - Charlotte M. Ocker - Louise Arnold - Mary Cook - Eliza Wierman - Sarah Wierman - Lydia W. Penrose - Martha Hamilton - Elizabeth Hamilton - Elenor Comly - Alvira S. Cox - Jacob Harris - Mary Harris - Mary Ann Harris - Jesse Cook - G. S. Faus - John Griest - Josiah Cook - Thomas T. Wierman - David Y. Beals - Nathan Griest - Cornelius Cook - Joseph A. Wierman - Wm Wierman - Geo Shaffer - Owen Griest - Alen Griest

#88 26th of 4th mo 1832   LEWIS HARRY-SARAH COMLY
Whereas Lewis Harry of Warrington Township in the County of York and State of Pennsylvania son of Jesse Harry late of the Borough of York and Mary his wife deceased and Sarah Comly daughter of Samuel Comly of Latimore Township in the County of Adams in the State aforesaid and Susanna his wife

MENALLEN MINUTES, MARRIAGES, & MISCELLANY

... this twenty sixth day of the fourth month eighteen hundred thirty two ... at Huntington.

		Lewis Harry
		Sarah C. Harry
Joel Garretson	Wm Wright	Samuel Comly
Peter Griest	Mary Kettlewell	Susanna Comly
Mary GriestR	ebecca Wierman	Ezra Comly
Isaac Tudor	Phebe Day	Lydia Comly
Abraham Cook	Matilda Wierman	Phebe Comly
Wm C. Wierman	Eveline M. Beals	Mary Wierman
Isaac P. Garretson	Charlotte M. Ocker	Joel Wierman
	Sarah Ann Pilkington	Lydia S. Wierman
	Susanna M. Lundy	Joseph Harry

#89 31st of 1st mo 1833   WILLIAM C. WIERMAN-SUSANNA MARIA LUNDY

Whereas William C. Wierman of Huntington Township in the County of Adams in Pennsylvania son of William and Sarah Wierman of the place aforesaid and Susanna Maria Lundy daughter of Benjamin and Esther Lundy (the latter deceased) of Washington City, District of Columbia . . . this thirty first day of the first month eighteen hundred thirty three . . . at Huntington.

		William C. Wierman
		Susanna Maria Wierman
Lewis Harry	Sam'l Comly	William Wierman
Wm Wierman	John Ocher	Sarah Wierman
John W-?-	Samuel Harris	Benjamin Lundy
Andrew -?-	John Stephens	Lydia T. Wierman
Josiah Penrose	A. B. Dimarce	Joel Wierman
Josias Garretson	George Bittinger	Eliza Wierman
Uriah Griest	Oliver Garretson	Sarah C. Wierman
Mary Ann Harris	Nathan Griest	T. T. Wierman
Hannah Wright	Joseph P. Harry	Joel Hendrix
	Phebe Comly	Amy Wierman

#90 30th of 5th mo 1833   WILLIAM UNDERWOOD-ALVINA GRIEST

Whereas William Underwood of Latimore Township in the County of Adams in the State of Pennsylvania son of Zephaniah Underwood and Hannah his wife of Newberry Township in the County of York in the State aforesaid and Alvina Griest daughter of Amos Griest and Phebe his wife all of Latimore Township in the County of Adams in the State aforesaid . . . this thirtieth day of the fifth month eighteen hundred thirty three . . . at Huntington.

		William Underwood
		Alvina Underwood
W. C. Wierman	John Stephens	Z. Underwood
Susanna M. Wierman	Phebe Comley	Hannah Underwood
Isaac Russell	Lydia Comley	Amos Griest
Jacob Howard	Isaac P. Garretson	Phebe Griest
May Hallowell	Barzillai Garretson	Edwin G. Vancise
Matilda Pilkington	Lewis Harry	Keziah Griest
Jane Cook Jr	Sarah C. Harry	Joseph Wickersham
Rebecca Wierman	Abel T. Wright	Rebecca Underwood

MARRIAGES

Matilda Wierman	John Vikes	Joseph P. Harry
Jane Wierman	Elisha Penrose	Amanda U. Griest
Sarah Ann Pilkington	Susanna Comley	Chas Underwood
Elizabeth A. Funk	Malinda Everitt	Mary A. Griest
Josiah Cook	Elizabeth E. Garretson	Jesse Underwood
John Griest	Joel Garretson	Jane W. Underwood
George E. White	Abel N. Russell	Nathan Griest
	Henry T. Wierman	Mary Ann Griest
	Sam'l Harris	Uriah Griest
	Wm. Wierman	Mary Griest
	Eliza Sheffer	Ruth Russell
	Eliza Wierman	Peter Griest
	A. B. Demarce	

#91 26th of 12th mo 1833   BARZILIA GARRETSON-MALINDA EVERITT

Whereas Barzilia Garretson of Newberry Township County of Adams and State of Pennsylvania son of John and Rebecca Garretson (the former deceased) of the same place and Malinda Everitt of Latimore Township County of Adams and State aforesaid daughter of Isaac and Rebecca Everitt . . . this twenty sixth day of the twelfth month eighteen hundred thirty three . . . at Huntington.

		Barzilia Garretson
		Malinda Garretson
Oliver Garretson	Isaac Tudor	Rebecca Garretson
Charlotte M. Ocker	Wm Wright	Rebecca Everitt
Amanda White	Phebe Wright	Joel Garretson
Sarah W. Russell	Ruth Russell	Elizabeth E. Garretson
John Ocher	Lewis Harry	Martha Everitt
David S. Beales	Hannah Wright	George W. Everitt
W. Fleming	Rachel Garretson	Isaac T. Garretson
M. Vanscoyoc	Phebe Comly	Mahlon Garretson
Wm. C. Wierman	Lydia Comly	Margaret Bonner
Joseph Harry	Jane Cook	Rebecca Bonner
Joel Wierman	Josiah Cook	John Everitt
Lydia S. Wierman	William H. Wright	Jesse Walker
	Rebecca Wierman	Wm Wierman
	Jane Wierman	Josiah Garretson
		Sam'l Comly

#92 30th of 3rd mo 1837   EDWIN G. VANCISE-MARIA M. GARRETSON

Whereas Edwin G. Vancise of Washington Township in the County of York and State of Pennsylvania son of Daniel Vancise and Elizabeth (now Boyles) and Maria M. Garretson of Latimore Township in the County of Adams and State aforesaid daughter of Joel and Martha Garretson . . . this thirtieth day of the third month eighteen hundred thirty seven . . . at Huntington.

		Edwin G. Vancise
		Maria M. Vancise
Jesse Cook	Susanna VanScoyoc	Joel Garretson
Rebecca Cook	Lydia Beales	Elizabeth E. Garretson

MENALLEN MINUTES, MARRIAGES, & MISCELLANY

William Ellis	Elizabeth Hess	John Griest
Abel Walker	Rebecca Miller	John Griest Jr
Maryann Walker	Lydia A. Wierman	Hannah Griest
Mary Wierman	William W. Wright	Isaac P. Garretson
Alvina S. Cox	Elizabeth Ellis	Louisa W. Garretson
Israel Cook	Sarah Jane Ellis	Peter Griest
Sarah G. Cook	Isaac Vale	Isaac Tudor
Joseph A. Wierman	Isaac Griest	Mary Tudor
Caleb Beales	Rebecca Griest	Joel A. Garretson
William S. Walker	Lydia Comly	John E. Garretson
Jacob Scholl	Phebe Comly	Louisa Ellis
Charles C. Price	Joel Wierman	Hannah Maria Garretson
Sam'l Comly	Mary Griest	Hannah Wright
Frederick E. Baily	Lewis Tudor	Huldah S. Penrose
Jane R. Smith	Martha Ann Tudor	Edith Griest
Matilda M. Pilkington	William H. Cook	Phebe Wright
Cornelius G. Cook	Joseph Russell	Susanna Brown
Isaac Cook	John Russell	Nathan Griest
	Acquilla P. Garretson	Mary Ann Griest
	Mary Ann Ellis	Hiram C. Metcalf M.D.

#93 28th of 3rd mo 1838   GEORGE WRIGHT-LUCY WRIGHT
Whereas George Wright son of John Wright and Alice his wife (the latter deceased) and Lucy Wright daughter of Thomas Wright and Ann his wife all of Adams County in the State of Pennsylvania . . . this twenty eighth day of the third month eighteen hundred thirty eight . . . at Monallen.

George Wright
Lucy Wright

Sam'l Hendricks	Sarah Ann Smith	John Wright
Martha Harris	Eliza Griest	Nathan Wright
William H. Wright	Rebecca Wright	Elizabeth Wright
Wm H. Wierman	William W. Wright	Leah Wright
Josiah Cook	Samuel H. Harris	Lydia C. Wright
Hiram T. Wright	Rebecca Ann Harris	Ruth M. Wright
Alec T. Wright	Mahlon Garretson	Jane Mary Weakley
John Griest	-?- Wright	Eliza Hewet
Barzillai Garretson	-?- Wright	Jane Wright
Jesse Russell	E. Wright Weakley	Ruth Anna Harris
Sarah Russell	Mary Wierman	
Joseph Sheetz	Ben'n Harris	Alvina S. Cox
Joel Hendricks	Joel Garretson	Ruth Wierman
John Becker	Charles S. Wright	Ann Wright
	Elijah Wright	Martha Wright
		Elizabeth Becker

#94 21st of 6th mo 1839   GIDEON WIDEMIRE-RUTH RUSSELL
Whereas Gideon Widemire of Clearfield County in the State of Pennsylvania son of Urbane Widemire and Magdalena his wife and Ruth Russell of Adams County and State aforesaid daughter of Joseph Griest and Rebecca his wife (the parents all deceased) . . . this twenty first day of the sixth month eighteen

MARRIAGES

hundred thirty nine . . . at Huntington.

		Gideon Widemire
		Ruth Widemire
Charles C. Price	Jesse Cook	Gideon Griest
M. R. Stewart	Rebecca Cook	Uriah Griest
Donah M. Stewart	Joel Garretson	Mary Griest
Andrew Graham	Elizabeth E. Garretson	Samuel Widemire
John E. Bonner	Jonah Garretson	John Russell Jr
Esther Moorhead	Elizabeth Garretson	Mary Ann Griest
Rebecca F. Bonner	William Ellis	Isaac Tudor
Rebecca H. Frazer	Lydia Ann Griest	Mary Tudor
Maria C. Jones	Hannah Griest	Phebe Wright
Sarah Funk	Martha G. Pearson	Joel Wireman
Mary L. Hammersley	Sarah H. Metcalf	Lydia S. Wireman
Emily Esther Moorhead	Catharine M. Ickes	Allen Griest
Jane Harvey	Hannah M. Garretson	Edith Griest
Israel Cook	Rachel E. Garretson	
Hannah Wright	-?- Garretson	
Rachel Wright	Jane L. Taylor	
Isaac Wright	Eliza J. Moorhead	
-?- Tudor	Hannah Kettlewell	
William H. Cook	Martha Ann Tudor	
Mary Griest	Mary A. Griest	
Caroline Griest	John E. Garretson	
Anne Wright		

#95 1st of 7th mo 1841   NATHAN SMITH-EDITH GRIEST

Whereas Nathan Smith son of Thomas Smith and Phebe his wife (the latter deceased) of Mc-?- Township, County of Bedford and State of Pennsylvania and Edith Griest daughter of Gideon Griest and Jane his wife (the latter dec'd) of Latimore Township, County of Adams and State aforesaid . . . this first day of the seventh month eighteen hundred forty one . . . at Huntington.

		Nathan Smith
		Edith Smith
Benjamin Harris	Hannah Wierman	Gideon Griest
Jane Harris	Edwin G. Vancise	Martha Griest
Martha Wright	William Ellis	Owen Griest
Charlotte Pearson	Joel Garretson	Ruth Smith
Joseph A. Wierman	Elizabeth E. Garretson	Mary Ann Griest
M. J. Thatcher	Phebe Wright	Nathan Griest
Mary Kettlewell	Joel Wierman	Mary Ann Griest
John Cook Jr	Lydia S. Wierman	Uriah Griest
Ruth Morthland	Isaac P. Garretson	Mary Griest
Allen Griffith	Louisa Garretson	Sarah Ann Griest
Sarah Griffith	Hannah Maria Garretson	Rebecca Griest
Israel B. Cook	Rachel Eliza Garretson	Martha T. Griest
Edward S. Walker	Oliver Garretson	Edith Griest
Israel Wright	Hannah Wright	Lydia Ann Griest
-?- Tudor	Rachel Wright	Elisha Griest
Henry C. Griffith	Wm W. Wright	John Griest

MENALLEN MINUTES, MARRIAGES, & MISCELLANY

Aran Cox
Sarah Cox
B. W. Vanscoyoc
Israel Tudor
Mary Tudor
Rebecca Everitt
Jane H. Hussey
Maria Griffith

Jesse Cook
Rebecca Cook
Josiah Garretson
Wm Wright
Joel Amos Garretson
William H. Cook

Rebecca Griest
Mary Griest
Philena Jane Griest
Content Griest
Almira Griest
Adela Jane White
John E. Garretson

#96 2nd of 3rd mo 1842   GEORGE HEWET-ELLEN WRIGHT
Whereas George Hewet of Monallen Township Adams County State of Pennsylvania son of George and Deborah Hewet (both deceased) and Ellen Wright daughter of William and Rachel Wright (the latter deceased) of the same place . . . this second day of the third month eighteen hundred forty two . . . at Monallen.

George Hewet
Ellen W. Hewet

Hannah G. Penrose
Laura Ellis
Sarah I. Ellis
Sam'l H. Harris
Cyrus Griest
Mary Ann Griest
Joel Garretson
Wm. E. Bailey
Sam'l E. Cook
Jn'o W. Cook
J. J. Wills
Elizabeth Ellis
Elizabeth Wright
Josiah Penrose
Hannah Leach
Ezekiel Hartzell
Geo Wilson Jr
Sarah Wilson
Jane Wilson
Joshua Vale
Leah Thomas
Eliza Hewet
Rhoda Warner
Thos McCleary
Wm Hewet

Caleb Ozbun
Ann Wright
Lydia Wright
Rebecca Wright
Julien H. Wright
Wm. H. Wright
Jane Wright
Jonah Cook
Mary Cook
Jesse Cook
Thos E. Cook
Wm Morrison
Alex Underwood
Dan'l S. Taylor
Wm H. McCreary
Conrad Wierman
Rebecca Wierman
Susan Wilson
Eliza Wilson
Emily Bateman
Ruth Morthland
Martha Harris
Maria Harris
Rebecca Ann Harris
George Griest
Laura A. Smith
David Wills

Wm Wright
John Wright
Nathan Wright
Abel T. Wright
Wm. B. Wilson
Joel Wright
John B. Wright
Geo W. Garretson
Isaac I. Wright
Elijah Wright
Jacob Joyce
Thos H. Wright
Geo W. Wright
Hiram T. Wright
Maria T. Wright
Ruth M. Wright
Jacob B. Hewet
Ruth Anna Wright
Jane F. Wright
Ann Wright
Leah Wright
William Ellis
Elihu Barnard
Jane Harris
Benj'n Harris

#97 30th of 6th mo 1842   EPHRAIM G. COX-MARY KETTLEWELL
Whereas Ephraim G. Cox of Carrol County in the State of Maryland son of George Cox and Sarah his wife of the County and State aforesaid and Mary Kettlewell daughter of Charles Kettlewell and Hannah his wife of the County of Adams in the State of Pennsylvania . . . this thirtieth day of the sixth

MARRIAGES

month eighteen hundred forty two . . . at Huntington.

		Ephraim G. Cox
		<u>Mary Cox</u>
Jesse Russell	John Tudor Jr	Charles Kettlewell
Oliver Garretson	Nathan Griest	Hannah Kettlewell
Gideon Griest	Mary Ann Griest	John R. Cox
Jane H. Harney	Susan J. Gardner	Hannah Kettlewell
Mary E. Pearson	Caleb Beales	Rebecca A. Gardner
Josiah Garretson	Leah W. Cook	Jane E. Marsh
Mary Griest	Rebecca Cook	Mary J. Metcalf
Maria C. Jones	Jesse Cook	Joel Garretson
-?- G. Reed	Owen Griest	Elizabeth E. Garretson
Mary F. Reed	Mary J. Stewart	Rebecca Everitt
Margaret C. Woolford	Emily C. Moorhead	Martha Everitt
Barbara Stickel	Louisa Wierman	Joel A. Garretson
Margaret Deardorff	Philena Jane Griest	Lydia A. M. Walker
George Deardorff	William H. Cook	Hiram Metcalf
Isaac Tudor	Isaac Wright	Sarah A. Metcalf
Mary Tudor	Mary H. Matier	Juliet M. Taylor
Rachel F. Deardorff	Sarah Cox	Joseph Taylor
W. W. Wright	Aaron Cox	Joel Wierman
Wm Stewart	Margaret Elliot	Lydia Silverman
Hannah Wright	Mary S. Hammersley	Rachel E. Garretson
Rachel Wright	Elizabeth Stiehe	Hannah M. Garretson
	Edwin G. Vancise	

#98 26th of 9th mo 1844   JOHN B. WRIGHT-MARY NEBINGER

Whereas John B. Wright of Monallen Township County of Adams and State of Pennsylvania son of Nathan and Elizabeth Wright of the County and state aforesaid (the latter deceased) and Mary Nebinger daughter of Robert and Elizabeth Nebinger of the County of York and State aforesaid . . . this twenty sixth day of the ninth month eighteen hundred forty four . . . at the house of Robert Nebinger in Lewisberry.

	John B. Wright
	<u>Mary N. Wright</u>
Joel Garretson	Nathan Wright
Lydia S. Wierman	R. Nebinger
Elizabeth M. Fuller	E. Nebinger
Benj'n Harris	Brooke Statler
Cyrus Griest	Julia Kirk
Jane Harris	G. P. Nebinger
Mary Ann Griest	W. P. Nebinger
Jesse Cook	Ann Nebinger
Rebecca Cook	Nancy Kirk
Gideon Griest	Martha H. Nebinger
Isaac Tudor	Elijah Wright
Job Hoopes	Mary A. Wright
Rhoda Hoopes	Joseph N. S. Wright
Louisa Kirk	Geo Nebinger
Elizabeth Field	Maria Nebinger

MENALLEN MINUTES, MARRIAGES, & MISCELLANY

Jesse Kirk	C. E. Nebinger
Joseph G. Starr	Rebecca Nebinger
Maria Williams	Chapman Nebinger
Matilda Church	Augustus Nebinger
	Robert H. C. Nebinger

#99 20th of 11th mo 1845   BENJAMIN W. VANSCOYOC-PRISCILLA ALLEN

Whereas Benjamin W. Vanscoyoc of Latimore Township in the County of Adams and State of Pennsylvania son of Enoch and Hepzibah Vanscoyoc of the same place and Priscilla Allen of Huntington Township county and state aforesaid daughter of John and Sophia Allen late of St Marys County in the State of Maryland deceased . . . this twentieth day of the eleventh month eighteen hundred forty five . . . at the residence of Elizabeth M. Fuller in Huntington Township aforesaid.

Benjamin W. Vanscoyoc
<u>Priscilla A. Vanscoyoc</u>

	Enoch Vanscoyoc
Mary Jane Stewart	Hephzibah Vanscoyoc
Jacob H. Gardner	Ruth Vanscoyoc
W. Stewart	Elizabeth M. Fuller
Dinah M. Stewart	Rachel M. Mott
Gideon Griest	Moses Vanscoyoc
Martha Griest	Mary Jane Tyson
Israel Cook	Elizabeth Fuller
George Hewet	Charles Kettlewell
Elizabeth Bridges	Hannah Kettlewell
Isaac Shelly	Jesse Cook
Maria Harris	Rebecca Cook
Maria S. Cook	Benjamin Harris
Mary Ann Allen	Jane Harris
Ruthanna M. Cook	

#100 26th of 11th mo 1845   MOSES D. PRICE-ANN WRIGHT

Whereas Moses D. Price of Gunpowder in the County of Baltimore and State of Maryland son of Mordecai Price of Samuel of the place aforesaid and Mary his wife and Ann Wright daughter of Samuel Wright of Monallen in the County of Adams and State of Pennsylvania and Elizabeth his wife . . . this twenty sixth day of the eleventh month eighteen hundred forty five . . . at Monallen.

Moses D. Price
<u>Ann W. Price</u>

John Wright	Isaac I. Wright	Mordecai Price of Sam'l
Franklin Davis	J. B. Wright	Elizabeth Wright
George Wilson Jr	Wm Ellis	Wm H. Wright
Waln Hoopes	Leah Wright	Jane Wright
Sam'l H. Harry	Jane F. Wright	Rebecca Price
H. S. Wright	Harry Bell	Martha H. Wright
Alice G. Wright	Elijah Wright	Mordecai Price Jr
David E. Cook	I. H. S. Wright	Deborah Price
David Bender	Mary A. Wright	Eliakim G. Penrose
Alexander Hutton	Louisa A. Smith	Rebecca Wright
Mary H. Wright	Maria L. Wright	Phebe M. Tudor

MARRIAGES

Robert H. Wright	Martha Harry	Mary Jane Griffith
Rachel Garretson	Mary Ann Griest	William H. Cook
Lydia H. Chapman	Mary Cook	Wm Wright
Oliver M. Price	Ruth Cook	Jesse Cook
Isaac F. Tudor	E. Wilson	Rebecca Cook
Sarah Wright	Ellen W. Hewitt	Nathan Wright
Samuel B. Wright	Ruth Anna Wright	Cyrus Griest
Jn'o B. Galbreath	Ruth M. Wright	Abel T. Wright
Mary I. Galbreath	Rebecca J. Bell	Jesse Cook
Sarah C. Wierman	Susan S. Wood	Mahlon Garretson
	Mary Ann Ellis	Charles S. Wright
	Josiah Penrose	Wm Wilson
	Wm W. Holzinger	Joel Wright
	Joseph A. Wierman	Jacob B. Hewitt
		George Hewett

#101 30th of 9th mo 1846   CHARLES S. WRIGHT-HANNAH G. PENROSE

Whereas Charles S. Wright of Monallen Township County of Adams and State of Pennsylvania son of John and Alice Wright of the County and State aforesaid (the latter dec'd) and Hannah G. Penrose daughter of Josiah and Rachel Penrose of the County and State aforesaid (the latter dec'd) . . . this thirtieth day of the ninth month eighteen hundred forty six . . . at Monallen.

                                                                                         Charles S. Wright
                                                                                         <u>Hannah G. Wright</u>

Jno B. Galbreath	Eliza Wilson	John Wright
Sarah Galbreath	Rebecca Wierman	Josiah Penrose
Louisa H. Smith	Phebe Day	Hannah Garretson
Ann Wright	Jane Wilson	Joel Wright
Tho H. Wright	Sarah Wilson	Nathan Wright
Charlotte I. Wright	Emily Bateman	Wm Wright
Rachel Wright	Lewis Tudor	Jacob B. Hewet
John McGrew	Martha Harris	Eliza Hewet
David Wills	Elizabeth Ann Cook	Martha H. Wright
Isaac I Wright	Lucy Wright	Rebecca Wright
Sarah G. Wright	Hiram S. Wright	George Hewet
Amanda E. Wright	Alice G. Wright	Ellen W. Hewet
Eliza Jane Garretson	Theodore Overholtzer	William H. Wright
Eliza Hoopes	Rachel E. Garretson	Jane Wright
Joel Wierman	Martha H. Tudor	John B. Wright
Lydia T. Wierman	W. W. Wright	Mary H. Wright
Waln Hoopes	Rachel Wright	R. H. Wright
Cyrus Griest	Maria Wright	Elisha Penrose
Mary Ann Griest	Ruth Anna Wright	Jane F. Wright
Hiram Griest	Leah Wright	Huldah S. Penrose
-?- Smith	Isaac Wright	Ruth M. Wright
Louisa Smith	Elijah Wright	Elisha G. Penrose
Lucy Ann Bowman	Mary A. Wright	Abel T. Wright
Mary Ann Ellis	Joseph H. S. Wright	
Sarah T. Ellis		

MENALLEN MINUTES, MARRIAGES, & MISCELLANY

#102 23rd of 10th mo 1846   ELISHA PENROSE-SAVANNA WRIGHT
Whereas Elisha Penrose of Monallin Township County of Adams and State of Pennsylvania son of Josiah Penrose and Rachel his wife of the county and state aforesaid (the latter deceased) and Savanna Wright daughter of William Wright and Rachel his wife of the county and state aforesaid (the latter deceased) . . . this twenty third of the tenth month eighteen hundred forty six . . . at Monallen.

	Elisha Penrose
	Savanna Penrose
Hiram T. Wright	Josiah Penrose
Martha H. Wright	Wm Wright
Rebecca Wright	Hannah Garretson
Samuel Way	Huldah S. Penrose
Josephine Smith	Charles S. Wright
Louisa Smith	Hannah G. Wright
Elizabeth Hewet	Abel T. Wright
Elizabeth Jane Cook	George Hewet
Francis F. Smith	Ellen W. Hewet
Jane Caufman	Isaac I. Wright
Benjamin F. Wilson	Sarah G. Wright
Sarah Wilson	Amanda E. Wright
Emily Bateman	Thomas H. Wright
Elizabeth Bosserman	John Wright
Martha Ann Bosserman	Jane F. Wright
Eliza Hewet	Ruth M. Wright
Mary E. Smith	Isaac Tudor
Elmira Day	Mary Tudor
Cyrus Griest	Joel Wright
Jane Wilson	Lewis Tudor
Ruth Wilson	Nathan A. Tudor
Elijah Wright	Benj'n Harris
Rebecca Wierman	Jane Harris
	George W. Wright
	Lucy Wright

#103 20th of 5th mo 1847   THOMAS PEARSON-MARIA E. GRIFFITH
Whereas Thomas Pearson of Washington Township in the County of York and State of Pennsylvania son of Amelia Griest late of Harrisburg (deceased) (formerly Pearson) and Maria E. Griffith daughter of Allen and Sarah Griffith of Huntington Township in the County of Adams and State aforesaid . . . this twentieth day of the fifth month eighteen hundred forty seven . . . at the house of the said Allen Griffith.

	Thomas Pearson
	Maria E. Pearson
Josiah Garretson	Allen Griffith
Huldah H. Griffith	Sarah C. Griffith
Rebecca Cook	Henry C. Griffith
Thomas G. Kennedy	Mary I. Griffith
Mary Ann Kennedy	Rebecca S. Griffith
Charles Kettlewell	Elizabeth Jane Cook

238

MARRIAGES

Joel Garretson	William Cook
Rachel Griffith	Sarah C. Griffith
Robert A. Tyson by request	Emeline Loyd
Peter Griest present at signing	William Tyson Jr
Mary Asper	Mary Jane Tyson

#104 26th of 8th mo 1847   EDWARD BROOKES-SARAH ANN GRIEST

Whereas Edward Brookes of Fawn Township York County in the State of Pennsylvania son of Thomas and Rachel Brookes of the same place and Sarah Ann Griest daughter of Gideon and Jane M. Griest of Latimore Township in the County of Adams and State aforesaid . . . this twenty sixth day of the eighth month eighteen hundred forty seven . . . at Huntington.

Edward Brookes
Sarah Ann Brookes

	Gideon Griest
Daniel P. Thomas	Martha Griest
Charles Kettlewell	Sarah Brookes
Elizabeth M. Fuller	Rebecca Griest
Rachel M. Mott	Owen Griest
Mary Jane Tyson	Nathan Smith
Maria Edith Pearson	Edith Smith
Lydia Ann Griest	Lydia Griest
Mary Jane Griffith	Elmira E. Griest
Rebecca Laura Griffith	Martha Jane Griest
Sarah Walker	Angelina Griest
Ruth Anna Walker	Eliza Griest
Allen Griffith	Jesse Cook
Sarah Griffith	Rebecca Cook
Josiah Garretson	Mahlon Garretson
William Tyson Jr	Eliza Garretson
Jacob Griest	Joel Garretson
Hiram Griest	John Kettlewell
William H. Cook	Hannah Kettlewell
Teresa J. Espy	Nathan Griest
Philena J. Griest	Edward S. Walker
Louisa Newcommer	Edwin G. Vancise
Angelina Griest	Lucinda M. Griest
Lucinda Scholl	William J. Walker
Aaron Cox	Peter Griest
Sarah Cox	John E. Garretson
Isaac Tudor	

#105 29th of 6th mo 1848   DAVID E. COOK-MARY McGRAIL

Whereas David E. Cook of Monallen Township in the County of Adams and State of Pennsylvania son of Isaac Cook and Sydney his wife both deceased and Mary McGrail of the township county and state aforesaid daughter of George McGrail and Mary his wife (both parents deceased) . . . this twenty ninth day of the sixth month eighteen hundred forty eight . . . at the house of Mary McGrail.

David E. Cook
Mary E. Cook

MENALLEN MINUTES, MARRIAGES, & MISCELLANY

George Hewet	John W. Cook
Cyrus Griest	Samuel E. Cook
Wm Wright	Margaret Cook
Gideon Griest	William W. Cook
Charles Kettlewell	Thomas E. Cook
Eli Leach	Sarah Wierman
Joel Garretson	Elizabeth Jane Cook
Jane Wright	Matilda Cook
Jane Harris	Charles D. E. Cook
Catherine E. Means	Jesse C. Wierman
Frederick Hartzel	Rebecca McGrail
Jane Hartzel	Eliza Ross
John Moose	

#106 25th of 1st mo 1849   JOSEPH M. SPENCER-LYDIA ANN GRIEST

Whereas Joseph M. Spencer son of Joseph Spencer and Lydia his wife of Clearfield County Pennsylvania and Lydia Ann Griest daughter of Uriah Griest and Mary his wife of York County and State aforesaid . . . this twenty fifth day of the first month eighteen hundred forty nine . . . at Huntington.

Joseph M. Spencer
<u>Lydia Ann Spencer</u>

Elizabeth E. Garretson	Abel T. Wright
Jane Harris	Lavinia Spencer
Sarah C. Griest	Miles S. Spencer
Edwin G. Vancise	Martha Harris
Mahlon Garretson	Lavinia H. Griest
Nathan Smith	Phebe M. Griest
Isaac Tudor	Elisha Griest
Mary Tudor	Rebecca Griest
Benj W. Vanscoyoc	Wm. E. Griest
Sam'l H. Harris	Malon Griest
William J. Walker	Edith Vale
Lucinda Griest	Eliza Garretson
Joseph G. Vale	Rebecca E. Vale
Nathan P. Griest	Gideon Griest
Annie Wright	Rebecca Griest
Edith B. Philips	Nathan Griest
Hannah Wright	Mary Ann Griest
Hannah M. Wierman	Almira E. Griest
Rachel Garretson	Philena J. Griest
Caroline G. Worley	Jacob Griest
Serina A. Albert	Content Griest
Josiah Garretson	Joel Wierman
Aaron Cox	Lydia S. Wierman
Isaac W. W. Pearson	Martha P. Garretson
Oliver Garretson	Edward S. Walker
Isaac Wright	

MARRIAGES

#107 24th of 1st mo 1849   HIRAM GRIEST-LOUISA ELLIS

Whereas Hiram Griest of Monallen Township in the County of Adams and State of Pennsylvania son of Cyrus and Mary Ann Griest and Louisa Ellis daughter of William and Elizabeth Ellis all of the township county and state aforesaid . . . this twenty fourth day of the first month eighteen hundred forty nine . . . at Monallen.

Hiram Griest
Louisa E. Griest

Jacob Peters Jr	John Bosserman	Cyrus Griest
Washington Morison	David Bender	Mary Ann Griest
Mary Ann Wierman	Emily Bateman	William Ellis
Amos J. Bender	Rebecca A. Harris	Elizabeth Ellis
Joseph M. Bender	Maria L. Harris	Josiah Wickersham
Hiram S. Wright	Elijah Wright	Jane E. Griest
Wm Bender	Conrad Wierman	George M. Griest
George W. Garretson	Maria L. Wright	Sarah Jane Ellis
Mary Cook	Ruth Anna Wright	Mary Ann Ellis
George Moore	Jacob B. Hewet	Maria E. Hunt
Anna E. Peffer	Eliza Hewit	Ann M. Griest
Thomas McCreary Jr	Joel Wright	Jesse W. Griest
George M. Cook	Thos Pearson	Cyrus S. Griest
David R. McCreary	Maria E. Pearson	Maria E. Griest
Reuben Wierman	W. W. Wright	Elizabeth Griest
Jane Wilson	Jane Wright	Waln Hoopes
Abel T. Wright	Josiah Cook	Sarah Ann Hoopes
Elizabeth S. Wright	Mary Cook	Ruth M. Wright
Nathan Wright	Wm Wright	Elizabeth Jane Cook
John Wright	Jesse Cook	Nancy J. Morrison
Joseph Joyce	David E. Cook	
Bemont Taylor	Mary Cook	George Hewet
Thomas H. Wright	W. Wilson	Ellen W. Hewet
George Wilson Jr	Charles S. Wright	
S. W. Estep	Jane F. Wright	
Wm. H. McCreary	Eliza Wilson	
Nicholas G. Wilson	George W. Wright	
John W. Hoopes	Sarah Wilson	

#108 24th of 4th mo 1850   THOMAS JONES-MARTHA HARRIS

Whereas Thomas Jones of Fawn Township York County and state of Pennsylvania son of Thomas and Martha Jones of the same place and Martha Harris daughter of Benjamin and Jane Harris of Butler Township in the County of Adams and state aforesaid . . . this twenty fourth day of the fourth month eighteen hundred fifty . . . at Monallen.

Thomas Jones
Martha H. Jones

Joel Garretson	E. J. Everitt	Benjamin Harris
Maria M. Vancise	George Hewitt	Jane Harris
Eliza Garretson	Ellen W. Hewitt	Rebecca A. Harris
Mahlon Garretson	Joseph Joice	Maria Harris
Nathan Smith	Jacob Kirk	Elizabeth A. Jones

MENALLEN MINUTES, MARRIAGES, & MISCELLANY

George W. Wright	Hannah Kirk	Julia Harris
Joel Wright	Jane Wright	Samuel H. Harris
David E. Cook	William H. Wright	Jesse B. Jones
Elizabeth Wright	Thomas E. Cook	Hiram L. Harris
George Wilson Jr	Jane C. Griest	Nathan Wright
Hiram T. Wright	Mary Garretson	Maria L. Wright
A. G. Garretson	John Wright	Ruth Anna Wright
John Bosserman	Anna M. Griest	Ruth M. Wright
David Wills	Eliza Hoopes	Jane F. Wright
John Garretson	Sarah Wilson	Eliza Wright
George Moose	Rebecca Wright	William Ellis
John Hoopes	Rebecca F. Griffith	William Wright
Caleb Beales	Mary C. Beales	Jesse Cook Jr
Anna E. Houck	Josephine Smith	Ruth Cook
George M. Cook	Maria E. Pearson	R. R. Everitt
Louisa Smith	Elizabeth Hewitt	Sarah M. Wright
Emily Bateman	Sarah T. Parker	Ruth W. Wills

#109 23rd of 6th mo 1851   WILLIAM G. CADWALLADER-REBECCA GRIEST
Whereas William G. Cadwallader of Mechanicsville in the County of Adams in the State of Pennsylvania son of William and Sarah Cadwallader of Washington (the latter dec'd) in the County of York and State aforesaid and Rebecca Griest daughter of Gideon and Jane Griest of Latimore (the latter dec'd) in the County of Adams aforesaid . . . this twenty third day of the sixth month eighteen hundred fifty one . . . at Huntington.

William S. Cadwallader
Rebecca G. Cadwallader

Mahlon Garretson	Amos Griest	William Cadwallader
A. N. Russell	Almira Underwood	Gideon Griest
Cyrus Blackburn	Isaac Tudor	Martha Griest
David Cadwallader	Mary Tudor	Angelina Griest
John Miller Jr	Lydia T. Wierman	Martha Jane Griest
Miles T. Spencer	Joel Wierman	Eliza Griest
Harrison N. Spencer	Jane Harris	Almira E. Griest
Isaiah Blackburn	Benj'n Harris	Edith Smith
Joel Brown	William Wright	Lucinda M. Griest
H. W. Wierman	Mary Ann Squibb	Phebe M. Griest
Lucretia M. Wierman	Charlotte Pearson	
Sarah A. Metcalf	Joel Wright	
Ruth M. Wright	Abel T. Wright	
Rachel E. Garretson		
Martha A. Tudor		
Content Griest		
Jacob Griest		

#110 29th of 12th mo 1853   WILLIAM CLEAVER-LOUISA W. GARRETSON
Whereas William Cleaver of Penn Township Clearfield County and State of Pennsylvania son of Andrew and Hannah Cleaver (the former dec'd) of the same place and Louisa W. Garretson daughter of Asahel and Mary Walker (the latter dec'd) of Washington Township in the County of York and State

MARRIAGES

aforesaid . . . this twenty ninth day of the twelfth month eighteen hundred fifty three . . . at Huntington.

		William Cleaver
		<u>Louisa W. Cleaver</u>
Nathan P. Griest	J. W. Pearson	Asahel Walker
Benjamin Shelly	Kezia Smith	George W. Cook
Theodore P. Wierman	Rachel Smith	William H. Cook
John A. Wierman	John Wolford	Ruth Anna Walker
J. Wm Wierman	Aaron Cox	Edwin G. Vancise
Sherman H. Smith	Sarah Cox	Maria M. Vancise
Charles W. Griest	Edith Vale	Lavinia Vancise
Phebe W. Wierman	Clara J. Wolford	Gideon Griest
Mary E. Sadler	Rebecca A. Fisher	Martha Griest
Anna E. Knause	Sophia Shuman	Sarah A. Metcalf
Mary E. Wierman	H. M. Wierman	Mary C. Beals
Solomon Myers	Mary Ann Wierman	Joseph Wierman
Rebecca Griest	Jesse Cook	Maria Louisa Vancise
Jemima Rush	Rebecca Cook	
Mary Griest	Jacob Griest	
Rebecca G. Cadwallader		Elizabeth C. Garretson
Anna Griest	Nathan Smith	
Oliver Garretson	Edith Smith	

<u>#111 25th of 10th mo 1854</u>   ABEL T. WRIGHT-JANE C. GRIEST

Whereas Abel T. Wright of Monallen Township Adams County and State of Pennsylvania son of William and Rachel Wright (both deceased) and Jane C. Griest daughter of Cyrus and Mary Ann Griest of the same Township County and State . . . this twenty fifth day of the tenth month eighteen hundred fifty four . . . at Monallen.

		Abel T. Wright
		<u>Jane C. Wright</u>
William Ellis	Maria L. Harris	Cyrus Griest
Joseph Joice	Mary A. Wierman	Mary Ann Griest
Josiah Cook	Ruth M. Wright	Samuel Cook
Jesse Cook	Rebecca Wright	Jane F. Wright
Joel Wierman	Mary A. Wright	Franklin Davis
Lydia S. Wierman	Elijah Wright	Ruth Anne Wright
William H. Wright	James Clayton Wright	Joel Wright
Jane Wright	H. A. Wright	Rachel Ann Griest
Thomas E. Cook	T. A. Wright	Cyrus S. Griest
Martha H. Wright	Deborah Farquahar	George Hewitt
Jesse C. Wright	Elcetta Griest	Ellis W. Hewitt
William E. Wright	Leah Cook	Thomas H. Wright
Samuel B. Wright	Louisa A. Smith	Charlotte T. Wright
G. S. W. Smith	Sarah Griest	Isaac J. Wright
Mary E. Tate	Joel Fisher	Rachel Wright
F. T. Tate	Rachel A. Wright	Amos Griest
Ruth W. Wills	Emily T. Wright	Margaret Griest
Nancy I. Morrison	Charles S. Wright	Hiram Griest
William W. Hewitt	Hannah G. Wright	Louisa Griest

MENALLEN MINUTES, MARRIAGES, & MISCELLANY

Emily Bateman
Sarah M. Wright
Sarah B. Wierman
Ruth Schriver
Rebecca A. Harris
Benjamin Harris

Martha Jane Cook
Willing C. Griest
Amos W. Griest

Jesse W. Griest
Ann M. Griest
Maria Edith Griest
Elizabeth Mary Griest

#112 23rd of 5th mo 1861   FRANKLIN W. COOK-EDITH ANN COOK
Whereas Franklin W. Cook of Monallen Township Adams County Pennsylvania son of Thomas E. and Mary Cook and Edith Ann daughter of Josiah and Mary Cook of the township, county and state aforesaid . . . this twenty third day of the fifth month eighteen hundred sixty one . . . at Monallen.

Franklin W. Cook
Edith Ann Cook

Thomas E. Cook
Mary T. Cook
Josiah Cook
Mary G. Cook
Jesse W. Griest
Martha Jane Cook
Charles J. Tyson
Maria E. Griest
Benjamin W. Cook
Martha C. Beals
Marcellious S. Cook
J-?- Cook
Henry Cook
Elmira J. Cook
Martha Ann Cook
Cyrus S. Griest
Letitia A. Griest
Cyrus Griest
Mary Ann Griest
George Hewitt
A. S. Wright
Jane C. Wright
Anna M. Griest

Hiram Griest

Azanath Wright
Sarah Wilson
Edith Griest
Maria W. Cook
Mary Ann Ellis
B. J. Houck
Annie F. Gitt
H. A. Wright
V. W. Mumma
Maria E. Cook
Amos Cook
Josiah W. Cook
Charles C. Cook
Sarah A. Cook
Hannah A. Hoopes
Jane Wilson
Beulah K. Shugh
Eleanora F. Wilson
Hannah B. Wilson
Ruth Wilson
Sallie M. Bender
Josiah Griest
Mary Ann Griest

#113 30th of 4th mo 1863   CHARLES J. TYSON-MARIA E. GRIEST
Whereas Charles J. Tyson of Gettysburg, Adams County, State of Pennsylvania son of Comly Tyson and Susan G. his wife of Philadelphia, state aforesaid and Maria E. Griest daughter of Cyrus Griest and Mary Ann his wife of Monallen Township Adams County State aforesaid . . . this thirtieth day of the fourth month eighteen hundred sixty three . . . at the house of Cyrus Griest.

Charles J. Tyson
Maria E. Tyson

William Ellis
Mary Ellis
Charles S. Wright
Hiram S. Wright

Martha Jane Cook
Henry Cook
Annie E. Cook
Seneca P. Broomell

MARRIAGES

Josiah Griest	Susan Sullivan
Mary Ann Griest	Cyrus Griest
Josiah Cook	Mary Ann Griest
Mary Cook	Hiram Griest
Ruth Bateman	Lavinia E. Griest
Mrs. Annie Gilt	Abel F. Wright
Andrew Koser	Jane C. Wright
Jesse M. Griest	Cyrus S. Griest
Josiah Griest	Letitia B. Griest
Lizzie A. Griest	Annie M. Griest
Isaac G. Tyson	Amos W. Griest
-?- Griest	Lavinia Griest
Jesse W. Griest	Mary Ann Ellis

#114 22nd of 3rd mo 1866   ANDREW KOSER-ELIZABETH M. GRIEST

Whereas Andrew Koser of Butler Township in the County of Adams and State of Pennsylvania son of Henry G. Koser and Margaret his wife of the same place and Elizabeth M. Griest daughter of Cyrus Griest and Mary Ann his wife of Monallen Township in the County and State aforesaid . . . this twenty second day of the third month eighteen hundred sixty six . . . at the home of Cyrus Griest.

Andrew Koser
Elizabeth M. Koser
Henry G. Koser
Margaret Koser
Cyrus Griest
Mary Ann Griest
Edith Griest
Josiah Griest
Mary Cook
Josiah Griest
Mary Ann Griest
Nathan Smith
Mary W. Smith
Charles S. Wright
Hannah S. Wright
Hiram Griest
Lavinia E. Griest
Abel Wright

John C. Brough
Elmer Cook
[the rest of
this column
is illegible]

#115 21st of 12th mo 1871   WM H. BLACK-EMILIE WRIGHT

Whereas Wm H. Black of Straben Township in the County of Adams and State of Pennsylvania son of Wm and Jane S. Black (the latter deceased) of the County and State aforesaid and Emilie Wright daughter of Charles S. and Hannah G. Wright of the County and State aforesaid . . . this twenty first day of the twelfth month eighteen hundred seventy one . . . at the home of Chas. S. Wright.

William H. Black
Emilie W. Black

MENALLEN MINUTES, MARRIAGES, & MISCELLANY

W. W. Bailey	Mary Ann Griest
Eliza R. Wright	Hiram S. Wright
Z. Hubbard Moore	Alice G. Wright
Rachie A. Wright	M. N. Wright
Amos W. Griest	Jane C. Wright
Lou A. Wright	Lizzie Wright
Jesse W. Griest	G. E. Wright
Sibilla E. Griest	Chas. S. Wright
Cyrus S. Griest	Hannah G. Wright
Letitia B. Griest	Ruth M. Wright
A. J. Koser	Jane Y. Wright
Lizzie M. Koser	John B. Wright
Wm. F. Penrose	Sue K. Black
	John H. Black

#116 21st of 2nd mo 1872   GIDEON SMITH-MARTHA JANE COOK

Whereas Gideon Smith of Pipe Creek in the County of Carroll in the State of Maryland son of Nathan Smith and Edith his wife (the latter dec'd) and Martha Jane Cook daughter of Josiah Cook and Mary his wife (the latter dec'd) of Menallen Township County of Adams State of Pennsylvania . . . this twenty first day of the second month eighteen hundred seventy two . . . at the house of Josiah Cook.

	Gideon Smith
	Martha Jane Smith
Hiram Griest	Maria K. Cook
Louisa E. Griest	Eli M. Hibberd
Jesse W. Griest	Sallie A. Cook
Sibilla E. Griest	Jesse Smith
Eliza R. Wright	Ruth Lizzie Griest
Amos W. Griest	Elizabeth Gainer
Jane C. Wright	Josiah Cook
Wm. Thomas Penrose	Frank W. Cook
Ellis W. Cook	Edith A. Cook
Willie H. Griest	Harry E. Cook
Geo. Edward Wright	Henry Cook
Elizabeth M. Koser	Frances A. Cook
Andrew J. Koser	Mary Ann Griest
Amos G. Cook	Josiah Griest
H. Bichie Day	Mary Ann S. Griest
Josiah W. Cook	Jesse Cook
Martha Smith	Jennie May Cook
	Mary Cook

#117 24th of 5th mo 1872   EDWARD A. RUSSELL-LOUISA A. WRIGHT

Whereas Edward A. Russell of Unionville, Center County, Pennsylvania son of Abel and Maude A. Russell and Louisa A. Wright of Monallen Township, Adams County Pennsylvania, daughter of Hiram S. and Alice G. Wright . . . this twenty fourth day of the fifth month eighteen hundred seventy two . . . at Flora Dale, Adams County Pennsylvania.

MARRIAGES

	Edward A. Russell
	Louisa A. W. Russell
F. C. Gitt	Hiram F. Wright
-?- Wright	-?- G. Wright
-?-	Lizzie Wright
Eli P. Garretson	Mary A. Russell
Frank Garretson	Mary Garretson
Susan Matthews	Elijah Wright
Carrie Vale	Mary Wright
Eliza K. Wright	John B. Wright
Ida C. Wright	-?- Wright
Ruth L. Griest	Ruth H. Wright
G. E. Wright	Chas. J. Tyson
-?- Penrose	Maria E. Tyson
-?- Slaybaugh	Hannah Garretson
-?- Underwood	Hannah G. Wright
-?- Thomas	Amon N. Griest
Catherine Thomas	

#118 5th mo 1872   ZIBA HIBBERD MOORE-LAVINIA GRIEST

Whereas Ziba Hibberd Moore of Adams County in the State of Pennsylvania son of Ziba Moor and Mary B. his wife the former deceased of Chester County and state aforesaid and Lavinia Griest daughter of Hiram Griest and Louisa C. his wife of Adams County in the State of Pennsylvania . . . this -?- of fifth month eighteen seventy two . . . at the house of Hiram Griest.

	Ziba Hibberd Moore
	Lavinia G. Moore
Jane C. Wright	Hiram Griest
Ann M. Griest	Louisa E. Griest
Charles J. Tyson	Mary B. Moore
Maria G. Tyson	Mary Ann Griest
Ruth L. Griest	Emma Griest
Maria R. Cook	Mary Ann Ellis
Josiah Griest	Harris Griest
Mary Ann Griest	Hadly Griest
Josiah Cook	A. J. Koser
Hannah G. Wright	Ella P. Thompson
Esther Morthland	Ella M. Griest
Eliza P. Wright	Esther H. Griest
Lizzie Wright	Della J. Griest
Ida Wright	Jesse W. Griest
Elijah Wright	Sibilla C. Griest
Mary A. Wright	Martha M. Thompson
Josiah W. Cook	Eleanor H. Moore
C. -?- Wright	Cyrus S. Griest
A. G. Cook	Letitia B. Griest
G. C. Wright	George W. Derby
Amos W. Griest	Sallie J. Derby
Mary Lizzie Griest	

MENALLEN MINUTES, MARRIAGES, & MISCELLANY

[pages 213 and 214 are illegible.]

#119 19th of 10th mo 1876   WILLIAM WITSON-JANE C. WRIGHT
Whereas William Witson of Mishar-?-, St. Joseph County State of Indiana, son of Micah and Mary Witson (both deceased) and Jane C. Wright daughter of Cyrus Griest (now deceased) and Mary Ann his wife of Menallen Township Adams County, State of Pennsylvania . . . this nineteenth day of the tenth month eighteen hundred seventy six . . . at the house of Mary Ann Griest.

William Witson
<u>Jane C. Witson</u>

Mary Ann Griest		William G. Miller
Elizabeth Gause		Annie W. Miller
Jesse Cook		Pearson Matthews
Josiah Cook		Elva W. Matthews
M. W. Cook		Hiram Griest
Hannah G. Wright		Louisa E. Griest
W. P. Glinson		Cyrus S. Griest
G. Edward Wright		Letitia R. Griest
E. Comly Tyson, Sr		Annie M. Griest
Josiah Griest		Charles J. Tyson
Mary Ann S. Griest		Maria E. Tyson
Ruth Lizzie Griest		Amos W. Griest
Esther Morthland		Eliza R. Griest
Sarah E. Vale		Emilie Belle Griest
Amos G. Cook	Lucy E. Koch	Mary E. Griest
Maria R. Cook	Annie Stinson	Florence Griest
Sallie P. Derby	Dennis Stinson	Mary H. Tyson
Mary Ann Ellis	Edwin C. Tyson	Adella Griest
Rachie A. Wright	Harris Griest	Lizzie Griest
		Hadley Griest

#120 25th of 12th mo 1878   CHARLES L. LONGSDORF-ELIZABETH WRIGHT
Whereas Charles L. Longsdorf of Williamsport, Lycoming County Pennsylvania son of Alexander and Rebecca Longsdorf (both deceased) and Elizabeth Wright of Menallen, Adams County, Pa. Daughter of Hiram S. and Alice G. Wright . . . this twenty fifth day of the twelfth month eighteen hundred seventy eight . . . at Flora Dale, Adams County, Pennsylvania.

Charles L. Longsdorf
<u>Elizabeth Wright Longsdorf</u>

J. B. Wright	
M. N. Wright	Hiram S. Wright
Mary Garretson	Alice G. Wright
Mary A. Wright	M. Alice Wright
Isaac J. Wright	
Sarah G. Wright	
Ruth M. Wright	
Jane F. Wright	
Rachie A. Wright	
Margaret J. Wilson	
George W. Wilson	

MARRIAGES

#121 14th of 7th mo 1878 JOHN HOWARD GOVE-MARY ELIZABETH GRIEST
Whereas John Howard Gove, Washington County, Nebraska, son of Moses Dennis Gove and Sarah B. Gove (the former deceased) and Mary Elizabeth Griest of Adams County Pennsylvania daughter of Hiram Griest and Louisa E. Griest and according to the laws of the state of Nebraska obtained a marriage license from the Judge of the County Court of Gage in said state . . . this fourteenth day of the seventh month eighteen hundred seventy eight . . . at the house of Jesse and Sibilla Griest, Otoe Agency, Nebraska.

                                                             John Howard Gove
                                                           Mary Elizabeth Gove

Mahlon H. Kent	Francis M. Barnes	Sibilla E. Griest
Annie R. Kent	Richard Dumbard	Ziba Hibberd Moore
William Turner	George Boyd	Lavinia G. Moore
Elizabeth Turner	-?- Deroin	Emma Griest
Maurice Walton	Jesse W. Griest	Mary L. Barnes
		Barclay White

[#122: Illegible. Looks like Hiram T. Harris and Miriam G. Wright 1875.]

[#123: Illegible. Looks like George E. Wright son of Charles S. Wright and Hannah Penrose to Jane Garretson Wright daughter of Isaac J. Wright and Sarah Garretson, 10th of 5th mo 1880 . . . at the house of said Jane's parents.]

#124 17th of 11th mo 1887 CHARLES MICHENER-FLORENCE GRIEST
Whereas Charles Michener of Butler Township, Adams County State of Pennsylvania son of Charles Michener and Rebecca S. his wife (the former deceased) of the city of Philadelphia and State of Pennsylvania and Florence Griest of Butler Township Adams County State of Pennsylvania daughter of Cyrus S. Griest and Letitia B. his wife of the same place . . . this seventeenth day of the eleventh month eighteen hundred eighty seven . . . at the house of Cyrus S. Griest aforesaid.

                                                     Charles Michener
                                               Florence G. Michener

Mary T. Michener	Cyrus S. Griest
E. Belle Griest	Letitia B. Griest
Frank Jarrett	Rebecca J. Michener
G. Wilmer Koser	Lydia W. Michener
Mary E. Griest	Ellen M. Michener
Lizzie Griest	Edward Mather
George G. Griest	Geo. B. Passmore
C. Arthur Griest	Lizzie B. Passmore
Maurice Griest	Seneca Broomell
Martha M. Jarrett	Rebecca J. Broomell
Sallie Jarrett	Samuel N. Broomell
Morris Jarrett	Mary E. Broomell
Sarah E. Jarrett	Ella Broomell
Charles J. Tyson	G. Lupton Broomell
Maria E. Tyson	John Mather
Hiram Griest	Ella M. G. Prickett

MENALLEN MINUTES, MARRIAGES, & MISCELLANY

Louisa E. Griest
Jane C. Whitson
William Whitson
Annie M. Griest
Elizabeth M. Koser
Andrew J. Koser
Amos W. Griest
Eliza R. Griest
Frederic Earl Griest
Sibilla E. Griest
Edwin C. Tyson
Mary W. Tyson

L-?-

Josiah W. Prickett
Esther Prickett
Mary A. Tyson
Z. J. Peters
M. Bushman
Marianna Hawxhurst
Bertha Hawxhurst
Gilbert Hicks
Israel Garretson
Rachel Garretson
Esther Morthland
Sarah E. Vale

#125 23rd of 2nd mo 1888   HADLY KENT-VIOLA WHITSON
Whereas Hadly Kent of the Township of Upper Oxford, County of Chester and State of Pennsylvania son of Joseph Kent and Maria Jane his wife (both deceased) and Viola Whitson of the Township of Menallen in the County of Adams and State aforesaid daughter of William Whitson and Elizabeth his wife (the latter deceased) . . . this twenty third day of the second month eighteen hundred eighty eight . . . at the house of William Whitson.

Hadly Kent
Viola W. Kent

Elizabeth W. Koser
Amos W. Griest
Eliza R. Griest
Esther -?-
Mary E. -?-
Charles G. Hewett
Hiram Griest
Louisa E. Griest
Annie M. Griest
Cyrus S. Griest
Letitia B. Griest
Sibbilla E. Griest
Maria E. Tyson
William Whitson
Jane C. Whitson
Maria K. David

[Right hand
column
illegible.]

#126 10th of 12th mo 1891   AMOS C. HARTMAN-RUTH EMMA BAIR
This is to certify that Amos C. Hartman of Bermudian in the County of York and State of Pennsylvania son of Samuel and Harriet Hartman and Ruth Emma Bair daughter of John and Lydia Ann Cook of near Dillsburg, York County and State of Pennsylvania . . . this tenth day of the twelfth month eighteen hundred ninety one . . . at Warrington Friends Meeting House.

Amos C. Hartman
Ruth Emma Hartman

Fannie M. Cook
J. Ernie Bair
Wm. R. Cook

Clara Wooden
Lillie Darone
Sallie A. Myers

MARRIAGES

Mary V. Cook	Albert C. Myers
E. W. Smith	Anna M. Smith
T. L. Hoopes	Sallie C. Meredith
M. M. Ramsey	M. G. Cooke
Hiram Griest	C. J. Cooks
Hannah Lerew	Miles H. Shearer
Carrie A. Cooke	Jene Lerew
Ira L. Heiges	Girlie Shearer
Minnie S. Heiges	Maud Anthony
May Anthony	R. M. Heeney
Lydia H. Underwood	Mary Lizzie Gove
Mayme Bushey	Alice R. Bentz
Abram R. Wills	J. K. Bentz
L. C. -?-	Birdie Anthony
Florence MacMillan	Mary L. Brenneman
T. G. Crall	Mary Keeney
Joseph B. Byers	James Crall
Franklin Cookson	Jennie Reed
Melissa Anthony	Sevilla Linebaugh
Teresa A. Elder	Minnie B. Kutz
William Anthony	Fannie W. Cooke
Lydia Ramsey	

#127 13th of 10th mo 1892   ADAM CLARK VROMAN-ESTHER C. GRIEST
Whereas Adam Clark Vroman of the city of Rockford County of -?- State of Illinois son of Alan Vroman (deceased) and Esther C. Griest daughter of Jesse Griest of the township of Menallen County of Adams and State of Pennsylvania and -?- (now deceased also) . . . this thirteenth of the tenth month eighteen hundred ninety two at the house of J. W. Prickett.

                                                    Adam Clark Vroman
                                                    Esther C. Vroman

[Witness list illegible.]

#128 4th of 8th mo 1898   GEORGE G. GRIEST-HARRIETT T. ASHER
Whereas George G. Griest of Guernsey, County of Adams and State of Pennsylvania son of Cyrus S. Griest and Letitia B. his wife the latter deceased and Harriett T. Asher daughter of Morris Asher and Regina his wife the latter deceased of New Haven, County of New Haven, State of Connecticut . . . this fourth day of the eighth month eighteen hundred ninety eight . . . at the home of Cyrus S. Griest.

                                                    George G. Griest
                                                    Harriett T. Griest

Cyrus S. Griest	A. J. Koser
Mary E. Griest	Elizabeth M. Koser
E. Belle Griest	William Whitson
Charles Michener	Sibbilla E. Griest
Florence G. Michener	Seneca P. Broomell
Lizzie Griest	Rebecca J. Broomell
Maurice E. Griest	C. J. Tyson
C. Arthur Griest	Maria E. Tyson

MENALLEN MINUTES, MARRIAGES, & MISCELLANY

Hiram Griest Eliza J. Griest
Louisa E. Griest

#129 21st of 11th mo 1900   CYRUS S. GRIEST-M. ALICE WRIGHT
Whereas Cyrus S. Griest of the Township of Butler, County of Adams and State of Pennsylvania son of Cyrus and Mary Ann Griest both deceased of the township of Menallen County and State aforesaid and M. Alice Wright daughter of Hiram A. and Alice G. Wright, former deceased of the township of Menallen and county and state aforesaid . . . this twenty first day of the eleventh month nineteen hundred at Menallen Meeting House.

Cyrus S. Griest
Mary Alice Wright Griest
Alice G. Wright
Hiram Griest
Maria E. Tyson
Charles Michener
Florence G. Michener
Alice M. Michener
O. Raymond Michener
E. Belle Griest
C. Arthur Griest
Maurice E. Griest
-?- Bailey
-?- Cook
-?- Cook
Hannah G. Wright
Elizabeth M. Koser

[Left hand column illegible.]

#130 23rd of 7th mo 1901   WILLIAM H. GRIEST-ROSE CHRIST
Whereas William H. Griest of the County of Adams and State of Pennsylvania son of Josiah Griest and Mary Ann his wife both deceased and Rose Christ of the city of Toledo, state of Ohio, daughter of Jacob H. Christ and Artemesia his wife both deceased . . . this twenty third day of the seventh month nineteen hundred one . . . at the house of Jesse and Lydia L. Smith.

Wm. H. Griest
Rose C. Griest

[No witness list found.]

#131 17th of 4th mo 1909   AARON I. WEIDNER-E. BELLE GRIEST
Whereas Aaron I. Weidner of the Boro of Arendtsville, County of Adams and State of Pennsylvania son of Jacob S. Weidner and Leah his wife, both deceased and E. Belle Griest of Guernsey, County of Adams and State of Pennsylvania, daughter of Cyrus S. Griest and Letitia B. his wife (the latter deceased) . . . this seventeenth day of the fourth month nineteen hundred nine . . . at the home of Cyrus S. Griest of Guernsey.

Aaron I. Weidner
E. Belle Griest Weidner

Mary E. Smelser	Elizabeth B. Passmore	Cyrus S. Griest
E. C. Smelser	Samuel H. Broomell	M. Alice W. Griest
W. W. Boyer	Mary E. Broomell	Mary E. Griest

MARRIAGES

Elizabeth Lott Boyer	Hanson P. Passmore	Charles Michener
	Frances B. Passmore	Florence G. Michener
	Mary H. Way	C. Raymond Michener
	Hiram Griest	C. Arthur Griest
	Maria E. Tyson	Lola W. Griest
	Elizabeth M. Koser	Katharene E. Griest
	Josiah W. Prickett	Elizabeth Griest
	Ella M. G. Prickett	Maurice E. Griest
	Mary H. Prickett	A. D. Taylor
	Mary E. Gove	H. Elizabeth Taylor
	Mrs. G. W. Wierman	Carrie Steinour Weaver
	Z. J. Peters	Nellie M. Taylor
	Mary Tyson Peters	Lizzie J. Raffensperger
	Edwin C. Tyson	Charles E. Raffensperger
	Mary W. Tyson	David T. Koser
		Sarah E. Koser

#132 5th of 7th mo 1917   FREDERICK E. PARSONS-MARY MURIEL TYSON
Whereas Frederick E. Parsons of Grand Rapids, County of Kent and State of Michigan son of Frederick E. Parsons and Mary his wife both deceased and Mary Muriel Tyson daughter of Edwin C. Tyson and Mary his wife of the Township of Menallen, County of Adams and State of Pennsylvania . . . this fifth day of the seventh month nineteen hundred seventeen . . . at the home of Edwin C. Tyson.

		Frederick E. Parsons
		M. Muriel Parsons
Edwin C. Tyson		Maria E. Tyson
Mary W. Tyson		Mary Tyson Peters
E. Corinne Tyson		Z. J. Peters
Bertha H. Tyson		Mary Kerlin Walters
Chester J. Tyson		Anna M. Black
Florence H. Carpenter		Alice L. Black
Harold E. Hawxhurst	Mary E. Gove	Clyde H. Lady
Hazel L. Hawxhurst	Mary E. Griest	Arthur E. Cook
Edna Kerr Tyson	E. Belle Weidner	Mabel Leonard
Wm. C. Tyson	A. J. Weidner	Annie Kurtz Sheely
Paul Sharpless	Florence A. Michener	Beula E. Harris
Wallace V. Peters	Elizabeth Griest	H. T. Weaver
M. Edith Peters	C. Arthur Griest	Emma C. Weaver
Esther Vroman Peters	Lola W. Griest	William G. Weaver
Donald C. Tyson	Eleanor R. Koser	Ethel M. Busby
Robert A. Tyson	G. W. Koser	Robert M. Eldon
Elizabeth C. Tyson	Anna M. Michener	Florence S. Eldon
Margaret J. Tyson	Mary H. Prickett	W. S. Adams
Frederick C. Tyson	Eleanor S. Prickett	Elizabeth P. Adams
Hiram Griest	Elizabeth A. Garretson	
Isaac Wilson	Eliza J. Griest	
Elizabeth Koser Wilson	Alvie F. Starner	
A. W. Griest	J. W. Prickett	
Eliza R. Griest	Ella M. G. Prickett	
Frederic E. Griest		

MENALLEN MINUTES, MARRIAGES, & MISCELLANY

#133 10th of 5th mo 1923 HENRY C. PICKERING-ESTHER VROMAN PETERS
Whereas Henry Comly Pickering of Woodbourne, County of Bucks and State of Pennsylvania, son of John Rowlett Pickering (now deceased) and Hannah Gillam Comly Pickering his wife and Esther Vroman Peters of Guernsey, County of Adams and State of Pennsylvania, daughter of Zachariah J. Peters and Mary Tyson Peters his wife . . . this tenth day of the fifth month nineteen hundred twenty three . . . at Friends Meeting house at Flora Dale, Pa.

Henry C. Pickering
Esther Peters Pickering

Amos W. Griest	A. J. Weidner
Eliza R. Griest	E. Belle Weidner
Elizabeth Griest	Edwin C. Tyson
Mary E. Griest	Mary W. Tyson
Reuben L. Underwood	J. W. Prickett
Alice L. Black	Ella M. G. Prickett
Anna M. Black	Mary L. Wood
Mary E. Gove	G. W. Koser
Elizabeth A. Garretson	Eleanor R. Koser
Isaac Wilson	Eva Cook Lady
Elizabeth Koser Wilson	Clyde H. Lady
B. A. Jones	Annie G. Harris
Rachel Jones	Florence G. Michener
Frederic E. Griest	
Elsie Singmaster Lewars	Geo. W. Peters
Ruth R. Himes	Blanche G. Peters
Betty R. Hersh	Katherine Toner
John Richard Sylvanus Williams	Hanson W. Peters
Lucille Orr Walton	Mrs. Anna Peters
Richard C. Walton	Jacob F. Peters
Flora Wrigley Wilson	Sadie Peters
Mary C. Bigham	Hazel Peters
J. Paxton Bigham	David Hunter Riddle
Alverta Rouser	Susan Phillips Butt
Harry L. Rouser	Charles S. Butt
Ruth A. McIlhenny	Lillyan Royer Dill
Mary K. Lewis	M. T. Dill
Stella Myers	Martha Campbell Dicken
Grover C. Myers	Bertha H. Tyson
M. Stockton	C. J. Tyson
Catherine Stockton	M. Alice Wright Griest
Ruth R. Swope	Hannah G. C. Pickering
J. Donald Swope	John R. Pickering, Jr
Emilie K. McDowell	G. Rugan Neff
J. C. McDowell	Thomas R. Franklin
Zachariah J. Peters	Eliza M. Ambler
Mary T. Peters	Annie F. Ambler
M. Edith Peters	Annie A. Mode
Wallace V. Peters	Bertha C. Comly
Eleanor M. Peters	Mary E. Newbold
F. Herbert Peters	Emily P. Shepherd

MARRIAGES

Maria E. Tyson	Edgar A. Shepherd
Carrie Peters	Anna Pickering Maris
Sara R. Simmons	Frank Maris
D. William Simmons	Anna B. Griscom
Eliza J. Griest	Elizabeth C. Tyson
Ethel Wright	Harvey D. Lewis
Beula E. Harris	C. Arthur Griest
Annie K. Sheely	Lola Wierman Griest
Elise Triebel	Katherine E. Griest
R. Albanus Acuff	Letitia B. Griest
Mary Knight Parry	Eleanor S. Prickett
Henry C. Parry	T. Stockton Matthews
W. C. Tyson	Wm. D. Himes
Edna Kerr Tyson	
Fannie Hubbard Acuff	

#134 31st of 5th mo 1924 RICHARD D. LAMBERT-ESTHER CORINNE TYSON

Whereas Richard Davis Lambert of the city of Lynn, County of Essex and State of Massachusetts, son of Walter Lambert and Elizabeth Davis his wife and Esther Corinne Tyson of the Township of Menallen, County of Adams and State of Pennsylvania, daughter of Edwin C. Tyson and Mary W. his wife . . . this thirty first day of the fifth month nineteen hundred twenty four . . . at Menallen Friends Meeting House, Flora Dale, Pa.

	Richard Davis Lambert
	Corinne Tyson Lambert
Edwin C. Tyson	Wallace V. Peters
Mary W. Tyson	M. Edith Peters
M. Muriel Parsons	Henry C. Pickering
Frederick E. Parsons	Esther Peters Pickering
Jacqueline Mary Parsons	Eleanor M. Peters
Maria E. Tyson	F. Herbert Peters
Z. J. Peters	Ella M. G. Prickett
William C. Tyson	J. W. Prickett
Edna Kerr Tyson	Eleanor S. Prickett
C. J. Tyson	Mary H. Prickett
Bertha H. Tyson	M. Alice Wright Griest
Donald C. Tyson	E. Belle Weidner
Robert W. Tyson	Beula E. Harris
Elizabeth C. Tyson	Ethel Wright
Margaret J. Tyson	A. I. Weidner
F. C. Tyson	Anna M. Michener
E. Philip Tyson	C. Raymond Michener
R. Stanley Tyson	H. E. Hawxhurst
Chester J. Tyson, Jr	Hazel Sutton Hawxhurst
Ralph W. Tyson	F. F. Sharpless
Dixie Paul Tyson	Caroline H. Sharpless
Alan H. Tyson	Paul Sharpless
Norman E. Tyson	Alice L. Black
Elizabeth D. Lambert	Anna M. Black
Walter D. Lambert	Nellie W. Wright

MENALLEN MINUTES, MARRIAGES, & MISCELLANY

Bertha B. Lambert	Ryland H. Wright
Mary B. Lambert	Rachel E. Jones
Mary L. Davis	Barzillai A. Jones
Elizabeth Rose Wilson	Arthur E. Cook
G. Wilmer Koser	Florence S. Eldon
Eleanor R. Koser	Robert M. Eldon
Margaret Koser Lynch	Lucille Orr Walton
Amos W. Griest	Richard C. Walton
Eliza R. Griest	Reuben L. Underwood
Frederic E. Griest	Irene E. Wolfe
Frederic E. Griest, Jr	C. A. Wolfe
C. Arthur Griest	Elizabeth P. Adams
Lola W. Griest	W. S. Adams
Letitia B. Griest	Dorothy Adams
Leslie H. Keller	Agnes Adams
Katherine T. Keller	Mrs. Mary D. Wolff
Mary C. Garretson	W. E. Wolff
Robert Garretson	H. T. Weaver
T. B. Matthews Swift	Emma C. Weaver
R. Alice Longsdorf	Ruth Baugher Wilson
Jane R. Bigham	John George Wilson
S. G. Bigham	Flora Wrigley Wilson
Louise Barnhart	William B. Wilson
Robert J. Walton	Mrs. Ira Baugher
Emma J. Walton	Ira Baugher
Mrs. Emma Hutton	Esther R. Baugher
Myrtle V. Wright	J. Wilson Baugher
T. Frank Wright	Rebecca Garretson
Ella E. Deardorff	Mary Swope Keith
William B. Deardorff	Esther Branfield Thomas
Mary A. Dull	Edmund W. Thomas
Edna Royer Rice	Marion Ball Dickson
A. E. Rice	J. McCrea Dickson
Annie Kurtz Sheely	Elizabeth A. Garretson
	Margaret V. Peters
	George M. Peters

#135 7th of 5th mo 1926   ROBERT W. TYSON-THELMA M. MUSSELMAN

Whereas Robert William Tyson of the Township of Menallen, County of Adams and State of Pennsylvania, son of Chester J. Tyson and Bertha his wife of the Township, County and State aforesaid and Thelma Marcella Musselman of Lemoyne, County of Cumberland and State of Pennsylvania, daughter of Christian M. Musselman and Marcella his wife . . . this seventh day of the fifth month nineteen hundred twenty six . . . at Menallen Friends Meeting House near Flora Dale, Pa.

		Robert W. Tyson
		<u>Thelma Musselman Tyson</u>
C. J. Tyson	Ralph W. Tyson	Frederic E. Griest, Jr
Bertha H. Tyson	Paul Tyson	Elizabeth A. Garretson
Donald C. Tyson	Alan Tyson	Beula E. Harris

MARRIAGES

Elizabeth C. Tyson	Norman Tyson	Wm. B. Deardorff
Margaret J. Tyson	Edwin C. Tyson	Ella E. Deardorff
Frederick C. Tyson	Mary W. Tyson	Mrs. Lloyd Orner
E. Phillip Tyson	M. Muriel Parsons	Lloyd Orner
R. Stanley Tyson	Jacqueline Parsons	W. E. Wolff
C. J. Tyson, Jr.	Z. J. Peters	Mr. & Mrs. N. Z. Hartzler
Max Mitchell Ferguson	Mrs Fannie Bucher	Mrs. W. E. Wolff
C. W. Trafford	Mr & Mrs John C. Behney	Martha V. Rupp
M. Edith T. Peters	Ruth H. Musselman	Mary A. Rupp
C. Arthur Griest	J. E. Musselman	Irene E. Wolfe
Florence G. Michener	Hazel M. Howard	Mattie E. Ryder
Elizabeth Hersh Peters	Marian Powell	M. Alice W. Griest
Wallace V. Peters	David V. Huff	Elizabeth P. Adams
Mary E. Gove	W. S. Nagle	W. S. Adams
C. M. Musselman	Estella Nagle	Agnes Adams
Mrs. C. M. Musselman	Lola W. Griest	Dorothy Adams
Harry W. Remer	Letitia B. Griest	C. Arthur Hertzler
Florence Remer	Katherine Griest	Elizabeth Griest
Mabel Witmer	Eleanor S. Prickett	C. A. Wolfe
Morris C. Witmer	Ella M. G. Prickett	Amos W. Griest
Gillette Peterson	Ethel Wright	Eliza R. Griest
Ruth Musselman	Isaac Wilson	Anna M. Black
David -?-	Frederic E. Griest	Alyce M. Baker
Lanais W. Musselman	Alice L. Black	Gertrude N. Stover
Mr. & Mrs. H. Musselman	Eleanor R. Koser	Chas. E. Stover
Anthony M. Ryder		Mrs. V. E. Shape
Elmira C. Ryder		Mrs. W. D. Mumma
Mrs. T. D. Wagaman		Mrs. Rebecca E. Gross
Claire Walters		Mr. & Mrs. A. C. Fickes
Dr. and Mrs. J. W. Bowman		
A. Rebecca Gould		
Mrs. S. W. Long		
Mrs. Robt. W. Sadlie		
Mrs. W. A. Nebinger		
Mrs. William A. Evans		
Jas. G. Haggerty		
Mrs. Isaac Rauck		
I. L. Rauck		

#136 28th of 5th mo 1927   CHARLES B. TILTON-ELIZABETH C. TYSON

Whereas Charles Bancroft Tilton of the village of Tarrytown, County of West Chester and State of New York, son of the late William Henry Tilton and Flora Bancroft Tilton Moore, his wife and Elizabeth Charity Tyson, daughter of Chester J. Tyson and Bertha H., his wife, all of Menallen Township, County of Adams and State of Pennsylvania . . . this twenty eighth day of the fifth month nineteen hundred twenty seven . . . at the home of Chester J. and Bertha H. Tyson near Flora Dale, Adams County, Pa.

Charles Bancroft Tilton
Elizabeth Charity Tilton

MENALLEN MINUTES, MARRIAGES, & MISCELLANY

C. J. Tyson
Bertha H. Tyson
Donald C. Tyson
Robert W. Tyson
Thelma M. Tyson
Margaret J. Tyson
Frederick C. Tyson
E. Phillip Tyson
R. Stanley Tyson
Ralph W. Tyson
Dixie Paul Tyson
Alan Tyson
Norman Tyson
Edwin C. Tyson
Mary W. Tyson
M. Muriel Parsons
Jacqueline Parsons
Eliza R. Griest
Frederic E. Griest, Jr
Geraldine L. Tyson
Flora Bancroft Moore
Isabella C. Tilton Roe
Jean McNair Woods
Marian M. Woods
Constance Roe Taylor
John K. Woods
William B. Deardorff
Margaret K. Peters
Geo. M. Peters
Ruth A. McIlhenny
Esther Branfield Thomas
Edmund W. Thomas
C. M. Musselman
Mrs. C. M. Musselman
Jas D. Hull
Mary Broomell Hull
Thos B. Hull
Helen Lamb Hull
Ida Cocklin
Alice Cocklin Sauder
Ruth M. Musselman
J. E. Musselman
A. E. Rice
Daisy Orner
Elizabeth Garretson
Sue C. Blasingame
Ralph H. Blasingame
Marjorie B. Lawrence
W. S. Adams
Elizabeth P. Adams

Mrs. J. Clark McCullough
Harold Ritchie McCullough
Eugene William Smith
C. W. Trafford
Beula E. Harris
Mary E. Gove
G. W. Koser
Eleanor R. Koser
Lucile Orr Walton
Susan Edith Black
Anna M. Black
Alice L. Black
Mary E. Griest
Florence G. Michener
E. Belle Weidner
A. I. Weidner
Robert Garretson
Mary Garretson
Martha Garretson
Ruth M. Garretson
Loretta Raffensperger
Charles A. Wolfe
W. E. Wolfe
Lillian Royer Dill
Elizabeth G. Royer
Ella E. Deardorff
Z. J. Peters
Mary T. Peters
M. Edith Peters
Wallace V. Peters
Elizabeth Hersh Peters
Eleanor M. Peters
Elizabeth Griest
M. Alice W. Griest
E. M. Prickett
C. Arthur Griest
Lola W. Griest
Irene Wolfe
Edna Ulrich
Eliza Spencer Large
Elizabeth McGeorge
Katherine L. McGeorge
Letitia Griest
Katherine Griest
Florence S. Eldon
Robert M. Eldon
Sarah Hamilton Mellor
Helen L. Mellor
Howard Mellor, M.D.
Vaun Gillette Peterson

MARRIAGES

Ethel Clapsaddle
A. T. Dill
Jean Dill
Betty Dill
Carl Arneson

#137 18th of 9th mo 1927   DONALD C. TYSON-IRENE KENYON
Whereas Donald Charles Tyson of Roslyn, County of Montgomery and State of Pennsylvania, son of Chester Julian Tyson and Bertha Hawxhurst Tyson his wife and Irene Kenyon of Gasport, County of Niagara and State of New York, daughter of Charles Kenyon and Florence Kenyon his wife . . . this eighteenth day of the ninth month nineteen hundred twenty seven . . . at the home of Charles Kenyon at Gasport, Niagara County, New York.

Donald C. Tyson
Irene Kenyon Tyson

C. J. Tyson
Bertha H. Tyson
Charles Kenyon
Florence M. Kenyon
E. Phillip Tyson
R. Stanley Tyson
W. C. Tyson
Edna Kerr Tyson
Alice L. Black
A. Ernest Ducher
Susan M. Reef
Joseph Reef
Frank A. Rinn
Roy H. Wilson
Ida Wilson

Adah M. Lord
Winifred Sherman
Clayton E. Sherman
Grace B. Gaskill
Marion B. Maynard
Raymond D. Sprout
Kate Chambers Sprout
William J. Roberts
Lillian M. Roberts
Leonora C. Sprout
Robert N. Maynard
Roy N. Maynard
Mildred W. Dunbar
Rika M. Ritzinthaler

#138 26th of 1st mo 1886   BARZILLAI A. JONES-RACHEL E. WRIGHT
Whereas Barzillai A. Jones son of Thomas Jones and Martha H. his wife, all of Carroll County, State of Maryland and Rachel E. Wright, daughter of Isaac J. Wright and Sarah G. his wife all of Adams County, State of Pennsylvania, having experienced mutual congeniality and connubial attachment have agreed to unite in the marriage contract with each other . . . this twenty sixth day of the first month eighteen hundred eighty six . . . in the house of said Rachel's parents.

Barzillai A. Jones
Rachel E. Jones

Isaac J. Wright
Sarah G. Wright
Harlan L. Group
Amanda E. Group
Arvinia M. Group
Harvey W. Group
Leander L. Group
Ira M. Group
Miriam G. Harris

Thomas A. Wright
Cora E. Wright
Terressa H. Wright
Ida O. Wright
George E. Wright
Jane G. Wright
Ryland H. Wright
William P. Wright
Henry R. Fuss

William W. Hewett
Ella T. Hewett
Charles G. Hewett
Ida L. Wright
Amos W. Griest
Eliza R. Griest
Annie G. Harris

MENALLEN MINUTES, MARRIAGES, & MISCELLANY

Edwin T. Harris
Isaac E. Harris
Beula E. Harris
Dorothy Adams

Jane Edna Fuss
Israel Garretson
Rachel Garretson
E. Walhay
Rachel Walhay

#139 22nd of 2nd mo 1927   JOSEPH I. STUBBS-ESTHER G. PRICKETT

Whereas Joseph Isaac Stubbs of Germantown, County of Philadelphia and State of Pennsylvania son of Daniel Walter Stubbs and Margaret Ludwig his wife and Esther Griest Prickett of the Township of Menallen and State of Pennsylvania Daughter of the late Josiah Prickett and Ella M. G. his wife . . . this twenty second day of the second month nineteen hundred twenty seven . . . at the home of Ella M. G. Prickett, Menallen, County of Adams, Pennsylvania.

Joseph I. Stubbs
Esther P. Stubbs

Ella M. G. Prickett
Mary H. Prickett
Eleanor Griest
Frederic E. Griest
Amos W. Griest
Frederic E. Griest Jr
Eleanor R. Kaltenthaler
H. D. Lewis
Mary R. Lewis
Alice L. Black
Anna M. Black
Lucille W. Walton
Daniel W. Stubbs
Florence A. Stubbs
H. L. Stubbs
Elma S. Stubbs
Chas F. Jago

Isaac Char
Samuel G. Brosius
Marion M. Brosius
L. Ada Criswell
D. F. Cochran
Mary E. Brilliage
Elizabeth Bollinger
G. W. Koser
Eleanor R. Koser
Stella Myers
C. J. Tyson
Bertha H. Tyson
Mary E. Gove
C. Arthur Griest
Lola W. Griest
M. Alice W. Griest
Beulah E. Harris
Edwin C. Tyson
Mary W. Tyson

W. E. Wolff
Mary D. Wolff
Mary G. Criswell
Reba C. Cochran
Florence D. Eldon
Robt. M. Eldon
Mary K. Walters
Albert John Ruppel
Elizabeth Hersh Peters
Wallace V. Peters
Elizabeth Griest
Myra E. Craighead
E. M. Craighead
Lida Beitzel
Anna J. Roberts
Arthur Roberts
Josephine E. Homberger
J. E. Hornberger
Mary H. Cessna
Ida Barbour
Mrs. Lottie Slaybaugh
Wm. J. Barbour
Golda Barbour

SOURCES AND ACKNOWLEDGMENTS

Menallen Monthly Meeting began keeping minutes for both the Men's and the Women's Meetings at their first meeting in 1780. The oldest books, as they became filled, were placed in the care of Baltimore Yearly Meeting and were eventually turned over to the Friends Historical Library, Swarthmore College, Swarthmore, PA, where they have been microfilmed and properly stored. I used microfilm of the Minutes and of the Marriage Certificates to produce this book. I abstracted the records and tried to include every name, including both the maiden and married names of women when possible. If the reader wants a more complete explanation of any item in this book, it can be found in the original at Swarthmore.

The marriage certificates are listed in chronological order and indexed as to husband, wife and parents. The Minutes are listed in alphabetical order, as are the Burials, and neither is included in the Index.

There are inscriptions from eight Quaker graveyards listed under Burials. The inscriptions for the graveyards at Menallen, Friends Grove and Huntington in Adams County, and Redlands in York County were obtained directly from the tombstones themselves. I gratefully acknowledge the help of my grandsons, Gerald C. Walmer and William K. Walmer and of my son Charles R. Walmer and his wife Carolyn Walmer in the often difficult and unpleasant job of recording these. The inscriptions in the other four graveyards—Old Griest in Adams County, and Warrington, Newberry and York in York County—were obtained from lists in the possession of Menallen Monthly Meeting.

I would also like to thank my sister Ann C. Higgins, for the drawings of the meeting houses; my son-in-law Joseph L. Marinucci, for executing the maps; my daughter Kathy W. Marinucci, for proofreading and editing and my brother William T. Tilton, for desktop publishing the final copy.

INDEX

The index on the following pages includes names found in the History and the Marriages. The husbands, wives, and parents are included, but not the witnesses. The wives are listed by both maiden name and married name.

Because the Minutes and Burials are listed alphabetically by last name they are not included in the index.

A

ALISON
  Elizabeth 199
  James 199
  Sarah 199
ALLEN
  John 236
  Priscilla A. 236
  Sophia 236
ASHER
  Harriett T. 251
  Morris 251
  Regina 251

B

BAIR
  Ruth Emma 250
BATEMAN
  Elizabeth 212, 213
  Mary 212
  Rebekah 213
  William 212, 213
BEALS
  Elizabeth 192
  Jacob 192
  Mary 202
  Rebecca 202
  Solomon 202

BERKHOLDER
  John 33
BISHOP
  Aaron 20
BLACK
  Emilie W. 245
  Jane S. 245
  William H. 245
  Wm 245
BLACKBURN
  Alice 190, 193, 196, 199, 207, 222
  Amy 205
  Anthony 209
  Elizabeth 192, 205, 209
  Isabel 207
  John 192, 196, 222
  Mary 196, 203, 209, 222
  Moses 203
  Rachel 190
  Rebecca 192, 203
  Sarah 199
  Thomas 190, 193, 196, 199, 205, 207, 209
  William 205
BOWEN
  Ann 199
  Anne 209
  Elizabeth 209
  Jane 191

Jonathan 199, 209
Lidia 204
Rebecca 191
Sarah 199
Susanna 204
Thomas 191, 204
William 204
BOYLES
  Elizabeth 231
BROOKES
  Edward 239
  Rachel 239
  Sarah Ann 239
  Thomas 239

C

CADWALADER
  William 18
CADWALLADER
  Rebecca G. 242
  Sarah 242
  William 242
  William G. 242
CHRIST
  Artemesia 252
  Jacob H. 252
  Rose 252
CIXON
  Elizabeth S. 14
CLEAVER
  Andrew 242
  Hannah 242
  John 16, 194
  Louisa W. 242
  Malinda G. 16
  Miriam 194
  Peter 194
  Rebecca 16
  Susanna 194
  William 242
CLINE
  Joseph 34
COMLEY
  Jacob 212, 215
  Samuel 215
  Sarah 212, 215
  Susanna 212, 215
COMLY
  Samuel 229
  Sarah 229

Susanna 229
COOK
  Anna Elizabeth 17
  Asahel W. 17
  David E. 239
  Edith Ann 244
  Elizabeth 17
  Franklin W. 244
  George W. 18
  Hannah 18, 20
  Hannah C. 17
  Hezekiah 19
  infant son 17
  Isaac 19, 226, 239
  Jacob 195
  Jess 32
  Jesse 29, 31, 33
  John 18, 20, 250
  John Jr 18
  John W. 17, 19
  Joseph 17, 19
  Josiah 244, 246
  Leah 18
  Lydia Ann 250
  Margaret 226
  Maria W. 16, 17
  Martha 17, 19
  Martha J. 17
  Martha Jane 246
  Mary 195, 244, 246
  Mary E. 239
  Ruth Emma 250
  Samuel E. 226
  Sarah 17
  Sidney 226
  Susanna 195
  Sydney 239
  Theressa Caroline 17
  Thomas 195
  Thomas E. 244
  twins 18
  Walker 17, 19
COOKSON
  Daniel 228
  Eli 17, 19, 228
  Elizabeth 190
  Franklin Eli 17, 19
  Jane 190
  Milton 19
  Milton V. 17
  Phebe 17, 19, 228

INDEX

Samuel 190
Sarah 228
COX
  Amy 222
  Elizabeth 191
  Ephraim G. 234
  George 234
  Joshua 222
  Joshua Jr. 222
  Maria 222
  Mary 234
  Nathaniel 191
  Sarah 234

E

ELGAR
  Joseph 200
  Margaret 200
  Mary 200
ELLIS
  Elizabeth 241
  Louisa E. 241
  William 29, 30, 31, 32, 241
  Wm 32, 33, 34
EPPLEY
  Phebe Jane 16, 17
EVERETT
  Elizabeth 228
  Isaac 228
  Rebecca 228
EVERITT
  Elizabeth 192
  Hamilton 229
  Hannah 203
  Isaac 192, 194, 197, 203, 229, 231
  Malinda 231
  Martha 192, 194, 197, 203
  Rebecca 229, 231
  Rebecca K. 229
  Susanna 194

F

FARQUHAR
  Alen 11, 199
  Allon 200
  Amos 200
  Benjamin 199
  Mary 200
  Phebe 199, 200
  Reachel 199
FISHER
  Alice 206
  Elizabeth 206
  Isaac 206
  James 206
FULLER
  Elizabeth M. 236

G

GARRETSON
  Abel 17, 19
  Alice 193
  Ann 15
  Anna Cook 17
  Anne 19
  Arnold 17, 19
  Arsenith 15
  Barzilia 231
  Benjamin 15, 20
  Content 208
  Daniel 17, 19
  Eli Penn 15
  Eliza Ann 17
  Elizabeth 228, 229
  Elizabeth V. 15
  Ezra 15
  Frank G. 15
  Hannah Ann 15
  infant not named 15
  Isaac 30
  Isaac F. 33
  Isaac H. 30
  Isaac P. 32
  Isaac T. 29, 33
  Israel 14, 16, 17, 19, 20
  Israel Jr 15
  Jacob 15, 20
  Jane 216
  Jean 193
  Jesse 15, 20
  Joel 215, 228, 231
  Joel V. 15
  John 193, 196, 208, 213, 215, 216, 219, 227, 228, 231
  John G. 19
  Josiah 15, 20, 29, 30, 31, 32, 34, 229
  Louisa 15

Louisa W. 242
Mahlon 32, 33, 34
Malinda 231
Maria 15
Maria M. 231
Martha 15, 215, 231
Mary 15, 196, 208, 213, 215, 219, 227, 228
Melissa 17
Oliver 29
Rachel 15, 219
Rebecca 231
Rebecca K. 229
Rebekah 213, 216
Rhoda 15, 16
Ruth 14, 16, 20
Samuel 193, 216
Sarah 249
Susanna 196
GIBBONS
　Daniel 218
　Deborah 218
　Hannah 218
　James 218
GILLINGHAM
　Chalkley 14
GOVE
　John Howard 249
　Mary Elizabeth 249
　Moses Dennis 249
　Sarah B. 249
GRIEST
　Alvina 230
　Amelia 238
　Amos 230
　Ann 198, 202
　Anna 18
　Belinda 18
　Cyrus 29, 31, 32, 241, 243, 244, 245, 248, 252
　Cyrus S. 249, 251, 252
　Daniel 22, 198, 202, 220
　David 202
　E. Belle 252
　Edith 233
　Elizabeth M. 245
　Esther C. 251
　Florence 249
　George G. 251
　Gideon 219, 233, 239, 242
　Hadley 20

Harriett T. 251
Hiram 20, 241, 247, 249
Jane 219, 233, 242
Jane C. 243
Jane M. 239
Jesse 249, 251
John 26, 29, 31
Joseph 198, 219, 220, 223, 232
Josiah 252
Lavinia 247
Letitia B. 249, 251, 252
Louisa 241
Louisa C. 247
Louisa E. 249
Lydia Ann 240
Maria E. 244
Martha 18
Mary 18, 198, 202, 220, 240
Mary Alice 252
Mary Ann 241, 243, 244, 245, 248, 252
Mary Elizabeth 249
Nathan 32, 33, 35
Phebe 230
Rebecca 219, 232, 242
Rebekah 223
Rose C. 252
Ruth 223
Sarah Ann 239
Sibilla 249
Susan 220
Thos. 18
Uriah 240
William H. 252
GRIFFITH
　Abner 213
　Allen 238
　Ann 190
　Eve 190, 191
　John 199
　Lidia 199
　Maria E. 238
　Mary 213
　Rachel 190
　Rebecca 191
　Sarah 199, 206, 213, 238
　Thomas 190, 191
　William 22, 206, 213
GRIST
　Ann 200, 201

INDEX

Daniel 200
Martha 201
Susanna 200
Willen 201
GUNKLE
   Ruth Anna 16

H

HALLOWELL
   Benjamin 16
   Benj'n 14
HAMMOND
   Alice 193
   Deborah 193
   Elizabeth 218
   George 193
   James 193, 201, 210
   Mary 201, 210
   Ruth 201, 218
   Thomas 201, 218
HAMMS
   Samuel H. 35
HANCOCK
   Elizabeth 206, 207, 208
   Hannah 208
   James 206, 207, 208
   Joel 207
   John 208
   Mary 207
HANNS
   Samuel 35
HARBOUGH
   Peter 208
   Sophia 208
HARRIS
   Benjamin 211, 214, 217, 223, 225, 241
   Bulah R. 223
   Elizabeth 217
   Hiram T. 249
   Jacob 214
   Jane 225, 241
   Martha 241
   Mary 214
   Miriam G. 249
   Rebecca 223, 225
   Rebekah 211, 214, 217
   Samuel H. 20
   Sarah 214

HARRY
   Jesse 229
   Lewis 229
   Mary 229
   Sarah C. 229
HARTMAN
   Amos C. 250
   Harriet 250
   Ruth Emma 250
   Samuel 250
HENDRICKS
   Alice 201
   Hannah 224
   Samuel 201
   Sarah 201, 224
   Stephen 201
   William 224
HEWET
   Deborah 234
   Ellen W. 234
   George 234
HEWETT
   Jacob B. 32, 33, 34
   Joseph 196
   Rachel 196
   Sarah 196
HODGSON
   James 189
   John 189
   Martha 189
   Rachel 189
HOOPES
   Amanda Rhoda 18
   Amy B. 18
   Angelina 18
   Elizabeth N. 16, 17
   Elmira 18
   Franklin Waln 18, 19
   Hannah 16
   Hannah A. 17
   Joel 15, 20
   Joseph Ellis 18, 19
   Lucinda 18
   Maria W. 18
   Mary Elizabeth 18
   Phebe Ann 18
   Reuben 18, 19
   Sarah Ann 18, 19
   Thomas L. 18, 19
   Waln 18, 19

HOUGH
  John 10, 11
HUSSEY
  Abigail 217, 225
  Amos 217, 225
  Hannah 217
  Mary 225
HUTTON
  Ann 194
  Benjamin W. 223
  Bulah R. 223
  Deborah 193, 202
  Hannah 194
  Jane 225
  John 194
  Levi 223, 225
  Levy 202
  Martha 202, 223, 225
  William 193, 202

J

JANNEY
  Joseph 11
  Mahlon 10, 11
JENNINGS
  Hannah 207
  Isabel 207
  Thomas 207
JOHN
  Abel 22, 205
  Elizabeth 193
  Isaiah 201
  Joshua 201
  Martha 201
  Mary 205
  Reachel 201
JONES
  Barzilla 15
  Barzillai A. 259
  Edwin Thomas 15
  Hiram Benjamin 15
  Martha 15, 241
  Martha H. 259
  Rachel E. 259
  Thomas 15, 241, 259
JOYCE
  Elizabeth 227
  George 227
  Margaret 227

K

KENT
  Hadly 250
  Joseph 250
  Maria Jane 250
  Viola W. 250
KENWORTHY
  Amy 205
  Hannah 208
  Mary 205, 207, 208
  William 205, 207, 208
KENYON
  Charles 259
  Florence 259
  Irene 259
  Martha 224
  Rogers 224
KETTLEWELL
  Charles 234
  Hannah 234
  Mary 234
KIRK
  Hannah 16
  Jacob 16
KOSER
  Andrew 245
  Elizabeth M. 245
  Henry G. 245
  Margaret 245

L

LAMBERT
  Elizabeth Davis 255
  Esther Corinne 255
  Richard Davis 255
  Walter 255
LONGSDORF
  Alexander 248
  Charles L. 248
  Elizabeth 248
  Rebecca 248
LUNDY
  Benjamin 230
  Esther 230
  Susanna Maria 230

INDEX

M

MCCREARY
  Samuel 20
  William 20
MCCREERY
  Alice 209
  David 209
  Sarah 209
  Thomas 209
MCCRERY
  Rachel 196
  Sarah 196
  Thomas 196
MCGEE
  Mary 222
MCGRAIL
  Elizabeth 203
  George 239
  James 22, 203
  John 203
  Mary 203, 239
  Rebecca 203
  Thomas 203
MCMILLAN
  Elizabeth 222
  Enos 227
  Jacob 227
  Joseph 222
  Ruth 222, 227
  Sarah 227
  Thomas 222
MICHENER
  Charles 249
  Florence 249
  Rebecca S. 249
MICKLE
  Rebecca 191
MILLS
  Elizabeth 193
  Henry 193
  Lydia 15
MOOR
  Mary G. 14
MOORE
  Benj'n P. 14
  Flora Bancroft Tilton 257
  Lavinia 247
  Mary B. 247
  Z. Hibbard 20
  Ziba 247
  Ziba Hibberd 247
MORTHLAND
  Esther 18
  Phebe 198
  Robert 198
  Ruth 198
  Wm 198
MORTON
  Hannah 194
  John 194, 196
  Mary 194, 196
MUSSELMAN
  Christian M. 256
  Marcella 256
  Thelma Marcella 256
MYERS
  Albert Cook 24

N

NEBINGER
  Elizabeth 235
  Mary 235
  Robert 235

O

OWEN
  John 206, 213
  Mary 213
  Sarah 206, 213

P

PARSONS
  Frederick E. 253
  Mary 253
  Mary Muriel 253
PEARSON
  Amelia 238
  Ann 192, 197
  Elias 22, 192, 197
  Elizabeth 192, 215, 221, 222
  Isaac 192, 215, 221, 222
  Maria E. 238
  Martha 197, 215, 224
  Mary 221
  Thomas 197, 224, 238

PELLETT
   Francis 205
   Mary 205
PENROSE
   Abigail 208, 219
   Amos 208
   Elisha 238
   Hannah 249
   Hannah G. 237
   Josiah 219, 237, 238
   Rachel 219, 237, 238
   Savanna 238
   Sophia 208
   Thomas 208, 219
PETERS
   Esther Vroman 254
   Mary Tyson 254
   Zachariah J. 254
PICKERING
   Esther Vroman 254
   Hannah Gilliam Comly 254
   Henry Comly 254
   John Rowlett 254
   William 11
PIDGION
   John 196
   Rachel 196
   Susanna 196
   William 196
PLANK
   Daniel 35
PLOCHER
   Thomas 33
POTS
   Alice 197
   David 197
   Deborah 197
   Johathan 197
POTTS
   Deborah 197
   Jonathan 197
PRICE
   Ann 236
   Mary 236
   Mordecai 236
   Moses D. 236
PRICKETT
   Ella M. G. 260
   Esther Griest 260
   J. W. 251
   Josiah 260
PROCKTER
   John 204
   Reachel 204
   Sarah 204

R

REESE
   George 14
RUSSELL
   Abel 246
   Content 208
   Edward A. 246
   Hanah 223, 224
   Hannah 208
   Jesse 208, 224
   John 208, 223, 224
   Louisa A. 246
   Maude A. 246
   Ruth 223, 232
   Sarah 224

S

SHION
   Michael 11
SINCLAIR
   Elizabeth 204
   Job 204
   John 204
   Reachel 204
SMITH
   Edith 233, 246
   Gideon 246
   James 204
   Jesse 252
   Lydia L. 252
   Martha H. 16
   Martha Jane 246
   Mary 204
   Nathan 233, 246
   Phebe 233
   Phebe Angeline 19
   Susanna 204
   Thomas 233
SPEAKMAN
   Ann 191, 195, 198
   Ebenezer 191
   Elizabeth 191

INDEX

Joanna 195
Joshua 191, 195, 198
Phebe 198
Susanna 195
SPENCER
　Joseph 240
　Joseph M. 240
　Lydia 240
　Lydia Ann 240
SQUIBB
　Joanna 195
　Robert 195
　William 195
STABLER
　Thomas P. 14
STEER
　James 11
STOUT
　Christian 29
STUBBS
　Daniel Walter 260
　Esther G. 260
　Joseph Isaac 260
　Margaret Ludwig 260
SWAIN
　Hanah 220
　James 220
　Susan 220
SWAYNE
　Francis 219
　Jane M. 219
　Sarah 219

T

THOMAS
　Abel 210, 218
　Eleanor 216
　Eli 218
　Elizabeth 218
　Ellen 210, 218
　Hannah 16
　Isaac 216
　Rachel 210
　Rebekah 216
TILTON
　Charles Bancroft 257
　Elizabeth C. 257
　William Henry 257
TUDOR
　Isaac 29, 31, 32, 34, 227

Martha 227
Mary 227
William 227
TYSON
　Bertha 256
　Bertha H. 257
　Bertha Hawxhurst 259
　Charles J. 244
　Chester J. 256, 257
　Chester Julian 259
　Comly 244
　Donald C. 259
　Edwin C. 253, 255
　Elizabeth Charity 257
　Esther Corinne 255
　Irene 259
　Maria E. 244
　Mary 253
　Mary Muriel 253
　Mary W. 255
　Robert William 256
　Susan G. 244
　Thelma M. 256

U

UNDERWOOD
　Alvina 230
　Charles 203
　Hannah 203, 230
　John 203
　Mary 203
　William 230
　Zephaniah 230
UPDEGRAFF
　Ambrose 190
　Elizabeth 190
　Joseph 190
　Susanna 190

V

VALE
　Ann 228
　Joshua 18, 19
　Mary G. 18
　Oliver 19
　Oliver G. 18
　Phebe 228
　Sarah 17
　Sarah E. 18

William 228
VANCISE
　Daniel 231
　Edwin G. 231
　Elizabeth 231
　Maria M. 231
VANSCOYOC
　Benjamin W. 236
　Enoch 236
　Hepzibah 236
　Priscilla 236
VROMAN
　Adam Clark 251
　Alan 251
　Esther C. 251

W

WALKER
　Abel 10
　Abner 214
　Asahel 18, 19, 242
　Benjamin 214
　Garretson 19
　John 18
　Lewis P. 19
　Lydia 18
　Lydia G. 18
　Mary 242
　Ruth 214
　Sarah 214
WAY
　Alice 222
　Hanah 222
　Samuel 222
WEIDNER
　Aaron I. 252
　E. Belle 252
　Jacob S. 252
　Leah 252
WHITSON
　Elizabeth 250
　Viola 250
　William 250
WICKERSHAM
　Anna 15, 16
　Edith 15, 17
　James 15
　Mary 15
　Mary Ann 15
　Robert 20

Ross 15
WIDEMIRE
　Gideon 232
　Magdalena 232
　Ruth 232
　Urbane 232
WIERMAN
　Alexander 225
　Hanah 221
　Hannah 212, 215, 217, 218, 224
　Harmon 210
　Henry 210
　Henry Senior 21
　Isaac 212
　Jane 225, 226
　Joel 217
　Mary 210, 221, 225, 226
　Nicholas 225, 226
　Phebe 220
　Sarah 221, 230
　Susanna 212, 215, 230
　Susannah 210
　William 212, 215, 217, 218, 221, 224, 230
　William C. 230
WILSON
　Alice 211
　Benjamin 205, 211
　George 205, 226
　Mary 226
　Sarah 205, 211, 226
　William B. 226
WIREMAN
　Emy 198
　Hannah 201
　Mary 198
　Sarah 201
　William Jr. 201
　Wm 198
WITSON
　Jane C. 248
　Mary 248
　Micah 248
　William 248
WRIGHT
　Abel T. 243
　Able T. 32
　Alice 209, 211, 227, 232, 237
　Alice G. 246, 248, 252

INDEX

Ann 190, 211, 214, 220, 232, 236
Benjamin 200, 202, 209
Chapman A. 16, 20
Charles S. 237, 245, 249
Deborah 197
Elijah 29, 30, 31, 32, 33, 34
Elizabeth 197, 205, 210, 211, 212, 217, 235, 236, 248
Ellen 234
Emilie 245
Franklin 20
Gartrude 189, 190
George 232
George E. 249
Hannah G. 237, 245
Hiram A. 252
Hiram S. 246, 248
Howard L. 16
Ida L. 16
Isaac J. 34, 35, 249, 259
Jane 200, 202, 209
Jane C. 243, 248
Jane Garretson 249
Joel 29, 30, 31, 32, 33, 212
John 190, 197, 200, 201, 205, 210, 211, 214, 217, 220, 227, 232, 237
John B. 16, 34, 35, 235
Jonathan 21, 22, 199, 212
Joseph 10, 11
Louisa A. 246
Lucy 232
M. Alice 252
Martha 202
Mary 212, 214, 235
Mary W. 16
Miriam G. 249
Nathan 217, 235
Phebe 220
Rachel 189, 210, 234, 238, 243
Rachel E. 259
Reachel 199
Rebekah 211
Richard M. 16
Robert N. 20
Robert W. 16
Ruth 201
Samuel 189, 190, 211, 236
Sarah 205, 227
Sarah G. 259
Savanna 238
Susanna 199, 200
T. 35
Thomas 232
William 210, 220, 234, 238, 243
William H. 29, 30, 32, 33

www.ingramcontent.com/pod-product-compliance
Lightning Source LLC
Chambersburg PA
CBHW062006220426
43662CB00010B/1251